Elbridge Durbrow's War
in Vietnam

ALSO BY RONALD BRUCE FRANKUM, JR.
AND FROM MCFARLAND

*Vietnam's Year of the Rat: Elbridge Durbrow,
Ngô Đình Diệm and the Turn in U.S. Relations,
1959–1961* (2014)

Elbridge Durbrow's War in Vietnam

The Ambassador's Influence on American Involvement, 1957–1961

RONALD BRUCE FRANKUM, JR.

McFarland & Company, Inc., Publishers
Jefferson, North Carolina

LIBRARY OF CONGRESS CATALOGUING-IN-PUBLICATION DATA

Names: Frankum, Ronald Bruce, 1967– author.
Title: Elbridge Durbrow's war in Vietnam : the ambassador's influence on American involvement, 1957–1961 / Ronald Bruce Frankum, Jr.
Description: Jefferson, North Carolina : McFarland & Company, Inc., Publishers, 2019 | Includes bibliographical references and index.
Identifiers: LCCN 2019030809 | ISBN 9781476677750 (paperback : acid free paper) ∞
ISBN 9781476636207 (ebook)
Subjects: LCSH: Durbrow, Elbridge, 1903–1997. | Ngô, Đình Diệm, 1901–1963. | United States—Foreign relations—Vietnam (Republic) | Vietnam (Republic)—Foreign relations—United States.
Classification: LCC E183.8.V5 F728 2019 | DDC 327.730597—dc2 3
LC record available at https://lccn.loc.gov/2019030809

BRITISH LIBRARY CATALOGUING DATA ARE AVAILABLE

ISBN (print) 978-1-4766-7775-0
ISBN (ebook) 978-1-4766-3620-7

© 2019 Ronald Bruce Frankum, Jr. All rights reserved

No part of this book may be reproduced or transmitted in any form or by any means, electronic or mechanical, including photocopying or recording, or by any information storage and retrieval system, without permission in writing from the publisher.

Front cover: (*left to right*) President Ngô Đình Diệm with Leland Barrows and Ambassador Elbridge Durbrow at the farewell dinner for Barrows, 1958 (Arthur Z. Gardiner Papers (2014-2031), Harry S. Truman Library & Museum)

Printed in the United States of America

McFarland & Company, Inc., Publishers
Box 611, Jefferson, North Carolina 28640
www.mcfarlandpub.com

Table of Contents

A Note on Sources and Names	vii
Preface	1
1. A Short Honeymoon in Saigon	5
2. "The Miracle Man of Vietnam": Durbrow and Ngô Đình Diệm Visit the United States	14
3. Formulating Vietnam Strategy, 1957	24
4. Funding the Vietnam Strategy, 1957	36
5. Planning for Victory: MAAG, Durbrow and Ngô Đình Diệm	52
6. The Politics of Opposition	65
7. The War at Home and on the Periphery: American Criticism of Ngô Đình Diệm	78
8. The Laotian Crisis, 1959	88
9. The Cambodian Affair, 1959	99
10. The Unending War of Respect: Colegrove Replaces Cambodia	110
11. National Assembly Elections and Question of Democracy	122
12. The Struggles of a Young Republic	135
13. American Lines Divide Over Vietnam	146

14. The Vietnam Triangle: Durbrow, Lansdale
 and Williams 157
15. Influencing Ngô Đình Diệm and the Abortive
 November 1960 Coup d'état 168
16. Durbrow's Last Days in Vietnam 184

Conclusion 196
Chapter Notes 199
Bibliography 251
Index 257

A Note on Sources and Names

The Department of State Central Decimal Files (Record Group 59) is a valuable source for understanding the diplomatic relationship during the Vietnam War. Each document in the series is stamped with a multi-alpha-numeric code. The first number in the code refers to the primary classification of the document. For this manuscript, classification code 6 (Political Relations of States) and code 7 (Internal Politics and National Defense Affairs) is used. The next set of alpha-numeric numbers refers to the country code. The Republic of Vietnam's code is 51K while the Indochina code is 51G. Following this data is a subject code. The following codes are used in this manuscript.

.00	Political Affairs—General
.00(W)	Political Affairs: Week Reports (Weekly reports on South Vietnamese political, military, and economic affairs.)
.001	Political Affairs: Communism
.022	Political Affairs: Government—Territory
.11	Political Affairs: Executive Branch of Government—Chief Executive
.13	Political Affairs: Executive Branch of Government—Cabinet; Ministry
.3	Political Affairs: Judicial Branch of Government
.34	Political Affairs: Judicial Branch of Government—Laws; Statutes
.5	National Defense Affairs—General
.5 MSP	National Defense Affairs: Mutual Security Program
.521	National Defense Affairs: Intelligence Activities—Biographical Data
.54	National Defense Affairs: Maneuvers; Troop Movements

.5511   National Defense Affairs: Organization—Personnel: Conscription
.58   National Defense Affairs: Missions
.5811   National Defense Affairs: Missions—U.S.

The date, which is proceeded by a solidus (/), is the final number. Thus, a document stamped 751K.00/4-2860 was one that was filed in the Internal Politics and National Defense Affairs classification for Vietnam under the general subject category of Political Affairs and is dated April 28, 1960. All of the Central Decimal Files listed for the period 1960–1961 in the chapter notes come from the microfilm series, *Confidential U.S. State Department Central Files: Vietnam, 1960–January 1963: Internal and Foreign Affairs*. Material from Record Group 59 that is dated before December 31, 1959, is also located in the National Archives and Records Administration at College Park, Maryland. This book also uses material from Record Group 84: Records of the Foreign Service Posts of the Department of State and the *Foreign Broadcast Information Service* (FBIS) files located in Record Group 263: Records of the Central Intelligence Agency. These documents consist of translated abstracts and full stories from Vietnamese language sources. When used, the documents are cited by indicating the date of the actual publication and then the date listed in the FBIS. The page number citations with the FBIS, which use a triple letter format, have also been modified to a single letter. Vietnamese newspapers are also used in this study. While reliability of this type of source might be called into question, it offers insights not available in diplomatic correspondence and often supplements those documents.

A final source that was most valuable to this study was the Papers of General Samuel T. Williams, who served as the chief of the Military Assistance Advisory Group in Vietnam for most of Durbrow's tenure. Williams and Durbrow had an uneasy relationship and it was Williams' extensive notes on his meetings with Ngô Đình Diệm that help to clarify the alternative reporting originating from the United States embassy in Saigon.

Preface

American historians of the Vietnam War have tended to divide the conflict into neat time periods, either by bookending their studies with significant events in the war or focusing on a specific presidential administration. In a war that defies the complexities of modern diplomacy, questions 20th century military tactics, and challenges the social and political norms of its age, it is not surprising that such a methodology has been employed. This approach is not flawed and many influential works have used it to examine a piece of the Vietnam War. However, the forced limits imposed by using American presidential terms or the self-imposed restrictions placed upon a study that introduces the insertion of American combat troops in 1965 and ends with their withdrawal in early 1973 begs the question of how the war should be viewed. Recent trends in Vietnam War historiography have finally acknowledged that in order to understand the War, the Vietnamese perspective is vital. This has allowed for a reexamination of the conflict and has provided a new foundation on which historians have argued the merits and consequences of America's twenty-five year involvement in Southeast Asia. Other studies, while still focusing on the American perspective, acknowledge the Vietnamese role in determining this most significant event in the post–Second World War era.

This study does not challenge the methodology employed by five decades of Vietnam War historians and, in many ways, is a reflection of it. Rather, it asks the simple question, "Who shaped Vietnam policy?" In its simplest essence, the present work examines the relationship that developed between United States ambassador to the Republic of Vietnam, Elbridge Durbrow, and the Vietnamese president, Ngô Đình Diệm. It is one that inspired hope at its beginning only to see that optimism slowly erode over the four years that Durbrow served in Saigon. The story is more complex, just as any study that involves the Vietnam War. The layers of internal conflict in Washington in directing American foreign policy in Southeast Asia intertwine with the rich, and complex, forces of ego and personality within Saigon.

Durbrow, and the individuals who served under him in Saigon, helped to shape the narrative of United States diplomacy in Vietnam. While it is true that foreign policy decisions about Vietnam and the emerging war were finalized within the Department of State, Department of Defense, and White House, it was Durbrow and his people that provided the data and perspective on which those decisions were made. Durbrow may not have been the one to confirm the final decision, but he was able to shape the conversation in the direction he believed to be the best option.

In this case, the best option did not include Ngô Đình Diệm as the future president of the Republic of Vietnam. Durbrow did not approve of his method of rule, while the Vietnamese president grew to distrust the American ambassador. The relationship soured during the years 1959 and 1960. As such, American telegrams and despatches originating from Saigon tended to reflect the negatives occurring in Vietnam at the expense of the real, if limited, progress. Durbrow made sure that he controlled the messages and data used to formulate policy. When Military Assistance Advisory Group (MAAG) commander General Samuel Williams, and then his replacement, General Lionel McGarr, attempted to counter Durbrow, the ambassador turned on them. Durbrow also blocked attempts by the Department of Defense to insert Colonel Edward Lansdale, a longtime and trusted friend to Ngô Đình Diệm, into Saigon at a critical time in 1960. It is true that Durbrow did defend Ngô Đình Diệm on a few occasions, as in the case of Vietnam's relationship with Cambodia in 1959, but he was motivated more by how his perception might be viewed in Washington than a genuine concern for Vietnam.

The events during Durbrow's tenure might seem benign when compared to the tumultuous years after 1963. Certainly the assassinations of President John F. Kennedy and Ngô Đình Diệm in November 1963, coupled with the upheaval in Vietnam afterwards, surpassed Durbrow's actions. However, by ignoring Durbrow's role, one loses his significance in affecting American action in Vietnam after his departure. By 1963, Ngô Đình Diệm had proven himself to be a liability to American objectives in Southeast Asia. Few within the Kennedy administration trusted his continued rule in Saigon and many believed his time was up. American policymakers maintained that Ngô Đình Diệm was obstinate to American advice, aloof to the concerns of his people, and dangerous to the American Cold War effort in Southeast Asia. The United States personnel in Vietnam who shared this opinion had reason for their concerns. Ngô Đình Diệm no longer trusted most Americans by 1963 and believed that they either did not share, or could not comprehend, his vision for Vietnam. Interactions between Ngô Đình Diệm and American diplomats in 1963 failed to alleviate these anxieties.

The origins of his distrust, however, did not begin during the Kennedy administration. The consequences of Durbrow's actions in Vietnam during his tenure as ambassador set the stage for the drama and tragedy that unfolded in 1963. Durbrow taught Ngô Đình Diệm how and why he should be leery of Americans who did not share, or were not willing to consider, his beliefs. Durbrow shaped the American narrative on who Ngô Đình Diệm would become and, through this process of a self-fulfilling prophecy, made it easier for it to occur. This interpretation does not excuse Ngô Đình Diệm from any wrong-doing, nor should one assume that this study seeks to place the blame entirely on Durbrow. Quite the contrary, the Vietnamese president made some serious mistakes and missteps in his descent from power and there were other Americans who mishandled Ngô Đình Diệm just as significantly as Durbrow. However, the significance of the relationship between Durbrow and Ngô Đình Diệm needs a place in Vietnam War historiography. It is important to understand how and why the American relationship with Ngô Đình Diệm arrived at a place in 1963 when the United States believed it better for the Vietnamese president to be eliminated rather than working with him towards a common objective. It is the hope that *Elbridge Durbrow's War in Vietnam* will offer some insight into this process.

1

A Short Honeymoon in Saigon

Elbridge Durbrow arrived in Saigon at an interesting time. Ngô Đình Diệm had just escaped an assassin's bullet and his brother, Ngô Đình Nhu, was on a world tour that included a stopover in the United States to prepare for Ngô Đình Diệm's return trip to that country. Durbrow would have little time to learn the subtleties of Southeast Asia before he would be tested as the third ambassador to the Republic of Vietnam. On February 22, 1957, Ngô Đình Diệm cut the ribbon to officially open the Ban Mê Thuột fair, one of the many functions that took up most of the president's days. Ngô Đình Diệm, accompanied by Đỗ Văn Công, Secretary of State for Agrarian Reform, and various members of the foreign diplomatic corps, then walked to the area designated for the day's speeches.[1] The path was lined by soldiers to protect Ngô Đình Diệm from over-eager Vietnamese who had come to witness the event and be in the presence of the then very popular president. There was one individual, a young man dressed in tan trousers with a jacket, who waited for the president's arrival for a different reason.

As Ngô Đình Diệm proceeded down the path, his would-be assassin, known only as Phùng, pointed a MAT-49 machine pistol at Ngô Đình Diệm, only to have photographers who were covering the event block his first attempt before he had a chance to act. Ngô Đình Diệm passed Phùng, still anonymous in the crowd, who, after a few seconds and four meters distances separated the two, took aim and fired one round before his pistol jammed. The bullet somehow missed Ngô Đình Diệm but hit Đỗ Văn Công instead. Guards surrounded Ngô Đình Diệm to protect him from another attempt and apprehended the failed assassin. Throughout the entire affair Ngô Đình Diệm remained calm, standing over his fallen cabinet member.[2]

Ngô Đình Diệm then delivered his speech and spent two hours at the fair, walking among the people, visiting the exhibits, and speaking with the participants. He was calm and attentive to the people and fair exhibits with no obvious effects of the events that had transpired earlier. It was not until the last half hour of his tour that security personnel made their appearance in strength. Until that point, Ngô Đình Diệm was exposed and vulnerable to another attack. Ngô Đình Diệm was not a stranger to vulnerability since his return to the country in 1954, and neither had he shied away from difficult and dangerous situations. What happened at Ban Mê Thuột on February 22 was one of many close calls that Ngô Đình Diệm had encountered. He would survive all, relatively unscathed, save one that would result in his death and the transformation of the Republic of Vietnam forever.

The February 22 assassination attempt, and Ngô Đình Diệm's response, made a lasting impression on those who had witnessed it. He proved himself to be in charge of the situation and confident in his ability to survive whatever challenge or obstacle was put before him. Much later, as the Ngô Đình Diệm-Durbrow relationship soured, the ambassador would comment that Ngô Đình Diệm had a messianic air about him and believed himself to be beyond such timid things as an assassination or coup d'état attempt. In 1957, at the start of the new relationship, Durbrow would have other ideas.

Speculation about the failed assassination attempt intensified while the Saigon Government's imposition of a news blackout increased the rumors and intrigue surrounding the event. The government's action was nothing more than an attempt to release an official statement before the numerous Saigon dailies or international press printed their versions of the event. This did not alter the speculation of what was considered a significant media story. The Republic of Vietnam went so far as to confiscate the March 5 edition of *Dân chúng* (The People), which had a story containing theories on the identity of Phùng and his motives, though Counselor of the Embassy in Vietnam Daniel Anderson believed the real reason for the confiscation was because the newspaper also had a story critical of Ngô Đình Diệm in the same issue.[3] This question of freedom of the press and how American and Vietnamese perceptions of it differed would become an important matter for the new ambassador as he navigated his way through the politics of Saigon.

Two theories emerged on why Phùng had tried to kill Ngô Đình Diệm. One explanation claimed that Phùng was a member of the Cao Đài and had tried to kill the president because of his position against that religious group in 1955 and for his failure to reconcile with the self-imposed exiled Cao Đài pope Phạm Công Tắc.[4] The Cao Đài had been active in the preceding weeks with anti-government activities, including staging protests against Ngô Đình Diệm and the Saigon Government during the filming of J.L. Mankiewicz's *The Quiet American* in Tây Ninh, which was the base province for the Cao Đài, and the alleged Cao Đài Liberation Group's attack at Trì Bình village in Tây Ninh. The action had resulted in the deaths of five Civil Action cadres. The second theory of Ngô Đình Diệm's would-be assassin was that he was a Communist agent, who might have had Cao Đài connections.[5]

Subversive activities, for whatever reason, and the intensification of the communist insurgency would become additional concerns for Durbrow as he attempted to wield American power, influence, and advice to a sometimes willing, sometimes hesitant, Ngô Đình Diệm. Ultimately, it was the issue of internal security and the question of Ngô Đình Diệm-sponsored reforms to alleviate the chief complaints of the subversives that led Durbrow to the extreme position of calling for alternatives to his rule. These issues would plague the United States–Vietnamese relationship.

Another issue that surfaced before Durbrow's arrival in Saigon on April 13 revolved around the influence of Ngô Đình Diệm's brother and sister-in-law who, like so many ruling families in Asian countries, and in the early 1960s within the United States, assumed official, and sometimes unofficial, positions of power in the government. Ngô Đình Diệm's younger brother, Ngô Đình Nhu, and his wife Trần Lệ Xuân, more commonly known as Madame Nhu, were slated for a world tour in 1957, with a stop in Washington, D.C., planned between March 17 and April 1. As the younger brother of Ngô Đình Diệm, Ngô Đình Nhu was considered one of his most ardent supporters and was believed to have a significant amount of influence with him.[6] Madame Nhu, who was the daughter of Vietnamese ambassador to the United States Trần Văn Chương, served as the official hostess for the Bachelor-President; she was also a member of the National Assembly and would later head the Vietnamese Women's Solidarity Movement. Ngô Đình Diệm trusted his brother and wife with his life and would later become their most zealous supporter as oppositionists and then Americans called for their removal.

Ngô Đình Nhu's visit prompted discussion of the Republic of Vietnam as well as speculative planning for a trip to the United States by Ngô Đình Diệm in May.[7] While nothing concrete was decided during the Ngô Đình Nhu visit and meetings—contact with him was considered as a courtesy call and nothing more—Ngô Đình Nhu did meet with United States President Dwight D. Eisenhower, Secretary of State John Foster Dulles, and various agencies within the State Department. A variety of issues were discussed with Ngô Đình Nhu during his visit, which foreshadowed some of the problems Durbrow would face as ambassador to the Republic of Vietnam.[8] Over time, Ngô Đình Nhu's role in the Saigon Government evolved. He would become the principle antagonist to Durbrow and his immediate counsel at the embassy while, at the same time, assume control over many of the programs targeted by the United States for reform. One interesting issue to emerge from the plans for the Ngô Đình Nhu's visit to Washington was a problem that many American faced in Vietnam and framed the larger differences between the two cultures and illustrated the differences of perception between the Americans and the Vietnamese. The issue was how one should address someone with a Vietnamese name.[9]

Because the Vietnamese name convention was opposite of the United States, where the first name appear at the end while the family name was first, Americans found it confusing as to how to address their Vietnamese counterparts. Ngô Đình Nhu maintained that the American practice afforded Ngô Đình Diệm less respect than he deserved, and compared the United States model to calling Eisenhower "President Dwight." Williams maintained that it had never been a problem before and cited several examples of Vietnamese referring to the president by his given name as well as his full name.[10] In William's conversation with Ngô Đình Diệm, Ngô Đình Diệm had always referred to the given name of a Vietnamese participant except when there were two or more individuals with the same name, which was not an infrequent occurrence. Williams also asserted that many, if not a majority of Vietnamese from the North, had the family name of Nguyễn; it would greatly confuse the matter to switch to the family name for the president, Ngô, and then proceed to do the same for his secretary of state and military officers. Eventually, Anderson asked Ngô Đình Diệm what he would prefer, to which he responded that Ngô was the correct usage and then blamed the French for starting the misuse of Ngô Đình Diệm.[11]

The Americans resolved the issue by using Ngô Đình Diệm's full name when possible and his family name when practical, though the record revealed an inconsistent naming practice at best. This naming convention would never catch on as Durbrow continued to refer to the president as Diệm and Americans thereafter followed suit. The whole episode demonstrated the difficulty that Americans in Vietnam faced and something that Durbrow would find increasingly irksome. An issue as simple as what to call the leader of the country took several of the leading American military and diplomatic figures in Vietnam, Honolulu, and Washington weeks to resolve and even then, after consulting the Vietnamese involved, failed to come up with a solution that satisfied all parties. If something as simple as a name stumped the Americans, the process of nation building, rehabilitation and resettlement of the Vietnamese refugees from the North, the effects of the French colonial occupation, the communist insurgency, and the social, economic, cultural, and political reforms sought by the Americans would prove to be a real challenge. It was this task that Durbrow had accepted when he agreed to become the third United States ambassador to the Republic of Vietnam and challenged him for nearly four years.

Ngô Đình Nhu's visit to Washington illuminated a series of economic and military problems which Durbrow would face. In his April 4 meeting with the members of the International Cooperation Administration from the Department of State, Ngô Đình Nhu outlined the Republic of Vietnam's philosophy in dealing with economic matters and mentioned the most pressing issues.[12] Ngô Đình Diệm's government worked to solve several problems at once rather than singling out individual issues to resolve independently. This was something that the Vietnamese would never be able to fully communicate to the Americans and caused unnecessary tension in later years. The method and priority of the Vietnamese use of resources and focus would often conflict with the goals and desires of the United States. It was not a malicious attempt to dismiss American advice or counsel, though many Americans believed this to be the case, but rather the byproduct of a different perspective on the important issues in the country and the way in which one went about resolving them.

Ngô Đình Nhu also highlighted some of the minor issues that would play an influential role in the relationship. One of the more important of these was communication, or the perceived lack of it.[13] This type of miscommunication between a large, sophisticated donor nation and a smaller, though growing in bureaucracy, former colonial country that was engaged in many different, complex programs, would serve as a catalyst for future problems between the United States and the Republic of Vietnam. Another related issue revolved around project-priority for aid already received in South Vietnam. Ngô Đình Nhu raised the issue of highway construction to demonstrate his point.[14] The Saigon Government wanted to develop a highway system that linked the already established and secure urban centers with the underpopulated plateau region to the north and northwest of Saigon in order to resettle and rehabilitate migrants or immigrants. The Vietnamese took the position that these highways would facilitate the relocation as well as provide the vital links necessary to provide social and economic benefits to induce people in the cities to leave. The highway system would also add a measure of security to the new population centers by providing easy access from military bases around Saigon.

The International Cooperation Agency in Vietnam rejected this plan and called for the use of the allocated resources to develop coastal, commercial highways to promote intra-coastal trading. While this would have the benefit of improving the economy, it would do nothing to alleviate the overcrowding in the cities or promote resettlement and improve internal security in the plateau region. This type of difference between the Vietnamese and the Americans in priority was not unique to the Republic of Vietnam but served as an added reminder of the difficulty that each country faced in working toward an independent, stable, and economically prosperous South Vietnam.

During the course of his Washington visit, Ngô Đình Nhu also addressed military considerations with the Americans.[15] The communist threat to internal security would consume more and more of Ngô Đình Diệm's time and energy in the years to come though at the end of March, he revealed the extent of his concern to Williams during a two hour conversation that included General Maxwell Taylor.[16] Ngô Đình Diệm expressed his anxiety over increased communist activities in Southeast Asia and specifically in Vietnam where the communist insurgency, still labeled by the United States as the Việt Minh, had engaged in propaganda designed to alienate the population away from Ngô Đình Diệm's rule. Tracts signed by members of the *Chi bộ của Đảng Lao động Việt Nam* (Worker's Party of Vietnam and often referred to as just the Lao động Party) called on the people to rise up against Ngô Đình Diệm and his American allies who were forcibly relocating people from the cities to the countryside.[17] Ngô Đình Diệm firmly believed in the danger of the communist menace and, according to Anderson, had become more sensitive to actions against his government that threatened the internal security of the country since the assassination attempt.

Ngô Đình Nhu continued this line of thinking in Washington. In answer to a question by Assistant Secretary of Defense Mansfield D. Sprague about the membership of the Lao động Party, Ngô Đình Nhu estimated that there was between 300,000 and 400,000 men organized into heavy divisions of approximately 12,000 men with significant artillery as was the *modus vivendi* in the Soviet and Communist Chinese armies. The Republic of Vietnam's Armed Forces numbered 150,000 strong and was organized into light divisions of 6,000 men.[18] Ngô Đình Nhu used these figures as well as the communist objective of the complete overthrow of his nation's government to press for an additional 20,000 to 30,000 men for the armed forces to absorb the initial shock of a Democratic Republic of Vietnam invasion and then have the means to counterattack.

Ngô Đình Nhu focused on using only Vietnamese troops in this potential scenario, unlike the 1950 Korean War that saw an infusion of American and United Nations personnel into that country. It was the consensus at the meeting that both the Americans and Vietnamese viewed this type of attack as part of a civil war.[19] This was an interesting point of view given the change of American thinking seven years later after Ngô Đình Diệm and Ngô Đình Nhu had been assassinated. The Americanization of the war after 1964 would not be restrained by 1957 thinking as the principle opponents to United States Armed Forces in Vietnam, Ngô Đình Diệm and Ngô Đình Nhu, were gone, and Eisenhower had left office after serving his two terms. What happened to cause such a radical departure from the sentiment of the April 5, 1957, meeting had its roots in the Durbrow era in the Republic of Vietnam and the American-encouraged coup d'état of Ngô Đình Diệm in November 1963.[20]

Another serious issue being discussed in Saigon during the weeks preceding Durbrow's arrival was the question of the status of Chinese minorities in Vietnam within the larger question of the role of the Saigon Government in the day-to-day activities of its people. Durbrow arrived in Saigon during a time that seemed to condone, and even promote, a serious inequality against the minorities in the South though it seems fitting to also mention that the

United States suffered from the same set of challenges in its own South. Land reform was another contentious subject.[21] Ngô Đình Diệm was faced with two potential problems related to this issue. The first dilemma dealt with the large tracts of land owned by French colonialist who had served as absentee landlords during the period of French rule in Indochina. They continued to lay claim to the land after the French were forced out of the country as a result of the 1954 Geneva Conference. There were other underutilized or unclaimed lands that had the potential to serve a real need for the Vietnamese. The second issue was the number of Vietnamese, either refugees from the North or individuals who found themselves without a livelihood when the French vacated South Vietnam. These individuals were without land or the prospects for prosperity. Ngô Đình Diệm sought to establish a land reform program that would marry these two problems together in order to solve both.

In doing this, Ngô Đình Diệm also sought to create a human wall of former military and anti-communist refugees along a north-south axis on the border of Laos and Cambodia. They would serve as a line of defense against the infiltration of North Vietnamese cadres into South Vietnam. Not only would a successful land reform program solve these social, economic and

Counselor of the United States Embassy Elbridge Durbrow (left) with author Charles Thayer and Marie Victoire Alphand, daughter of the French ambassador during his assignment to Moscow after the end of the Second World War. Charles W. Thayer Papers (2008-1030) (Harry S. Truman Library and Museum).

internal security concerns but, if done properly, would highlight the very real differences between the Republic of Vietnam program and the failed land reform efforts in North Vietnam. Ironically, this program would run its course during Durbrow's tenure as ambassador and would surface occasionally, and sometimes significantly as in the case of the Agroville Program, to serve as another source of American frustration toward Ngô Đình Diệm.[22]

The final issue Durbrow faced was Ngô Đình Diệm's proposed return trip to the United States that was eventually set for May 5, less than one month after Durbrow officially took over for G. Frederick Reinhardt. Ngô Đình Diệm wanted to investigate industries that could be exploited in the Republic of Vietnam as well as drum up support for the South Vietnamese cause by attending functions sponsored by the American Friends of Vietnam and Michigan State University.[23] The primary purpose of the trip was to reaffirm the strong connection between the United States and the Republic of Vietnam during the period of transition from Reinhardt to Durbrow. While there was no indication that United States foreign policy toward South Vietnam was in jeopardy or even undergoing a review, it was important for Ngô Đình Diệm to publicize the unique relationship he shared with the Americans not only to his fellow countrymen but also the world.

Two weeks before Durbrow arrived in Saigon, the Republic of Vietnam's National Assembly convened for its first regular session in 1957.[24] Trần Văn Lắm, president of the body, delivered the opening speech during which he reviewed the status of the Republic and the expectations of things to come. Among the goals of the National Assembly were the creation of a Constitutional Court and National Economic Council. Both of the bills introducing these organizations would remain in the forefront of South Vietnamese politics; it would not be until the final months of Durbrow's four years in Saigon that each would become a reality. The incessant delays in establishing these agencies as well as unanticipated delays in the creation of other agencies within the government designed to make the Republic stronger remained a source of contention for Durbrow and fed the growing frustration during his time in South Vietnam. Durbrow, like most Americans in Vietnam, was a project-oriented problem solver. Ngô Đình Diệm took on a more holistic approach that seemed to many Americans to be unfocused.

All of this was not to suggest that only negative issues confronted Durbrow when he arrived in Saigon. Former ambassadors Donald R. Heath and Reinhardt had left a country that had survived a division near its 17th parallel and saw the end of one hundred years of French colonialism that had done nothing more than, in the opinion of Franklin Delano Roosevelt, milked that country for all it was worth.[25] The Republic of Vietnam increased its population by an estimated 810,000 during the 300 days following the signing of the July 1954 Geneva Agreement and struggled through the process of resettling these new citizens, who often had left the North with nothing but what they could carry on their backs, while managing the affairs of those who had suffered during the Japanese occupation during the Second World War and the French attempt to re-exert its control in the region in what would become known as the First Indochina War.[26]

Ngô Đình Diệm had successfully led the country after Geneva, had survived his battles with the Cao Đài, Hòa Hảo, and Bình Xuyên in 1955, helped to proclaim a Republic, and oversaw its first Constitution.[27] Vietnam had survived but there was still much to do before it could find itself secure among the stable countries of the Free World, safe from an outside threat and prospering under an expanding economy. Ngô Đình Diệm had much to do to achieve these results and expected that a powerful and sympathetic United States, which actively participated in the exodus of North Vietnamese to the South and committed itself through the Michigan State University Group and government agencies to help achieve his goals and objectives, would be a willing partner. This, however, depended upon the working and diplomatic relationship between Ngô Đình Diệm and the primary United States representative to his country, Elbridge Durbrow.

This story is one that highlights the possibilities, explores the opportunities lost, and examines the frustration and disappointment from both sides. While Durbrow would leave the country at the beginning of May 1961 and would be far removed from the events of November 1963 when those involved in Vietnamese-American foreign policy abandoned Ngô Đình Diệm, it was his force and direction that began the ending of the special relationship shared by the United States and the Republic of Vietnam. When he handed over the ambassadorship to Frederick E. Nolting, Jr., the damage had been done and the fate of Ngô Đình Diệm and later his country were sealed.

2

"The Miracle Man of Vietnam": Durbrow and Ngô Đình Diệm Visit the United States

Two days before Durbrow's plane would land at Tân Sơn Nhứt airfield in Saigon, on April 13, a murder in the capital occurred that served as an introduction for Durbrow into the mystery and intrigue that was Saigon. Lucien Cannon, the head of the Canadian delegation of the International Control Commission (ICC), was murdered in his sleep on the night of April 11 in the Canadian compound, the apparent victim of three knife wounds to the heart. The murder of such a prominent foreigner in Saigon, especially one that held such a position in the much contested ICC that was responsible for the carrying out of the 1954 Geneva Agreements, altered Durbrow's transition into his ambassadorship. This event, added to the many other Vietnamese issues related to the internal security, diplomacy, economy, society, and personalities of the Republic of Vietnam, would test Durbrow. In some ways, it never really gave him a chance to ease into what would become one of the most contentious and controversial American ambassadorships that the United States operated in the late 1950s.

The strange and strained circumstances around the death of Lucien Cannon were not the main focus of Durbrow during his first few weeks in the Republic of Vietnam though the episode introduced him to life as an ambassador in Southeast Asia. Durbrow had to learn quickly the subtleties of Vietnam and the foreign diplomatic corps in Saigon as well as establish himself as the new ambassador with the United States embassy. Throughout the affair, he proved himself loyal to his staff and conscious of the entitlements associated with diplomacy.[1]

Durbrow, when not involved in assisting with the case, was deeply engrossed in planning for Ngô Đình Diệm's return trip to the United States. Though in Saigon for less than one month, Durbrow would travel with Ngô

Đình Diệm and accompany the president while he was in Washington. During this time Ngô Đình Diệm outlined his philosophy, goals, and objectives for the Republic of Vietnam as well as how he expected the United States to aid in his vision. The meetings would set the tone for the early Ngô Đình Diệm–Durbrow relationship as the issues that would occupy the two men, many of which had already been introduced, were discussed and analyzed by the leaders and representatives of the two countries.

Planning for Ngô's return trip to the United States began well before Durbrow arrived in Saigon or presented his credentials to Ngô Đình Diệm. In March, during the Nhus' world tour stopover in Washington, discussions regarding the official visit were reviewed, which brought about the frenzied set of telegrams on the subject of how to address Ngô Đình Diệm. The United States trip would be a significant event in the early tenure of Ngô Đình Diệm as president of the Republic of Vietnam. It would be the most important event since the 1955 referendum that brought him into power and key to his continued support both within South Vietnam and from the international community. The trip would also be important for Durbrow as he sought to establish himself as the leading American representative to this Southeast Asian country and as a confidant and advisor to Ngô Đình Diệm.

The trip, therefore, had a special significance to each man. Ngô Đình Diệm needed to reaffirm his position of importance within a dynamic and often diffused American Cold War foreign policy. This would assure continued United States support for South Vietnam in its struggle against the communist insurgency and the threat from North Vietnam. Ngô Đình Diệm also attempted to guide American aid and assistance in the direction that he believed would be the most useful for the continued success towards a stable and prosperous independent state that was tied to the United States but also operated in a leadership position within Southeast Asia. For Durbrow, the visit would give him the opportunity to learn more about how Ngô Đình Diệm operated, what Ngô Đình Diệm believed the Republic of Vietnam needed and whether that matched his assessment, and begin the relationship between these two strong-willed and determined men. While much would happen during Ngô Đình Diệm's visit to the United States, the issues and problems that they would face in the years to come would surface in these few weeks in May.

A few days after Durbrow presented his credentials to Ngô Đình Diệm, Christian G. Chapman, from the political section of the embassy, forwarded to the ambassador a proposed schedule for Ngô Đình Diệm's visit as talking points for Durbrow's meeting with the president on April 20 as the two went over the agenda.[2] Durbrow provided Ngô Đình Diệm with options that limited what Ngô Đình Diệm had originally planned or substituted what the Department of State thought would be a better use of Ngô Đình Diệm's time, as well as easier to accomplish, given the logistical requirements during the trip. Planning for the trip and the trip itself, in many respects, symbolically framed the Durbrow–Ngô Đình Diệm relationship.

Ngô Đình Diệm asked for more than he needed or really wanted, and Durbrow and the Department of State half-responded to the Vietnamese requests and substituted alternatives that sometimes fit into the original request, but often were generated by an American belief that they knew better than Ngô Đình Diệm what he wanted or needed. In the case of the trip to the United States, Ngô Đình Diệm's request for a visit to Fort Benning was replaced by a trip to Fort Belvoir, while he had to select two of the three options in his visit to his old stomping grounds: the two Maryknoll Fathers facilities at Lakewood and Ossining, or Seton Hall—because of logistics.[3] Ngô Đình Diệm's trip to New York, where he had planned to attend functions sponsored by the American Friends of Vietnam was altered to focus on the Far-East American Council of Commerce and Energy while his trip to Akron, Ohio was cancelled and his visit to Detroit was coupled with the Michigan State University meetings. Other than the proposed agenda, Chapman only asked Durbrow to inquire to what extend Ngô Đình Diệm was interested in highways so that the embassy could begin preparing an appropriate brief for circulation. Durbrow and Ngô Đình Diệm went over the schedule on April 20 and subject to a slight modification came to a consensus.[4]

The next task for the embassy was to find out who was going to join Ngô Đình Diệm for the trip and prepare biographies for distribution in Washington. This process highlighted another significant characteristic of Durbrow's tenure as ambassador: his trust and delegation of responsibility to his senior staff as well as his real need of the entire staff to handle the details as he transitioned into the position. This characteristic, while not unique in diplomatic circles to Saigon, still foreshadowed the significance of senior staff in assisting and influencing Durbrow's actions toward the end of the decade. In April 1957, Durbrow relied entirely on Anderson and Chapman to identify Ngô Đình Diệm's entourage and prepare the necessary background information for Washington. This was done in a timely matter so that Anderson could transmit the data to the Department of State by April 30.[5]

After Anderson forwarded the official party biographies to Washington, Durbrow composed two telegrams explaining what Ngô Đình Diệm might be interested in discussing based on his interactions with the president earlier in the week and through his conversations with Anderson and Chapman.[6] Durbrow maintained that Ngô Đình Diệm was bound to bring up highway construction to improve the Republic of Vietnam's roads for military and economic purposes and would probably ask for additional engineers to help with the Vietnamese efforts. Ngô Đình Diệm had a very specific plan in place that was not in accordance with the views of the United States Operations

Mission (USOM). Durbrow believed Ngô Đình Diệm was also likely to want to discuss the Đa Nhim Hydroelectric Project, land settlement, agrarian reform, industrial development, and petroleum and mineral surveying.

Durbrow also mentioned projects related to the military, including equipment for the Civil Guard and additional assistance to the Self-Defense Corps, funding for an increase of the Armed Forces, American personnel replacements for the French mission that was preparing to leave, and possible United States intervention in SEATO for the South Vietnamese in its fight against the insurgency and threat from the North Vietnamese.[7] Durbrow also thought Ngô Đình Diệm would call for more assistance to promote Vietnamese education as well as propaganda efforts to spread the story of the Republic of Vietnam to the North through medium wave, and the world through short wave, transmissions. Finally, Durbrow expected Ngô Đình Diệm to bring up the problem of Chinese citizens in Vietnam and defuse what was becoming a brewing crisis of interest for the United States. Ngô Đình Diệm had issued a series of decrees that increasingly restricted Chinese-owned business and called for the Chinese in Vietnam to obtain Vietnamese citizenship or leave the country.

The second telegram, sent two hours later, focused specifically on the Chinese issue. Durbrow recommended that the Department of State use Ngô Đình Diệm's visit to outline the American concern with Ngô Đình Diệm's policies and how it affected the role that the United States expected the Republic of China to play in the region. In 1957, the United States preferred to use the Republic of China as a counterweight to the communist influence spread by the People's Republic of China rather than relying on the Republic of Vietnam, which was still in its infancy. The Republic of China played the role as leader of the Free World nations in Asia and the Pacific and, accordingly, received the bulk of American attention and resources. Ngô Đình Diệm did not agree with the proposed role of the Chinese in the region and, in fact, maintained that the Republic of China's influence did not even extend to the minority Chinese population in Vietnam.

Ngô Đình Diệm was more concerned with lessening the economic hold of the Chinese in South Vietnam and forcing them to either become official citizens of the country or leave. Durbrow's position, and recommendation to Washington, differed. He argued that Ngô Đình Diệm must be made to understand that the United States respected Saigon's efforts to incorporate all of the people within its borders into the Republic but could not accept the process by which Ngô Đình Diệm was attempting to do this. It lessened the prestige the Republic of China held in the region and accomplished nothing more than to create tension within the Chinese-Vietnamese community and between the two Republics.[8]

On May 1, Nguyễn Hữu Châu, Secretary of State at the Presidency and

Secretary of State ad interim for Internal Affairs, forwarded to Durbrow a copy of a telegram that Ngô Đình Diệm sent to the Vietnamese embassy in Washington that day, which outlined his proposed agenda for conversations in Washington.[9] They met on May 3 to go over the agenda and seek clarification on the major political, economic, and military points that Ngô Đình Diệm wished to discuss.[10] On the political front, Ngô Đình Diệm had formulated a strategic concept for unifying Southeast Asia against the communists through the strengthening of SEATO's relations with anti-communist nations, improving internal security, and reorganizing the administrations and economies of the countries to stabilize the financial institutions and eliminate smuggling and corruption. Durbrow reported that Ngô Đình Diệm was particularly concerned with contraband, the opium trade, and illegal financial transactions.

On the economic front, Ngô Đình Diệm wanted to maintain the level of United States assistance to his country in order for the Republic to continue its movement toward a stable economy. American aid helped Ngô Đình Diệm balance his budget, maintain the standard of living for the Vietnamese people, and establish an equitable taxation system. Ngô Đình Diệm also wanted to have discussions on the adverse effect of rice sales by the United States that lowered the price as well as the extent to which the United States made the Republic of Vietnam participate in triangular aid. Ngô Đình Diệm and Nguyễn Hữu Châu also desired VN $365,000,000 (U.S. $5,069,444) to help offset the refugee relief aid spent in 1955 though Durbrow warned them against seeking this money as the fiscal year had ended for the United States and too many Washington officials were averse to compensating the Vietnamese for overspending. Ngô Đình Diệm, however, found it difficult to accept such an argument from Durbrow, especially as the money had gone toward refugee relief and the outstanding loans could not be paid off, which had the unfortunate result of setting off currency inflation. Ngô Đình Diệm and Nguyễn Hữu Châu also forewarned Durbrow of the Saigon Government's focus on resettling the Central Highlands, and creating a more sophisticated highway system to support this resettlement, forming what Ngô Đình Diệm had described as a human wall protecting the Republic of Vietnam from infiltration from Cambodia and Laos.

Regarding the military, Ngô Đình Diệm was adamant about increasing the size of the Armed forces by 20,000 men at the lower end of the pay scale. This would enable the Republic of Vietnam to increase its Armed Forces while staying within its budget and allow released professional soldiers the opportunity to resettle into the lands comprising of Ngô Đình Diệm's human wall. Durbrow was not impressed by Ngô Đình Diệm's plan and warned him that it would not receive sympathetic consideration. The 20,000-man debate would remain a source of contention throughout Durbrow's time in Saigon.

Durbrow concluded his meeting with Ngô Đình Diệm and Nguyễn Hữu Châu by advising them to focus on the most fundamental of issues while in Washington rather than trying to discuss everything, especially when many of the subjects the Vietnamese had planned to discuss could be worked out between the USOM and Saigon officials. Durbrow tried to advise Ngô Đình Diệm on Washington politics and how to play the game. Ngô Đình Diệm, through his experience of the United States trip, would find that Washington politics were not as difficult to traverse as that of Saigon. Whether he was correct in his assessment was less important than the fact that Durbrow failed to make a strong impression on Ngô Đình Diệm on how to conduct his trip while the reception he received confirmed to Ngô Đình Diệm that he understood Washington better than the American ambassador.

Durbrow's warning that many of the issues on Ngô Đình Diệm's agenda needed to be dealt with in the Republic of Vietnam by the USOM proved true early in the trip. The Administrator General of Foreign Aid, Vũ Văn Thái, and Director General of Planning, Huỳnh Văn Điểm, met with the Director of the Office of Southeast Asian Affairs, Kenneth Young, and the Deputy Regional Director for Far East of the International Cooperation Agency, Paul Summers, on May 7 to review economic aid in the Republic of Vietnam.[11] Vũ Văn Thái and Huỳnh Văn Điểm brought up a number of projects that the Vietnamese planned to pursue with American assistance, including a glass factory, cement factory, and industrial development center. On the question of agrarian reform, which involved releasing United States money to begin financing down payments to landlords for purchase of their land, and Triangular Francs, the Vietnamese were told that the USOM was the appropriate agency for these discussions, just as Durbrow had forewarned.

For the Vietnamese, the USOM had either been too slow or less than enthusiastic about the Vietnamese projects or positions, and had failed to satisfy the Saigon Government. The natural next step for the Vietnamese was not to amend their position to compromise with the Americans in Vietnam but to appeal directly to Washington. Unfortunately, United States decision-making did not work in the same way. Young and Summers were not about to overrule their experts in the field to satisfy the Vietnamese concerns. This created a situation in which both sides would, over time, become frustrated with the other. For the Vietnamese, the Americans seemed too intransigent in their position and failed to take into consideration the expertise of the Vietnamese. For the Americans, the Vietnamese seemed unwilling to compromise even though it was the United States who was paying the bill. The monetary commitment meant that a certain degree of control was expected while compromise needed to be initiated by the Vietnamese who were, self-admittedly, still learning how to govern their country.

Ngô Đình Diệm, with Durbrow, first met with Eisenhower on May 9 at the White House.[12] Ngô Đình Diệm spent most of the forty-five minute conversation with Eisenhower comparing the North Vietnamese military with that of the Republic of Vietnam and elaborated on the weakened position South Vietnam had in its armed forces as a result of the French organization and lack of confidence in the fighting spirit of the Vietnamese. His main objective was to outline the need for the additional 20,000 men to bolster his defenses and make it possible to counter-attack after the inevitable North Vietnamese invasion was blunted. Ngô Đình Diệm made it a point to describe the unlikelihood of Cambodia, Laos, and Thailand coming to the defense of South Vietnam, as well as the weakness of other available SEATO forces. In addition to Thailand, whose priority would be to protect its own extended borders with Laos, only Pakistan and the Philippines were likely contributors, and neither had a force large enough to commit a part of it to the Republic's defense.[13] Ngô Đình Diệm also highlighted the theme of the Republic of Vietnam surviving under his leadership when the supposed international experts believed he would fail. He asserted to Eisenhower that he had survived and thrived when almost all around him had given him up. This entitled him to a bit of stubborn pride but also a belief that he knew and understood his country and people much better than his Vietnamese critics and certainly more than the American experts in South Vietnam. This position would lead to several clashes in the years to come and eventually result in his downfall.

Later in the day, Ngô Đình Diệm met again with the same group minus Eisenhower to re-iterate some of his main points on the military and diplomatic situation in the Republic of Vietnam.[14] Ngô Đình Diệm focused on the incursions from Cambodia and Laos into the northwestern part of the Republic and briefly outlined his human wall strategy. Dulles was specifically interested in Ngô Đình Diệm's take on the situation in Laos as well as a better understanding of his stance regarding the Chinese minority problems.[15] The Vietnamese president argued that the situation in Laos was becoming complicated with the return of Prince Phetsarath Ratanavongsa who threatened the position and power of Deputy Prime Minister and Minister of State Katay Don Sasorith. Ngô Đình Diệm informed Dulles that Katay had threatened a coup d'état against Phetsarath should he assume power and aid the communist insurgent group, the Pathet Lao. If this were to happen, Ngô Đình Diệm predicted direct North Vietnamese involvement in the affair and a widening of the war.

While the situation in Laos was troublesome, the Chinese minority problem bothered the Americans more than Ngô Đình Diệm had realized, even if he did not fully understand or empathize with the American position. Dulles introduced the topic into their discussion by stating that the United States was an ally of both the Republic of Vietnam and the Republic of China and was concerned that this problem might create a situation that would destabilize the Free World alliance. Ngô Đình Diệm maintained that assimilation in Vietnam and in Asia and the Pacific in general had been going on for years though the situation in the Republic of Vietnam was different than other cases because the Vietnamese and Chinese shared racial and cultural similarities.[16] Both Ngô Đình Diệm and Walter Robertson, who was present at the meeting, argued that the Vietnam-born Chinese wanted to remain in Vietnam rather than be deported to Taiwan, though they had different motives for this decision. Through the course of the discussion, Ngô Đình Diệm remained consistent with his earlier position regarding the Chinese question even if his policies and decrees caused angst for the Americans, who believed the issue had international, rather than local, repercussions.

Ngô Đình Diệm's Washington portion of his trip went well, though United States officials were unable to acquire from him assurances of changing his stance on the Chinese minority problem. Ngô Đình Diệm and his entourage were able to meet face-to-face with their American counterparts and through this process gain a better understanding of the Americans in Washington who decided United States policy in Southeast Asia. The trip also had the advantage for Durbrow and Ngô Đình Diệm to come to a greater understanding of one another in what would become one of the more important relationships to exist between the two countries. Durbrow was present at the major meetings in Washington and witnessed how Ngô Đình Diệm acted; he saw the Vietnamese president's passion but also experienced his mandarin-nature. Likewise, Ngô Đình Diệm had the opportunity to assess Durbrow and his commitment to his new post as ambassador.[17]

In Saigon, a story making the headlines was the confirmation that the Republic of Vietnam had requested all French military mission personnel to vacate the country. The French had organized their withdrawal to end on July 31 and the United States had already made plans to take over their responsibilities. The termination of the French mission touched off another controversy between the United States and France as the French in Vietnam asserted that the order was inspired by the Americans rather than from Ngô Đình Diệm. From the United States embassy in Paris, the new ambassador there, Amory Houghton, argued that the French would view any American move to replace them as confirmation of United States duplicity in the Republic of Vietnam.[18] This line of thinking was standard among western diplomats at the time; they never acknowledged that Ngô Đình Diệm was capable of guiding foreign policy on his own. Moves such as the termination of the French mission had to be inspired by the United States, for Ngô Đình Diệm would never have the force to act alone. This type of thinking eventually led the United States into the fateful decision in 1963 to terminate its relationship with Ngô Đình Diệm.

Ngô Đình Diệm returned to the Republic of Vietnam on May 23 to streets lined with Vietnamese cheering him while flags, streamers, and a hastily-constructed arch marked his return home.[19] While the half-day holiday for schools and government workers may have accounted for some of the crowd, there was a general feeling of appreciation for Ngô Đình Diệm by the people of Saigon, who were aware of the significance of the trip. The simultaneous release of messages on May 27 from Ngô Đình Diệm and Eisenhower pointed out the success of the trip and the continued good relations between the countries. It also did much to bolster Ngô Đình Diệm's prestige in the Republic of Vietnam.[20] He had established himself as an undisputed leader and confirmed publicly the alliance between his country and the United States as a result of the visit. With this important event out of the way, Ngô Đình Diệm returned to the everyday problems of his presidency, some more serious than others, while Durbrow continued his lesson on Vietnam, its politics, personalities, and particularities.

One individual who would prove himself to be important in that education was Wolf Ladejinsky, who had served as a land reform advisor in the United States Overseas Mission from 1954 to 1956 and then as an advisor to Ngô Đình Diệm. Ladejinsky had been witness to the creation of the Republic of Vietnam, deeply involved in the United States efforts to resettle and rehabilitate the northern Vietnamese refugees who had arrived during Operation Exodus and served as one of the confidants to Ngô Đình Diệm during his rise to power.[21] Ladejinsky's position with Ngô Đình Diệm, and his influence on him, was confirmed to Durbrow shortly after their return to Saigon. On May 25, Ladejinsky and Ngô Đình Diệm met, during which time the question of the Chinese minorities arose.[22] Ngô Đình Diệm continued to maintain that the situation was an internal matter and not as serious as the Americans had made it out. Ladejinsky conceded the internal nature of the problem but convinced Ngô Đình Diệm to seek out the Chinese minister Yuan Tze-Chien in order to maintain relations between two of America's staunches anti-communist allies in Asia.

When Durbrow met with Ngô Đình Diệm on May 28, Ngô Đình Diệm discussed the overall effect of the Vietnamese laws on the Chinese and, without mentioning Ladejinsky, told Durbrow that he planned to meet with Yuan to sort out the problem. Durbrow was able to assess in Ngô Đình Diệm the willingness to listen to American advice, which would lead him to some unfortunate assumptions later in his ambassadorship. This type of reasoning and relation building would prove critical in the days to come.

Ngô Đình Diệm's trip to Washington was a milestone in the early political career of the Vietnamese president, but it was also an important moment in the young relationship with the new American ambassador. Both men observed the other during the high profile trip. Ngô Đình Diệm was able to assess the skill and commitment of Durbrow in his new assignment while

Ngô Đình Diệm's words and actions helped the ambassador in learning his lessons about Vietnam. Returning from the trip, each man still had much to learn about the other though there would be ample opportunity to do so as Vietnam faced the many challenges and obstacles it had as it developed into a stable Republic and worked to assume a position of leadership in Southeast Asia.

3

Formulating Vietnam Strategy, 1957

After his return to Vietnam, Ngô Đình Diệm concentrated on foreign and domestic policy while still basking in what was considered a successful trip.[1] Durbrow's return to Saigon was also focused on Vietnamese diplomacy as he continued to find his way as United States ambassador. One of the first crises to greet Durbrow was the detainment of a Cambodian military aircraft that had landed at Tân Sơn Nhứt airport without clearance on May 28.[2] The crew of two Cambodians and three Frenchmen were held, so Durbrow reported, in retaliation for an earlier incident with Cambodia where twenty Vietnamese had been arrested for accidently crossing the shared border. The Frenchmen were released after the intervention of the French embassy, but the Cambodians were held until Phnom Penh promised to release the detained Vietnamese patrol.[3] The incident, though minor, when compared to the events that would follow in the coming years, foreshadowed a real obstacle for Durbrow as he dealt with the Vietnamese and Southeast Asians. Nothing seemed easy to solve nor as simple as it might appear when first encountered. The situation with Cambodia continued to be a source of tension and frustration for Durbrow, the Americans, and the Vietnamese.

On July 18, a group of armed individuals attacked the Bác dạy area in Châu Đốc and killed eighteen Vietnamese, including two Civil Guard personal who went to protect the villagers. A third Civil Guard member was seriously wounded but managed to call in reinforcements, which forced the attackers to retreat. This attack served as a catalyst to intensify the deteriorating relationship between the two countries. Two individuals involved in the Châu Đốc massacre were arrested at the beginning of August and were sentenced to death. They were reportedly followers of Ba Cụt.[4] The arrests helped keep the incident alive in the press and among the people.

The conflict between the two countries reached a high enough intensity by mid–August that the CIA included it in its August 15 Weekly Summary.[5] The United States intelligence briefing focused on the maritime conflict that included the insertion of Cambodian marine garrisons on the smaller islands of Île a l'Eau and Île du Milieu and Cambodia navy exercises in the Gulf of Siam, which included the sailing of an LSIL through disputed waters. The Cambodians also announced the insertion of two 40mm artillery guns on the Île a l'Eau. Unlike Ngô Đình Diệm, who saw the French as the main instigators of Cambodia's aggressive moves against his country, the CIA suggested that the French advisers aboard the ships may have helped to restrain more aggressive action. This point was echoed by the United States embassy in Phnom Penh. There was a real American concern for the Republic of Vietnam's response to the Cambodians and their insertion of their own forces on the island of Phú Quốc to the southeast of the Cambodian-held islands.

While Ngô Đình Diệm considered aggressive actions against the Cambodians, whom he claimed had seized the islands in order to add insurgents in the Cà Mau region of the Mekong Delta, the United States worked to de-escalate the situation. Both countries received American aid, which would likely be used against the other in a conflict, but the real concern was the level of instability an armed clash would have in the region. The United States needed both countries to participate in their anti-communist alliance in the region while any hostility between the two American allies would diminish the role of the United States in Southeast Asia. Given this real possibility and the attitude of the French who had been forcibly replaced by the United States, Ngô Đình Diệm's assessment of the situation was not unreasonable.

The American embassy in Phnom Penh also reported on the deteriorating relationship between the two countries.[6] When Ambassador Carl Strom met with the new prime minister Sim Var on August 8, he brought up the frontier incidents, especially the offshore island situation. Sim Var responded by focusing on the aggressive nature of the South Vietnamese, who he considered no better than their northern brethren. Sim Var pointed towards earlier French failure to resolve the border issue between the two countries but also blamed the Vietnamese for ignoring Cambodian protests of incursion. In response to the border incidents, the Americans in Cambodia recommended that the United States not become involved, in order to avoid appearing to side with one country over the other.[7]

Durbrow echoed this recommendation on August 14, adding that he and Williams had on several occasions urged Ngô Đình Diệm to work with the Cambodians to resolve the crisis. Durbrow advised against high-level talks initiated by the Americans.[8] Later, in September, Durbrow also shied away from referring the situation to the United Nations General Assembly.[9] Strom reaffirmed this position after a meeting with Sim Var, who had just met with Ngô Đình Diệm on the occasion of the departure of Prince Norodom

Sihanouk from Cambodia.[10] When Strom brought up the possibility of a joint border patrol between the two countries, Sim Var ignored the suggestion though the Cambodian prime minister agreed with the United States' need to have the two countries in the region settle their differences. While tensions were high, the Republic of Vietnam representative in Cambodia, Ngô Trọng Hiếu, was encouraged by the Cambodian press reports of Sim Var meeting with Ngô Đình Diệm and reported to Edmund Kellogg, American Counselor of the embassy in Phnom Penh, of his optimism.[11]

This optimism did not last long, however. On September 3, *Dépêche du Cambodge*, a paper under Sim Var's control, published a front-page article about the establishment of approximately twenty Vietnamese military outposts along their shared border.[12] The article argued that the real purpose of the Vietnamese was to intimidate Cambodia and destroy its neutrality. Ngô Đình Diệm informed Durbrow that he had authorized Civil Guard and custom border patrols along the border to prevent smuggling and other illegal activities but held back from deploying an Army of the Republic of Vietnam (ARVN) division in the Seven Mountains region north of Rạch Giá where activity was intense because he feared how the Cambodians would react.[13] The Cambodians continued to press the matter with their embassy in New Delhi, India with a press release accusing the Vietnamese of placing military reinforcements on the border, calling for compulsory recruitment in the Vietnamese Armed Forces (presumably to attack the Cambodians), and a condemnation of Ngô Đình Nhu who, upon his return from a trip to the United States, had allegedly issued an inflammatory statement against the Cambodians.[14] As the Americans attempted to get the full story, they found little more than two perspectives and much animosity.[15]

When confronted about the article, Sim Var stated that the Vietnamese were chasing Hòa Hảo forces, but they were also pillaging and looting Cambodian villages in the process. The Vietnamese responded to this allegation by not only denying it but also calling for Cambodian observers at the Vietnamese outposts.[16] The real problem was the unwatched border and the ability for armed groups to cross it with ease. One such force, formed in June, may have been the source of the initial Vietnamese incursion and Cambodian concern. This new threat emerged in Châu Đốc on the Cambodian border in An Giang Province. A group led by Michel Nguyễn Văn Lanh, also known as Nguyễn Long Châu, organized about 200 lightly armed men recruited mostly from the Hòa Hảo sect.[17] As reported by the Counselor of the United States Embassy for Political Affairs, Thomas D. Bowie, this new group used superstition and threats of violence to intimidate the people in their area of operation. They also thrived in a space that was being used by communist insurgents, who had attached an advisor to the group, even though they had alienated the local population because of their terroristic actions. While

3. Formulating Vietnam Strategy, 1957

Bowie did not think this new threat warranted the press it had received in Vietnamese-language newspapers, it was this type of activity that Ngô Đình Diệm needed to curb with his Self-Defense Force and Civil Guards, both of which were under scrutiny by the Americans. It should not be surprising that Ngô Đình Diệm also focused on this region and the Cà Mau peninsula as possible areas to expand agricultural enterprises, as well as resettlement projects for released military personnel, in order to counter this new type of threat.[18]

While subversive organizations like the Nguyên Châu group made matters more difficult in the western provinces of South Vietnam, Ngô Đình Diệm was adamant about the role of Cambodia in directly and indirectly aiding the insurgents. When he and Durbrow met with Admiral Stump and Williams on September 16, Ngô Đình Diệm reaffirmed his belief that the insurgents were using Cambodia as a sanctuary and were regularly supplied by roads through Laos and Cambodia from North Vietnam.[19] Durbrow's summary of the conversation included his own assessment that grudgingly confirmed, to a certain degree, Ngô Đình Diệm's position but also raised the possibility that Ngô Đình Diệm was overreacting in order to secure additional American aid. Durbrow also expressed concern over a recent request by Acting Minister of Defense Trần Trung Dũng to Stump in which he brought up the increase of the Vietnamese Armed Forces by 20,000.[20] The ambassador also questioned the extent of Ngô Đình Diệm's concern as another way to influence the United States decision to support the Self-Defense Force to 60,000. Durbrow concluded that the increase in insurgent activity might also be explained by increased banditry rather than an organized attempt to assassinate. While Durbrow hedged his concern with the possibility that Ngô Đình Diệm was correct, it was clear that he was beginning to question Ngô Đình Diệm's perspective. This would prove critical as the relationship between the two men deteriorated.

Durbrow, like Ngô Đình Diệm, worked to find the right strategy to promote Vietnamese diplomacy. For Ngô Đình Diệm, it was a necessity born from the need to be seen as legitimate and not under the auspices of the United States. As such, he promoted foreign dignitaries coming to the Republic of Vietnam and set aside significant time for overseas trips.[21] Durbrow wanted to project an image of a stable, rationale free world ally who was united in the common course of anti-communism in the summer 1957, even when it intersected domestic policy. Durbrow spent a considerable amount of energy, resources, and attention on improving Saigon's diplomacy with other countries in the region. Ngô Đình Diệm's announcement of foreign trips was encouraging but Durbrow was always seeking something more. On June 8, the two men met and discussed the Republic of Vietnam's relationship with Cambodia and Laos. This was especially important given recent events in the region. Durbrow had an opportunity to influence Ngô Đình Diệm toward American thinking though he was still cautious about asserting himself so early in his ambassadorship. This would change with time.

Ngô Đình Diệm used 1957 to increase his presence abroad with trips to the United States, Thailand, Australia, India, and the Republic of Korea. Durbrow believed that these first contacts with the Vietnamese president would serve him well, but it would also benefit the United States. The leaders on his itinerary "probably will be impressed by Ngô Đình Diệm's combination of scholarship with tough, single-minded devotion to his concept of the national good." Durbrow continued in his assessment, "US foreign policy objectives will be well served if Diem conveys the implicit, but perhaps unspoken, message to many people of Asia that truly nationalistic states, with economic systems of their choice, can develop their material resources and cultural identity with American moral and material support, and without fear of becoming the victim of a new colonialism."[22] The attempt to insert Vietnam into American Cold War strategy as a recipient of untarnished American aid and as a product of Western values and benefits was not surprising.

Regarding Laos, Ngô Đình Diệm also made pointed remarks about his northwestern neighbor while discussing the general foreign policy situation. He believed that relations between the two countries were good, though he did not think Laotian leadership was very strong. He lamented that Katay Don Sasorith might not have enough money to bribe party leadership in his country to form a government, suggesting an inferior brand of democracy when compared to Vietnam, though the practice of bribery for support was not uncommon in his country.[23] Durbrow did not record an assessment of the Laotian situation though he framed the discussion not in a regional context but rather as part of the Cold War where the United States would encourage Vietnamese actions to improve its position in the region as a counter to the Communist Chinese. Durbrow thought globally while Ngô Đình Diệm was focused on the region. This difference of perspective would become more pronounced as time passed.

Laos continued to be a source of concern for Ngô Đình Diệm as well as the United States. When Durbrow and Ngô Đình Diệm met with Senator John Sparkman (D-Alabama) and the Chief of Staff for the Senate Foreign Relations Committee, Carly Marcy, on September 23 in Saigon, Ngô Đình Diệm reminded the Americans that the communist insurgents were using Laos to send weapons to their bases in Cambodia and the Republic of Vietnam.[24] Not only did Ngô Đình Diệm fear for his country, he predicted that the failure to stop this movement would lead to communist takeovers in both countries. The Americans were not blind to the precarious nature of the stability in Laos, given the recent difficulties in forming a cabinet. When Leonard Bacon, Counselor of the Embassy in Laos, met with Katay on September 25, he outlined three real dangers to continued United States–Laotian relations, including their negotiations with the Pathet Lao, the subversion in the provinces and the irregular use of aid funds.[25] On the question of the Pathet Lao, Katay maintained that they were an extension of the Vietnamese communists and acknowledged their importance in allowing them access to Laotian roads to the RVN. The convergence of Laos and Cambodia to the future of the RVN was clear to most in 1957, though future American actions would opt for neutrality and a blind eye rather than heading off the problem before it became unmanageable.

Durbrow's early introduction into the mysteries of Saigon, which began with an attempted assassination of the president and the murder of a diplomat, was significant. Throughout his tenure, intrigue would fill his days while his and his embassy's interpretations of events varied from the serious to the absurd. In the case of the latter, Durbrow reported on the removal of a large portrait of Ngô Đình Diệm from the façade of Saigon's City Hall as a sign that the government was working to decrease the "cult of personality" criticism emerging from the Saigon intellectuals.[26] He would later learn that it was simply being cleaned. Rumors were numerous in Saigon, while the ability to sift through them for truth would constantly challenge Durbrow. One recurring rumor was the possibility of a coup d'état to unseat Ngô Đình Diệm. On June 4, Durbrow reported the unusually intense rumor about the imprisonment of Ngô Đình Diệm in Dalat, with varying justifications for the move, ranging from Vice President Nguyễn Ngọc Thơ's rift with the president over economic issues to the military's dissatisfaction of not being paid. While Durbrow confirmed the rumors' fabrication, including the one that suggested the United States had initiated Ngô Đình Diệm's imprisonment, he did report the strong likelihood that the origins of the rumors were French sources.[27]

Ngô Đình Diệm had requested the removal of the remaining French advisors and other military personnel from the Republic of Vietnam, which had not been kindly received by the former colonial ruler. Even before Durbrow arrived in Saigon, the relationship between the French and Vietnamese was strained. In the post–Geneva Conference environment, the French held on to the little control they had while Ngô Đình Diệm worked diligently to release Vietnam from the last vestiges of colonialism. Durbrow, thus, arrived in the middle of this struggle. Throughout June, he had to deal with French criticism of American replacements of its advisor teams even though, as he pointed out, the move was agreed to and documented from as far back as December 1955.[28] The effects of the French were felt through the actions of the overseas Vietnamese in France as well as plots and actions that emerged to destabilize or remove Ngô Đình Diệm from power. One such movement to form was the Vietnamese National Salvation movement led by Nguyễn Văn Tâm, Trần Văn Hữu, Nguyễn Văn Xuân, and Nguyễn Văn Hoan. This

Vice President of South Vietnam Nguyễn Ngọc Thơ at the Independence Day celebration parade, October 26, 1959. Arthur Z. Gardiner Papers (2014-1510) (Harry S. Truman Library & Museum).

group called for a change of government, which prompted the pro–Saigon daily *Tự do* (Freedom) to label them as traitors.[29]

Another source of opposition, closer to home, was connected to Phan Quang Đán, who had been vocal in the controversies surrounding the repatriation of Chinese-born Vietnamese. His name surfaced occasionally when calls for reforming Ngô Đình Diệm's government were made. These movements of intrigue were often repeated in Cambodian newspapers which did not help to improve Vietnamese relations with that country.[30] When Ngô Đình Diệm met with Durbrow on June 10, he specifically pointed to Phan Quang Đán as the main instigator, calling him "the most convincing liar in Viet Nam."[31] Durbrow pressed Ngô Đình Diệm on how he felt about the then leader of the Democratic Bloc. The president responded that it was better to ignore him. Still, Durbrow sensed that there was more to this situation than Ngô Đình Diệm let on. He worried that Ngô Đình Diệm was concerned about the rumor campaign but unsure on how to respond to it though he feared that Ngô Đình Diệm might make "precipitous action without thinking."[32] Durbrow's insight here was accurate, as Phan Quang Đán would play a leading role in trying to undermine Ngô Đình Diệm, while Ngô's failure to respond in a suitable manner influenced Durbrow's position as he reported future events.

Phan Quang Đán continued to oppose Ngô Đình Diệm and put forth his Democratic Bloc as the only real opposition to the coalition of organizations that supported Ngô Đình Diệm. He would be critical of many of the moves of the Saigon Government and work to support those people in Vietnam who suffered from its actions.[33] Even when praising government action, such as the Saigon-Biên Hòa road project, Phan Quang Đán was able to find fault with the Saigon Government. In an article in his newspaper, *Thời luân* (Commentary), Phan Quang Đán argued that the new highway would "have a deep and realistic influence not only in the economic, but also in the psychological and political fields."[34] He, however, criticized Ngô Đình Diệm for not giving the people whose homes were affected by the highway project the time to move and receive compensation as outlined in article 20 of the Vietnamese Constitution. He also used *Thời luân* to voice the concerns of other Vietnamese people and organization against Saigon Government action.

On August 25, *Thời luân* published a lament from Chinese merchants who had seen their livelihood decline since the passage of Ordinance 53, which prohibited foreigners from practicing eleven professions in Vietnam. It printed an appeal by reserve soldiers who had not been demobilized despite completing their two years of service.[35] He was also critical of the trial of the twenty-three Bình Xuyên personnel who were being charged with a breach of internal security under Article 146 of the Military Law and amended Penal Code for their role in the 1955 uprising in Saigon.[36] He argued that death penalties for eight of the men and the other, less harsh verdicts were too severe. Bowie, who reported to Washington on Phan Quang Đán's position, relied on three individuals for his report, all of who were anti–Ngô Đình Diệm. This trend of reaching out to the opposition and reporting their perspective would become the standard in Durbrow's embassy.[37]

In the confrontation between Phan Quang Đán and Ngô Đình Diệm, it did not help the Saigon Government that the offices of *Thời luân* and another oppositionist newspaper *Tân Dân* were attacked and the editions ready for distribution were destroyed.[38] About thirty individuals who were attending a Harbor Workers' mass meeting organized to denounce the newspapers left after the meeting was over to destroy the newspaper offices. A third daily, *Tự do*, which was friendly to the government, was attacked for denouncing the destruction. Condemnation of the attacks continued and was joined by a fourth paper, *Ngôn luận* (Opinion).[39] The attacks occurred during the week of September 13 while Ngô Đình Diệm was in Australia, though Durbrow reported that it was clear the action had the approval of the Saigon Government. Earlier accounts from the United States embassy characterized the pro–Government papers as barely mentioning the event, though Durbrow later reported on September 21 that the *Times of Vietnam* used an editorial to deplore the sacking of the offices and wished that the attackers had used different means of demonstrating their views.[40]

The American reports of a lack of pro–Government press on the event were somewhat misleading, as it filled all Vietnamese newspapers for the next two weeks. While some newspapers, such as *Ngôn luận*, condemned Phan Quang Đán for exploiting the Bình Xuyên defendants to further his own political career, presumably through publicity, and *Cách mạng Quốc gia* (National Revolution) questioned the defending of "culprits whose guilt is as clear as day," not all newspapers neglected the consequences of the original article and the drama that followed.[41] *Tự do* was quite critical of Phan Quang Đán's article but condemned the sacking of *Thời luân*'s offices as well as the *Dân chúng* publishing house that printed the newspaper.[42]

The destruction of the *Dân chúng* publishing house was front page news on all of the Saigon dailies on September 9.[43] The Chinese newspapers *Sun Wun Jih Pao* and *Yuan Tung Jinh Pao* both provided narratives of the events while *May Jih Luan Zan*, the Chinese-language daily, offered a reporter's eyewitness account of the original demonstration as it began at the dock warehouse.[44] The *Vietnam Press* enumerated all of the damage suffered by both *Thời luân* and *Tân Dân*.[45] While Durbrow was technically correct that the pro–Government newspapers, as a whole, did not share any sympathy to the destruction of the newspapers involved in the controversy, he reported only a portion of what was going on in the Vietnamese press. Newspaper stories about the destruction, its costs and effects on the lives of those associated with the organization, and the role of the press in Vietnam, were predominant in the newspapers. *Cách mạng Quốc gia* and *Đan Nguyên* continued to provide accounts as Durbrow had initially stated but there was no absence of press disagreement with them. Many newspapers rallied to the cause and condemned the actions even in the face of continued threats to their person and organization. The domestic upheaval surrounding the newspapers would eventually relax though such concerns were always prevalent under the surface of the Saigon political scene. Indeed, Durbrow would learn quickly that the dynamics of Saigon politics was complex and sometimes contradictory. This was true not only with the Vietnamese intelligentsia that served as a constant source of trouble for Ngô Đình Diệm but also the French who did not plan to leave Vietnam quietly.

Both Williams—who had been in Vietnam longer and had dealt with the French duplicity before—and Durbrow worked with Ngô Đình Diệm to ease the transition. It was clear, however, that Ngô Đình Diệm did not want to go easy on the French. In a September 27 meeting with Durbrow, he clearly indicated his displeasure with the French and told Durbrow that he would ask their Cultural Mission to leave if they did not withdraw their intelligence agents and return certain buildings that had been promised to the Republic of Vietnam.[46] For Ngô Đình Diệm, the French were the source of most of this discontent in Vietnam and the main instigators of rumor and intrigue designed to thwart his progress and remove him from power. Durbrow's challenge was to sift through real and imaginary French moves as he charted the United States' path for Vietnam to productive membership in the international community of nations.

While Durbrow and Ngô Đình Diệm navigated rumor and intrigue, of immediate concern to Ngô Đình Diệm upon his return to Vietnam was the construction of several highways which would connect urban centers and provide both economic and security opportunities between the southern and northern regions of the country. Durbrow and Ngô Đình Diệm had discussed the Saigon-Biên Hòa project before the Washington trip and it, along with other ideas, resurfaced in early June. Amidst a reoccurring conversation about the size and role of the Civil Guard, Durbrow worked with Ngô Đình Diệm to finalize the road projects. On June 18, Durbrow, Williams, and Director of the USOM Leland Barrows met with Ngô Đình Diệm to discuss priorities for the road construction.[47] While the 18-month Saigon-Biên Hòa project was settled upon, and construction begun on July 23, Williams kept pushing for a Ban Mê Thuột–Ninh Hòa road in order to ease the movement of material from Nhà Trắng to the Central Highlands.[48]

Ngô Đình Diệm agreed with Williams' logic, but he wanted priorities to be pushed further north, with the road from Ban Mê Thuột to Kontum via Pleiku taking precedent. Ngô Đình Diệm worried over how those in the northern part of the country would feel if a more southerly approach was taken. In reality, Ngô Đình Diệm wanted the northern region opened for refugee resettlement and serve as a barrier against Northern incursions. He also envisioned a plan to discharge 3,000 servicemen per month to populate the 300,000 hectares of land in the Sóc Trăng–Cà Mau–Bac Lieu region. Both areas were under threat by the insurgents.[49] The conversation on the roads was significant, if only because it reaffirmed the differences in strategical thinking between Ngô Đình Diệm and the Americans.[50]

Domestically, land reform continued to be a focus for Ngô Đình Diệm and a challenge for Durbrow. In his July 7, 1957, anniversary speech, Ngô Đình Diệm lauded his land reform accomplishments, which he included as increasing land available for tenant farmers, increasing contracts between landowners and tenants, and loaning money to farmers and cooperatives to increase production."[51] The reality of the situation was not as positive. The Vietnamese people in the countryside had to contend with more than one challenge as they navigated between landowners, the Saigon Government, and the insurgency. Landowners, often absentee, charged for the use of land that sometimes generations of Vietnamese had worked, while the insurgents encouraged their refusal to pay rent and instead pay tribute to them. Ngô Đình Diệm's intrusion was perhaps not as direct; he had ordered the purchase of land in the vulnerable regions to the northwest of Saigon and along the border of Cambodia

Director of the United States Operations Mission in Vietnam Leland Barrows (*left*) with Ngô Đình Diệm at the Presidential Palace in Saigon, 1958. Arthur Z. Gardiner Papers (2014–2025) (Harry S. Truman Library & Museum).

and then set it aside for troops on active duty to work with their families and then take over once their service commitment was complete.⁵² Ngô Đình Diệm hoped that this process would then encourage the people working nearby lands to purchase outright rather than pay the insurgents tribute. As Durbrow and Ngô Đình Diệm worked out their relationship, others in Vietnam with a longer history in the country warned Durbrow of potential trouble with the Ngô family.

At the new United States Consulate in Huế, the American views on the Ngô family were quite strong. After a failed attempt by Durbrow to meet Ngô Đình Diệm's brother Ngô Đình Cẩn through a visit to their mother, the American consul, Robert Barbour, wrote a scathing despatch to Washington in which he characterized Ngô Đình Cẩn as an "aloof and skittish individual" who was said to "rule Central Viet Nam with an iron and bigoted hand."⁵³ Throughout his report Barbour loathingly described the failure of Ngô Đình Cẩn to meet with Durbrow, which he saw as a deliberate slight. Barbour followed up his reporting of Ngô Đình Cẩn in early September with a despatch about how the Revolutionary Workers' Party planned to reorganize later in the year at its national convention in Saigon. The party would have both Ngô Đình Nhu and Ngô Đình Cẩn as its leaders. Barbour warned that if the reorganization happen, it would be difficult to diminish the political influence of Ngô Đình Cẩn.[54]

Another source of complaint for Ngô Đình Diệm came from individuals within the Saigon community who had access to American embassy staff. The reports of meal time conversation made their way to Washington and helped to create an image of Ngô Đình Diệm that was used to later establish American policy in Vietnam. Embassy member Robert Jelley reported one such conversation on September 18 that took place with Vietnamese National Assembly Deputy Nguyễn Văn Báu. During the course of their conversation and three bottles of wine, Jelley reported that Nguyễn Văn Báu lamented the "mandarin mentality" of those in charge in the northern region of the Republic.[55] In addition to criticizing Ngô Đình Diệm's family, while praising the president, Nguyễn Văn Báu also indicated that the National Assembly had little control over any matter of importance and commented on the inability of the northerner, in reference to Ngô Đình Diệm and his family, to understand the southerners. Nguyễn Văn Báu would not be the first to complain, nor would he be the last, but the constant reporting of only those who criticized the Saigon Government made their way into reports to Washington.

The events with Cambodia, the Saigon intelligentsia, and the negative reporting from Huế limited the honeymoon period for Durbrow. He had landed an ambassadorship in a country that was progressing forward but still deeply dependent upon the United States for its survival. After the Ngô Đình Diệm trip to the United States, Durbrow learned just how significant his challenge was and, through that, how difficult it would be to gather all of the principle actors together to accomplish the American goals for Vietnam. Even as he did this, Durbrow had to reconcile the fact that Vietnam's goals were not always the same as those of the United States. His path in Vietnam would be a difficult one, but not one, at least in 1957, that he felt was beyond his talent. It would be some time before this possibility occurred to him.

4

Funding the Vietnam Strategy, 1957

One of the recurring issues between Durbrow and Ngô Đình Diệm was the amount of aid the Republic of Vietnam received from the United States. The fiscal year 1958 was no exception. While Durbrow and Williams had been deflecting anxious questions about the amount of aid for most of Durbrow's young tenure as ambassador, the situation became more pronounced in October. On October 1, Durbrow and Williams met with Ngô Đình Diệm, Secretary of State for the Interior Nguyễn Hữu Châu, Acting Minister of Defense Trần Trung Dũng, and Assistant to the Minister of Defense Nguyễn Đình Thuần.[1] The principle purpose of the meeting, called by Ngô Đình Diệm, was to discuss the proposed reduction of American spending on the South Vietnamese military, which was estimated at twenty percent. Barrows had met with Nguyễn Ngọc Thơ earlier to inform the Vietnamese of the anticipated cuts and the expectation that the Vietnamese would make up the difference based on increased Treasury receipts.[2] Nguyễn Hữu Châu maintained that the Saigon Government could not fill the gap by doubling its ten percent contribution to the military budget because of lower than anticipated tax revenue, which had been originally based on USOM predictions. Essentially, he argued that the Vietnamese were relying on revenue anticipated by faulty data. The shortfall could not be managed by the Vietnamese. This was probably not the best way to start what would be a contentious conversation.

Williams took a more conciliatory approach to this issue, maintaining that the establishment of a priorities list for economic and military spending would help deal with the situation; Durbrow was more determined in his line of debate. This was not a predetermined strategy but more of a reflection on how the two men differed in dealing with the Vietnamese. Over the course of the next three years, Williams followed a methodology that involved listening to and talking with his counterparts. Initially, Durbrow acted the same, but as his ambassadorship continued he changed to a position where talking, or dictating, to the Vietnamese became his standard. The evolution of this process would not only strain the Williams-Durbrow relationship but would have dire consequences to the American position in Vietnam by the time John F. Kennedy entered the White House in 1961.

As the conversation continued, Nguyễn Hữu Châu brought up the issue of the Civil Guard and the Self-Defense Corps again. He argued that these units were critical to Vietnam's military strength and needed to be expanded, basically reiterating the position the Vietnamese had been advocating for the past several months. When Durbrow asserted that funds would need to be diverted from other projects to support those two organizations, it changed the course of the conversation and revealed Durbrow's changing perception of the Vietnamese president. Ngô Đình Diệm maintained that the needs of the military outweighed the needs of the economy, to which Durbrow took exception. For the Vietnamese, a strong military was essential if reunification negotiations were ever to proceed in earnest with the North Vietnamese. Ngô Đình Diệm also worried over the real possibility that the Republic of Vietnam would become isolated in Southeast Asia, considering the neutralist and questionable policies in Cambodia and Laos, and the political instability in Thailand. He culminated his argument with the proposal that the United States increase its military spending in Vietnam at the expense of Cambodia and other neutral countries which were, in fact, receiving aid from the Communist nations as well. What Ngô Đình Diệm argued, in essence, was that Vietnam should be rewarded for its unwavering support of the Free World's fight against the Communist Bloc at the expense of those who were less worthy allies.

Durbrow was not swayed by this line of reasoning. He argued that Cambodia received a much smaller aid package from the United States than Vietnam and any decrease to it would not make up the difference. He ended the conversation by telling Ngô Đình Diệm that the MAAG and USOM would continue to study the issue and provide recommendations. He would not provide any decisions until that point. The next day, Ngô Đình Diệm requested another visit with Durbrow on a separate matter but brought up the same topic at the end of that conversation. Both meetings forced Durbrow to the conclusion that Ngô Đình Diệm was only concerned with military strength and security. He reported to Washington that Ngô Đình Diệm had neither the desire nor willingness to understand the need to build up the economy, which Durbrow had argued would serve the Vietnamese better in gaining regional allies and provide future stability. Durbrow's remarked that Ngô Đình Diệm was more interested in a "strong, well-trained, loyal military machine, and he does not believe that economic development serves to assure the continuance of his regime."³ Whether accurate or not, this type of developing perspective created a dangerous path in working with the Vietnamese.

Durbrow was clearly influenced by Barrows and the USOM, which had become increasingly frustrated with the lack of progress with American-led initiatives in the Republic of Vietnam. Ladejinsky also served on Barrows' side, urging Ngô Đình Diệm to work closely with USOM experts on a number of issues.⁴ It did not help the economic front that Ngô Đình Diệm and the Vietnamese consistently clashed over the road building scheme and other issues. As Ngô Đình Diệm remarked to Durbrow at the end of their October 2 conversation, the "miracle" of Vietnam that had been reported in the United States was more flattering then it was realistic.⁵ There were problems that still existed in the Republic of Vietnam and Ngô Đình Diệm fought for every dollar of United States aid. For him, this assistance was a matter of survival and no sum could be too large. Durbrow had the luxury of being more sparing with American dollars.

One example of the differences between Ngô Đình Diệm and Barrows' USOM that helped to maintain the level of tension between the two was the scheme of General Lê Văn Kim, who Williams had wanted to replace General Hoàng Văn Lạc in Huế. Lê Văn Kim had tried to bypass Ngô Đình Diệm's plans in the Central Highlands by establishing resettlements based on a Russian model.⁶ Rather than resettle individuals on two or three hectares of land as Ngô Đình Diệm had wanted, Lê Văn Kim called for the clearing of one-hectare pilot farms, which would be seeded while those resettled watched and learned how to maintain it. Once the pilot farm was established, each person would be given four hectares. Essentially, this doubled the land envisioned, which would, as Ngô Đình Diệm complained to Williams, denude the forests.

Ngô Đình Diệm was more angered by the USOM attitude, which had accepted Lê Văn Kim's plan and moved forward with it, because it assumed that Ngô Đình Diệm had approved it. When Ngô Đình Diệm expressed his displeasure, the USOM representatives informed him that they would not change course nor would they release funds for Ngô Đình Diệm's original plan until he could prove that it would be successful. Ngô Đình Diệm was clearly angered by Lê Văn Kim's actions and confronted him, and he was also justified in his attitude towards those Americans who moved forward with a major plan without his approval, and then compounded the problem by refusing to work with the Saigon Government to resolve the conflict.

When Nguyễn Hữu Châu met with Durbrow again on October 30 to discuss the Self-Defense Force, he reiterated Ngô Đình Diệm's conviction of its importance in countering the Communist threat. Nguyễn Hữu Châu informed Durbrow that if the United States did not pay its "'promised' share, the Vietnamese would have to find money for the Self-Defense Force by taking it away from some other important project or borrowing from the Treasury."⁷ Durbrow used the words "promised share" in his reporting to Washington though there was no corroborating evidence to suggest that Nguyễn Hữu Châu used such language. Durbrow did report his concerns to Nguyễn Hữu Châu about the lack of organization, chain of command, and training system for the Self-Defense Force. Whether this was a defensive reflex to Nguyễn Hữu Châu's words or a real concern, even if already mentioned by the ambassador on a few different occasions, was less important that the fact that this Vietnamese concern was, as Durbrow remarked, still being investigated by the Country Team; that is, there was no progress to report.[8]

While Durbrow was intransigent, Williams was willing to continue the discussion. During their December 3 meeting, Ngô Đình Diệm requested that Williams help to accelerate the process to procure American rifles for the Civil Guard.[9] Williams reiterated that the USOM could not proceed with arming the Civil Guard until there was an approved organizational table. While Durbrow would have left the conversation stand at that point, Williams asked Ngô Đình Diệm if he thought it was expected that MAAG prepare the organizational table. It was at this point that Ngô Đình Diệm asked not only for a United States point of view on the Civil Guard but also for a few sample table of organizations so he could study them to make sure the Americans understood his concept. At issue here was whether the Vietnamese had the resources and expertise to create a table of organization for the Civil Guard. Durbrow interpreted their delays as a result of disorganization and confusion, while Williams saw the issue as one of expertise. MAAG had been going through the same process for the Vietnamese Army for over a year and Williams understood the magnitude of the complexity involved. Rather than withholding weapons with a demand for the document, Williams offered a way for the process to move forward, even though he informed Ngô Đình Diệm that the Michigan State University Group was opposed to the president's plan.

Another example of Ngô Đình Diệm's trust of Williams and worry over Durbrow occurred during a December 20 meeting when Ngô Đình Diệm complained that Durbrow seemed to dismiss Ngô Đình Diệm's arguments for the need for improved roads, an improved Civil Guard, and the need to resettle the Central Highlands, suggesting that the latter was improvised, but listened to Minister Counselor of the French Embassy, M. Michel Wintrebert, during their meeting with him as they inspected the Ban Mê Thuột area on December 18–19.[10] Wintrebert discussed the importance of the region as the best line of defense against a northern attack. Ngô Đình Diệm remarked to Williams that Durbrow "was very much impressed to hear this from a Frenchman," though Ngô Đình Diệm had been making the same argument since the ambassador arrived in Vietnam.[11] It seems that the two also shared a more personal relationship than Durbrow had with the president. Both seemed to be able to joke with one another without finding cause for offense.

Williams understood Ngô Đình Diệm and the problems he faced. For example, after Ngô Đình Diệm returned from his Christmas trip to Bổ Túc and Pleiku, he maintained that he needed new tents, cots, and bedrolls.[12] Williams offered Army equipment but Ngô Đình Diệm wanted items from the Sears and Roebuck catalog. While the two went back and forth on the tents and equipment, Ngô Đình Diệm told Williams that he would pay for everything from his own resources but would need at least five tents because he often took a group with him on his visit to the Central Highlands. Williams suggested, to the delight of Ngô Đình Diệm, that if he wanted to toughen up his ministers, he could have them sleep on the ground rather than in the tents. This type of exchange, in jest, was absent in the Durbrow–Ngô Đình Diệm conversations.

In fact, Durbrow reported to Washington that the purpose of all of Ngô Đình Diệm's trips at the end of the year was to show the members of the Diplomatic Corp in Saigon that the resettlement camps were progressing well, to offset the criticism from the same group.[13] The Diplomatic Corps had also been critical of the Self-Defense Forces and the security in the Mekong Delta, and Durbrow mused that Ngô Đình Diệm also intended these trips to counter those feelings. While it was certainly possible that Ngô Đình Diệm had these as some of his motives, to assign his movement in the countryside solely for the purpose of influencing the Diplomatic Corp seemed a little narrow. Ngô Đình Diệm also made trips without the Diplomatic Corp during 1957 and would continue to do so until the end of his time in Vietnam. How, and whether, Durbrow reported on these trips to Washington would be telling.

Ngô Đình Diệm's trips held several purposes. He wanted to understand what was occurring in the countryside in order to better plan for the future. He needed to check up on his subordinates to make sure they were carrying out their orders properly. Most important, Ngô Đình Diệm wanted to have a visible presence in the countryside, to reassure the people who continued to suffer from a colonial past and an insecure present. Security was a significant concern for Ngô Đình Diệm just as it was for Durbrow. On October 4, Durbrow circulated a memorandum to American officials in Saigon about the increase in attacks in the countryside, including the assassination of the District Chief and his family in Mỹ Tho. He established a series of restriction for travel as well as protocol of individual travel outside of the urban centers.[14] This action came as a result of an October 2 meeting with Ngô Đình Diệm, during which the Vietnamese president informed him that he had credible evidence of potential Communists attacks against Americans.[15]

Durbrow's report to Washington and his actions after his conversation with Ngô Đình Diệm suggest that he did not take the threat too seriously, though he did release his official warning. Durbrow read more into the conversation, especially when Ngô Đình Diệm suggested that American journalists refrain from meeting opposition politicians in "dark small alleys" at night, though he had no problem with the same journalists meeting the opposition leaders in more secure areas. Ngô Đình Diệm's remarks about the secretive nature of the opposition leaders were not lost on Durbrow, who apologized for his cynicism in reporting the threat. By questioning the sincerity of the warning in his reporting, Durbrow began to create the foundation for future reports that questioned the goodwill of Ngô Đình Diệm.

Ngô Đình Diệm's warning became real on October 22 when an explosion, presumably a stick of dynamite, occurred within the Five Oceans Bachelor Officers Quarters in Saigon. The explosion injured a group of United States Army officers who were standing in front of the military billet. The attack, which happened at 7:25 a.m., was followed by a second ten minutes later at the Metropole Hotel, which housed enlisted men. In all, thirteen men were injured, though none were killed.[16] A third bomb exploded at the United States Information Service (USIS) library at approximately 1:08 p.m.[17] The damage was extensive, but there were no serious casualties. Almost all of the Vietnamese daily newspapers published statements from the State Department and the Saigon Government claiming that the attacks were initiated by the Communist insurgents.[18] When Durbrow met with Ngô Đình Diệm on October 22 to discuss the attacks, he acknowledged the accuracy of the information provided but then questioned Ngô Đình Diệm on whether these same intelligence sources had concrete information about whether the Pathet Lao were communist.[19] Ngô Đình Diệm indicated that he did have the evidence, though he did not think the Laotians would believe it. It seems strange, given the day's events, that Durbrow would switch the conversation to Laos and that he needed Vietnamese proof of communist influences of the Pathet Lao.

When Ngô Đình Diệm met with Williams on October 24, he showed his concerns over the wounded soldiers and informed the general that a Laotian had been arrested on an Air Laos flight to Vietnam after he was caught with a box of detonators.[20] The Laotian claimed he was going to use them for fishing. However, there were some organizations that used the attacks to discredit the Saigon Government. The Voice of the National Salvation Movement, a clandestine radio station, broadcast several reports about the day. On October 23, it argued that whether the attacks were inspired by the Communist insurgents, the reality was that because the United States supported Ngô Đình Diệm, it should expect to suffer either directly or indirectly. It also reported that the Saigon Government was incapable, despite millions of American dollars and years of training, of protecting the people of Saigon.[21] The media in Hanoi followed a similar line of argument in its reporting of the attacks.²² Eventually, other Vietnamese dailies editorialized on the bombings. *Ngôn luận* called them, "the insane and barbarous acts of a wild animal," while *Cách mạng Quốc gia* maintained that the acts were "contemptible terrorism."²³ By November 8, the Central Intelligence Agency maintained that the wave of anti–American attacks was over, though it noted that continued assassinations and other acts of terror against the Vietnamese were still possible.²⁴

Another issue facing Durbrow and Ngô Đình Diệm was a controversial Government measure that attempted to disband more than 300 labor organizations for failing to possess authorization certificates from the Ministry of the Interior. The Vietnamese press was critical of this move, despite Ngô Đình Diệm's claim that many of the groups were fronts for Communist activity. *Dân chúng* argued that the Saigon Government's actions against the labor unions was unconstitutional, while *May Jih Luan Zan* published a letter from the Vietnamese General Confederation of Labor about the move against its members.²⁵ Neither paper was punished for publishing stories that were not favorable to Saigon's policies.

Intertwined with this domestic turmoil was the problem of Cambodian-Vietnamese relations. Cambodia continued to be an issue for Durbrow as he sought to relieve tension along the border, as well as enhance South Vietnam's image around the world. Reports continued to emerge of cross-border incursions and raids, such as the one that the Cambodian newspaper *Sống chung* reported on October 15.²⁶ The *Sống chung* story highlighted a Vietnamese commando raid from An Giang province into the village of Khánh An. The newspaper claimed that eight villages had been ordered to evacuate from the border, and when the villagers of Khánh An refused, the population of approximately 100 people was detained. While there was no confirmation of the events as described in the article, this type of reporting helped maintain the level of intensity and animosity that kept tensions high.²⁷

The next challenge in October occurred when Penn Nouth, the Cambodian representative to the United Nations, made a speech in the General Assembly which implied, if it did not directly single out, the negative role of the Republic of Vietnam in Southeast Asia.²⁸ While Durbrow saw these moves as purely political, he recommended against action because it would most likely be ineffective. Durbrow saw the two sides as over-emotional in their debate on the border dispute, which was curious, as there was evidence of communist incursions from Cambodia into South Vietnam that seriously affected internal security.²⁹

While there was a 3,000-man force from the 11th Light Division that was engaged in the Delta region near the border of Cambodia, it was focused on the Việt Cộng and other dissent groups. Ngô Đình Diệm dismissed the Cambodian complaints, citing their need to be noticed. He denied the idea that the South Vietnamese were building up forces along the border beyond the primary mission of dealing with the insurgents and continued to press the Americans on the role of the French in influencing Cambodian policy. In a conversation with Williams, Ngô Đình Diệm claimed that half of the French aid to the Cambodians was used for currency manipulation and opium traffic, the profits of which the French ambassador and secret service manipulated for their own clandestine activities.[30] Ngô Đình Diệm did not provide any evidence for these accusations.

When United States ambassador to Cambodia Carl Strom met with Sim Var to discuss the situation, he learned that the Cambodians were eager to end the conflict but were concerned that the Vietnamese had not responded to the protests they had filed.[31] Ngô Trọng Hiếu, the Vietnamese representative in Cambodia, had also failed to provide evidence that the Communists were sending weapons to the insurgents across the border. The Cambodians did not seem to want to address the issue until the Vietnamese initiated the conversation and provided tangible proof. Strom recommended that Durbrow share Sim Var's remarks and concerns with Ngô Trọng Hiếu to which Durbrow agreed though he reiterated his desire not to have the United States intervene in this affair with the Vietnamese for fear that they would resent such actions.[32] Less than a week later, Durbrow switched his position and thought it not prudent to relay the conversation in specifics. Durbrow was very concerned about perception and worried that both sides would use the United States to their advantage. He did not want the American position in Southeast Asia compromised.[33]

Significant to the Vietnamese-Cambodia rift was the very real disadvantage of the Vietnamese insurgents negotiating with the Cambodians. The two sides met in October for two and a half weeks and issued a five-point communiqué that suggested the possibility of closer relations.[34] For the Vietnamese, the emerging relationship confirmed that Cambodia's neutrality was in name only, while the United States worried about how it would affect a non-communist Cambodia. There was also a concern that the Vietnamese insurgents' representatives were speaking for all Vietnamese to the exclusion of the Saigon Government. The consequences for the Vietnamese-Cambodian border dispute, should the Cambodians allow this, did not bode well for the future stability of Southeast Asia.

The two sides continued to bicker as they worked to figure out a solution to this lingering controversy. Both Sim Var and Ngô Đình Diệm called for negotiations without proceeding to the next step. Ngô Đình Diệm told Durbrow on October 17 that he approved of a Cambodian incursion 500 meters into Vietnam to engage with insurgents but was angered by the fact that the Cambodians had not told ARVN about the operation in advance. Ngô Đình Diệm suggested that had they done so, the two sides could have coordinated and done a more effective job, but also at play was the idea that the failure to communicate the plans in advance was a slight to the Vietnamese.[35] It did not help that Ngô Đình Diệm was losing faith in Ngô Trọng Hiếu. Ngô Đình Diệm believed that he was too timid.[36] Whether Ngô Đình Diệm was justified in his assessment, it helped to reinforce Durbrow's growing notion that the Vietnamese president had a shrinking circle of confidants beyond his family.

Ngô Trọng Hiếu met Durbrow for the first time on October 24 to discuss the media campaign.[37] He wondered why the editor of the *Times of Vietnam*, Gene Gregory, an American, would write so dismissively about Prince Norodom Sihanouk. Ngô Trọng Hiếu was most likely referring to an October 19 article in the *Times of Vietnam*, which accused the Cambodians of tolerating a Hòa Hảo presence in their country. The article set off another round of media jabs by each nation.[38] The implication was that because he was an American, he was sponsored by the United States Government. Durbrow dispelled that notion and countered with an implication that someone in Saigon was influencing Gregory. When Ngô Trọng Hiếu claimed he was at a loss as to who this would be, that is, not naming a member of the Ngô family, Durbrow doubted this innocent in his report to Washington.

There was no question in Durbrow's mind that Ngô Đình Diệm or Ngô Đình Nhu was behind the media attacks, a point to which Ngô Trọng Hiếu indirectly confirmed when he told the ambassador that Ngô Đình Diệm was in no mood to work with the Cambodians as long as their media blitz about Vietnamese troops along the border continued. The war of words persisted when an *Agence Kampuchea Presse* story reported demonstrations by Cambodians in Trà Vinh province against Vietnamese troop concentrations along the border.[39] The Vietnamese denied the allegation and the demonstrations. Edmund Kellogg, Counselor and Consul General of the Embassy in Cambodia, confirmed that Ngô Trọng Hiếu was near the end of his usefulness after their meeting on October 29.[40] Kellogg described Ngô Trọng Hiếu as tired, discouraged, and voicing his desire to resign.

The border dispute helped to illuminate Durbrow's personality, style of leadership, and feeling towards Ngô Đình Diệm. He was concerned about perception, at times, more than the actual situation. For Ngô Đình Diệm, the Cambodians were neutralists who were influenced by the French to serve against the best interests of the Vietnamese. In dealing with his western neighbor, Ngô Đình Diệm was less concerned about perception and more with the real threat that Cambodia imposed by its diplomacy and unsecure border. Internal security was paramount and a necessary requirement for economic revitalization and the future of the Republic Vietnam. As Williams would point out in a letter to Stump on October 18, this growing distinction was worrisome: "Frankly, I can't help but feel the relationship between the GVN and ourselves (Military excepted) is not as cordial as it was a few months ago."[41] The only variable added during this time was the introduction of Durbrow as ambassador.

In addition to the border dispute, Durbrow had to contend with the Vietnamese press, whose sponsorship in part by the Saigon Government gave it credibility as the voice of Ngô Đình Diệm. The *Times of Vietnam* offered two editorials on the rule of Sihanouk in Cambodia that increased the ire of the Phnom Penh leadership. Kellogg met with Sim Var on October 22 to discuss the October 11 editorial. Sim Var argued that the insulting language to Sihanouk, calling him a "hypocrites [sic], spoiled child, kept child" was provocative in a time when the Cambodians were planning to negotiate with the Vietnamese at their request.[42] While Kellogg had to smooth the way for Sim Var, Durbrow needed to present a stronger position against these intentional provocations.

Cambodia was not the only area of concern for Durbrow as he built his relationship with the Vietnamese. While the situation in Laos might not have been a high priority for Durbrow, it was for the Vietnamese. On November 2, Nguyễn Ngọc Thơ and Nguyễn Hữu Châu met with Durbrow to express their concern over the increased Communist presence in Laos and their fear that South Vietnam was being boxed in by its neighbors.[43] Earlier that day, Prime Minister Prince Souvanna Phouma and the Chairman of the Political Delegation of the Pathet Lao, Phoumi Vongvichit, had signed a political agreement in which the Pathet Lao turned over the provinces of Sam Neua and Phong Saly.[44] In return, the Pathet Lao forces were integrated into the Royal Laotian Army and a coalition government was created that would lend legitimacy to the Pathet Lao as a political force. While the CIA indicated in a November 30 report that there was some movement in the anti-communist propaganda campaign in the country as well as the introduction of 200 police in each of the Northern provinces, the Pathet Lao representatives in the Laotian cabinet were creating obstacles to the governing of them. The new possibility of a legitimate Pathet Lao organization that still had the support of the North Vietnamese caused worry for Ngô Đình Diệm.[45] When Ngô Đình Diệm met with Williams on December 3, the two briefly discussed Laos and the integration of the Pathet Lao in the Royal Laotian Army.[46] Ngô Đình Diệm complained that the Laotian officials were not taking the Pathet Lao forces seriously and had no contingency in place should they begin to make trouble.

While Ngô Đình Diệm expressed his concerns, the Vietnamese dailies offered a different perspective. *Dan Nguyên* argued that the agreement boded well for the people of Southeast Asia and expressed a hope that the Communists in North Vietnam would follow suit. *Lê Sống* (Reason to Live) maintained that the settlement was more a result of the Pathet Lao exhausted from its struggle and realized that it could not be supported from Peking or Hanoi.⁴⁷ The effects of the merger would not become clear until 1958.

Cambodia and Laos were at the forefront of Ngô Đình Diệm's exchanges with Durbrow, though domestic actions involving the Saigon government caused greater concern for the ambassador. The conflict between Phan Quang Đán and the Saigon Government continued into October, with *Đan Nguyên* issuing a series of articles designed to discredit him. In its September 28 issue, it published an article based on an earlier one by Hilaire du Berrier that suggested a link between Phan Quang Đán, though not naming him directly, and the Office of Strategic Services (OSS) at the end of the Second World War.⁴⁸ This was followed by an October 3 article that asked Phan Quang Đán to answer two questions: Was he a spy for the OSS, and did he live at the expense of the OSS?⁴⁹ The newspaper also rejected his response to du Berrier's charges against him, citing his connection to opium smuggling and other criminal activities and asserting that only other criminals were aware of such criminal activities. *Thời luân* responded to the charges with a detailed timeline of Phan Quang Đán's life as well as details on how he had been slandered in the past.⁵⁰

This interaction intertwined with a Government lawsuit against *Thời luân* for articles "harming national interest and for public defamation."⁵¹ The trial, which was supposed to begin at the start of October but was delayed until the end of the month, was designed to put pressure on the newspaper, which was the voice of the Democratic Opposition Bloc. *Thời luân* again found an ally in *Tự do*, which published an editorial on October 4 that enumerated the need of having *Thời luân* and the Democratic Opposition Bloc in a free Republic of Vietnam.⁵² *Thời luân* did not back down in its publications, even after one of its Sunday supplements was seized. On October 13, the newspaper called on the Saigon Government to reimburse it for damages suffered in September, printed reports of support for it from the Vietnamese people, and made calls for democracy in the Republic.⁵³ On October 12, one charge against *Thời luân* by the Ministry of Economics was dismissed by the Court of Assizes.⁵⁴

Thời luân was not alone in voicing its dissent. On November 19, *Dân chúng* issued an editorial that called for the press to unite against the threat, perceived or real, of intimidation against it.⁵⁵ The newspaper asserted that all members of the press needed to rally together, not only to support *Dân chúng* which had suffered earlier and was the victim of several bomb threats, but also to support any organization that was the focus of an anti-free speech campaign. Both *Thời luân* and *Dân chúng* printed stories designed to counter alleged government abuse, whether it was an attempt to suppress it or the labor unions.⁵⁶ *Ngôn luận* started a series of articles towards the end of November in which it questioned the effectiveness of the government's anti-communist policies.⁵⁷ *Tự do* took on the National Revolutionary Movement's newspaper, *Cách mạng Quốc gia*, which maintained that the labor unions needed to be disbanded because the ranks had been filled by communists.⁵⁸ These newspapers represented an opposition press that was active and vocal in its reporting and dissent.

The question of American aid to the Republic was never far from the minds of the Vietnamese. During a November 22 trip to visit refugee villages and inspect the road work to the north of Saigon, Ngô Đình Diệm again referred to the necessity of maintaining the aid packet if not increasing it.⁵⁹ Ngô Đình Diệm used polite, but strong, wording to express his worry over the proposed aid cuts and used the trip to remind Durbrow of the need for more roads at the expense of quality. This fit into the Vietnamese notion of holistically dealing with the multitude of problems confronting the Republic of Vietnam. Ngô Đình Diệm was faced with a Laotian border that harbored the Pathet Lao, a neutralist in name only Cambodia, and increased insurgent activities in his own country. He led the fight in these battles while at the same time trying to provide leadership in the lesser developed countries against Communism. United States aid was essential to overcome these problems and Durbrow had a difficult time convincing Ngô Đình Diệm that these monies were going to be less available in the coming year.

Durbrow needed to convince Ngô Đình Diệm that the United States remained a staunch ally and attempted to do so by enumerating the many American contributions to Vietnam. Using various funds, including monies from Defense Support, Technical Assistance, and un-programmed funds, the United States would contribute at least $185 million to the Vietnamese. The Americans also pushed other loan considerations such as the Development Loan Fund to bring the total up to near $200 million.⁶⁰ Durbrow also hoped to gain favor by informing Ngô Đình Diệm that MAAG had approved an increase to the Self-Defense Force to 43,500. While it was still 16,500 shy of the total needed by Ngô Đình Diệm, he hoped the compromise would satisfy the Vietnamese president.

When Durbrow and Ngô Đình Diệm met on November 27 during a luncheon for Vice Admiral Wallace Morris Beakley, the two again discussed the 1958 aid package. Ngô Đình Diệm had already heard from Trần Văn Chương that the aid package had been settled and hoped Durbrow could provide the details. Because he had not received official word from Washington, Durbrow offered only the vague information that it would be higher than the $180 million that had been discussed earlier when the cuts were announced.⁶¹ While Durbrow did not provide details, he did take the opportunity to stress how important it was for the Vietnamese to work closely with the USOM to help justify all expenditures. Ngô Đình Diệm complained of the USOM examining every request in minute detail, rather than just getting the job done. For Ngô Đình Diệm, the USOM process was cumbersome and inefficient when speed and agility was needed most. For all his understanding of the West, Ngô Đình Diệm did not accept the funding process, which made it more difficult for Durbrow to operate in Vietnam.

While Ngô Đình Diệm's complaints about the USOM fell on deaf ears with Durbrow, Williams was a more sympathetic listener. When the two met on December 3, Ngô Đình Diệm informed the General that he was able to get bulldozers from the French because they did not care how they were used, while the USOM categorized each bulldozer and only allowed it to be used for that purpose, even if it was at hand and idle.[62] Over time, the constant requests and expressions of displeasure accumulated, which helped push the ambassador towards the breaking point in his relationship with Ngô Đình Diệm.

The final aid package was revealed to the Vietnamese on November 29.[63] Both Williams and Durbrow summarized the meeting with Ngô Đình Diệm and his principle cabinet officials, though the two written remembrances were a little different. Durbrow reported that a conversation took place, during which he outlined the funds available to the Vietnamese for 1958. Williams reported the same numbers but also included Durbrow's justifications for this level of assistance, which included a failure of the Vietnamese to explain their need for additional funding on certain projects, the inability to use money already allocated, and the inability to be firm on priorities. Durbrow characterized the meeting as "frank but friendly" and noted that Ngô Đình Diệm was obviously disappointed.[64] Williams summarized the first part of the meeting, which was dominated by the Americans, with Ngô Đình Diệm's initial response when told that the aid for Vietnam was good; he answered with only one word: Why?[65]

This opened the conversation to all of the participants at the meeting with such subjects as the Self-Defense Force, resettlement, and continued cooperation between the Vietnamese and USOM taking center stage. The Vietnamese were not impressed with the 43,500 man compromise for the Self-Defense Force. Nguyễn Hữu Châu considered the budget inadequate because there were already more men in the organization than the United States budget allowed, which would require the Vietnamese to cover the additional costs. There were no additional funds available in the Vietnamese Government. Ngô Đình Diệm stressed the importance of the resettlement, with demobilized military personnel, of the High Plateau in Central Vietnam.

When Durbrow agreed on the importance of the resettlement, Ngô Đình Diệm asked him when the tractors that the United States had promised would arrive. Williams reported that this remark went unanswered. Durbrow did not mention the exchange. Instead, he reported to Washington that Ngô Đình Diệm was satisfied though disappointed at the end of the conversation, while

4. Funding the Vietnam Strategy, 1957 49

Williams's recollections did not offer any assessment of how Ngô Đình Diệm felt at the moment. It was curious that the two leading Americans in Vietnam would report the same meeting differently but, then again, each had a different perspective on Vietnam and on its leader.

Ngô Đình Diệm was so concerned about the cut in budget that he requested another meeting with Durbrow the next day.[66] The two traversed the same topics that they had had earlier, though Ngô Đình Diệm offered the observation that the Vietnamese people might call for a neutralist policy so that the government could spend more on the economy and reduce military expenditures. While Ngô Đình Diệm rejected that idea, the implied threat was real if conveyed in an amateurish way. Durbrow responded to the warning by reiterating that the Vietnamese could apply to the Development Loan Fund. He informed Washington that Ngô Đình Diệm would probably continue to plead his case though, it was clear that he did not have the sympathetic ear of the ambassador. However, Durbrow did request a review of the 1958 aid package from Washington, though the assistance amounts did not change. While Ngô Đình Diệm expected an increase in funds as a result of the review, Durbrow knew this not to be the case as early as mid–December, and rather than tell him outright, only encouraged him to apply for more Development Loan Funds.[67]

Even as Ngô Đình Diệm worried about the America aid package, he had to contend with those working around him. Ngô Đình Diệm was at ease when speaking to Williams and their relationship was different than the one he shared with Durbrow. The president expressed his frustration about the government officials, and presumably intelligentsia and opposition politicians in Saigon, who conveyed a defeatist attitude when speaking with the Americans. Wolf Ladejinski had told him that defeatist rumors were spreading through government agencies and had made their way to the embassies in Saigon.[68] Ngô Đình Diệm complained to Williams that these individuals stayed in Saigon and did not see the support or progress made in the countryside. It frustrated him that their words were considered. Williams agreed and then provided some reassurance that he did not fall into that trap. This disconnect would intensify as the years progressed and, as Durbrow moved further from Ngô Đình Diệm, it would become a significant source of contention.

Another problem for Ngô Đình Diệm that needed to be addressed was the quality of information he received from those around him. At the end of 1957, this was best expressed in the continued struggle to get the road from Kontum to Mo Doc completed. When Ngô Đình Diệm and Williams met on December 13, they spent the better part of their meeting discussing the road. Ngô Đình Diệm needed the road to be finished before the end of 1958 in order to secure the Central Highlands, which he considered the most strategic priority at the time.⁶⁹ Williams agreed, and instead of chastising the president, as had Durbrow and Barrows before, he worked with the Vietnamese to figure out what needed to be done. Williams also informed Ngô Đình Diệm of the key changes in Vietnamese personnel that had taken place in the project, of which Ngô Đình Diệm had no knowledge. After their informed discussion, in which Williams offered American engineers and other experts to assist in the project, Ngô Đình Diệm asserted that "if a 'revolution' is necessary to get results on the road, then a revolution it must be."⁷⁰ This conversation served as the starting point for several trips and briefings that joined together various Vietnamese departments and American personnel who all shared the same objective. It ushered in a spirit of cooperation that was truly needed in Vietnam but was limited to the American military.

The year 1957 ended with a certain level of uncertainty but also a hope of progress in the New Year to come. While the Vietnamese were faced with a cut in American aid, it did not stop their desire to continue to build up their armed forces, including the Civil Guard and the Self-Defense Force. Ngô Đình Diệm spent a few of the last days of the year visiting the Central Highlands, including two resettlement projects of demobilized soldiers at Bổ Túc and Katun, which were north of Tây Ninh.⁷¹ He also visited Pleiku and Kontum in an effort to get a sense of what was happening in this strategic

Ngô Đình Diệm on one of his main inspection trips to the countryside, 1959. Arthur Z. Gardiner Papers (2014-1393) (Harry S. Truman Library & Museum).

area of the country. These trips, as with all of the ones taken in 1957, pointed to a leader who was genuinely worried about his country as well as how his country was perceived internationally. It was curious that these two qualities would be the ones that Durbrow highlighted as lacking in Ngô Đình Diệm as his tenure as ambassador progressed. Cambodia continued to be a source of controversy, especially with the possibility that the Cambodians indicated a plan to establish navigational aids on the contested Poulo Panjang islands to ease transit to the their new port at Kompong.[72] The two countries had a long history of mistrust and nothing in 1957 helped to assuage it. By the end of 1957, Ngô Đình Diệm had traveled 57,498 miles, taking him to the United States, Thailand, Australia, the Republic of Korea, and India.[73] He had spent fifty-four days abroad. He also made twenty inspection trips within Vietnam for a total of 7,098 miles travelled. For any detractors of the Vietnamese president who claimed that he ruled from Saigon, these numbers offer an alternative narrative. It was one that the Americans respected, though that would change over time.

5

Planning for Victory: MAAG, Durbrow and Ngô Đình Diệm

The year 1958 started off in dramatic fashion, when, on January 4, a large-scale raid was executed by Communist insurgents against a French rubber plantation in Minh Thành, approximately 85 km north of Saigon.[1] The attackers, dressed in khaki-clad ARVN uniforms, took a significant amount of money and then looted and burned the plantation's facilities and equipment. The group quickly overwhelmed the eighty Civil Guards on the estates of *La Societe des Cauotehouc d'Extreme Orient*. During the raid, the plantation workers were subjected to lectures about the benefits of life in North Vietnam and warned not to continue supporting the Saigon Government. This event marked what would be a difficult three months for the Saigon Government and Durbrow, as each navigated the dangerous topics of family, money, Cambodia, and the Civil Guard. Each subject challenged Durbrow as he worked with the Vietnamese, while it tested everyone's patience as both sides adjusted their perspective of each other.

By the end of 1957, Durbrow had joined the ranks of those who questioned the role and value of Ngô Đình Diệm's family. Durbrow's progression against the Ngô family was evident in his reporting of his first conversation with Bishop Ngô Đình Thục, brother of Ngô Đình Diệm, who the ambassador had a chance to meet for the first time during Cardinal Francis Spellman's visit to the Republic of Vietnam. The conversation centered on how one might counter communist propaganda, which gave Durbrow an opening to ask for a definition of Personalism. This term had made its way into Ngô Đình Diệm's speeches in the latter part of 1957. Personalism would emerge as the ideological and spiritual response to Communism, and Ngô Đình Trúc offered only a general, vague statement about it to Durbrow.[2] While Durbrow still grappled with what Personalism meant, he reported that the Vietnamese people would "be as much impressed, if not more so, by evidence of honest and selfless officials at all levels and by continued improvements in the standard of living, in short, by good government, as by a fine formulation of ideals."[3] This type of passive-aggressive snub would become more common as Durbrow's time in Vietnam continued.

Like Durbrow, Robert Barbour, in the American Consul in Huế, also continued his criticism of the Ngô family in Central Vietnam. He reported on a denunciation campaign in Quảng Nam Province, which had rounded up suspects, many of whom he claimed were probably innocent, based on his sources.[4] Vietnamese newspaper referred to this as the Đại Lộc Affair.[5] Barbour maintained that Ngô Đình Diệm was angry about what amounted to an excessive zeal by his brother and the newly installed Province Chief, Hồ Liêm, but would probably not take any action. Barbour offered no evidence as to why he believed Ngô Đình Diệm would take no action other than the implied reason that he would not counter Ngô Đình Cẩn. It was this type of assumption that would lead the Americans into an increasingly hostile situation with Ngô Đình Diệm.

The affair itself was initiated by Phạm Xuân Áng, the District Chief of Đại Lộc, which was located within the province. He was responding to the Quảng Nam Province Chief, Nguyên Hòa Phạm, who believed it was time for a Communist Denunciation Campaign.[6] Phạm Xuân Áng had been appointed the chairman of the board for a local re-education course. Former members of the Communist insurgency, who had been appointed to important roles within this organization, took advantage of their new power to begin what witnesses called a campaign of terror against people who may or may not have been associated with the insurgency in the district.[7] The former Việt Minh rounded up 360 other self-confessed Việt Minh, which then led to an estimated additional 1,000 arrests. These individuals were then allegedly tortured into confession.

According to seven witnesses, who published a letter in *Tự do*, they appealed to Phạm Xuân Áng but he failed to address the issue and, instead, shielded those responsible for the questionable acts.[8] In none of the newspaper reporting, done chiefly by *Tự do*, was the old or new Province Chief or Ngô Đình Cẩn mentioned, nor was there an implied connection with either man. In Ngô Đình Diệm's conversations with Durbrow and other Americans, he never mentioned the affair, or as Barbour reported, his anger over his brother's actions. Thus, while it was possible that Barbour's reporting was accurate, there was no collaborating evidence to support it, and neither could his conclusions about Ngô Đình Diệm's possible non-action be buttressed by other evidence. It was clear, however, that the campaign did occur and had run amok. It was interesting that Barbour called for an end to such campaigns and more emphasis on social and economic assistance at a time where Ngô

Đình Diệm was contemplating ending economic programs to fund the deficit in the military budget. Something had to give during this critical time.

Barbour also wrote a high-handed dispatch about his first encounter with Ngô Đình Cẩn, who had rebuffed meetings with Americans, including Durbrow.[9] The meeting itself did not offer any new insight. Barbour dismissed Ngô Đình Cẩn's complaint about giving Vietnamese surplus cheese and powdered milk because it was foreign to their diet with the implied comment in his report that the Vietnamese should be happy that the Americans sent food. Barbour characterized Ngô Đình Cẩn as one who epitomized "all the extreme features of the Huế environment—ultra traditionalism, xenophobia, conservatism, and a general distrust of things or ideas new or foreign."[10] Barbour went into the meeting with certain expectations and did not seem to attempt to sway from these preconceptions in his reporting. He did add a note at the end of the dispatch asking that it not be shared with any Vietnamese or foreign government official, which at least acknowledged that he knew the inflammatory nature of his words.

Others who voiced their opposition in conversations to officers in the American Embassy included the Minister Counselor of the French Embassy, Michel Wintrebert, who maintained that Ngô Đình Diệm needed to be more flexible when dealing with others. "Ngô Đình Diệm was reluctant to compromise," the Hanoi-born Frenchman argued, "with an opponent or an enemy."[11] He asserted that Ngô Đình Diệm had given some freedom to the press and hoped that it would filter to the political sphere. While the remarks were noted as being friendly, it was interesting to speculate exactly how Ngô Đình Diệm was to compromise with an enemy whose sole purpose was the destruction of his government. This type of reasoning was not unique to the French; Americans would soon be voicing similar ideas much to the chagrin of Ngô Đình Diệm.

Just as domestic turmoil caused Durbrow and other American diplomats to call into question the actions of Ngô Đình Diệm and his family, so did the Vietnamese position toward the Cambodians. The situation with Cambodia did not seem to improve with the New Year. Ngô Đình Diệm was adamant in his refusal to believe that the Cambodians could, or would change. In a January 8 meeting with Williams, while they were again speaking of the status of various road projects, Williams asked the president if arrangements could be made with the Cambodians to clean out the bandits operating along the border. Ngô Đình Diệm responded emphatically that it could never happen.[12] He asserted that the Cambodians could not be trusted and maintained that the only way to make them change was to cut United States aid. Ngô Đình Diệm would continue this line of thinking much to the chagrin of many Americans. The Cambodians continued to put public pressure on the Vietnamese.

On January 20, Durbrow learned through an Associated Press report that the Cambodians had issued a statement to the United Nations which indicated that the Cambodian minority in Vietnam was the victim of genocide and that tens of thousands of innocent Cambodians had died as a result of the conflict between Saigon and the insurgents.[13] It turned out that the information was not accurate; Cambodia's Permanent Mission to the United Nations had earlier sent a brochure to United Nations members but not to the organization itself, which outlined the long repeated history of Cambodian-Vietnamese conflict along its border.[14] Throughout early February, there was much discussion on how to handle the Cambodian action with the Vietnamese. The Americans were undecided until they could get a sense of the Cambodian's intentions and recommended simply ignoring it.[15] When Strom reported that the Cambodians had no intention of commenting on the contents of the brochure to the United Nations, it seemed that the policy of ignoring it would prevail.[16] While the actual incident was benign in the end, it was these types of actions that helped the lingering controversy continue.

While Ngô Đình Diệm and Durbrow were at an impasse over Cambodia, Ngô Đình Diệm pushed the issue with Williams. During their January 23 meeting to discuss the road building status, he brought up the issue of Cambodia, asserting that the Communist insurgents had agents in the Government and Sûreté who used their positions of influence, and bribe money from the Soviet Union and China, to progress their aims and buy National Assembly members and higher-level officials.[17] Ngô Đình Diệm did not offer proof to Williams and the conversation return to the roads without a Williams' respond. Still, Ngô Đình Diệm would continue to press the Cambodian issue to the Americans with the hope that some type of favorable outcome would result that diminished the United States relationship with Cambodia to the benefit of the Republic of Vietnam. It was not just Ngô Đình Diệm that argued for the Vietnamese side. When Durbrow and Ngô Đình Nhu met on January 30, Ngô Đình Nhu maintained that the Cambodians were worried about their increased isolation as Vietnamese diplomacy strengthened its ties to other countries in Southeast Asia.[18] He argued that the Cambodians did not want to resolve the border dispute because it gave them a way to exert pressure against the Vietnamese and internationally publicize their rift. Certainly the pamphlet distributed earlier bears this out even though it was the general consensus of both the Americans and Vietnamese that Cambodia had not planned to pursue the pamphlet further than its distribution.[19]

No sooner had the pamphlet crisis subsided when another replaced it. The Vietnamese had called a meeting for February 25 with the Cambodian and Laotian negotiating teams to discuss the implementation of the 1954 Paris Accords.[20] The Vietnamese representative, Ngô Trọng Hiếu showed up an hour late, after the other participants who were also joined by a Frenchman, had crafted a motion of regret against the Vietnamese action. Ngô Trọng

Hiếu called for a reconsideration of the agenda, which had been approved two months earlier without objection, and also indicated that the Paris Accords had lapsed. Cambodian Prime Minister Penn Nouth informed Strom that this action had called into question Vietnamese-Cambodian relations and reopened the possible avenue of the United Nations to address Cambodian grievances. He maintained a similar line with the Belgian Minister in Cambodia, whom he met on February 26, who reported to Strom that Penn Nouth was very emotional and disheartened by the Vietnamese insult, asserting that the Vietnamese-Cambodian relationship would never improve until the Vietnamese began treating the Cambodians as equals.[21]

When Durbrow and Ngô Đình Diệm met on February 27, the ambassador questioned him about the snub.[22] The Vietnamese president argued that the Cambodians had included the French in the meeting after he had specifically asked that they not be involved in the preliminary discussions at the technical level. Ngô Đình Diệm believed that it was necessary to work out the details of the Paris Accords and determine how much was owed each country before the French became involved. He maintained that inclusion of the French would lead to failed talks though he also, to the surprise of Durbrow, claimed that the French were being very helpful in the matter. There was no logic to this inconsistency.

In addition to Cambodia, Laos also remained a focus for Ngô Đình Diệm in the New Year. When he met with Williams on January 23 to discuss the progress of the roads, the two quickly came to the issue of Laos and its internal security problem.[23] Williams asserted, and Ngô Đình Diệm agreed, that there was a need for greater coordination between the Vietnamese and Laotians on their common border. For Ngô Đình Diệm, his frustration revolved around the North Vietnamese using the roads in eastern Laos to help support the insurgency in the South and his inability to counter that usage or force the Laotians to intervene. Ngô Đình Diệm used this issue to bring up, again, the possibility of a road from Kontum to Huế, with a shorter loop around the foothills to the northwest that were used by the enemy. Ngô Đình Diệm argued that he needed the road to gain control of the area. Without that control, the population would become demoralized by the constant insurgent activities. When Williams asked him where the money would come from to build such a road, Ngô Đình Diệm responded that it did not matter where the money came from and that he would find it somewhere. Ngô Đình Diệm believed this area critical to the survival of the Republic and the key to preventing the insurgents from gaining the support of the people. Williams understood this more so than Durbrow and Barrows.[24]

The issue of road development and other infrastructure improvements was a constant obstacle to good relations between Ngô Đình Diệm and the USOM. Any hope of an improved relationship between Ngô Đình Diệm and

Barrows was diminished early in the New Year when they clashed over a USOM interpreter. Ngô Đình Diệm explained to Williams on January 23 that Barrows refused to give the name of an interpreter who had asked a series of unusual questions to the Province Chief of Tây Ninh, and then handed Barrows an order from the Minister of Interior that stated all Americans must go through the Ministry to get information from Vietnamese.[25] When Ngô Đình Diệm called in the Minister, Nguyễn Hữu Châu, he showed Ngô Đình Diệm a different order that did not include all of Vietnam but only that one interpreter. The false order was created, allegedly by the interpreter, to sow disharmony between the Americans and Vietnamese. Ngô Đình Diệm asked Barrows for the name of the interpreter so that he could be prosecuted but Barrows refused because the document had a Top Secret rating. Barrows' action frustrated Ngô Đình Diệm, who thought the USOM was protecting someone who was linked to the Communists and was feeding false information to the USOM. That information then made its way to the Embassy and helped to inform critical decisions. For Ngô Đình Diệm, this type of obstruction was far too familiar and only helped to further alienate the two.

The Saigon Government and USOM also conflicted over the National Budget and the ability of the Vietnamese to make up the deficit caused by the cut in United States aid.[26] Ngô Đình Diệm argued to Williams at the same meeting that the USOM demanded a 1,400 million piaster contribution to its military budget when the Vietnamese had set its contribution at 900 million. Ngô Đình Diệm complained to Williams that the USOM would only help if the Vietnamese tax receipts were inadequate and that he did not expect such a surplus. He also maintained that any real surplus should go into Vietnam's reserves. The main issue, beyond the dollar amount, was the USOM going over the budget "with a microscope" rather than allowing the Vietnamese to manage their own money. While he did not state it directly to Williams, implied in the conversation was the question of trust and control. As the year progressed, these issues would continue to plague that relationship as well as the one between Ngô Đình Diệm and Durbrow. In fact, Ngô Đình Diệm would comment to Williams in March that the "USOM has no perspective, no preoccupation with its work. That they always want to study the problem and be sure there are no risks. That they never get down to business."[27] This level of frustration would not diminish over time.

The level of acrimony between Ngô Đình Diệm and the Americans was heightened by the unresolved, at least from the Vietnamese perspective, issue of American aid to the Republic of Vietnam for 1958. On February 3, Durbrow and Ngô Đình Diệm met for three hours to discuss the subject. Durbrow reported that the conversation was friendly, frank, and fruitful.[28] He had requested the meeting to review the aid package while Ngô Đình Diệm informed the ambassador that he had not requested a meeting until he had all of the budget and revenue numbers available. With those in hand, Ngô Đình Diệm surprised Durbrow by informing him that the Saigon Government had 900 million piasters available from excess revenue from taxes (600 million piasters) and 1957 surplus (300 million piasters).

Unfortunately for Durbrow, Ngô Đình Diệm had already earmarked all of the excess review from taxes to existing projects such as road work, canal clearing, dredging and paying for 17,500 Self-Defense Force personnel not covered by the United States while the remaining surplus was set aside from export subsidies and settlements with the Cambodians as a result of the Paris Accords. Essentially, Ngô Đình Diệm made sure to highlight the fact that the Saigon Government was using all of its revenue for existing, legitimate projects designed to increase infrastructure, improve diplomatic relations in the region, and protect itself against the insurgency.[29] Durbrow was faced with the only option of urging Ngô Đình Diệm to spend some of the surplus to the Military Budget and shift some 1957 military expenditures savings to the 1958 budget.

As the two continued their conversation, Ngô Đình Diệm's real concerns surfaced. He complained, again, about the slowness of the USOM. Durbrow countered that the Vietnamese were as responsible for the delays as the USOM. Where Williams might have shown empathy, even if he did not agree, Durbrow seemed reluctant to give in to these complaints. Ngô Đình Diệm also brought up his frustration at seeing Vietnam's aid cut when it had been a steadfast ally in the Free World and he had served as a spokesman against the Communist threat. Durbrow replied that the United States appreciated his efforts and that Vietnam's aid had not been cut proportionally. Missing the Vietnamese point, Durbrow suggested to Ngô Đình Diệm that if his country contributed more to its military budget, it would greatly impress the United States and prove that Vietnam was doing all it could to achieve economic independence. For Ngô Đình Diệm, Vietnam was at a critical crossroads and the next year would make or break the country. The Communist insurgency was increasing its activity and the demand on Vietnamese resources was stretching them thin. Vietnam needed more, not less. More than once, Ngô Đình Diệm had told Durbrow and other visiting Americans that Vietnam was not doing as well as the American press had reported in 1957. It was difficult to determine if those Americans knew this, or refused to sway from their own narrative.

The February 3 conversation, however, did mark a change in Vietnamese strategy. Shortly after the meeting, Vũ Văn Thái informed Barrows and Durbrow that he hoped the ambassador's talk with Ngô Đình Diệm had convinced him of the need to contribute more and suggested that Ngô Đình Diệm might accept a compromise where the Saigon Government contributed half of the difference to cover the military budget.[30] On February 6, Nguyễn Ngọc Thơ saw Barrows and offered another solution to the deficit that had the Vietnamese contributing 956 million piasters (an increase of 56 million piasters) and the United States covering the rest. This solution also had the Vietnamese take over the 170 million piaster obligation for land development from the Americans.[31] Durbrow strongly recommended that the United States accept the compromise. He had received what he wanted from the Vietnamese: a larger monetary commitment while still holding his ground. In many respects, Durbrow won his political battle while the Vietnamese were able to fight for another year.

One consequence that resulted from all of the questions and controversy surrounding the military budget was the Civil Guard. Much of the early part of March focused on that group as Ngô Đình Diệm and Durbrow again clashed over the differences between American and Vietnamese priorities and realities. On February 26, Durbrow sent Ngô Đình Diệm a letter on the Civil Guard that addressed the Vietnamese plans for the organization.[32] After consulting with the Country Team, Durbrow noted only one major difference between the Vietnamese and American plans. The Vietnamese maintained that the Civil Guard needed to be under the military while the Americans believed it should fall under the Ministry for the Interior. The difference in organizational responsibility was significant. The Americans, with the backing of the Michigan State University Group, argued that the Civil Guard was a civilian police force rather than a paramilitary force. As such, to place it under the Ministry for Defense did not make sense. There were specific reasons for this position though Durbrow's letter did not list or imply them other than making the argument that in peacetime, the Civil Guard would work closely with other police agencies. Durbrow also argued that the United States had assisted in the creation of police forces around the world but always with the understanding that they were not attached to, or linked with, the military. Why the United States considered the Vietnamese situation similar to earlier instances of assistance was not enumerated. Durbrow did note, however, that the United States was prepared to provide equipment for thirty-five mobile and seventy fixed Civil Guard companies.

Durbrow and Ngô Đình Diệm met the next day, February 27, with Nguyễn Hữu Châu also present. The question of the Civil Guard was discussed early in the conversation.[33] Ngô Đình Diệm was adamant that it be placed under the Ministry of Defense, to which Durbrow repeated his same position that all previous attempts by the United States to assist countries with police forces came under the control of a civilian organization. While Ngô Đình Diệm envisioned a 50,000-man force, he was quick to reassure Durbrow that the Civil Guard was not designed to challenge the military. He also questioned Durbrow on whether a change of name to National Guard would help alleviate concerns. Durbrow was firm in responding. He did not think that Congress would fund equipment, arms, training, and provide other assistance for a 50,000-man force nor would it continue to fund an organization attached to the Ministry of Defense. Durbrow believed Ngô Đình Diệm was using the Civil Guard to increase the size of his military beyond what the Americans thought was necessary. It was a reasonable assumption though it was also true, from a Vietnamese perspective, that the force was necessary, given the immensity of the challenge at hand and the prospects for increased conflict in the future.

Durbrow made it clear to Ngô Đình Diệm that a larger military, at the expense of building up economic infrastructure, would not solve Vietnam's problems. Durbrow implied that because the United States had already discussed the needs of the Vietnamese military, this attempt at increasing personnel under the guise of the Civil Guard was bound to fail. Ngô Đình Diệm disagreed with Durbrow. Infrastructure improvements meant nothing if the Communist insurgency continued to have a presence among the people. He needed a Civil Guard that was large enough and armed sufficiently to deny them this opportunity to influence the Vietnamese. The conversation ended with Durbrow urging Ngô Đình Diệm to give the American position serious consideration to which Ngô Đình Diệm agreed with the caveat that the issue would be raised again the next week and include Williams and Barrows.

That meeting occurred on March 5.[34] The group discussed a number of issues, including roads and bridges, first. Nguyễn Hữu Châu reiterated the Vietnamese desire to place the Civil Guard under the Ministry of Defense to provide internal defense, which he argued was a larger mission than a Ministry of Interior–led police force. The Vietnamese held that the Civil Guard would engage with Communist insurgents and rebels rather than just bandits and petty criminals. As such they needed to be better equipped, larger in size, and able to coordinate with ease with the military. Durbrow replied that he thought the two sides were "in agreement on about 95% of the concept."[35] He argued that if the Vietnamese accepted the American proposal of 100-man companies, it would have a stronger force than any American state police. At this point, Nguyễn Hữu Châu injected that the companies needed to be 125- or 150-man strong.

While Williams tried to get the conversation back to the issue of organization, Barrows jumped in and argued that the question of size of the companies needed to be resolved, as the Country Team had agreed on 100. At this point, Williams, perhaps a little frustrated, argued that the size of the force did not matter. A 200-man company would work and the 100-man proposal was based on individual responsibilities within a company. If Nguyễn Hữu Châu wanted 125-man companies, it was fine though it would require a change to the Table of Organization and Equipment (TO&E) that MAAG had prepared. Williams was not worried about the size of the individual companies and did not want to get bogged down on that detail. Williams continued to assume the role of facilitator when Nguyễn Hữu Châu tried to make other changes.

The Vietnamese wanted the 5,000 Gendarmerie included in the 55,000-man Civil Guard.[36] While Williams agreed that the Gendarmerie should remain in the military budget, as they would eventually become the Military Police for the Armed Forces, he argued against including them in the Civil Guard as that was now being considered as a civil police force. He recommended that the idea be dropped and it did not make its way into future deliberation. It seemed that Williams had earned the trust of the Vietnamese and his ideas and arguments were heeded. The same could not be said for Durbrow or Barrows.

The two sides continued their discussion on organization with Ngô Đình Diệm acknowledging the American position that it would be easier to get money for the Civil Guard if it was attached to the Ministry of Interior. However, he asserted that these two forces needed to be under one Ministry, to avoid competition and improve coordination. Ngô Đình Diệm feared the possibility of rivalry between the Ministries of Interior and Defense and maintained that the Civil Guard needed military status to avoid potential obstacles towards achieving its ultimate objectives. Neither side seemed willing to budge on this issue which did not bode well for the next related topic on how the Civil Guard would be equipped. The Vietnamese wanted heavier equipment and weapons for the Civil Guard which seemed, to the Americans, to place it on equal footing with the military.

The Americans entered the March 5 decision believing, as Durbrow commented, that they were very close to agreeing on a concept for the Civil Guard. They left the meeting, as Barrows would enumerate, with four major differences. The Vietnamese wanted the Civil Guard organized as a separate force under the Ministry of Defense that would be under military law and discipline. It wanted companies greater than 100 men and it required heavier equipment and weapons. Barrows maintained that there were difficulties for each point and Williams expressed a hope that an agreement could be reached soon so that weapons could make their way to the Civil Guard. Durbrow ended that portion of the discussion by reaffirming that the Civil Guard did not belong under the Ministry of Defense. Williams tried to ensure that Barrows and Durbrow did not get bogged down on details but he stood little chance of bridging the gap that divided the two sides.

The situation worsened when Nguyễn Hữu Châu sent the Americans his list of heavy equipment requirements for the Civil Guard on March 6. This revised TO&E called for equipment for 55,000 men, which included fifteen armored companies, twenty-one horse cavalry companies and 225 light infantry companies.[37] The TO&E asked for more helicopters than the Vietnamese

Armed Forces possessed, though there was nothing included for maintenance and support units. The 1,900 horses required for the cavalry included gas masks but made no provisions for veterinary care. It was a shockingly amateurish document. Durbrow met with Ngô Đình Diệm the next day, March 7, at the former's request before his departure to the United States. Ngô Đình Diệm had hoped to talk about public works projects he had planned to take with the extra revenue from 1957.[38] Durbrow took the opportunity to review the detailed TO&E that Nguyễn Hữu Châu had sent.

He reported that he told the Vietnamese president that he needed to be as frank and firm as he ever had; the new concept for the Civil Guard would be better equipped than the current Vietnamese military, which was unacceptable to the Americans. Durbrow argued that the United States had given other countries money for police training with the qualification that they would be civil police forces. The revised TO&E made it impossible for Durbrow to argue that the Civil Guard was a police force but, rather, an extension of the military units already in existence. There was no way to justify the amount of hardware requested for the role of the Civil Guard as protectors of internal security. Durbrow made it clear that this latest Vietnamese request was unreasonable and would not be approved of in Washington.

Durbrow then told Ngô Đình Diệm that if he felt so strongly about this new TO&E for the Civil Guard that he would try to promote it in Washington, even though he had just remarked that it would not be approved, but that he, as a friend of Vietnam, urged Ngô Đình Diệm to seriously reconsider and accept the American concept.[39] What Durbrow did not know, however, was that Ngô Đình Diệm was under the impression that Nguyễn Hữu Châu had shared the new TO&E with Williams and that it had received the General's approval. This did not occur, which might have made the omission more serious had it not been for Williams' relationship with Ngô Đình Diệm.

Soon after Nguyễn Hữu Châu had delivered the TO&E to Durbrow, the Secretary of State for Defense, Nguyễn Đình Thuần, met with Williams to gauge his reaction to the document.[40] Nguyễn Đình Thuần informed Williams that the Ministry of Defense had not seen the paper and wondered if Williams had been consulted. Williams had not and recommended that the TO&E be withdrawn. Early on March 10, Nguyễn Hữu Châu telephoned Counselor of the American Embassy, Howard Elting, as Durbrow had returned to the United States earlier in the month, to set up an appointment as he had just left from a meeting with Barrows.[41] Barrows met with Elting first and told him that the Vietnamese had revised their Civil Guard numbers back down to 30,000 and that Ngô Đình Diệm had instructed Nguyễn Hữu Châu to withdraw the TO&E. When Elting finally met with Nguyễn Hữu Châu, the latter told him the same thing and made the excuse that the document he had sent was for a future concept rather than a current request.

5. Planning for Victory 63

The Vietnamese realized that they had made a significant error with this document and needed to avoid potential future embarrassment.

Ngô Đình Diệm attempted to sidestep the awkwardness over the situation on March 8.[42] He avoided speaking about the Civil Guard with Elting that day, but had a three-hour meeting with the British ambassador to Vietnam, Roderick Parkes, during which the issue was addressed. Ngô Đình Diệm reaffirmed his insistence that the Civil Guard be placed under the Ministry of Defense.[43] When asked if he thought there could be a compromise, Ngô Đình Diệm responded that he needed to do what he thought was right even if, as the Americans had told him, he could get the equipment with fewer obstacles by doing what they proposed.[44] He told Parkes that he could not justify following this American advice, as it would not be proper, but that it could also be used against him by the Americans in the future. He ended the conversation with a curious statement that he was, "very pleased because this shows that the Americans now trust me and accept what I am trying to do."[45] Parkes interpreted this statement as one where Ngô Đình Diệm did not want to hurt this new, trusting relationship by being obstinate about the Civil Guard. Presumably, however, Ngô Đình Diệm had already heard from Nguyễn Đình Thuần about how Williams had reacted to the TO&E and was setting up a situation that would allow him to save face over this fiasco.

In order to avoid another potentially embarrassing confrontation, Nguyễn Hữu Châu asked Williams to meet with him on March 12.[46] He offered Williams a new TO&E, which he assured the General was very different from the one sent earlier, and asked for his opinion as to whether he should forward it to the embassy. Nguyễn Hữu Châu repeated the story that the first TO&E was a concept that had been developed after Durbrow had asked for long range future plans for the Civil Guard but that the current TO&E dealt with the immediate situation. Through the course of their combined review of the document, Nguyễn Hữu Châu seemed focused on making sure that the Americans would not react negatively towards the Vietnamese requests. The American record of the meeting made him appear deferential and apologetic to Williams. This very well may have been the case as he had failed to get Williams approval of the first TO&E that had caused Ngô Đình Diệm so much embarrassment. Williams agreed that the document was more balanced but he cautioned Nguyễn Hữu Châu that the Country Team still believed that Ngô Đình Diệm wanted to create a paramilitary force rather than a national police force.

After this interaction, Nguyễn Hữu Châu met with Elting and handed him the new TO&E.[47] While the revised document called for Civil Guard companies of 158 men rather than the 100 men in the Country Team's recommendation, Elting maintained that the document would need to be studied and deflected the Vietnamese comment that Williams had earlier stated it did not matter how many men were in a company. When Williams met with Ngô Đình Diệm on March 26, the two had a much more relaxed conversation about the Civil Guard.[48] Ngô Đình Diệm, who had just returned from the Philippines, compared the two countries and their attempts at creating a Civil Guard. The Philippines' force was under the Defense Ministry but was attempting to move it under the Ministry of Interior, which he thought was a mistake. Ngô Đình Diệm claimed that too many Americans were fond of the Philippines; he singled out the personnel of the Michigan State University Group who travelled there on the weekends. Ngô Đình Diệm maintained that because the Republic of Vietnam was much smaller than the Philippines and the United States, it had different needs. The conversation did not progress much further on the subject. Ngô Đình Diệm reaffirmed that he had an ally in Williams while making it clear that the MSUG and USOM were not being helpful.[49]

One of the casualties of this Civil Guard episode was Nguyễn Hữu Châu. On March 29, he visited Elting at his house to inform him that he had submitted his resignation that morning. Nguyễn Hữu Châu blamed the ever-growing Cần Lao Nhân Vị Cách Mạng Đảng's (Personalist Labor Revolutionary Party, or Cần Lao Party) influence in the Government, as it had attacked him both personally and professionally.[50] Elting speculated that the resignation was spurred by his attempts to divorce the sister of Madame Nhu and her family's reaction to it. It was also a reaction to the increased influence of the Cần Lao Party as well as a protest to the growing authoritarianism of the Ngô Đình Diệm government. Elting was not privileged to the information about Nguyễn Hữu Châu's failure to show Williams the first TO&E which Durbrow used to have his frank and firm conversation with Ngô Đình Diệm. No record exists of the Vietnamese president's reaction to Durbrow or how he handled it with Nguyễn Hữu Châu, but it seems reasonable that Ngô Đình Diệm was not pleased with Nguyễn Hữu Châu and let him know about it. Ngô Đình Diệm did accept the resignation in early May and by Presidential Decree 13, Nguyễn Đình Thuần, Director of Cabinet at the Ministry of Defense, replaced him.[51]

The episode with the TO&E was a foreshadowing of the problems to come. Both the Vietnamese and Americans had established very different paths to arrive at the same destination. Ngô Đình Diệm was adamant that he knew the proper way to proceed and did not appreciate it when Durbrow or members of the Country Team opposed his plan of action. Whether it was the TO&E, Cambodia, road development, or how to handle members of his extended family, the two sides jockeyed for power and position at almost every turn, often times with Williams acting as the mediator or facilitator. It resulted in a difficult path toward progress and one that had a high probability of ending with a break between the president and ambassador.

6
The Politics of Opposition

In the midst of the Civil Guard controversy, another disturbing event occurred within Saigon that centered on the role of the Vietnamese press. The episode served as a reminder for Durbrow that he was dealing with a young, still developing, Republic. It also remained a point of contention between the Americans and Ngô Đình Diệm as he defined his vision for Vietnam. The opposition newspaper, *Thời luân*, had published several editorials, stories, and letters that criticized the Saigon Government. On March 1, it printed an article, titled "Letter to My National Assembly Deputy" which criticized the Saigon Government and made some remarks that were deemed as pro–Communist propaganda. As a result, the edition was seized.[1] On March 5, *Thời luân* editor, Nghiêm Xuân Thiện, gave a press conference to discuss the actions taken against his paper.[2] A *Dân chúng* editorial criticized him for failing to address why his paper was seized and also praised *Ngôn luận* for publishing excerpts of the March 1 article.[3] *Ngôn luận* argued that the article was propaganda that encouraged the Communist insurgents. It rejected the message that praised North Vietnam while criticizing the South.[4] *Tự do* maintained that the article added nothing constructive to the continued growth of the Republic of Vietnam though it did offer a March 13 editorial that agreed with many of the points in the earlier article.[5] *Tự do* argued that *Thời luân* inadvertently praised Communism because it did not understand the local and international situation with which the Saigon Government was forced to deal.[6]

On March 13, Nghiêm Xuân Thiện was served with a summons to appear in court as a result of the article.[7] He received a ten-month suspended sentence and was fined 100,000 piasters.[8] More importantly, the Government removed its authorization for the paper to publish. *Tự do* responded to the event by printing a warning to the Saigon Government to listen to the people, who were now in greater numbers reading *Thời luân*, before its forced closure.[9] In another move, the Court of appeals upheld the sentence against

Thời luân for libel against the Economic Police and Army, which had been tried earlier, on March 19.[10] Nghiêm Xuân Thiện received a 20,000 piaster fine and had to pay 100,000 piasters to the Economic Police Service. He received a 10,000 piaster fine in the case against the Ministry of Defense and had to pay one piaster in damages.[11]

The closure of *Thời luân* was greeted with concern. *Tân Dân* asserted that it marked the "death of a vanguard fighter in the struggle for freedom of the press."[12] The loss of the newspaper had damaged the American perspective of Ngô Đình Diệm, especially for those already concerned about his rule. These events, coupled with the arrest of nine newsmen who were allegedly Communist agents charged with subverting the press, including men from three newspapers—*Sài Gòn Mới* (New Saigon), *Lê Sống, and Buổi sang* (Morning Post)—that were pro–Government, intensified the already frail relationship between the Government and the press.[13] These events, and the announcement of the arrest of a Vietnamese who was employed by the USIS as a journalist, set the tone for the spring and summer months.[14] Add to that the confirmation of the bubonic plague in Long Điền District, Phước Tuy Province and at the Long Hai resort, and the prospects for a calm 1958 waned.[15]

On March 29, Phi Vân, the editor of *Dân chúng*, was arrested.[16] In its editorials, *Dân chúng* had supported the earlier arrests but questioned whether all individuals involved were actually Communists. Other editors of *Dân chúng* issued an editorial on April 2 questioning the reason for the arrest.[17] It acknowledged writing a series of editorials about individual freedoms that found criticism in the Saigon Government but argued that if these were the justification for the arrest then Phi Vân should not have been held accountable for their actions. They speculated that he was arrested for being a communist though the paper had been founded by those who had fled the North in 1954–1955 to escape communism. Regardless, the paper hoped for answers while its principle editor was detained.

Elting offered a confidential comment in his April 6 Weekly to Washington that more arrests were expected and that the Saigon Government had a document that revealed the extent of Communist subversion in the press.[18] On April 12, Phan Quang Đán announced that he planned to start a new newspaper, *Thiết Thực* (Truth) though Elting thought it unlikely that he would be granted a license given his close connection with Nghiêm Xuân Thiện and his leadership in the opposition.[19] The newspaper announcement was a part of a larger move by Phan Quang Đán to take his Republican Party out of the opposition bloc so that it could concentrate on the 1959 legislative elections.[20] Phan Quang Đán withdrew as the Secretary General of the Democratic Party and was replaced by Hoàng Cơ Thùy.[21] This shake-up was the first of many as the elections drew nearer. On April 29, Phan Quang Đán announced that he would apply for legalization of the Liberal Democratic Party, which would have similar objectives to the Democratic Party.[22] He would remain a voice of opposition to Ngô Đình Diệm and eventually gain favor in the American Embassy.

The role of the press went through a period of self-reflection and review as a result of the arrests and suspension of *Thời luân*. On April 19, a press officer for the Ministry of Interior told twenty editors of the leading Saigon newspapers that they needed to provide accurate and verifiable news stories in order to be a worthwhile contributor to the Republic.[23] *Ngôn luận* offered an editorial on April 21 that reaffirmed this position and openly wondered why a disciplinary council had not already been set up.[24] *Dân chúng* also voiced an opinion in the discussion when its April 25 editorial reaffirmed the value of the Fourth Estate in the Republic as defenders of the people's interests and an advocate of freedom and democracy.[25] All of this discussion culminated in the Ministry of Information creating a Council that established control over the press by its own representatives in order to regulate itself and avoid adverse publications. The new disciplinary council was made up of twelve publishers with a rotating chairman and secretary. It would examine cases of any violation of discipline and hand out punishments as needed.[26] Elting believed this new measure resulted from the Ministry of Interior's request to form a Press Office so that questions asked by the media would get accurate answers.[27] He reported that the press would probably react with passive resistance and the office would eventually die out as had its predecessor, the Newspaper Publishers Association.

The role of the press in the Republic of Vietnam and how Ngô Đình Diệm responded to it would become increasingly important to those Americans who reported back to Washington. Few, however, were willing to listen to Ngô Đình Diệm's side of the controversy without judgments. Williams was an exception and when they met on May 24, the issue of the press entered their conversation. Ngô Đình Diệm maintained that the Communists benefited from the freedom of the press that existed in South Vietnam.[28] He argued that the press was a principle instrument of the communists in Vietnam and that they used it to make gains even as they were failing in the countryside. The press, he argued, only reported the sensational and the negative. The newspapers were only interested in profit.

When Williams pressed him to provide specific newspapers that fell into this category, Ngô Đình Diệm responded that it was a general situation. Ngô Đình Diệm admitted that he did not think that the newspaper editors or publishers were Communists but that they accepted articles from them without review or confirmation. The two then discussed censorship, with Ngô Đình Diệm arguing that it was necessary but not yet in place in Vietnam, while Williams cautioned him that some outside of the country believed that censorship existed already. To some extent, both arguments were correct. While Ngô Đình Diệm might not have been directly involved in the press, members of his family and some within his Government did exert pressure on the Saigon newspapers though there was still an opposition press in Vietnam that thrived.

An example of this was the announced suspension of *Buổi sang* for financial reasons, though Elting reported that its former editor, Văn Hoan, believed Ngô Đình Diệm forced the suspension as part of a plan to ease General Mai Hữu Xuân out of leadership in the military, as he was connected to the newspaper through family ties.[29] The financial reasons, as reported by Elting, were connected to the Government-controlled distribution agency refusing to handle *Buổi sang*, thereby making it impossible for the newspaper to continue to function. On May 31, *Công nhân* suspended publication due to an "interior reorganization," though *Tự do* argued that too many papers relied on sensational reporting in a highly competitive market, which caused some newspapers to stray from responsible journalism. The implication was that this was what had happened to *Buổi sang* and *Công nhân*, though in the case of *Công nhân*, the Vietnam General Confederation of Labor, which controlled the newspaper, met on May 18 and voted to rescind its right to publish because it had received court summons for slander and for printing false news.[30]

While the Americans reported on the challenges to the freedom of the press in Vietnam back to Washington, there was also an increased reference to the frustration felt by members of the embassy staff and USOM towards Ngô Đình Diệm and his government. On March 28, Elting and Arthur Gardiner met with Ngô Đình Diệm and his Secretary of State for Public Works and Commissions, Trần Lê Quang, to discuss roads.[31] Ngô Đình Diệm wanted to shift focus away from building and improving route 21 to focus on route 19, which held more military and economic significance for the future of Vietnam. He had met with Williams on March 26 to discuss the issue, as he often did to get a sense of the General's perspective before he broached the subjects with the Embassy or Country Team members.[32] When Ngô Đình Diệm started to discuss the same topic with Elting and Gardiner, Elting interrupted him to let him know that Williams had already discussed their earlier conversation in detail. As Elting would remark, "I did this in the hope of forestalling a repetition of the three and one-half hour session he had had with the General."[33] While it was true that Ngô Đình Diệm and Williams had long conversations, the one on March 26 was not exclusively about roads. Ngô Đình Diệm and Williams discussed a number of topics with both men interjecting during the conversation.

When Ngô Đình Diệm met with Durbrow, American visitors, or members of the Country Team or USOM, he did have a tendency to dominate the conversation. The Americans would increasingly view this as aloofness and did not appreciate getting a lecture on the importance of one project or a lesson in history on Vietnam. Elting wanted to stave off a three and one-half hour lecture on the value of Route 19 to the security of Vietnam. While there was nothing to suggest that this was the intention of Ngô Đình Diệm, he would have surely engaged them in a conversation long enough to ensure that they understood his position and were willing to consider it. More often than not, the American perception was that Ngô Đình Diệm prolonged and dominated the meetings to eliminate the possibility of a counter-argument, and because he liked to hear himself speak. Neither was quite accurate; as in so many cases in Vietnam, perception often trumped reality when it came to American-Vietnamese relations.

The growing frustration with Ngô Đình Diệm surpassed the passive-aggressive approach offered by Elting, with two messages authored by individuals who were already on record as opposing Ngô Đình Diệm. On April 10, Barbour sent a despatch titled "Cracks in the Citadel Wall," in which he reported the anonymous complaints of some lower level officials and Huế intellectuals to the rule of Ngô Đình Diệm and Ngô Đình Cẩn.[34] Barbour began his document by again characterizing Central Vietnam's conservativism and resistance to things foreign or different. He argued that those who had approached him or members of the Consulate in Huế were still in support of Ngô Đình Diệm, but that this support had waned. While he did not identify any of the individuals by name, he did give some general characteristics: they were between twenty-five and forty years of age, had studied in France or Britain, and they were not organized.[35] Barbour maintained that one complaint was that Ngô Đình Diệm's family, specifically Ngô Đình Nhu and Ngô Đình Cẩn, who held places in government, had failed to reach the people; he made no mention of the numerous trips Ngô Đình Diệm had made to the Central Highlands in 1957 or 1958. There was a general complaint of corruption though the real disputes seemed to be more with personal activities. Barbour reported complaints about Ngô Đình Cẩn prohibiting bars and dances. He also tried to control local newspapers and limited permits needed for political groups to meet. These young intellectuals, as Barbour referred to them, also worried about their inability to get visas to travel abroad. Those abroad, he was told, feared to return because they did not believe they would ever get to leave again. Nothing was mentioned about Vietnamese conscription, which some of these young Vietnamese intellectuals would have to confront when they did return.

Barbour lamented what he believed was the Central Vietnamese administrations' inability to deal with the dissatisfaction of the intellectuals' dissent. He concluded that the Americans in Huế needed to work with the intellectuals to deflect their discontent in order to stave off the possibility that they would turn to the Communists. He noted that he shared the beliefs and arguments of the dissenting intellectuals and would offer strategies on how the United

States could work with them to keep them away from the Communists as an alternative to Ngô Đình Diệm.

On April 15, Bowie sent a despatch summarizing two conversations with Vietnamese leaders that criticized Ngô Đình Diệm's rule.[36] During his Vietnamese lesson with the Director of Information and of the Press, Nguyễn Ngọc Chạch, Bowie was present when National Assemblyman Nguyễn Văn Báu paid him a visit. Nguyễn Văn Báu, who had been educated in Paris and served as a Colonial Administrator before the Republic of Vietnam, talked openly about the failures of the Saigon Government. Both Vietnamese, who Bowie ranked as second echelon in the Government, complained that the Provincial leaders needed to know their people better and that the National Assembly should have a more important role in governance. Both believed that only the Ngô family made the important decisions while their voices were not heard. Bowie commented that the men had never met and that each was anti-communist and a nationalist. They both implied in their conversation that they wished the United States would, in Bowie's words, "grant more freedom to the Vietnamese."[37] It was interesting, given the Vietnamese reputation for being reserved, that two men who had never met each other had such a meaningful conversation in front of a high-ranking American official. While it was possible that the coincidence of the meeting when Bowie was present was real, it was also possible that the meeting was staged for the benefit of the American. Regardless, Bowie's report was yet another negative despatch about Ngô Đình Diệm in which views were reported without confirmation, in which the reporting officer was clearly in accord with the perspective.[38]

Not all of the negativity or American frustration with the Vietnamese was unwarranted. However, some of these frustrations were shared by Ngô Đình Diệm. There were often complaints about the inability of the Vietnamese to get things done. One clear example occurred on May 29 when Ngô Đình Diệm and Williams organized a meeting to discuss the state of the Vietnamese logistics system. Williams brought with him Brigadier General Gunnar Carlson, the Deputy Chief, MAAG for Logistics and Administration, while Ngô Đình Diệm included his logistics chief, Lieutenant Colonel Nguyễn Văn Mạnh, as well as Nguyễn Văn Thuận, among others.[39] The purpose of the meeting was to get a sense of the needs and excesses of equipment for the Vietnamese based on the current TO&Es. Carlson noted that neither the Engineers nor Air Force had submitted inventories. When the Vietnamese Chief of Military Engineers, who was also present, started to complain about the lack of equipment and the poor existing state of what he had, first Williams and then Ngô Đình Diệm interrupted him to ask him when he would provide an inventory. According to Williams' records, the Chief had no idea about his inventory and told the president two months. This type of indecision or failure to be aware of one's responsibilities plagued the Vietnamese army.

Both Carlson and Williams expressed frustration during the meeting with the inability of the Vietnamese to provide basic inventories and also understand the importance of such lists to justify continued expenditures by Congress and the USOM in Vietnam. However, in this case as with many that involved Williams, Ngô Đình Diệm was on their side. As Carlson and Williams continued to press, Ngô Đình Diệm eventually interrupted the conversation to state that the necessary inventories would be submitted as needed. The interactions, as the meeting continued, reaffirmed the frustration that some Americans had with the Vietnamese. and vice-versa. At any one point, Carlson, Nguyễn Văn Mạnh, Nguyễn Văn Thuận, and Williams interrupted each other to point out that some assertion made by one was incorrect. However, unlike other meetings between Americans and Ngô Đình Diệm, the frustration was not directed at Ngô Đình Diệm and he was a more sympathetic figure to the American military representatives present. When Ngô Đình Diệm met with Durbrow and others from the Country Team, the situation was different.

There was also frustration on the Vietnamese side, though its expression was often less subtle and more embarrassing for the Vietnamese than the Americans. On June 3, Ngô Đình Nhu gave an interview to Didier Lambert, Director of *La Vie Française*, who published it in the *Journal d'Extreme Orient*.[40] Ngô Đình Nhu spoke well of the Vietnamese-French relationship but use the forum to criticize the United States and its Aid Program. Ngô Đình Nhu signaled out the USOM and its obstruction, obstinacy, and unrealistic expectations. While the remarks were critical of the Americans, the Embassy did not feel it could demand a retraction, though it reported that the USOM and the Saigon Government had been working more closely together. After the fallout from the interview, Elting reported that the American reaction made Ngô Đình Nhu realize that he had made a mistake.[41] He also related the Vietnamese response, which was that Ngô Đình Nhu had been misquoted; Ngô Đình Nhu indicated in private conversations that this was the case. There was nothing in Elting's communiqué that suggested the Americans were convinced of this mistake. Vietnamese concerns about Americans in their country was also explored in an June 11 *Người Việt Tự do* article that criticized United States aid workers in Vietnam and suggested that these Americans were "more or less 'disgusted' by their responsibility; they lack determination and initiative."[42] *Người Việt Tự do* also criticized the Americans for failing to build better relations with the Vietnamese and understanding Vietnamese culture.[43]

If the negative reports from Huế and the constant strain between the Americans and Vietnamese in Saigon were not enough, the issue of Cambodia continued to provide an underlying tension between all involved in Vietnam. Cambodia did not take center-stage during the early spring. However, there were still outstanding issues that plagued the relationship. The Cambodians had issued complaints about the treatment of Khmer minorities in the Cochin-China region, which had been enumerated in the earlier controversial pamphlet. The murder of a monk at a pagoda in the village of Le Tri, Tri Ton District, Châu Đốc Province resulted in much activity though both the Cambodians and Vietnamese had different versions of the events that had taken place.[44] The frontier between the two countries remained unstable as both sides violated what the other believed to be the border, which included clashes between the two armies. There were also instances of Vietnamese removing Khmer villagers and then destroying their villages, kidnappings, and mass arrests while sovereignty over islands in the Gulf of Siam and disputes about the use of the Mekong River by the Cambodian Navy kept the tension high.[45] With Durbrow out of the country and Williams sick, Vietnamese-Cambodian relations was not a high priority for the United States though that would change into the early summer months.

By early June, the Department of State expressed concern about the deteriorating relations between the two countries. Walter Robertson, Assistant Secretary of State for Far Eastern Affairs, instructed the embassies in Saigon and Phnom Penh to discretely indicate to both governments the need to avoid action that would hamper relations as well as encourage finding the path toward improvement.[46] Even as the United States decided to become more proactive in the situation, the Vietnamese were working to improve relations. Ngô Trọng Hiếu informed Strom that they had settled the case of Cambodian naval vessels on the Mekong and had indirectly appealed to Sihanouk to have the Cambodian press stop its propaganda campaign against the Vietnamese.[47]

In a conversation with the Vietnamese Secretary of State for Foreign Affairs Vũ Văn Mẫu, however, Elting received a different perspective. Vũ Văn Mẫu confessed that he was confused by the Cambodians, who claimed that 600 Vietnamese in army uniforms attacked Cambodians on Cambodian soil, then simultaneously stated that there were no Vietnamese insurgents in Cambodia, and that the attack had been, in fact, conducted by Vietnamese insurgents.[48] Vũ Văn Mẫu also informed Elting that Penn Nouth had secretly traveled to Hong Kong for several days to engage the Communist Chinese in helping them improve their new port. Robertson, in a document drafted by Joseph Mendenhall, denied the Vietnamese claim, suggesting instead that the Cambodian actions had been favorable to the Free World and advised Elting to remind the Vietnamese of the American desire of improved Vietnamese-Cambodian relations.[49]

While Vũ Văn Mẫu expressed concern, other Vietnamese were more optimistic. The Vietnamese had begun conversations with the Cambodians on the stalled financial settlement while Ngô Trọng Hiếu had been instructed by the Foreign Ministry to be as friendly as possible with his Cambodian counterparts.[50] While the Vietnamese made it clear to Durbrow, who had returned from Washington, that Vietnamese action was restricted so long as the Cambodian press continued to insult Ngô Đình Diệm, there were signs of a possible improvements. Indeed, the Cambodians did not make it easy. On June 14, *Réalités Cambodigennes,* a publication whose political articles were cleared by Sihanouk, published an "Open Letter to Vietnam." It focused on the "Vietnamization" of hundreds of thousands of Cambodians who lived in the Cochin-China region.[51] The *Réalités Cambodigennes* article affirmed that the Cambodian government could never allow these Cambodians to be forcibly denationalized and called upon the Saigon Government to work with their minority peoples instead of alienating them.

The war of words took on a more serious tone as the Cambodians increased the rhetoric of a potential conflict with both the Republic of Vietnam and Thailand, who shared its western border.[52] Durbrow denied any possibility of armed conflict between the two sides, especially given MAAG's close relationship with the Vietnamese Armed Forces. This, however, did not stop the rumors circulating Phnom Penh and Saigon. Strom learned on June 23 that the Forces Armées Royales Khmer Chief of Staff Lon Nol went to assess, firsthand, the nature of an incident involving an unidentified force that had surrounded the village of Ban Pak Nhay in the northeastern part of the country near the Republic of Vietnam's border.[53] Meanwhile, a parachute battalion was being readied to move into region 5 where the village lay. Strom called for calm but also offered several possible explanations, including the most obvious, which was that it was a Việt Cộng force. The hope was to minimize the drama of this alleged incident and maintain Cambodian-Vietnamese relations as best as possible.

Strom's hope was dashed on June 25 when Sim Var issued a proclamation that publicized a Vietnamese invasion of Cambodia that began with Ban Pak Nhay on June 18.[54] He called upon the Cambodian people to rally against the invading troops, which he claimed were being reinforced for a larger offensive into Cambodia. A Royal proclamation followed that had the Vietnamese not only in Ban Pak Nhay but also in the villages of Kompadon and Oyadao, which were also situated in Stung Treng province.[55] The proclamation listed twenty-nine major violations of Cambodian territory by the Vietnamese since the beginning of 1957 in addition to countless minor violations. The proclamation ended with a call for the United States to intervene and, failing that, the United Nations.

Strom acknowledged that the United States had to accede to the Cambodian request before the incident grew into something more than it really was though he thought, given all of the evidence available, that the Cambodians were exaggerating the claims in order to force the Vietnamese to amend their diplomacy towards them.[56] If this was true, it was a dangerous and misguided attempt as the Vietnamese, given their negative disposition towards the Cambodians, would not give in to idle threats or possible blackmail. Vũ Văn Mẫu responded with an editorial in the *Vietnam Press* which not only denied the Cambodian accusations but offered several instances where the Cambodians had violated Vietnamese territory, attacked Vietnamese military and civilian personnel, moved the border markers between the two nations, and launched an unwarranted media attack against the Vietnamese and their government.[57] Vũ Văn Mẫu claimed that the Vietnamese only wanted good relations with the Cambodians and asked, "What Machiavellian designs do they nourish in seeking to create misunderstandings in domestic and international opinion on [the] origins [of] these frontier incidents?"[58] While few Americans would agree with the musing of Vũ Văn Mẫu or his claims that the Vietnamese were innocent, the two diametrically opposed sides of this increasingly combative battle of nerves was the last thing that the United States needed or wanted.

As the incident developed, the Americans in Saigon tended to dismiss the Cambodian claim, given the prolonged accounts of similar, unsubstantiated reports coming from the Cambodian press. While Durbrow did not exonerate the Vietnamese for their part in the deterioration of the relationship, he also did not think it was appropriate for him to go to Ngô Đình Diệm and request negotiations, as Strom had advocated, when the intensity of the Cambodian propaganda against the Republic of Vietnam continued unabated.[59] On June 26, the situation began to resolve into something clearer though the participants were not aware of it at the time.

Vũ Văn Mẫu issued another communiqué on that day that tied the current crisis with a June 7 prison break, which the Vietnamese claimed was supported by the Cambodian Army.[60] He alleged that the prisoners made their way to Ban Pak Nhay and were picked up by trucks to be moved further inland. When the Civil Guard units pursuing the prisoners were confronted by the Cambodian Army, which was patrolling within Vietnamese territory according to his story, they were attacked. These attacks occurred on three separate occasions. While the Americans may have been skeptical of the Vietnamese version of the events, as they were of the Cambodian side of the story, Williams and General Edwin Hartshorn, Chief of MAAG in Phnom Penh, were able to meet and compare information.[61]

The two concluded that after the June 7 attack on the prison camp, a small group of ARVN soldiers were dispatched near the Cambodian border and were reinforced after the Civil Guard units were attacked on June 15. They agreed that it was possible that some of these troops crossed the poorly marked border in pursuit of the prisoners but that all had returned to their base, which was sixty kilometers inside of the Republic of Vietnam, by June 22. There was no evidence to suggest, however, that the Vietnamese had occupied Ban Pak Nhay or the other villages as was suggested by Sim Var or the Royal proclamation. Given this evidence, Durbrow argued against any United States intervention in the matter and purposely did not try to see Ngô Đình Diệm without instruction and especially given the earlier confrontation about the Civil Guard.[62] This may have been the right strategy, though by ignoring Ngô Đình Diệm, it also left open the possibility that the ambassador was considering the Cambodian claims. Durbrow was strenuous in his support of the Vietnamese side of the conflict though it was not clear if he ever shared that with Ngô Đình Diệm.

Despite this American information, the Cambodians continued to insist that the Vietnamese were still occupying Ban Pak Nhay. Strom learned on June 26 that Cambodian intelligence believed there were two battalions of the 181st ARVN regiment near the village with an additional eighteen battalions, including an armored reconnaissance battalion, heading toward Stung Treng. When pressed, however, the Cambodians told Strom that their information came from a civilian source.[63] Had the information been accurate, it would have constituted a major international incident, but the movement of so many troops could never have escaped the attention of the Americans. Durbrow confirmed this but also cautioned that it was important to have the Canadians accompany any Polish or Indian investigations of the occupation so that the false rumors were not confirmed.[64] There was a real concern that some members of the International Control Commission might cause problems by supporting the Cambodians over the Vietnamese.

Most observers of this potential crisis were at a loss to the degree to which the Cambodians pursued their claim. The French ambassador in the Republic of Vietnam, Jean Payart, did not understand the Cambodian king's insistence on issuing a proclamation about this one event when so many other violations of the border by both sides had occurred. Payart believed the Cambodian Government to be "irresponsible and insensitive to [the] general international situation."[65] Ngô Đình Diệm and Ngô Đình Nhu continued to dismiss the Cambodian claims while ridiculing their effort to get troops to the imaginary front and pointing out that if the Vietnamese were to invade, it would be toward Phnom Penh rather than the northeastern part of the country.[66] Both also believed the June 7 attack against the prison and recent Cambodian moves were designed to justify an increased Communist Chinese presence in their country. Ngô Đình Nhu went further by adding that the only reason Sihanouk accused the Republic of Vietnam of violating Cambodian territory was his desire to increase Cambodia's prestige at the expense of South Vietnam. He also thought Sihanouk's neutrality was really an attempt to wait and see whether the Communists or the West prevailed in Southeast Asia.⁶⁷ This was a type of neutralism that neither Ngô Đình Nhu nor Ngô Đình Diệm could accept.

When Strom met with the Cambodian Foreign Minister, Trương Cảng, on June 26, the Cambodians continued to maintain that the Vietnamese were entrenched around Ban Phak Nhay, though it was possible that they originally violated the border in pursuit of the prisoners.⁶⁸ Trương Cảng admitted that the Cambodians had the ninety prisoners who had requested asylum and confirmed that Cambodia would return any of the prisoners who were Vietnamese but would have to weigh the cases of anyone who was Cambodian to determine the merit of their request. He told Strom that the only thing the Cambodians wanted, at that moment in time, was the withdrawal of the ARVN forces. As the situation became clearer, Strom reported that he believed that Vietnamese soldiers had entered Cambodian in battalion strength to pursue the prisoners and most likely stayed around Ban Pak Nhay for several days.⁶⁹ He did not think any Vietnamese remained in Cambodia and that the continued Cambodian troop movements and public declarations were designed to invoke an international condemnation of the Vietnamese. When he confronted Penn Nouth on June 27, there was a certain backing away from some of the more extravagant claims though they still insisted on confirmation that the Vietnamese had withdrawn.⁷⁰

The Vietnamese reaction to the Cambodian actions was restrained. The Saigon Government and its representatives in Cambodia continued to deny the charges against it, and though there was some Vietnamese propaganda that attempted to turn the focus towards Cambodian violations into Vietnamese space, it was not as provocative as the Cambodian efforts.⁷¹ The same was true with the Vietnamese press, for the most part. Several newspapers expressed concern over the incident, such as *Người Việt Tự do* and *Sài Gòn Mới*, though the *Vietnam Press* tempered its concern with a reminder of the Cambodian violations in the Republic of Vietnam.⁷²

There was an unrealized hope that the events of June, which had seen a heightened tension in Southeast Asia and had shifted the focus away from the Communist insurgency threat, would resolve itself with clearer heads. The natural animosity between the Cambodians and Vietnamese, reinforced by centuries of conflict and two different cultures, was never going to disappear, but it was the hope of the Americans in Saigon and Phnom Penh that both sides would see the consequences of their folly before either made an egregious error. For the Cambodians, the alleged invasion did not occur, which might have caused some embarrassment and a need to avoid further humiliation, and coupled with the need to resolve the financial settlement from the Paris Accords, forced the issue. Sihanouk needed Ngô Đình Diệm to make some concessions in order to save face. However, for the Vietnamese, the necessity of compromise was overshadowed by the relentless Cambodian

6. The Politics of Opposition

press campaign against the Saigon Government and a distaste for Cambodians in general. Ngô Đình Diệm believed Sihanouk to be self-centered and self-interested while his opinion of the military strategy and prowess of the Cambodian army was already established on the record.[73] The strong personalities at play in this crisis, backed by equally strong American embassy opinions, made it difficult for the situation to resolve itself by the end of the month. As July approached, the extent of the drama made itself truly known.

Neither the Vietnamese nor the Cambodians were willing to concede ground on the crisis. Each side offered the possibility of concessions though neither followed through to the point that the border dispute could be resolved to their mutual satisfaction. The situation became even more complicated when, on July 23, Sihanouk announced Cambodia's recognition of Communist China.[74] That action changed the overall tenor of both the American and Vietnamese perspective towards Cambodia while, the lingering debate over the border marker continued to plague their diplomatic relation. The recognition confirmed to Ngô Đình Diệm that the Cambodians could not be trusted; it, and the way the Cambodians handled the Ban Pak Nhay episode, meant that the Vietnamese would have no tolerance to future Cambodian actions that threatened to harm the role and position of the Republic.

7

The War at Home and on the Periphery: American Criticism of Ngô Đình Diệm

In the early stages of the border dispute, General John O'Daniel, former MAAG chief, visited the Republic of Vietnam from May 19 to June 17. O'Daniel, who had been invited back by Ngô Đình Diệm, served as the chairman of the American Friends of Vietnam. This group was active in the United States in promoting Vietnamese interests as well as sponsoring programs and conferences designed to educate the American people on the Vietnamese plight. After reporting his observations and conclusions, O'Daniel made a recommendation that foreshadowed the troubles of the Durbrow period and beyond. He maintained that the American approach in Vietnam "should be that of a member of a team, not merely as a teacher or coach of the team, since being too aloof and official makes Americans little different in approach from the French."[1] O'Daniel also recommended that the United States minimize the importance of its role in sponsored projects so that the Vietnamese felt in control. His advice would be repeated by others in the years to come but usually by those who aligned on the side that opposed Durbrow and his team after they had moved against Ngô Đình Diệm.

O'Daniel's perspective would have been warmly received by Ngô Đình Diệm during the prolonged crisis with Cambodia. Durbrow had initially been the team player that O'Daniel advocated by supporting the Vietnamese position, though that may have come about through a defense of his own position rather than a defense of the Vietnamese. Cambodia continued to occupy the time of the Americans in Vietnam, though other challenges would soon emerge to test Durbrow, Williamds, and the Country Team.

When Durbrow met with Ngô Đình Diệm on September 4, he urged him to initiate a collaborative action to move the border marker. Ngô Đình Diệm agreed but, having already offered to re-position it, was reluctant to reinitiate the process for fear that Sihanouk would use it against the Vietnamese. Ngô Đình Diệm was convinced that "Sihanouk had worked himself into [a] corner from which he cannot get out gracefully and therefore [was] planning [a] bombastic propaganda campaign in [an] effort [to] gain sympathy [from] other nations and get himself out of [the] dilemma he cause by recognition CHICOMs."[2] Durbrow believed that Ngô Đình Diệm was not willing to make any further concessions, as it would be seen as a sign of weakness and used by Sihanouk for propaganda. Ngô Đình Nhu confirmed this sentiment during his meeting with Durbrow the next day. He argued that the Vietnamese had made a good faith effort to jointly move the marker and could not do it unilaterally as it would cause Sihanouk to lose prestige. Durbrow confessed in a telegram to Washington, though not to Ngô Đình Nhu, that he did not understand "this type of Oriental 'logic.'"[3] It many respects, Durbrow's statement was more true than he cared to admit. Even after being in Saigon for over a year, he did not understand the Vietnamese or Southeast Asians. This was his single greatest flaw as ambassador and would serve as the catalyst in breaking with those Americans who did understand Ngô Đình Diệm and the Vietnamese; it would also aid in his final break with Ngô Đình Diệm.

Other events occurred during the Cambodian border dispute that would have lasting effects on the Vietnamese-American relations during Durbrow's tenure. On July 10, party leaders for the National Revolutionary Movement and the Citizens Rally met in Saigon to become one party. This was something that Ngô Đình Diệm and Ngô Đình Nhu had instructed to happen.[4] While there were several members of the Citizens Rally that did not merge, the two groups reorganized into a new National Revolutionary Movement on July 11. Former president of the Citizens Rally and new vice president of the National Revolutionary Movement Trương Vĩnh Lê told Chalmers B. Wood, Second Secretary of the American embassy, that the fusion was designed to prevent Communist infiltration at the lower levels of the party as well as strengthen the overall organization. Wood agreed that the risk was real but his concern, in reporting of the event to Washington, was the lack of a real two-party system in Vietnam.

The Vietnamese Socialist Union was small and divided while the Democratic Bloc had been splintered by the departure of Phan Quang Đán, who was politically inactive, as his Liberal Democratic Party had yet to receive permission to form. Wood was also concerned by the increased role that Ngô Đình Cẩn would play in the Central Committee of the National Revolutionary Movement and the effects of his rivalry with his brother Ngô Đình Nhu for leadership. Wood saw a greater internal threat of instability within the organization than an outside threat of Communism. The lack of a legitimate opposition party would continue to concern Durbrow and his Embassy through the rest of the decade.

The domestic political scene and the continued tension with Cambodia gave Durbrow much to think about. These musings were expanded with a renewed crisis in Laos. Laos was experiencing its own set of circumstances that threatened the stability of the region. Prince Souvanna Phouma, the leader of the Lao Lam Lao Party, was unable to form a cabinet that met the approval of the conservatives and the newly formed anti-Communist party, the Committee for the Defense of the National Interests (CDNI).[5] The CDNI wanted two-thirds of the fourteen-member cabinet but had been offered only five seats. Added to the mix was the Communist Party's Neo Lao Hak Xat, who also wanted representation, and used rumors of North Vietnamese intervention if they were excluded. When the Laotians did form a government, it comforted Ngô Đình Diệm, who told Williams that Laos was not a problem.[6] The new Laotian Prime Minister, Phoui Sananikone, declared, on September 2, that his government opposed the Communists' attempts to subvert governments and would side with those who defended traditional democratic principles.[7]

The emerging Laotian situation, coupled with the rumors of Cambodia's possible recognition of North Vietnam at the end of November, increased the importance of Laos as it related to United States and Vietnamese diplomacy in Southeast Asia. On December 2, Durbrow reported the Country Team's recommendation that the Vietnamese provide some type of assistance to Laos.[8] The Vietnamese Army had already been discussing possible action and had sent several Civic Action teams to help the Laotians develop a similar program. The Country Team suggested other efforts that included Vietnamese assistance in resettlement and agricultural development programs, coordinating information programs, road development, and assistance in moving supplies through Vietnam. The American Embassy and MAAG Laos concurred with all of the suggestions save expanding South Vietnamese informational activities in Laos except among the Việt Cộng present in that country.[9] While much of the energy and focus of the United States and Vietnam had been on Sihanouk and Cambodia, the role of Laos in Southeast Asia's future emerged with greater significance.

These regional views were important, but it was the immediate problem in South Vietnam that dominated Durbrow's attention. On August 10, the Việt Cộng launched a major raid against the French-owned Michelin rubber plantation in Dầu Tiếng, the second such attack in 1958.[10] The installation was completely destroyed. The CIA offered an assessment that concluded that the 400 heavily armed forces marked a new campaign, bent on causing large-scale economic damage to the Republic of Vietnam. By attacking the French-owned company, it was hoped that the Saigon Government would find it harder to attract foreign investments into its country. Ngô Đình Diệm had visited the plantation at the end of July and unconfirmed reports received at the American embassy in Saigon suggested that the target was selected because Ngô had made the trip.[11] Ngô Đình Diệm discussed the attack with Williams when they met on August 14.[12] He argued that the Vietnamese defenders had failed in their responsibilities to defend the plantation. They had been forewarned of a possible attack but were not on alert or organized to defend. Ngô Đình Diệm used the attack as another example of why the Civil Guard needed to be trained in anti-guerrilla operations.

When Ngô Đình Diệm and Williams met again on August 22, the Vietnamese president informed the General that insurgents had infiltrated the plantation.[13] This move was another example of the Việt Cộng attacking a successful economic development project in order to disrupt Government progress in the countryside. Another French-owned rubber plantation was attacked at the end of September.[14] As the trend toward targeted assassinations and the destruction of economic commodities increased, Ngô Đình Diệm's insistence of the need for a more powerful Civil Guard also increased.

When Durbrow, Williams, and Ngô Đình Diệm met with the Secretary of the Army Wilber Brucker on September 3, the nature of the threat from the North and Ngô Đình Diệm's strategy to defeat it were discussed.[15] Ngô Đình Diệm focused on the three major issues for Vietnam's defense: conscription, roads, and communications equipment. These were not new items for discussion and Ngô Đình Diệm used the meeting with Brucker to highlight the need for improvements. While the conversation took the usual, unsurprising path, as did most of the ones with Ngô Đình Diệm involving these subjects, what was significant was the comments written in pencil by Williams on his copy of the memorandum. They represented confirmation of the break between Williams and Durbrow as well as Williams' frustration with the ambassador and the Country Team. When the group discussed Việt Cộng training tactics and strategies, Brucker commented that they were doing so in the open. When Durbrow replied that the strategy was secret, Williams wrote the comment, "Stupid remark."[16] To suggest that the Việt Cộng strategy of conducting guerrilla attacks and arming the people to also attack was a secret plan was too much for Williams, though Ngô Đình Diệm did not counter the suggestion in the conversation.[17]

The animosity that was festering in Saigon among the Americans was also evident in their relations with the Vietnamese. Ngô Đình Diệm had already expressed his concern in working with the USOM. During a September 10 meeting with Williams, Ngô Đình Diệm shared his frustration in dealing with Durbrow.[18] Williams and Ngô Đình Diệm had a good working relationship, and while Williams was careful not to side against the ambassador when dealing with the Vietnamese, he did occasionally empathize with Ngô Đình Diệm. Earlier, Ngô Đình Diệm had asked Durbrow for information and advice about the relationship between civil and military agencies when a country was placed under military control. Durbrow interpreted that as a request for information about Civil Defense. When Williams informed the Vietnamese president of this, Ngô Đình Diệm was adamant that he had made himself clear. After Williams explained that he too had misunderstandings with civilians when using military terms, Ngô Đình Diệm suggested that Durbrow attend the National War College so that he could get training as others in the State Department did. In essence, Ngô Đình Diệm wanted Durbrow to be informed so that his requests would not be misunderstood. Williams was probably the only American in Saigon at the time to whom Ngô Đình Diệm could openly express his frustration with Durbrow. That channel would remain open as long as Williams was in Vietnam.

In the same meeting, Ngô Đình Diệm complained about the USIS and its disinterest in working with the Vietnamese to establish a radio station to broadcast to the North. This was one of the topics during Brucker's visit that Williams took issue with when Durbrow explained the American position. Ngô Đình Diệm asserted that the USIS personnel believed themselves superior to the Vietnamese and were complacent with what they were doing. Again, Ngô Đình Diệm could share his frustration with Williams without fear of reprisal. The Vietnamese were ready to launch the station but needed USIS assistance. Both Ngô Đình Diệm and Williams felt the urgency of the situation given Hanoi's advantage in radio propaganda and the potential for Cambodian broadcasts once Communist Chinese equipment was received.

If Williams and Ngô Đình Diệm shared growing feelings of frustration with Durbrow, they also conspired to ensure that the best plan for Vietnam moved forward. During a September 23 meeting, Ngô Đình Diệm discussed the issue of pay for the Self-Defense Force, a topic that had received attention and some controversy earlier.[19] The Country Team had agreed to a 43,500-personnel force budget in which the Saigon Government contributed 300 of the 1,000 piaster salary for each participant. During the conversation, Ngô Đình Diệm informed Williams that some personnel in the Central Region would work for only 600 or 700 piasters. After learning this, Williams asked Ngô Đình Diệm not to discuss this topic with anyone. Williams was worried about defending the justification for continued United States support for the program and believed public knowledge of the Vietnamese savings would jeopardize its future. When Williams reported his conversation with Ngô Đình Diệm to Durbrow, he left out this section.[20] While there were numerous issues with this decision that would further the split between Williams and Durbrow, the interaction showed a level of confidence and trust between the two that was not evident between Ngô Đình Diệm and Durbrow.

Williams was one of only a few American allies to Ngô Đình Diệm. The list of potential opponents seemed to be getting longer now that Durbrow headed it. On October 1, the CIA daily briefing indicated that Ngô Đình

Diệm's "dictatorial rule" was threatening his position, and that members of the Army, his cabinet, and influential Vietnamese had begun to increasingly criticize Ngô, who was seen as isolated from the people and dependent upon a small group of advisors, headed by Ngô Đình Nhu.[21] The briefing asserted that Ngô Đình Nhu was feared and hated and used the Cần Lao Party, of which he was the head, to further his ambitions. It concluded that there was too much of an emphasis on internal security and not enough focus on economic progress which, when coupled with the methods of the Cần Lao Party, was causing further discontent among the Vietnamese people. While Country Team, Embassy, and Consulate members had been reporting this progression during most of 1958, whether out of concern, frustration, or misunderstanding, the CIA briefing was significant for it was the first echo of the thoughts of those who expressed concern about Ngô Đình Diệm and his continued rule.

One of the influential Vietnamese was Ngô Trọng Hiếu, who had been the Vietnamese representative to Cambodia for nearly two and a half years and had been embroiled in the border marker incident. When he met with Wood on October 8 to discuss Vietnamese-Cambodian relations, the topic of the *Times of Vietnam* and its articles that had caused the problems with Sihanouk arose. Ngô Trọng Hiếu argued that because the newspaper was under the control of Ngô Đình Nhu, the Americans needed to discuss with him the role of the newspaper and exert influence on him if the Americans wanted the tone of the publication changed.[22] Ngô Trọng Hiếu had presented inconsistent leadership as Vietnam's representative in Cambodia and had swayed from optimism to pessimism several times since the June incident. Wood also pointed out that Ngô Trọng Hiếu had been close to Ngô Đình Nhu but their relationship had deteriorated and, coupled with his alleged dishonest activities, may have resulted in his observations about Ngô Đình Nhu. However, Wood argued that Ngô Trọng Hiếu's comments were consistent with others he had heard and should, therefore, be acknowledged.

While no one individual was directly linked to the CIA daily briefing as the source for its assessment, it seems reasonable that Wood's report played a contributing role. Another constant source of criticism of Ngô Đình Diệm that reached its way to Washington came from the overseas Vietnamese in France. Many of these individuals lost resources and prestige with the fall of former Vietnamese emperor Bảo Đại in October 1955 and blamed Ngô Đình Diệm for their plight. In the midst of the October 26 anniversary celebrations, two anti–Ngô Đình Diệm pamphlets reached the American embassy in Paris, enumerating the evils of the Vietnamese president.[23] Given the wording and the images used, the Counselor of the Embassy, Randolph Kidder, connected the pamphlets with Phạm Huy Cơ, who represented Phan Quang Đán's Democratic Party in Paris, and his colleague, Huỳnh Công Hậu. The overseas

Vietnamese, who had no vested interested in a Saigon Government led by Ngô Đình Diệm, were allowed their voice of dissent by the continued reporting of their words and actions. Kidder met with the French officer in charge of Vietnamese affairs, J. Duzer, on October 21, who had also received the pamphlets, though he thought the source of them was General Lê Quang Vy.[24] Over time, this had a cumulative effect that became significant regarding the continued rule of Ngô Đình Diệm.

The opposition to Ngô Đình Diệm also was the origin of innumerable rumors about the Saigon Government and specifically the Ngô family. Duzer confirmed that he had heard stories about discontent in the Vietnamese military, but he saw the source of this discontent as personal and financial rather than connected to the Ngô family.[25] Williams and Ngô Đình Diệm discussed this on October 30 in the aftermath of their meetings with Brucker and Admiral Felt.[26] The two reviewed the various anecdotes emanating from the Army, which Ngô Đình Diệm claimed was initiated by French agents. What was remarkable about the exchange was not the information but clear level of trust and respect between the two individuals that seemed to be absent when Ngô Đình Diệm discussed similar sensitive matters with Durbrow or Barrows. In fact, when Williams commented on the degree and depth of the information Ngô Đình Diệm provided visiting dignitaries, he responded that one of the reasons he did this was because it forced Durbrow and Barrows to listen and learn. This mutual level of failed understanding of perspective between the president and the ambassador would become more evident and serious as the nature of events worsened in the Republic of Vietnam.

Another source of rumors against the Ngô family was Takehiko Nishiyama, the attaché from the Japanese Embassy in Saigon. On December 2, he met with R.E. Jelley, who was assigned in the Economic Section of the Embassy, to discuss a number of issues.[27] Nishiyama told Jelley that he had had discussions with Intellectuals who were associated with the University of Saigon and had expressed their discontent with Ngô Đình Diệm's rule. He did not reveal his source though his assessment reaffirmed the position many within the American embassy in Saigon had established. On December 12, Heavner forwarded a memorandum from the USIS Branch Public Affairs Offices in Huế, written by David Hitchcock, that outlined the complaints of the Huế intelligentsia that had emerged in that country with the opening of the University of Huế in 1957 and the expansion of the hospital in that city.[28] Hitchcock, who had been in Vietnam for nearly two years, had established contacts with the leading professionals and intellectuals to further the USIS mission. He reported that these individuals, all of whom had returned to Vietnam from Europe, primarily France or the United States, had trouble adjusting to the strict life in Huế. This included their ability to drink and dance though there was also a concern about freedom of expression. The principle focus of the complaints centered on Ngô Đình Cẩn, who had already been the subject of numerous reports, and how he controlled the region. The implied trepidation, however, was really on the inability of Ngô Đình Diệm to rein in his brother and what appeared to be a lack of understanding of the worries, expressed by the Huế intellectuals, of the Saigon Government.

While the criticism of Ngô Đình Diệm from the Vietnamese in France was intense, several individuals were able to garner the attention of American embassy officials there as were Vietnamese visiting Paris.[29] Nguyễn Văn Cẩn, a Vietnamese Deputy in the National Assembly, met with Kidder on January 17 to discuss the 1959 National Assembly elections and his wavering of whether to run again. Nguyễn Văn Cẩn complained about the limited role of the Assembly in governing the country and the poor quality of the National Assembly members. While Nguyễn Văn Cẩn did not endorse the Vietnamese who opposed Ngô Đình Diệm in Paris, save for the vocal Nguyễn Hữu Châu, his implied message was that there was dissent in Saigon and the legitimate forums for governance were not being taken advantage of by Ngô Đình Diệm. Nguyễn Văn Cẩn later told the Chief of the Mission to the North American Treaty Organization and European Regional Organizations W. Randolph Burgess that he had decided not to run for reelection because of his disillusionment with the National Assembly, the cost of the campaign, and the possibility of his defeat. He wanted to stay in Paris if he could get his family out of Vietnam, though he did not think he would be able to do so and, therefore, planned to return to Vietnam.[30]

Not all of the reports emanating from Saigon were negative. Wood forwarded a conversation he had with Nguyễn Phương Thiệp, who served as the Secretary General of the National Assembly and was the editor of the Weekly *Gazette de Saigon*, a publication that was rarely mentioned in the daily *Foreign Broadcast Information Service* from Vietnam.[31] Nguyễn Phương Thiệp was a supporter of Ngô Đình Diệm who claimed that the Vietnamese people admired their president. When the two spoke of the National Assembly, Wood interpreted their conversation as Nguyễn Phương Thiệp not being too interested in discussing it, though he did indicate that his job was difficult because he needed to spend much of his time showing those under him how to do their jobs. This remark was significant, though it was not commented on by Wood. The Republic of Vietnam was still very young and many of those in positions of power did not know how to perform their jobs. Ngô Đình Diệm recognized this and assigned a few individuals, who had experience, with increasing responsibilities. Those who were not a part of this group claimed nepotism or favoritism, deflecting their deficiencies onto what they saw as a corrupt system rather than acknowledging them. While it was true that Ngô Đình Diệm became too reliant on a few individuals as the Republic matured, his starting point for this practice was based on the realities of the situation.

In the backdrop of the political intrigue and bickering, the internal security of the Republic of Vietnam loomed. The Vietnamese had been successful in thwarting attacks against Americans and Vietnamese celebrating the anniversary of the Republic, but the threat level was still high. Ngô Đình Diệm continued to press home the need for additional or improved roads in Vietnam to better connect the country militarily and economically, and touted the level of success of the Self-Defense Force. When Williams and Ngô Đình Diệm met on November 13, the topic came up early in their conversation.[32] Ngô Đình Diệm praised the work of the Self-Defense Force in Central Vietnam, though he did admit that the pay for one Self-Defense Force member was split between two people; this was another fact not transmitted to Durbrow. Ngô Đình Diệm argued that the greater efficiency of the Self-Defense Force meant that they could assume a more significant role in the static defense in the countryside, which would free up Civil Guard units for continued training.

Ngô Đình Diệm argued, to a sympathetic audience, that the Self-Defense Force and Civil Guard needed to be better trained and equipped to fulfill their roles. Williams agreed and also mentioned that the Civil Guard had lost five million dollars because their mission had not been clearly defined. The loss of money came as a result of the USOM rather than MAAG; Williams suggested that Ngô Đình Diệm speak with Durbrow, Barrows, or Gardiner. Ngô Đình Diệm complained that they were waiting to hear from Washington, though when Williams urged him to speak with them again he did, though there was no record of that conversation. Williams had the ability to speak directly to Ngô Đình Diệm and he responded, in part, because Ngô Đình Diệm knew that Williams had his best interest in mind. That was reinforced by other high-profile visitors to Vietnam. When Deputy Assistant Secretary of Defense for the Military Assistance Program Charles Shuff visited Ngô Đình Diệm on November 14 with Williams and Durbrow, he reaffirmed Williams' commitment to Vietnam. Williams was "a man who does not hesitate to bang on tables and make his requirements known and who has your best interest at heart," he asserted during the meeting.[33] The record during Durbrow's tenure as ambassador does not reflect a similar reinforcement for him with other visitors to Vietnam.

In another instance, Ngô Đình Diệm informed Williams that members of the Self-Defense Force could replace vacancies in the Civil Guard. Williams cautioned him against using the word integration and instead recommended calling it reinforcing to avoid members of the USOM speaking out against the strategy. In trying to muddle through the obstacles and regulations imposed by the USOM and Country Team, Ngô Đình Diệm had a willing ally in Williams.[34] In the same December 8 meeting, Ngô Đình Diệm complained that the road project from Bến Giang to Đắk Lê was delayed because the USOM

7. The War at Home and on the Periphery 87

called for a bulldozer with 100 horsepower but the only ones available were the 95 horsepower Oliver and the 102 horsepower Caterpillar. According to Ngô Đình Diệm, the USOM wanted new specifications to fit one of the two available bulldozers before the road project progressed. His frustration, which was shared by Williams, centered on the fact that the project needed to start during the dry season or an entire year would be lost.

Ngô Đình Diệm also complained to Williams about the USOM's insistence of using their method of building roads and ignoring Vietnamese knowledge and experience in working in their region. Ngô Đình Diệm told Williams that he thought the USOM engineers believed the Vietnamese to be ignorant. The USOM engineers wanted to build roads with a thick base of rock and sand with irrigation ditches on either side without asphalt. The Vietnamese wanted a thin layer of rock, sand, and asphalt, but the Americans overruled them. As a result, the roads, built to American specifications, became wavy because of the Vietnamese soil and climate, with rocks sticking out of it like thorns.[35] After the failure, the USOM ordered the Ministry for Public Works to order asphalt for the roads. Ngô Đình Diệm worried that the USOM would lose prestige by this mistake, and asked Williams not to relay his perspective on the situation. Even though Ngô Đình Diệm and his government had significant issues with the USOM, it still was political enough to publically recognize its contributions. On the occasion of Barrows' return to Washington, ending his time with the USOM in Vietnam, *Cách mạng Quốc gia* saw his departure as a loss for South Vietnam: "Leland Barrows helped the southern government tremendously in its economic recovery and brought new, vital forces to the Vietnamese people."[36] However, it was these types of delays and procedures that boggled the Vietnamese president and cause him to become more firm with certain Americans in Saigon, which did not help his long term plans or tenure in office.

The issues confronting Vietnam, and the growing list of individuals opposed to Ngô Đình Diệm's rule, emboldened Durbrow to take a stronger stand. As his tenure in office progressed, the earlier remarks and advice by O'Daniel seemed more distant and less likely to be acted upon. As such, Durbrow seemed to be moving away from the principle American advocate of the Vietnamese leadership and toward the role as one of its most prominent detractors.

8
The Laotian Crisis, 1959

By the beginning of 1959, the Cambodian incident that had taken up so much of the time and resources of the United States and South Vietnam seemed to have settled. Durbrow could report in his January 3 weekly telegram that the Vietnamese press had been restrained since September and had even refrained from comment when Sihanouk suspended relations with Thailand at the end of 1958.[1] The three month truce in the press between the two countries and the real likelihood of a settlement on the border marker meant that other, more significant, issues could garner focus. The Country Team was anxious to move forward in retraining and reequipping the Civil Guard as it believed warranted and also help to arrest the Communist program of assassinations that had averaged between fifteen and thirty-five per month through 1958.[2] Ngô Đình Diệm agreed with these objectives though he also continued his push to build new roads in isolated spots in the northern part of South Vietnam in order to maintain a government presence in that region. He wanted to counter the Communists who had had uninterrupted access since the 1954 Geneva Agreements. The continuing saga of Cambodia, coupled with a new border crisis in Laos, and a change in American leadership in Southeast Asia and Washington all contributed to a Vietnam policy that was interrupted more than it was addressed.[3]

The situation in Laos became more critical in the opening days of 1959 as the North Vietnamese switched their attention to that country, forcing the South Vietnamese and United States to respond. On December 14, 1958, two days before the announcement that Laos and the Republic of Vietnam would elevate their diplomatic representation to the ambassadorial level, a company of North Vietnamese troops established three outposts approximately five kilometers inside of Savannakhet Province in Laos, in the villages of Ban Tarouna, Ban Kapai, and Ban Tavigne.[4] The initial report had the invading force as three regiments, which had penetrated sixty miles into Laos, though that estimation was quickly revised to three battalions that had advanced six miles.⁵ In reality, only three companies had moved across the border within a five-kilometer stretch.

The breech into Laos was significant for Vietnam, as Ngô Đình Diệm had been continually warning the Americans that the North Vietnamese would use Laotian territory to transport personnel and equipment into Cambodia and eventually the Republic of Vietnam. The move was also seen as a possible attempt to support the Neo Lao Hak Xat, the communist party in Laos, which was suffering as a result of increased Laotian political stability. A daily briefing from the CIA for January 3 argued that the North Vietnamese move into Laos would trigger the ICC to reactivate in Laos and would then be used as a safeguard against attempts to suppress the Neo Lao Hak Xat by the Laotian Government in Vientiane.⁶ Earlier, *Le Journal D'Extreme-Orient* attempted to quell rumors that the violation of Laotian territory was the signal for a coup d'état, though few believed such a force could help engineer such an action.⁷

The North Vietnamese responded to the Laotian allegations with a December 29 communiqué from Premier Phạm Văn Đồng. He claimed that Laotian aircraft had violated North Vietnamese airspace on seven different occasions over the provinces of Nghệ An, Tân Hoá, and Sơn La and had conducted a military, propaganda, and espionage campaign in the Hoàng Lập region.⁸ The Laotians denied the allegations, which were not given much credibility by the Americans in Vientiane, though Counselor of the Embassy in Laos Leonard Bacon offered American support and advice to the RLG response once it had been formulated.⁹ The Neo Lao Hak Xat party newspaper *Lao Hak Xat* also reported that its members had been arrested and persecuted by the Vientiane Government; this report was also dismissed by Deputy Prime Minister Katay Don Sasorith.¹⁰

The initial Saigon response to the incursion came from Ngô Đình Nhu, who met with Durbrow on January 7.¹¹ While Ngô Đình Nhu believed the military move was serious, he argued that it had been going on for some time and that the operation had been carried out by security forces rather than elements of the People's Army of Vietnam. Ngô Đình Nhu argued that the purpose of the operations was several fold. The North Vietnamese wanted to put pressure on the Laotian Government and support the Neo Lao Hak Xat, though it also aimed to prepare the local Laotian population and the Montagnard people in the region to assist in the movement of personnel and supplies to Cambodia. This line of reasoning was one that both Ngô Đình Nhu and Ngô Đình Diệm had maintained for some time. Ngô Đình Nhu worried about the quality of the Laotian officer corps, who had been trained by the French, and confirmed the need for the Vietnamese to aid in the development of the Laotian Armed Forces as had been planned earlier. The position was in line with Ngô Đình Diệm's desire to see the Republic of Vietnam was the bulwark against Communism in Southeast Asia and the Pacific. The Saigon Government wanted to take a leadership role in the region though it needed to settle its own affairs before it could do so.

On January 7, the United States learned that the North Vietnamese had withdrawn from the three original outposts that had caused the consternation, only to penetrate the border at three new spots in the southeastern region of the country.[12] While the United States was eager to publicize these new incursions, there was reluctance to do so if it resulted in the return of the ICC to Laos. The assumption was that the North Vietnamese wanted this to happen so that the ICC team would help them report the suppression of the Neo Lao Hak Xat by the government. Because the incursions were on the smaller scale, Washington's answer was to encourage a minimal response by Laos to the North Vietnamese rather than exaggerating the situation. The belief was that the North Vietnamese wanted a Laotian overreaction in order to escalate the situation.[13]

When Durbrow met with Vũ Văn Mẫu on January 8, the two discussed the North Vietnamese incursion and the possible Vietnamese response.[14] Vũ Văn Mẫu argued that his country's security was potentially threatened, something Ngô Đình Diệm and Ngô Đình Nhu had maintained, and that Vietnam might need to appeal to the Southeast Asia Treaty Organization (SEATO) to deal with the matter. Like the ICC, the United States did not want to involve SEATO because it would cause the Polish and Indian members of the ICC to react negatively and work to reactivate the ICC in Laos. Durbrow made sure to press this point to Vũ Văn Mẫu who agreed though he reserved the possibility of approaching SEATO if the situation worsened.

The Vietnamese press started to cover the events in earnest on January 9. *Cách mạng Quốc gia*, in expressing its alarm over the movement of North Vietnamese troops, argued that the action signaled that country's support for the Pathet Lao, while *Sài Gòn Mới* and *Dai Ha Jih Pao* argued that the North Vietnamese provocation was at the orders of the Soviet Union and China.[15] The *Times of Vietnam* maintained the position that North Vietnam acted as it did because of the stability established in Laos after it had reached an agreement with the Pathet Lao and had incorporated members of the Neo Lao Hak Xat into its government. Laotian neutrality was a danger to Hanoi and it used the troop movement to threaten it as well as Laotian stability.[16] Most of the other Saigon dailies followed this line of reasoning in the early days of the crisis.

Ngô Đình Diệm's position on the situation was revealed on January 10 when he met with Durbrow, Williams, and Gardiner. In response to Durbrow's query, Ngô Đình Diệm asserted that the Laotian government was weak and needed to take a stronger stand.[17] He told the Americans that he planned to appeal to the ICC concerning the North Vietnamese activities near the demilitarized zone, including Laotian territories, because it threatened South Vietnam.[18] Again, Durbrow took the lead in trying to convince Ngô Đình Diệm not to pursue this route, maintaining that the Laotians were planning to go to the Secretary General of the United Nations, Dag Hammarskjold, because they did not want the ICC reactivated. It was not clear why Ngô Đình Diệm pursued this line of reasoning, as Ngô Đình Nhu and Vũ Văn Mẫu had already been informed, though this may have been a test, as all three American principles were with him at the time. While not included in Williams' memorandum of conversation, Durbrow did report that Ngô Đình Diệm agreed with the Laotian plan to send a note to Hammarskjold and did not seem concerned with any repercussions with the ICC Saigon investigating the situation though he did agree that the reactivation of ICC Laos was not preferable.[19] When Elting met with Vũ Văn Mẫu on January 14, the Vietnamese foreign minister confirmed that Ngô Đình Diệm agreed with the American position and added that an ICC team would find it difficult to move through the jungle to investigate the incursions in the Vietnamese territory. It would probably find nothing though the action would signal to Hanoi that the South Vietnamese were well aware of their activities.[20]

The hope that the situation would be handled discretely by the Laotians was challenged when Bacon learned that Prime Minister Phoui Sananikone had not only received permission to send a note to the Secretary General but also requested special powers from the Laotian National Assembly based on the idea that the incursion was a national danger.[21] It did not help that some Vietnamese newspapers, like *Cách mạng Quốc gia*, were lamenting that Vietnam, Cambodia, and Laos could not militarily ally themselves to defend against Communist threats and called for a strengthening of SEATO to deal with issues like the current one.[22] Like Cambodia earlier, the United States did not think the situation merited the attention the Laotians were potentially planning to give it and worried that exaggerating the incursion would play into the hands of the Communists.

This concern was real as demonstrated by the Laotian drafts of a communiqué, which was delivered to the French to pass along.[23] The document was written as if the Laotians had already been in contact with Hammarskjold, which they had not, and that they asked the Secretary General to take action against Hanoi. Because North Vietnam was not a member of the United Nations, Hammarskjold could not do this and would most likely defer to the ICC and a reactivation of it in Laos. It also had the possibility of legitimizing the Vietnamese Communists by allowing it direct contact with Hammarskjold. Dulles agreed with the French position and encouraged Bacon and the Embassy to make sure the Laotians did not pursue the request for any type of United Nations observer.[24] The United States did not have to worry long that the Laotians would intensify the incident.[25]

The Americans learned from Laotian Permanent Representative to the United Nations Ourot Souvannavong on January 15 that he had been instructed by Vientiane to consult with Hammarskjold and other friendly groups in the United Nations.[26] When the Secretary General told him it was impossible to take action against the North Vietnamese, he agreed that the best course of action was to send a letter to the Secretary General outlining the situation, which was transmitted on January 16.[27] Souvannavong made it clear that the Laotian Government did not want the ICC reactivated for the same reasons as the Americans. The Laotians recognized that the incident was minor, but they took exception to Hanoi's propaganda campaign against Vientiane, which tried to shift the blame to them.

While it seemed safe to assume that the Laotians and Vietnamese would not act to reactivate the ICC in Laos, there was still concern that original members of the committee would work towards that goal. The January 17 CIA daily briefing reported that India, as chairman of the ICC for the Indochinese states, was taking steps to reactivate the ICC in Laos and was planning for a "Laos Committee" to meet in Saigon to review Hanoi's accusations of American and Laotian violations of the 1954 Geneva Agreements.[28] Because of the ineffectiveness of the ICC in Laos in identifying and reversing Communist activity, its potential reconstitution was seen as a victory for the Communist who could use it to further its propaganda and muddle the real situation in Southeast Asia.

When United States ambassador to Laos Horace Smith returned to Vientiane, he made a courtesy call to Minister of Foreign Affairs Khamphan Panya to get a review of the situation and Laotian actions since his departure in early January.[29] He confirmed Souvannavong's meeting with Hammarskjold who, he maintained, had expressed his sympathy with the Laotian plight. Khamphan Panya informed Smith that if the Secretary General was unable to intervene on the Laotian's behalf, his government might ask the Security Council to do so though the hopes for a successful outcome were hampered with the real possibility of a Soviet veto for any action. On this same day, the Laotian legation in Saigon issued a six-point communiqué that maintained the incident had been designed to pressure its government to support the Neo Lao Hak Xat and revive the ICC in Laos. Because the move was designed to support propaganda and political ends, the communiqué asserted that the Vientiane Government would not engage in polemics with the Vietnamese Communists.[30]

As the situation progressed, the United States could rest assured that the Laotians would not make any moves to help reactivate the ICC, though it did learn on January 24 that Phoui Sananikone, after receiving special powers from the National Assembly for a period of twelve months, announced a reorganization of his government.[31] While there was no early conversation about the reorganization, it did signal that the current crisis was far from over. However, like many other political situations that involved conflicting personalities and egos, the Laotian state of affairs was far from stable.

On February 7, the CIA daily briefing indicated that the Laotian Government was considering a denunciation of the 1954 Geneva Agreements.[32] It indicated that this move was in response to its inability to accept American military training facilities because of the treaty. Such a move had the potential to escalate the military tension in Southeast Asia as Hanoi would see it as a threat as would the Pathet Lao, whose existence in Laos would become more endangered. The move was not favored by the French who would most likely see a diminishing of influence in the country nor other countries involved in maintaining the peace since 1954. On February 11, the Laotian Government made the announcement that it was no longer bound by the 1954 Geneva Agreements.[33]

The Laotians argued that they had fulfilled their obligations as outlined under the agreements and that they were no longer necessary. Two immediate, and significant, consequences of the action were the possibility of American military training for Laotians and the prevention of reactivating the ICC in Laos. The Vietnamese press supported the Laotian decision. In a February 14 editorial, *Tự do* asserted that, "the Royal Laotian Government's decision was appropriate and logical. It serves as a definite answer to the plots and aggressive acts of the Red Chinese–Viet Cong bloc."[34] The Chinese-language daily, *Van Juo Jih Pao*, praised the Laotians and reaffirmed the Laotian right to request military aid from the United States.[35] While news of the denunciation, or fulfillment, was being discussed, Souvannavong met again with Hammarskjold.[36]

The Secretary General wanted to get a Laotian reaction to having him meet with representatives from India, Poland, and Canada separately, and not as ICC delegates, to have them approach Vientiane and Hanoi about using the United Nations to solve their problem.[37] Parsons, who met with Souvannavong on February 11, expressed American skepticism about such a tactic, just as Americans had done so earlier whenever the ICC or the nation-delegates to the ICC where mentioned in a possible solution. However, Acting Secretary of State C. Douglas Dillon favored the position that if the Laotians insisted on United Nation observers, then only one nation needed to be approached so any possible ICC connection could not be established.[38]

The United States was concerned about the Laotians accepting Hammarskjold's approach because it would provide legitimization to a country that was not recognized by the United Nations. There was also the possibility that the United Nations arbitrator would side with the North Vietnamese, which might humiliate the Laotians, while the involvement of the Secretary General could also bring in the Security Council and thus the Soviet Union.

None of these potential consequences were worth any possible benefits derived from United Nations participation.

The Laotian announcement of its fulfillment of the 1954 Geneva Agreements, and the alternative explanation that it renounced the document because of the underlying concern for the United States as it sought to maintain its diplomacy in Southeast Asia, was important. The notion of renunciation was significant after the Republic of Vietnam's action to not abide by the same Agreement because it had not been a signatory of it. On February 16, Smith met with Phoui Sananikone to determine the exact Laotian position regarding the Agreements.[39] He confirmed that the Laotians had fulfilled their obligations towards the Agreements; it had not denounced them but had settled them. As a result, Phoui Sananikone argued that the Laotians had the right to import weapons needed for their defense, thus negating these important articles in the 1954 Geneva Agreements. While the decision did allow the United States the possibility of aiding the Laotians, which was something that Ngô Đình Diệm had also encouraged by his offer of aid, it did open the possibility for an effective Communist propaganda campaign against Laos as well as increased military activity originating from the North Vietnamese.

Smith recommended, and the Prime Minister agreed, that the Laotian Government issue a communiqué explaining their action so that the denunciation rumor would not take. The American suggestions included a statement that Laos had no intention of letting foreign troops enter its border, increasing its border security, creating new military installations, or participate in any military alliance.[40] The first three points were not included in the statement that Phoui Sananikone had had his foreign minister, Khamphan Panya, draft. The American version was something that both the British and French strongly supported as their domestic press had been increasingly reporting the renouncement rumor and feared further escalation in the region as a result.[41] The Laotians issued the statement on February 18.[42]

Not only were the British and French anxious with the Laotian decision. Ngô Đình Diệm expressed a similar concern when he met with Admiral Felt, Williams, and Durbrow on February 16.[43] Felt, who had already visited Laos on his trip, was surprised to hear Ngô Đình Diệm claim that a crisis was brewing in Vientiane. When the Political Advisor to the Commander-in-Chief, Pacific, John Steeves, who was also present at the meeting offered that the crisis had to do with the possible postponement of the upcoming elections for a year, Ngô Đình Diệm corrected him. The crisis Ngô Đình Diệm envisioned was one within the Laotian Cabinet about the question of representation. Ngô Đình Diệm predicted that the meeting to determine this might lead to a fall of the government. He was waiting to proceed with a plan to ask the Laotians to help fill border posts between the two countries so that they could more easily control the border against future incursions. Ngô Đình Diệm did not seem concerned about the language the Laotians used regarding their ending of the 1954 Geneva Agreements; he was more concerned about a Laos strong enough to protect its side of the border, so that the Vietnamese could do the same on their own.

The position of Vietnam in Laos also caused concern for some of the United States' allies. The French ambassador in Vientiane, Oliver Gassouin, had repeatedly told Smith of his concern about the increased role of the Vietnamese in Laotian affairs. While Gassouin thought that Ngô Đình Diệm had good intentions, he believed that the Vietnamese president's ultimate goal was to be the head of an anti-communist coalition in the region. Implied in that statement was that the coalition would also be anti-colonial.[44] Durbrow countered Gassouin's allegations and doubted, as Gassouin had implied, that Ngô Đình Diệm was planning to use Laos as the "spearhead" for an anti-communist crusade in Southeast Asia.[45]

As the situation proceeded, Smith reported on February 19 that the Laotians had agreed to accept Hammarskjold's offer of sending a mediator on the border issue with North Vietnam though he had not been able to confirm if only one of the three ICC members or the whole group would deliver the message to Hanoi.[46] No sooner than this had been reported to Washington, Smith learned that Ourot Souvannavong had been instructed to ask Hammarskjold to delay all action for twenty-four hours.[47] News of the alleged denunciation and the twenty-four hour delay did not dissuade Hammarskjold. who still believed that any of the three members of the ICC, acting independently of one another and not in the capacity of that organization, could approach Laos and the North Vietnamese and offer their services as a neutral intermediary.[48]

Hammarskjold, who was also about to depart for a planned trip to the region, confirmed that he had no intention of going to Hanoi unless the Laotians suggested it. This fit into the American plans though the composition of the potential intermediaries was still an issue.[49] With this possibility in play, Christian Herter, acting for Secretary of State Dulles, who was seriously ill, informed Smith that he needed to continue to press upon the Laotians that the United States was still wary about United Nations involvement unless they approached Hammarskjold with the same plan already developed by the Secretary General but not including the three former members of the ICC Laos.[50]

Meanwhile, Smith and the other Americans involved were working on damage control over the use of the words denunciation, renunciation, or fulfillment, which had caused some trouble with the British and the French. Smith argued that all American sources of information needed to use the word fulfillment in order to lessen the potential diplomatic damage the action might take.⁵¹ On February 21, United States ambassador to the United Nations, Henry Cabot Lodge, Jr., learned that Ourot Souvannavong's new instructions, the reason for the twenty-four hour delay, were to request Hammarskjold to ask if the Indian delegate to the ICC would act alone as the intermediary to the North Vietnamese to see if they would accept United Nations involvement in the dispute.⁵² Hammarskjold agreed to the Laotian request though he acknowledged to Lodge that the United Nations had limited powers to act; Hammarskjold was also concerned about a recent *New York Times* editorial, titled "Realism in Vietnam," that praised the Laotians for courageously denouncing the Geneva Agreements.⁵³ The editorial called for the United Nations to step in and settle the matter.

While Cambodian matters replaced Laos for the next several weeks, the level of distrust and intrigue remained high. In early March, members of the Neo Lao Hak Xat alleged that the Vientiane Government was making mass arrests of its party members for trying to instill communist ideology in the people. At the same time, large numbers of Neo Lao Hak Xat members were resigning from the party.⁵⁴ Prince Souphanouvong also began calling for a reactivation of the ICC in Laos with greater vigor.⁵⁵

The possibility of a resolution to the Laotian situation emerged after Hammarskjold's visit to Vientiane in mid–March. Kellogg learned from the Lao Charge in Cambodia that he had received word that an arrangement had been achieved between Vientiane and Hanoi as a result of Hammarskjold's visit though he had no details about it.⁵⁶ Smith, however, confirmed that the announcement had been premature. When he met with the Laotian Foreign Minister Khamphan Panya on March 20, he raised the issue of the arrangement but learned that none existed. Hammarskjold had only promised to consult with the Indian delegates to the ICC to see if they would be interested in acting alone as an intermediary.⁵⁷

Throughout the entire Laotian affair, the United States and the Republic of Vietnam worked hard to make sure that the ICC in Laos was not reactivated. Both countries had lost faith in the ability of that organization to effectively work in the country and neither believed that the organization could withstand the onslaught of propaganda emitting from Hanoi without indirectly working for the Communists. The Indian delegate to the ICC, who also served as Chair of the group, disagreed with this position. When Hammarskjold visited New Delhi in early April and asked the chairman of the International Commission for Supervision and Control, Manilal Jagdish Desai, for India's help in mediating the border dispute between Laos and North Vietnam, it was not surprising that the Indians agreed to the request so long as the ICC in Laos was reactivated.⁵⁸ During his conversation with Desai, this position was confirmed with the proposal having members of the Laos ICC group meet in Saigon to discuss the Laotian–North Vietnamese border situation.⁵⁹ Smith had cause for concern at this stance, as he did for the announcement by Hammarskjold that the ICC still legally existed and therefore would be the group the Laotians would need to first consult before any additional actions by the United Nations could be taken in the region.⁶⁰

The Laotians shared the American and Republic of Vietnam view about the ICC. Ourot Souvannavong confirmed that the Laotians did not want the Indian representative to intervene, with or without the Laos ICC but, rather, the Vientiane approach was to seek the assistance of the Secretary General.⁶¹ The Laotians also planned to protest any ICC meeting dealing with the border solution that took place outside of Laos. These positions received strong support from the United States. The situation turned decidedly worse when, on May 11, two Pathet Lao units stationed in Luang Prabang, estimated at 500 troops in strength, which were designated to be turned over to the Laotian Army, fled instead.⁶² The immediate United States fear was that Communist countries would again call for the reactivation of the ICC Laos in order to thwart retaliatory action from Vientiane against Neo Lao Hak Xat leaders under custody.

Both Communist China and North Vietnam called for an end to the persecution of the units and a return of the ICC and labeled the Laotian action against Neo Lao Hak Xat leaders and the Pathet Lao as violations against the 1954 Geneva Agreements. In reporting the event, *Cách mạng Quốc gia* praised the Laotian decision to go after the units so that they would not be a future threat, while *Tự do*, also fearing that the force would form the nucleus for a renewed civil war, supported by the North Vietnamese, called for similar measures.⁶³ Durbrow met with Lalouette and Parkes on May 20 to discuss the new developments.⁶⁴ Both the French and British believed it would be difficult not to reconvene the ICC in Laos, especially if fighting erupted between the two sides. For his part, Lalouette believed it imperative that the French continue its role in Laos and that the Laotian army train quickly. There was no record of Durbrow's response as the discussion turned to Cambodia. The Soviet Foreign Minister, Andrei Gromyko, continued to maintain the pressure by announcing on June 1 that the Soviet Union and United Kingdom, as co-chairs of the 1954 Geneva Conference and Agreement, would discuss the Laotian situation and reconvene the ICC in Laos.⁶⁵ When coupled with the escape of the Pathet Lao group that had refused reintegration into the Royal Laotian Army, the situation in Laos did not look promising.⁶⁶

On June 6, the Council of Ministers in Laos declared the Pathet Lao soldiers military deserters, which negated any charge that the Royal Laotian Government had not fulfilled its obligations under the 1954 Geneva Agreements.⁶⁷ This pronouncement was designed to counter the propaganda originating from Hanoi and Peking that insisted the ICC be reconvened in Laos and that the Pathet Lao and members of the Neo Lao Hak Xat continue to be persecuted. The burgeoning crisis in Laos overshadowed events in Cambodia and Vietnam for a brief time. While Durbrow did not play a prominent role on the American side, he did work with Ngô Đình Diệm to push for the non-reactivation of the ICC in Laos. The two could agree on issues of mutual concern, but as 1959 continued, such issues were few and far between, which did not help an already unhealthy relationship.

9

The Cambodian Affair, 1959

While the Laotian crisis continued to capture the attention of the Americans as they dealt with Southeast Asia, Cambodia and Sihanouk once again became a focal point. The uneasy calm that had settled during the opening weeks of the New Year soon return to the new norm of intrigue, distrust, and declining relations that all parties had come to know. During a February 2 meeting between Williams and Ngô Đình Diệm, the president asked whether the General had any information about Sihanouk ordering the questioning of his generals as to whether any American military personnel had tried to get information from them or advise them.[1] While Williams did not, he promised to contact MAAG Cambodia and the CIA about this matter. The purpose of the question was linked to Ngô Đình Diệm's claim that Sihanouk believed the Vietnamese were planning a coup d'état against him.[2] The source of the rumor, according to Ngô Đình Diệm, was the French, who were advising Sihanouk about the Vietnamese plot and sheltering and aiding opposition leader Sam Sary.[3] Earlier, at a public rally in Phnom Penh, Sihanouk claimed that secret documents seized from Sam Sary's supporters proved that his group wanted to overthrow him.[4] The Cambodian claim and rumors foreshadowed a difficult time for Vietnamese-Cambodian relations, which did not suit Durbrow or the Americans in the midst of the Laotian affair.

The war of rumors escalated on February 12 when the French Press Attaché to Sihanouk, Jean Barre, informed the American Embassy that Sihanouk wanted better relations with the Republic of Vietnam, even though the Prince had evidence that Ngô Trọng Hiếu was involved in a plot to overthrow him.[5] The message was mixed, not unlike much of Sihanouk's dealings with Vietnam. Regardless of reality, the numerous rumors floating around in February pointed to deteriorating relations between Vietnam and Cambodia at a time when the United States needed a unified front. The day after this information was received, Ngô Trọng Hiếu's official vehicle was stopped at the border between Cambodia and Vietnam and searched by Cambodian police and customs agents.⁶ This was done despite the fact that the car was occupied by Ngô Trọng Hiếu and flew the Vietnamese flag. As he was well known to the border guards, there was no support for a case of mistaken identity or a harmless misunderstanding. It seemed evident, as other official cars were not stopped, that Ngô Trọng Hiếu was being targeted and that the intimidation techniques were a result of an order from the officers' and custom agents' superiors. Ngô Trọng Hiếu's car was stopped and searched three additional times between February 13 and February 16.⁷

On February 17, the *Vietnam Press* reported that a group of sixty men, who had attacked an Agricultural Development Center a few weeks earlier, had been based in Cambodia.⁸ The attack was significant because of its size and its target. Ngô Đình Diệm had worried over increased attacks against such centers by the Việt Cộng in order to disrupt the progress they had made. The origins of the attack also caused concern for the Vietnamese as it was further evidence that Sihanouk did not have control over his border with Vietnam. Coupled with the increased threat along the border with Laos, the Vietnamese sense of insecurity was heightened.

Vietnam's relations with Cambodia took another turn for the worse when Durbrow received a Cambodian communiqué that linked Vietnamese soldiers with Cambodian dissident Dap Chhuon and his activities in Siem Reap.⁹ The Cambodians had ordered the arrest of Dap, who learned of the action and fled into the forests; the Cambodian Government communiqué claimed that two uniformed South Vietnamese soldiers and a radio transmitter were found in Dap Chhuon's villa, as were documents which proved a link between Dap Chhuon's treasonous activities and foreign elements, presumably the South Vietnamese and Americans.¹⁰ When confronted with the news at a dinner on February 23, Nguyễn Đình Thuần and Vũ Văn Mẫu both tried to downplay the possibility as well as the significance of the story, though Durbrow reported that each was uneasy with the news.¹¹ Durbrow, for his part, emphasized the seriousness of the report if it were true, as it confirmed some of Sihanouk's suspicions and legitimatized his anti–Vietnamese rhetoric and action. Durbrow's concern was shared by other ambassadors in Vietnam, including France's Roger Lalouette.

The next day, Nguyễn Đình Thuần telephoned Williams to give him an assurance from Ngô Đình Diệm that no ARVN officers or men were involved in Cambodia, nor were the Vietnamese involved in sending arms, ammunition or radio equipment to Cambodia.¹² Ngô Đình Diệm confirmed the Vietnamese position to the Australian ambassador to Vietnam, Frederick Blakeney. Ngô Đình Diệm maintained throughout the episode that Dap Chhuon was not a revolutionary.¹³ The Vietnamese issued a denial in the *Vietnam Press* on February 24.¹⁴ This was followed by a February 26 editorial in *Cách mạng Quốc gia* which argued that Sihanouk needed to stop blaming others for the consequences of his siding with the French and Communist Chinese. It argued that Dap Chhuon and Sam Sary were patriots and that Sihanouk was using them to deflect his actions.[15]

Sihanouk continued to focus on the theme of foreign entanglement in his country and issued a statement that answered the Vietnamese claims of Dap Chhuon's loyalty. He responded by arguing that, "even Jesus Christ had His Judas."[16] He also asserted, using written confessions by Dap Chhuon's mistress and by his brother, that Nguyễn Văn Nhieu, a representative of Vietnam in Cambodia, had attended the conference in Siem Reap. This had been earlier reported, though no name given, by *Le Dépêche du Cambodge*, which argued that "Under cover of protestations of friendship, a conspiracy was patiently being hatched."[17] The Cambodians were determined to make sure that the Republic of Vietnam was embarrassed by the failed coup d'état.

The French Foreign Office's Indochina Section blamed the new intrigue on Ngô Đình Nhu and Ngô Đình Cẩn. It also attributed much of the heightened tension to Sihanouk who, it concluded, tended to blame the Americans for Vietnamese actions because it thought that the Americans controlled them and could stop an act before it started.[18] The head of the section argued that the Americans needed to respond to Sihanouk but had to do so in a "direct, sympathetic, full of soothing words, and responsive" way.[19] The French argued that Sihanouk's appeal to the United States to halt Vietnamese intrigue was real and that the United States had to check Ngô Đình Diệm in order to stop Vietnamese subversion in Cambodia. It was clear from the exchange that Ngô Đình Diệm was right to assume that he had no allies in France. In fact, a CIA daily briefing in March argued that the French were trying to attract Laos and Cambodia into a new French Community and that they believed the United States responsible for the abortive coup d'état in Cambodia and the Laotian statement regarding the 1954 Geneva Agreements.[20]

The next step in this latest controversy between the Vietnamese and Cambodians was debated in early March by the Americans. Durbrow asserted that Sihanouk had reason to suspect his neighbors and that this might have been the impetus behind claiming the plots against him; he warned against a statement that gave the impression that the United States was backing the Cambodians at the expense of the Republic of Vietnam, for fear that Ngô Đình Diệm or Ngô Đình Nhu would use it to support Dap Chhuon or Sam Sary.[21] This would realize the self-fulfilling prophecy that guided Sihanouk's actions. Durbrow also acknowledged that American support, real or imaginary, for Sihanouk over Ngô Đình Diệm caused the latter to become increasingly wary of the ambassador. The Cambodians, for their part, increased the intensity of the crisis by requesting the recall of Nguyễn Văn Nhieu from Cambodia because of his role in the Dap Chhuon affair.[22]

Durbrow consulted with the ambassadors of France, Australia, and

Britain on March 1 about the Cambodian situation.[23] Lalouette had had a conversation with Ngô Đình Nhu about the alleged Vietnamese plotting in Cambodia though Ngô Đình Nhu proclaimed his innocence. While Lalouette maintained that Ngô Đình Nhu was not actively plotting against Sihanouk, he thought it possible that Ngô Đình Nhu still believed Dap Chhuon could force a change in Cambodia. While Durbrow did not record the impressions of the British or Australians, Strom did speak with the Australian Minister Francis Hamilton Stuart on March 2 about Ngô Trọng Hiếu.[24] Stuart had earlier had a conversation with Madame Lê Văn Trọng, the wife of the Press Attaché for Ngô Trọng Hiếu and also the owner of the house in which he stayed, who informed him that the Cambodians wished to start anew with the Vietnamese but that Ngô Trọng Hiếu stood in the way. As Ngô Đình Diệm had officially recalled him on March 2, Ngô Trọng Hiếu was to go to France for a few months, and plans to transfer him to Thailand had been abandoned, it appeared that the possibility of improved relations existed.[25]

Strom followed up with Phạm Trọng Nhân, who took over in Ngô Trọng Hiếu's absence to confirm Stuart's report. Though he was able to confirm that a note was delivered that expressed concern about Ngô Trọng Hiếu's activities and worries for his safety, it did not mention the possibility of a new start with Vietnam.[26] While he did not receive a written message to these effects, he did confirm that an oral message was delivered that indicated the Cambodian Government wanted to forget the past and that the focus of the problem was Ngô Trọng Hiếu rather than the Saigon Government. During this time, Strom left Phnom Penh as ambassador to be replaced by William Trimble on February 19. Kellogg assumed the principle duties in Cambodia until Trimble arrived on April 11.[27]

Again, the French inserted themselves into the Sihanouk letter as they had in Vietnam and Laos. The French told Deputy Chief of Mission for the United States embassy in France, Cecil Lyon, that the United States needed to make Sihanouk realize that his neighbors had reason to be afraid of Cambodia's actions as it related to Communist China. He, however, did not blame Ngô Đình Diệm for the misunderstanding and instead focused on Ngô Đình Cẩn.[28] When the French ambassador to the United States, Hervé Alphand, met with Herter on March 4, he also called for a favorable reply to Sihanouk's letter as well as another firm talking to with Ngô Đình Diệm.[29] Herter replied by letting Alphand know that the French were acting in a way that damaged Franco-American relations in Cambodia by informing both Sihanouk and Ngô Đình Diệm of matters without consulting the United States which made it difficult for the Americans to manage the situation.

While there was some backlash to the French involvement in the current crisis between Cambodia and Vietnam, there was also concern about how far the United States could push Vietnam on the matter. Durbrow made it clear that Ngô Đình Diệm had not been pleased with him in their most recent interviews and thought it would be difficult for him to get a positive statement about Cambodia given his mood. It did not help matters, in Durbrow's mind, that Dap Chhuon had been killed by Cambodians on March 3 thus ending any possibility of using him to make changes in Cambodia or the Vietnamese press lamenting his death as a lost opportunity for Cambodia.[30] The Cambodians reported that they had extracted a confession from Dap Chhuon before his death and also had found important documents dropped during the chase that led to his capture before he was killed.[31] Because of the strained relationship with the Vietnamese president, Durbrow used intermediaries to gauge Ngô Đình Diệm's attitude towards the Cambodians.

On March 6, Hamilton Fish Armstrong met with Ngô Đình Diệm over breakfast and discussed the situation.[32] Ngô Đình Diệm told him that Sihanouk could not be trusted and that he was impossible to work with because of his unpredictability. He also complained about Sihanouk's "Russian technique" of voicing his complaints about other countries or leaders through the press or radio rather than using diplomatic channels. Ngô Đình Diệm was clearly referring to the number of speeches Sihanouk had made after the plot was revealed that implicated the Republic of Vietnam while ignoring the opportunity to resolve the issue in private communication between the two countries.[33] When Ngô Đình Diệm met with John D. Rockefeller III, on March 5, the latter tried to get a sense of whether Ngô Đình Diệm was willing to work with the Cambodians and came away less optimistic than before he started. Durbrow, in summing up the two meetings, worried over Ngô Đình Diệm's unwillingness to work with Sihanouk, but he did agree that getting a statement from Ngô Đình Diệm was desirable.[34]

Durbrow met with Ngô Đình Diệm on March 7 to discuss the Sihanouk letter and the possible responses to it.[35] The idea was to let Ngô Đình Diệm know that the Americans valued Vietnamese and Thai input to make sure that neither country was blindsided by Eisenhower's response to it. Durbrow emphasized that it was important to make sure that Sihanouk did not turn exclusively to the Communist Chinese but not lead him to believe that the United States was siding with Cambodia over Vietnam. Durbrow also provided a draft of a possible Vietnamese response to the letter which alluded to a strengthening of relations between the two countries. Ngô Đình Diệm read the draft and then discussed with Durbrow, in what the ambassador recounted as a "pleasant and reasonably moderate" matter, the difficulties in dealing with Sihanouk.[36] When Ngô Đình Diệm repeated his position as he had relayed to Armstrong and Rockefeller, Durbrow used this argument to call for a more forceful representation to the Cambodians so that they would know Vietnam was their friend rather than their adversary.

Vũ Văn Mẫu met with Durbrow later in the day and conveyed Ngô Đình

Diệm's concern that a Republic of Vietnam response incorporated into an American response might be used by the Communist as evidence that Vietnam was a satellite of the United States.[37] Vũ Văn Mẫu did hand Durbrow an aide memoire that outlined the Vietnamese position. It argued that the Republic of Vietnam did not have the ability to threaten the integrity and independence of the Cambodians nor did the Cambodians have the ability to do the same to Vietnam. The document asserted that Vietnam was willing to participate in normal relations with Cambodia if the Cambodians respected the independence and integrity of Vietnam.[38] The Vietnamese aide memoire was much more forceful a response than Durbrow expected after his meeting with Ngô Đình Diệm. He noted that Ngô Đình Nhu had entered the president's office as he was leaving and concluded that this accounted for the stronger response to the earlier proposal.

While it was possible that Ngô Đình Nhu influenced on Ngô Đình Diệm on this matter, it was equally probable that Ngô Đình Diệm did not need that encouragement. His mood toward Durbrow might not have softened, as the ambassador believed, and Ngô Đình Diệm simply wanted to avoid another uncomfortable situation with him. Ngô Đình Diệm was clear in his earlier conversations with Durbrow, Armstrong, and Rockefeller that he did not trust Sihanouk. In a more private conversation with Williams on March 11, Ngô Đình Diệm also revealed that he believed all of the personnel in the American embassy in Phnom Penh opposed him.[39] This was also reflected in a *Cách mạng Quốc gia* editorial the same day that questioned Cambodia's relationship with the Communist Chinese while delaying integration of effective border operations with Vietnam.[40] Williams did not comment directly to, or did not record, this accusation though he did promise to ask the Chief of MAAG in Cambodia, General Edwin Hartshorn, to see if there was any evidence to support this point.

The arrival of Hammarskjold to Cambodia, coupled with the death of Dap Chhuon, promised the possibility of a solution to the current crisis. Sihanouk's newspaper *Réalités Cambodigennes* published a special edition on March 10 that indicated the Prince would share the documents seized during the Siem Reap raid but fully believed the Secretary General would act impartially to help those at fault see the errors of their ways.[41] Implied, of course, was that the Republic of Vietnam was the guilty party in need of guidance. For his part, Hammarskjold made it clear that his role while in Cambodia was to listen to Sihanouk but not get personally involved or commit the United Nations to participating in the controversy. He also offered no comments regarding the Laotian–North Vietnamese border incident during a dinner party hosted by the French ambassador to Cambodia, Pierre Gorce, on March 10.[42] When Gorce urged him to visit Saigon to help with the Vietnamese-Cambodian situation, Hammarskjold told him he could not because then he would also be obligated to visit Hanoi.⁴³ This did not bode well for Sihanouk if he planned to use the Secretary General's visit for propaganda or to demean Ngô Đình Diệm. Hammarskjold met with Sihanouk and had a conversation that was described as very general by his personal assistant, Wilhelm Wachmeister. Upon his departure on March 13, Kellogg reported that he believed the visit, Dap Chhuon's death, and Sihanouk's announcement that he would depart on March 23 for a three-week trip for medical reasons to France, meant that the situation was diffused for a while.⁴⁴

Kellogg's hope of a peaceful transition away from the crisis was short-lived. The very same day as Kellogg filed his report, the Cambodians issued a communiqué that linked the arrest of twenty-four former Khmer Issarak chiefs in Svay Rieng Province to Sam Sary. The group was preparing to invade Cambodia with an army of Khmer recruited from South Vietnam.⁴⁵ The communiqué also maintained that Sam Sary was in South Vietnam though another report had him fleeing to the United States. It also stated that these leaders were to assemble between twenty to thirty men each who would be armed and funded by Sam Sary via Vietnamese military posts near Cambodia. The groups would then attack Cambodian police posts along the border while Sam Sary took his forces against Phnom Penh.⁴⁶ The South Vietnamese denied the allegation and offered Phnom Penh another chance to act responsibly in order to reestablish good relations with the Vietnamese.⁴⁷ *Dan Nguyên* pointed out the inconsistency of the Cambodian claim that Sam Sary was both in South Vietnam and the United States.⁴⁸

As this exchange occurred, Durbrow had also learned that the Cambodian representative to Vietnam, Siem Hieng, was returning "provisionally" to Phnom Penh and did not know if he would return to Saigon.⁴⁹ The combination of events suggested that far from being resolved, the disputes between Cambodia and Vietnam were as strong as ever. In reporting the events, Durbrow asserted that, even though the Vietnamese reply to the Cambodian claims was tempered, it fell short of expressing the desire to respect Cambodia's sovereignty because Ngô Đình Diệm and Ngô Đình Nhu had guilty consciences resulting from their failed attempt to overthrown Sihanouk.⁵⁰ While this may have been true, it was a rather strong observation to make without having laid down the groundwork for such a position. Sihanouk's behavior had been erratic towards not only the Republic of Vietnam but also the United States and Thailand. He had accused all three of plotting against him at any one time during the early months of 1959. That Durbrow singled out the Vietnamese provided some insight to his position toward Ngô Đình Diệm, Ngô Đình Nhu, and the Saigon Government.

Ngô Đình Diệm and Ngô Đình Nhu certainly had cause for a change of government in Cambodia. *Réalités Cambodgiennes* issued an editorial on March 14 that compared the Soviet Union and the West in their approach towards Cambodia. The editorial sided with the Soviets, suggesting that they were friends of Cambodia because they respected its neutrality. The West, it continued, was harming its relationship with Cambodia by aiding individuals like Dap Chhuon, who sought to align Cambodia with the West against the Soviets.[51] Less than a week later, *Réalités Cambodgiennes* released a letter from Ngô Trọng Hiếu to Dap Chhuon, which it apparently seized during the earlier raid, that implicated him in the plot to overthrow Sihanouk.[52] Kellogg, reacting to this release, urged Washington to move forward with the planned Eisenhower letter responding to Sihanouk's earlier appeal and warned that every day without the president's letter caused Cambodians to feel that the United States was siding with the Republic of Vietnam. As a result, many Cambodians were moving from being suspicious to openly hostile towards Americans in Cambodia.[53] Ngô Đình Diệm's response to the letter came much later when he met with Williams at the end of the month. Ngô Đình Diệm argued that the Photostat of the letter printed in *Réalités Cambodgiennes* showed only one fold and an envelope too small for it to fit into without multiple folds. Williams did not pass along this news to Durbrow.[54]

Allegations against the Americans were added to those targeting the Vietnamese when Son Sann and others tied the United States to the intrigue against Sihanouk.[55] These new statements put Kellogg and his embassy staff in a difficult position. He needed a public statement to deny the charges; the longer the delay, the more likely the Cambodians would be to believe the rumors. Kellogg also needed the presidential reply to Sihanouk's letter, which had been going through a series of revisions to gauge both Republic of Vietnam and Thailand reaction. The situation was not helped by the publication of the March 17 Vietnamese communiqué which responded to the March 13 Cambodian statement. The Vietnamese had circulated their response to all of the diplomatic missions in Phnom Penh, which made it difficult for the United States to refer to it in its presidential response without appearing to shun Sihanouk. It was also published in the *Vietnam Press*.[56]

When Durbrow met Vũ Văn Mẫu on March 24 to discuss the latest version of the American statement, he stressed the inopportune publicity of the Vietnamese communiqué and the difficult position in which it put the United States. The Eisenhower letter could not reference it without appearing to endorse it. Because the United States feared that Cambodia would continue to move towards Communist China, it did not want to give it a push.[57] The communiqué also raised the issue of a joint border patrol between the Vietnamese and Cambodians, which allowed for another discussion of Cambodian neutrality. On March 24, another Cambodian communiqué asserted that the groups operating on the border were Vietnamese, which made them an internal affair for Vietnam. The Cambodians maintained, therefore, that a suggestion of a joint operation was akin to a military alliance. The communiqué stressed that this would violate its neutrality as well as the 1954 Geneva Agreements, which prohibited such an action.[58]

The latest communiqué did not dissuade the Vietnamese from trying to work toward some type of border control. Durbrow met Vũ Văn Mẫu on March 25 and brought up the Cambodian argument, only to be told that the Vietnamese still believed some type of effective border control could be arranged between the two countries.[59] Throughout all of this exchange of official communiqués, the United States continued to work on its response to Sihanouk, which finally arrived on March 29. Sihanouk's reaction to the letter was cautiously favorable.[60] This, coupled with his delayed departure for France for medical reasons on March 30, helped to calm down the situation.[61] Both Cambodian and Vietnamese press agencies agreed to a truce, which held up fairly well during the month of April, though there were incidents of news stories that threatened to break the peace.[62]

The prospects of calm were reinforced by an April 30 speech by Son Sann, during his visit to Vientiane on what was described as a goodwill tour. Son Sann maintained that Cambodia worked upon "the principles of peaceful coexistence which have no other purpose than peace and good neighborliness externally, and economic and social development, maintenance of order and tranquility, internally."[63] While the speech was given during a dinner hosted by the Royal Lao Government, it was clear that the intended audience extended far beyond the borders of Laos. The United States Embassy in Cambodia also confirmed that the speech was a major policy statement by a source close to Son Sann.[64]

On May 3, *Réalités Cambodgiennes* offered a possible compromise to the Vietnamese ten-mile pursuit proposal along the border.[65] It acknowledged that the Cambodians were also worried about the internal security problem in Vietnam and how it might affect their border, though the newspaper fell short of accepting any responsibility for the continued existence of the Vietnamese insurgents operating in both countries. The new Cambodian approach as outlined in *Réalités Cambodgiennes* was much more sympathetic to Saigon's plight, and offered Trimble and Washington some hope.[66] C. Douglas Dillon, as acting Secretary of State, instructed Durbrow to act upon the *Réalités Cambodgiennes* article, and encourage Saigon to accept an offer to exchange information about border crossings by dissidents. Dillon maintained that this acceptance was a first step towards greater cooperation between the two countries.[67] Trimble reported on May 7 that the border marker, which had been the original cause of this dispute, had been moved back to its original position, though Durbrow could not confirm this with Vũ Văn Mẫu when he asked about it.[68]

When Trimble met with Son Sann on May 12, he once again tried to encourage better Cambodian-Vietnamese relations using the plan of shared communications on personnel movement along the border as an opportunity to bring up the subject. Son Sann responded that the Cambodian army had been cooperating but that the Vietnamese were not; Durbrow had received the opposite report from the Vietnamese.[69] Son Sann complained of a Vietnamese diplomatic note that accused the Cambodians of harboring insurgents fleeing from the Vietnamese military as well as hosting a clandestine Khmer radio station that was broadcasting anti–Sihanouk messages. For his part, Trimble listened and also acknowledged that he and Durbrow were under instructions to work to improve the situation. However, the Americans were limited in their ability to make a substantive change in the diplomatic environment without becoming too involved in the internal politics in Saigon and Phnom Penh. Trimble had a similar conversation with the Defense Minister Lon Nol.[70]

While Trimble took a more direct approach with the Cambodians, Durbrow still preferred something more subtle. Durbrow remained convinced that the United States needed to move slowly if it were to assume the role of mediator between the two countries. He feared that Ngô Đình Diệm would be unreasonable if it were obvious the United States intended to become more involved, as Ngô Đình Diệm had been consistent in his complaint that the West did not understand the duplicity of Sihanouk.[71] Durbrow wanted to move slowly but also worked on the French to manage Sihanouk or recruit another country to serve as an intermediary or help to find a solution. He mentioned Burma, Laos, and Australia as possible candidates. He also preferred more clandestine meetings between representatives rather than using the existing militaries to initiate communications. While either approach to the problem had potential, Durbrow's method ran the risk of further alienating Ngô Đình Diệm, who despised the French and needed a quick resolution to the Cambodian affair in order to focus all of Vietnam's attention on the insurgents.

It did not help, in Durbrow's mind, that the Vietnamese continued to treat the Cambodians as adversaries. When Durbrow met with Vũ Văn Mẫu on May 22, he praised the Cambodians for suspending the pro–Communist newspaper *Hoà bình Trung lập* (Peace-Neutrality) that had broken the truce, and lamented the Vietnamese decision to delay the passage of a Cambodian coastal patrol vessel traveling down the Mekong River to the Navy Yards at Subic Bay in the Philippines for scheduled repairs.[72] Implied in the conversation was that the Cambodians were being reasonable and the Vietnamese were not. Perhaps as a result of this perspective, Vũ Văn Mẫu informed Durbrow that the Vietnamese had agreed to a secret meeting between the Cambodian Vice Premier, Nhiek Tioulong, and Vice President Nguyễn Ngọc Thơ, only to be informed by Son Sann that no meeting could take place because rumors about it had appeared in Saigon, negating the necessary secrecy. Vũ Văn Mẫu believed Son Sann delayed in order to have the meeting take place

9. The Cambodian Affair, 1959

after Sihanouk returned from France. Nevertheless, he used the incident to counter Durbrow's contention that the Cambodians were working towards a resolution and the Vietnamese were not.

The possibility of a compromise continued to elude the United States as it sought to shore up the unlikely alliance between the Republic of Vietnam and Cambodia. Both sides expressed an interest in better relations but neither seemed willing to go the extra step to finalize that possibility. Press truces were announced and then broken while offers to resolve the problems emerged only to be sidetracked by something else.[73] For Trimble, and Strom before him, as well as for Durbrow it led to a certain amount of frustration. For the Durbrow–Ngô Đình Diệm relationship, which was already strained, this added stress helped to tip the balance and cause Durbrow to become more negative as it pertained to Ngô Đình Diệm's rule and future. As events proceeded, Durbrow would increasingly call for greater pressure on Ngô Đình Diệm to improve relations with Cambodia and more openly side against Ngô Đình Nhu, who he believed was the ringleader in Vietnamese attempts to subvert Sihanouk's rule.[74] These pressures, coupled with the declining levels of progress in the Republic of Vietnam on a variety of fronts, would further pit the two men against one another.

10

The Unending War of Respect: Colegrove Replaces Cambodia

While the United States was distracted by the events in Cambodia and Laos, the situation in the Republic of Vietnam grew steadily worse. When Ngô Đình Diệm met with Williams and Durbrow on April 9, he started their conversation with an update of the internal security situation. The first four months of 1959 had seen a marked increase in the number of Việt Cộng attacks, assassinations, and acts of sabotage.[1] Of particular concern for Ngô Đình Diệm was the Montagnard population in the Central Highland region. Ngô Đình Diệm had concentrated on this area for most of Durbrow's time in Vietnam and continued to press for resources to link the Montagnards by road. This would not only improve living conditions and economic benefits but also provide a means to offer security against the insurgents, who had had an unfettered presence in the area since the 1954 Geneva Agreements. Ngô Đình Diệm was concerned about the provinces bordering Cambodia and the insurgents' ability to cross into that country to seek protection. He also worried over the unwillingness of Sihanouk to work jointly with the Republic of Vietnam to cut off their safe haven. For Durbrow's part, he reported the conversation, as Williams had done, but also suggested that Ngô Đình Diệm's focus on the increased violence, which he thought "probably has some basis in fact," was really an attempt to influence the United States not to reduce its military budget in South Vietnam for FY 1960.[2]

The Vietnamese had been working on the Americans in Saigon in preparation for the FY 1960 military budget deliberations before the Ngô Đình Diệm, Williams, and Durbrow meeting. Nguyễn Đình Thuần and Durbrow discussed the possible scenarios regarding the military budget on April 8.[3] Nguyễn Đình Thuần argued that if Saigon had to increase its contribution to the military budget because the United States put its focus on economic development, it would impede the progress, or fail to counter the worsening conditions, of the internal security situation. He also argued that USOM

10. The Unending War of Respect

Ngô Đình Diệm (*near lamp*) and J. Graham Parsons (*right center*) with Elbridge Durbrow (*second from left*), Arthur Z. Gardiner (*second from right*), April 1959. Arthur Z. Gardiner Papers (2014-1540) (Harry S. Truman Library & Museum).

bureaucracy would slow down economic improvement; this had been a consistent and common complaint of the Vietnamese for Durbrow's entire tenure. Durbrow interpreted Nguyễn Đình Thuần's arguments differently than they were intended. He asserted that Ngô Đình Diệm wanted a stronger military budget because it had fewer restrictions than economic development dollars. This would allow Ngô Đình Diệm to invest in "his own pet economy projects without any USOM 'interference.'"[4] Durbrow asserted that if the Vietnamese were required to contribute more to their military budget, they would create a more realistic plan than what had been seen in the past. Durbrow was most likely referring to the absurd Self-Defense Force organizational chart that had surfaced the previous year.

When Parsons visited Vietnam at the end of April, Durbrow reported that Ngô Đình Diệm had emphasized the increased Communist insurgent activities in order to lay the groundwork for the Vietnamese justification for continued or increased military funding.[5] Ngô Đình Diệm also maintained his line of argument that placed blame for the increased activities on the French Colonials, who wanted to see the return of their empire at the expense of the new countries in Southeast Asia. While there was no record of Parsons' response to Ngô Đình Diệm's accusations about the French, he did emphasize the American position that it was necessary to focus on economic development and improve the living standard in order to rally the people to the side of the government and improve internal security. While an increase in the military budget might help, Parsons advocated the economic development focus. As the situation continued to deteriorate in South Vietnam, this line of thinking became more frustrating for Ngô Đình Diệm as he dealt with Durbrow and the Americans.

Parsons' trip to Southeast Asia marked a turning point in American relations with Ngô Đình Diệm. He was not impressed with the Vietnamese leader and, as a rising star in the Department of State, he had an opportunity to support Durbrow's efforts to mold Ngô Đình Diệm into something that the Americans wanted. On May 5, Parsons, from Seoul, was able to transmit his evaluation of his meeting with Ngô Đình Diệm as well as his impressions of the Vietnamese-Cambodian disagreement.[6] He acknowledged Ngô Đình Diệm's concern about Vietnam's internal security and the Vietnamese belief that Cambodia's position towards border security made the situation even worse, though he was not convinced by the Vietnamese argument that it was pointless to negotiate with Sihanouk. Parsons concluded that Ngô Đình Diệm's mandarin "authoritarian background" and simplistic solutions to the problems were more to blame.[7]

Parsons did not believe any accommodation was possible between the two countries, and implied it was Vietnam's fault, as that country had attempted to overthrow Sihanouk. He stated this as a "proven fact" though he offered no evidence for this absolute judgment. Parsons recommended that the United States warn Ngô Đình Diệm against further action and threaten, if necessary, to withdraw a portion of its aid if it impressed upon him the seriousness of the American concern. He also suggested that the United States pressure the French into curbing their colonial intrigue in Phnom Penh and, with Sihanouk, to allow for a settlement between the two countries. Durbrow sent a telegram to Washington that affirmed Parsons' position and offered further evidence from a ninety minute "lecture" Ngô Đình Diệm had had with him, Williams, and Stump during a dinner on May 6.[8]

It was a reasonable assumption that Durbrow was able to influence Parsons' assessment or at least confirm his already solid assumption about the rule of Ngô Đình Diệm. Durbrow had turned decidedly against Ngô Đình Diệm by this point and was unabashed, at least in private, in his desire to turn the Vietnamese president toward his way of thinking. In telegrams, he increased the use of words that portrayed Ngô Đình Diệm as an obstinate authoritarian.[9] While the extent to which Durbrow was working against Ngô Đình Diệm was not widely known, it was clear to Williams that the situation had changed. Durbrow's remarks were so pointed against the Vietnamese president during a May 5 Country Team meeting that Williams had Brigadier General J.B. Lambert record his recollections. Lambert's remembrances included Durbrow relaying a conversation he had with Parsons during his visit in which he outlined his plan of "'taking a club' to the President."[10] According to Lambert, Durbrow planned to tell Ngô Đình Diệm that Congress would never offer more than its current level of $130 million to the Vietnamese defense budget if Saigon did not take a serious effort to resolve its difficulties with Phnom Penh. Durbrow wanted to assert that Vietnam's internal security situation would vastly improve with peaceful relations with Cambodia.

This line of thinking was one that Durbrow knew would not work with Ngô Đình Diệm, which might be why he wanted to threatened future military aid. Durbrow did acknowledge that Ngô Đình Diệm did not like him. Lambert underlined this part of his memorandum to Williams and that Durbrow expected a very difficult remainder of 1959. Durbrow's solution was to strike at the president, question him on the rule of the Cần Lao Party in Vietnam politics, and threaten aid with the backing of Washington. With this approach, Durbrow concluded that, "the only thing we can do is batten down the hatches, be firm, and work our way through it."[11] Throughout this meeting, which included Gardiner, USIS member Darrell Price, and William Colby, who was the assistant to CIA Station Chief, Nicholas A. Natsios, Lambert was under the impression that Parsons agreed with everything that Durbrow proposed.[12]

While Durbrow had made his intentions known within the Country Team, reports originating from the American Embassy in Saigon help to reinforce the image of Ngô Đình Diệm losing control of the situation. On May 14, Barbour and Myriam Johnston from the USIS met with Võ Lang, the brother of Võ Văn Hái, who served as Ngô Đình Diệm's private secretary. Võ Lang, described as a longtime supporter of Ngô Đình Diệm, was visiting Vietnam from France. He argued that the Vietnamese president had changed and had "surrounded himself with a coterie of sycophants and petty tyrants."[13] He also asserted that the people genuinely detested Ngô Đình Diệm because he had become aloof to their needs. Neither Barbour, Johnston, nor Kidder, who wrote the despatch for the conversation, questioned how Võ Lang was able to come to these conclusions. He was not in a position to observe who surrounded Ngô Đình Diệm, and neither was there evidence he travelled to gauge the views of the people, other than visiting Saigon, Huế, and Dalat. Nonetheless, these types of negative reports continued to originate in the embassy and were very rarely countered by any positive reactions for the Saigon Government.

Durbrow continued to maintain the position that Ngô Đình Diệm was highlighting increased insurgent activity in preparation for the 1960 aid contributions; the reality was that the Việt Cộng had altered tactics to focus on sabotage by targeting equipment used for agricultural and land development programs.[14] Ngô Đình Diệm was concerned enough by the change in strategy that he brought Williams in to a conference on June 4 to make sure that Gardiner was truly aware of the extent to which the Việt Cộng had damaged the important equipment used in these projects.[15] Ngô Đình Diệm informed Williams that he was aware that some Americans understood the seriousness of the new situation and he was not exaggerating it for his own benefit. He was clearly referring to Durbrow, and Williams made sure that this vague reference was included in his summary report to Durbrow. The change in tactics also had another consequence that would play a significant role in the last year of Durbrow's time in Saigon. It reintroduced an American who had a long history with Ngô Đình Diệm and was one of the few men whom the Vietnamese president trusted.

On June 4, in a memorandum for Regional Director, Far East, Office of Assistant Secretary of Defense for International Security Affairs Rear Admiral Edward O'Donnell, Colonel Edward Lansdale voiced his concern about the change of tactics as reported by Durbrow.[16] Lansdale maintained that an appraisal of the new techniques was required to better understand the level of internal security in the Republic of Vietnam. He also asked the question, "Will the U.S. mission in Vietnam be able to evaluate the effectiveness of their own programs and personnel accurately enough for a sound judgment by the U.S.?" Lansdale was aware that the situation between the Country Team and Durbrow on one side, and Williams and MAAG on the other, was strained. He and Williams would form an alliance to combat the growing anti–Ngô Đình Diệm feelings emanating from Americans, and some Vietnamese, in Saigon. Just as the crises in Cambodia and Laos drained away the energy and resources needed to fight the insurgents in the Republic of Vietnam, the internal bickering and clash of personalities threatened to divide American attention at a time when it needed to listen to, and work with, its ally in Saigon.

Before this took place, however, Cambodia and Laos still served as the main source of tension between the Vietnamese president and American ambassador. Durbrow and Ngô Đình Diệm clashed on Sihanouk and Cambodia's relationship with the Republic of Vietnam. When the two met on June 1 after a joint meeting with Admiral Paul Blackburn and Williams, Durbrow brought up the earlier indications that the Cambodians wanted better relations and coordinated border control.[17] Durbrow informed Ngô Đình Diệm that he had been instructed by Washington to aid in these efforts once Sihanouk had returned to Cambodia, though he did not indicate that he and Trimble were the ones who asked to be instructed in this line of persuasion. He asserted to Ngô Đình Diệm that progress in the relationship was imperative, and that the view from Phnom Penh was that the Vietnamese were behind the anti–Sihanouk efforts in Cambodia and Vietnam. Throughout the hour-long conversation, it appeared that Durbrow was not willing to give in to any of Ngô Đình Diệm's counter-explanations for Vietnam's position as it related to Cambodia. There was no record of Ngô Đình Diệm's reaction to Durbrow's insistence, though it most likely added to the accumulating record maintained by the Vietnamese president to remind him that Durbrow was not his closest American ally.

A *Réalités Cambodigennes* article in early June, announcing that Sihanouk wished to meet with Ngô Đình Diệm to discuss their mutual problems and concerns, opened a new round of discussions and debate among the principles in Saigon.[18] When asked by Washington to confirm whether the offer was genuine, Durbrow was reluctant to confirm this with Ngô Đình Diệm; Vũ Văn Mẫu was away from Saigon or he would have approached him.[19] Durbrow gave no reason for not wanting to ask Ngô Đình Diệm directly, though he did offer that Lalouette had also heard that Sihanouk was drafting a letter of invitation. Durbrow may have wanted to avoid another dispute with Ngô Đình Diệm about Sihanouk, whom he knew the Vietnamese president did not trust, or he was waiting to insert himself into the situation when he knew he might be more effective. Both Durbrow and Lalouette believed that any meeting between the two Southeast Asian leaders needed to be preceded by a preparatory meeting such as the one that had been planned between Nguyễn Ngọc Thơ and Nhiek Tioulong. Durbrow requested Lalouette's assistance in making this happen, as he knew that Gorce had a much stronger relation with Sihanouk than did Trimble, who was still relatively new to his post.

The atmosphere in early June seemed to suggest that a meeting was possible. The Cambodians had just completed an operation to eliminate a group of Vietnamese insurgents who had crossed into Cambodia between June 7 and June 12. Cambodian reports of the operation suggested that several dozen insurgents were killed, wounded, or captured, which indicated that Cambodia could both pursue a neutralist policy by not allowing enemy combatants into their territory and also support the Vietnamese struggles by denying Cambodia as a safe haven to those against peace and the law.[20] *Tự do* also mentioned the attack and identified the Vietnamese as remnants of the forces of Ba Cụt.[21]

Durbrow did learn that both Sihanouk and Ngô Đình Diệm agreed to a meeting in principle and that it would take place in July. Durbrow recommended moving forward with a preparatory meeting which Washington agreed upon; the United States had seen enough of Sihanouk's antics to more closely align themselves with Saigon's view of the Cambodians.[22] When Vũ Văn Mẫu returned to Saigon from his trip to Vientiane where he was working out an agreement regarding Laotian use of the port at Tourane, Durbrow queried him on the Cambodian situation. He learned that the prospects for the meeting was real and that Ngô Đình Diệm was willing to discuss the financial aspects of the 1954 Geneva Agreements that had been delayed for so long. However, Ngô Đình Diệm was not willing to discuss the Khmer living in Vietnam or Cambodian usage of the Mekong River in the Republic of Vietnam because of Cambodia's recognition of Communist China.[23] Durbrow pushed for a secret emissaries meeting before the heads-of-state conference so that any obstacles to a final agreement between the two countries could be settled, which would allow for a more successful experience. When Durbrow mentioned the Tioulong-Nguyễn Ngọc Thơ option, Vũ Văn Mẫu speculated that this would not work because Son Sann was jealous of any added prestige Tioulong might earn from the success of such a meeting. Durbrow continued to press, though he reported that he was not confident that such talks would occur, despite the benefits they would add to a Sihanouk-Ngô Đình Diệm conference.[24]

Further efforts at ensuring a successful conference by inserting preparatory talks were hampered when Durbrow learned from Lalouette that Sihanouk wanted to meet with Ngô Đình Diệm on June 26, after Indonesian president Sukarno left Phnom Penh.[25] Durbrow rejected this idea, as he believed Ngô Đình Diệm would see the move as an attempt by Sihanouk to plan a propaganda event, as he had done in Thailand the previous year. Lalouette also informed Durbrow that Sihanouk had planned to bring Tioulong with him to see Ngô Đình Diệm, which countered Vũ Văn Mẫu's assertions that Tioulong had lost stature in the Cambodian Government. For Durbrow, the question became whether the Vietnamese were trying to thwart the conference by sabotaging any preliminary meetings or were simply misinformed about the nature of politics in Phnom Penh. The role of the French was not considered.

Trimble did mention the role of the French in the process, however. On June 16, he reported that Gorce did not believe a preliminary meeting was necessary or even desirable, because it might insult Sihanouk who was considered the originator of the proposal.[26] Trimble did not want the United States to act along as a third-party to the agreements in insisting that preliminary talks were necessary. He worried that it would place the United States in a position where it would be solely responsible for the failure if the conference did not occur. He also reported, as Ngô Đình Diệm had for some time, that Sihanouk believed himself to be a diplomat with superior powers, able to bring about a solution to a problem once he became involved in it. In short, Sihanouk had built up a self-image as one who merely needed to participate in order to bring resolution; this was a characteristic that Ngô Đình Diệm loathed and one of the reasons why he did not trust him.

Durbrow's position was backed by the Vietnamese. Nguyễn Ngọc Thơ also believed it essential that a preliminary meeting take place and Vũ Văn Mẫu had written his similar position in a long memorandum to Ngô Đình Diệm.[27] Nguyễn Ngọc Thơ, however, worried that Ngô Đình Diệm had given up the idea of such a meeting because Sihanouk's only purpose was to come to Saigon for propaganda. That is, there was no need to prepare and work out an agreement when the likelihood of a meeting was slight. Durbrow asserted that Ngô Đình Diệm was waiting for Sihanouk to extend his list of demands beyond the acceptable range so that he could prove that Sihanouk was not desirous of peace, but rather using the opportunity to increase his prestige at the expense of the Vietnamese. Ngô Đình Diệm could also tell the Americans, though Durbrow might have implied it himself, that, "I told you so," when this occurred.[28] This position received some credence when Gorce told Trimble on June 16 that no advanced preparation was needed and that he strongly opposed them because the meeting had been "Sihanouk's brainchild and he would regard any advice re: planning as unwarranted interference."[29] Ngô Đình Diệm was justified, in this case, in not trusting Sihanouk, or the French in Cambodia, who he believed to be poorly advising the Cambodians. This position, however, ran counter to what Durbrow and the Americans wished to see accomplished in Southeast Asia and would continue to cause discord in Saigon.

The prospects for talks improved after Son Sann approached Trimble after the Queen's dinner for Sukarno on June 20. Son Sann maintained that Sihanouk saw the meeting as a conversation rather than negotiations.[30] If this were true, it eliminated some of the concerns that Ngô Đình Diệm and the Americans had about Sihanouk's purpose. While Son Sann used the meeting's aims to counter Ngô Đình Diệm's desire not to discuss Cambodian minorities in Vietnam or the 1954 Geneva Agreements, he did confirm that the meeting was more for show than substance. This encouraged both the Americans and Vietnamese and diminished some of the earlier concerns about preliminary meetings and agenda. When Durbrow met with Vũ Văn Mẫu on June 22, he learned that the Foreign Minister was leaving for Paris so that his wife could receive treatment for an illness, and would not return until mid–July.[31] He wanted the meeting to occur after his return and relayed that Ngô Đình Diệm wanted an informal meeting, though he thought Sihanouk wanted a formal one. Clearly the two sides had not been able to communicate their preferences to each other, though, with the aid of the United States and France, it would slowly become clearer. For the remainder of the month, Gorce, Trimble, Lalouette, and Durbrow worked towards making sure that a meeting took place.[32] The Cambodians agreed to delay the talks until late July or early August, as Son Sann was also scheduled to go to France, and the Eighth National Congress of the People's Socialist Community (Sangkum) would be finished.[33]

The French were encouraged with the prospects for discussions between Cambodia and Vietnam and worked with the Americans to see it happen. However, it was not always clear that the French and Americans had the same information or objectives. Lalouette met with Durbrow on July 1 so that he could debrief the American ambassador on his trip to Phnom Penh. He also had met with Ngô Đình Diệm on June 30 and reported that the Vietnamese president had agreed to discuss any subject with Sihanouk, including the condition of Cambodian minorities living in Vietnam and the transition along the Mekong River.[34] Durbrow had met with Ngô Đình Diệm earlier and received an adamant refusal to discuss these two subjects, which meant that either Ngô Đình Diệm was telling the Americans and French different things or the French were trying to manipulate the meeting. While Durbrow was not willing to come to either conclusion without more information, he did fear that the mixed messages might sabotage the conference.

Lalouette also confirmed that the meeting between Sihanouk and Ngô Đình Diệm would have to be delayed until after Son Sann returned from France and that the trip had been planned for some time before Sihanouk's efforts to meet with Ngô Đình Diệm.[35] Both men agreed that any delay brought the possibility that some incident might occur that would derail the talks and thus lose the chance for a possible improvement of relations between the two countries. There were a few instances that threatened to do so. One involved a Vietnamese Civil Guard who was kidnapped by Cambodian troops on June 24.[36] The other ongoing event was the transmission of a clandestine radio broadcast originating from Thailand, the Republic of Vietnam, and Cambodia from the Voice of Khmer Freedom Movement that the Cambodians wanted to stop. Both Son Sann and Nong Kimny requested Trimble to ask the American embassies in Bangkok and Saigon to put pressure on their host governments to end these radio attacks against Sihanouk.[37]

When Durbrow met with Nguyễn Đình Thuần on July 8, he again brought up the issues surrounding the anti-Sihanouk broadcasts and informed him, via Trimble, that Sihanouk had gone out of his way to avoid anti–Vietnamese statements during the Sangkum Conference.[38] Durbrow was not convinced when Nguyễn Đình Thuần told him the broadcasts had originated in Cambodia and not the Republic of Vietnam. While Nguyễn Đình Thuần confirmed that Ngô Đình Diệm was reluctant to discuss the minority question and the Mekong, countering what Lalouette had told him earlier, there was a general sense that all issues were open for review and that no lasting agreements would be made during the meeting. The proceedings were disrupted later in the evening on July 8 when five Americans were attacked in Biên Hòa by the Việt Cộng, killing two and seriously wounding another.[39] The two MAAG advisors, Major Dale R. Buis and Master Sargent Chester M. Ovnand, were watching a film when the attack occurred. Two Vietnamese were killed trying to stop the attack.[40] The incident was a reminder that the internal security situation in the Republic of Vietnam was still far from stable.

On July 13, *Réalités Cambodigennes* announced that Sihanouk would travel to Vietnam in early August.⁴¹ He would be accompanied by Penn Nouth, Lon Nol, and Nhiek Tioulong for a two day visit.⁴² The party would arrive in Saigon on August 3 and depart on August 5. The possibility of a successful visit was confirmed by both Ngô Đình Diệm and Ngô Đình Nhu on July 23. Both believed that the meeting would bring about better relations.⁴³ *Cách mạng Quốc gia* declared that the meeting was promising for the development and promotion of friendly relations.⁴⁴ The Cambodians wanted the agenda to include Khmer minorities in Vietnam, application of the 1954 Geneva Agreements, foreign broadcasts aimed against Sihanouk, the border, and commercial exchanges. Vũ Văn Mẫu believed the atmosphere for positive talks was good while everything seemed ready to proceed.⁴⁵

The meeting proceeded without any serious setbacks while all of the public utterances followed typical diplomatic lines.⁴⁶ During their conversations, Ngô Đình Diệm and Sihanouk or their foreign ministers discussed border control, the Paris Accord, navigation of the Mekong, Cambodian use of the port of Saigon, the islands in the Gulf of Siam, and the Khmer minorities in Vietnam. While no written agreements were reached, Vũ Văn Mẫu believed that Sihanouk had behaved very well during the trip and seemed to be more cognizant of the Communist threat in Cambodia and the rest of Southeast Asia.⁴⁷ On his return to Phnom Phenh, Sihanouk remarked that the results of the summit were promising while Ngô Đình Diệm was cautiously optimistic.⁴⁸

Sihanouk's appraisal of the meeting was enumerated in an August 8 *Réalités Cambodgiennes* article as well as editorials in the same publication which were written by Jean Barre, Sihanouk's press advisor.⁴⁹ While the Vietnamese were publically expressing the same attitude, Ngô Đình Diệm informed Elting on August 10 that he had been forceful with Sihanouk about Cambodia's "peaceful coexistence," as it had been described in the *Réalités Cambodgiennes* article. Ngô Đình Diệm argued that such a policy did not work in a country where the Communists were trying to achieve domination.⁵⁰ Whether the two sides agreed, or agreed to disagree, in their post conference assessments, they did achieve something by meeting in what the Americans believed was a "good general atmosphere."⁵¹ However, during this potential historic conference, Durbrow and Williams were not in Saigon due to another event that had occurred earlier. Both had been recalled to Washington to address a series of newspaper articles written by Albert Colegrove.

Colegrove, a staff writer for the Scripps-Howard Newspaper Alliance, had published a six-part series of articles that criticized the Saigon Government and called into question the integrity of the American aid program in the Republic of Vietnam. The articles, which appeared between July 20 and July 25, were printed in the *Washington Daily News*.⁵² Published shortly after Eisenhower signed the Foreign Aid authorization bill, the timing of the articles required a strong response from American officials. They also resulted in hearings by the subcommittee on the Far East and the Pacific within the Committee on Foreign Affairs in the House of Representatives and hearings before the Subcommittee on State Department Organization and Public Affairs of the Committee on Foreign Relations in the United States Senate which included testimony by Anderson, Parsons, Durbrow, Williams, and Gardiner among many others.[53]

Colegrove, who had visited Vietnam between June 16 and July 4, charged the American aid program with inefficiency and mismanagement. He was also critical of certain Vietnamese who he asserted were corrupt. The charges were serious enough and had received such attention in the United States that the Americans in Vietnam could not ignore them. Both Williams and Durbrow categorically denied Colegrove's accusations and began to gather evidence to counter them. Durbrow recommended that the charges that Vietnam was running a police state and American officials were influencing journalists to not report the truth be countered by demonstrating that the exact opposite was happening. It would be easy to point to the August 30 National Assembly elections as well as several articles in the Saigon dailies that offered a freedom of opinion. Colegrove's assertions of prisons and concentration camps overflowing with political prisoners could be easily explained by the fact that Vietnam had to deal with not only the Communist insurgents but also members of the Bình Xuyên and Hòa Hảo as well as Vietnamese involved in the failed coup d'état against Ngô Đình Diệm in 1954. He estimated that there were about 10,000 political prisoners in re-education camps with another 30,000 incarcerated for ordinary crimes.[54] In connection to this accusation, Vice Consul at Huế, Theodore Heavner, visited one of the camps cited by Colegrove on June 19 to offer his own assessment, which was not as negative as what was published.[55]

The Vietnamese issued their own condemnation of the Colegrove articles. The *Vietnam Press* reprinted a version of the Colegrove interview with Ngô Đình Diệm, which countered what Colegrove had printed while the *Times of Vietnam* published editorials that condemned his articles.[56] The Minister for Information, Trần Chánh Thành, distributed a rebuttal to the assertion that the Vietnamese press was censored with specific examples of how papers criticized some of the Saigon Government actions and the National Assembly election bill.[57] While Colegrove printed that *Người Việt Tự do* was suspended because it had criticized the government, the reality was that this had occurred because its editor was arrested for passing bad checks. Both the Vietnamese and Durbrow could not help but mention that many of Colegrove's assertions were also being reported by the Hanoi press. Trần Chánh Thành maintained that the Colegrove articles and those who gave them credence were a gift to the North Vietnamese, who had devoted much of the airtime for Radio Hanoi to discuss what was argued.[58] *Chuông Mai* (Morning Bell) called upon the Americans to view their aid to Vietnam as not a favor but as a duty and asked rational Americans to counter the slander Colegrove offered.[59] The American Friends of Vietnam also issued a lengthy rebuttal of the Colegrove criticisms on August 24.[60]

Ngô Đình Diệm maintained that Colegrove's sources were mostly individuals who had been influenced by communist propaganda, members of the Đại Việt party or others closely associated with the former French colonials, or individuals who were just dissatisfied with the Saigon Government.[61] He also argued that Colegrove had misquoted or misrepresented the answers he provided the journalist when the two met briefly.[62] It seemed that the United States Senate agreed with this assessment. On August 13, Senator Mike Mansfield (D–Montana) released a statement that signaled the end of the Senate hearings. In it, he maintained that, "such problems as may affect the aid program in Viet-Nam are not peculiar to that country but affect the aid program generally."[63]

The effects of the Colegrove articles on Ngô Đình Diệm were subtle and significant. When Durbrow and Williams returned to Vietnam, they assured the Vietnamese president that the matter had been taken care of and that their presence in Washington limited any potential for long-lasting negative repercussions.[64] Durbrow reported that Ngô Đình Diệm sarcastically told him that he was convinced that it was a waste of time to go back to Washington when there were other pressing matters that needed the Americans attention, such as Laos.[65] Ngô Đình Diệm had called in Durbrow, Williams and Gardiner earlier, upon their return to Saigon, to have them briefed by Colonel Nguyễn Khánh, who served as the Permanent Secretary General for National Defense, on the situation in Laos and the possibility that the Pathet Lao was about to commence a general offensive against the Royal Government.[66]

Durbrow continued to try to convince Ngô Đình Diệm of the limited consequences of the Colegrove articles though Ngô Đình Diệm remained shaken by the criticism. Ngô Đình Diệm told the ambassador during a two-day trip to inspect the Central Highlands that if the Colegrove articles were a representation of the American idea of freedom of press then he wanted no part of it.[67] The Colegrove articles reaffirmed to Ngô Đình Diệm that there were Americans in Vietnam who opposed his continued rule. While Ngô Đình Diệm did not necessarily need this confirmation, it did occur at a time during which the Vietnamese and Cambodians should have been celebrating a turn in relations. Instead, it served as a reminder to Ngô Đình Diệm that he was more isolated than he either needed or wanted to be and Durbrow did little to ease this concern.

11

National Assembly Elections and Question of Democracy

Many in Vietnam and those Americans interested in the future of the country looked to the August 30 National Assembly elections as an indicator of how far Ngô Đình Diệm had gone in developing his Republic. While much of the attention of the summer 1959 had been devoted to the Cambodian and Laotian situations, as well as the Biên Hòa attack against MAAG personnel and the Colegrove Articles, there was interest in the upcoming elections. They served as an opportunity for the Republic of Vietnam to showcase its progress, as well as reaffirm that it stood as the bulwark against Communist encroachment in Southeast Asia.

On June 25, 1959, Ngô Đình Diệm confirmed Law 19/50 and then Law 20/50 the next day, establishing the procedures and conditions for the next set of National Assembly elections in the Republic of Vietnam.[1] In the new Republic, the 1959 elections were significant because they served as a benchmark for how well the Vietnamese had adapted democratic principles into their political system. The elections also served as a predecessor for the 1961 election that would determine if Ngô Đình Diệm would remain as president. Law 19/50 did not offer anything too unusual. Each deputy would represent 55,000 voters, which was a decrease from the previous election and had caused some concern but nothing significant. Vietnamese had to be eighteen to vote while candidates had to be at least twenty-five years of age and had satisfied their military commitment. Candidates received Government money from local committees equivalent to 72 piasters ($1.00) per voter to be divided impartially among the candidates. This was doubled from the previous election. Law 20/50 established the campaign season, limited to two weeks, for the August 30 election and enumerated how a candidate could get on the ballot.

There were some significant changes from the 1956 election laws. In addition to the change in the number of people each delegate represented, the new laws eliminated the twelve deputy positions in the National Assembly that had been reserved for refugees who had fled the North after 1954. This worried many of the northern refugees, who believed that they now would not be represented. In order to make sure that there was less opportunities for fraud or intimidation, voters had to provide both their identity and voting cards at the balloting stations but were allowed to put their completed ballots in a sealed envelope while alone in a closed booth. In 1956, ballots were distinguished by color and voting done in the open, which made the notion of a secret ballot suspect. Overall, the lessons learned from the 1956 experience where applied to the 1959 election with the hopes that the process would be smoother and without incident. Still, there was some criticism of the election law and procedures.

On July 6, Second Secretary of the United States embassy, Chalmers Wood, had a conversation with Lê Si Ngạc, who served as the Director of the Faculty of Engineering.[2] Lê Si Ngạc expressed his concern about the election law's provision that allowed the Saigon Government to pay the expenses of the candidates; he argued that this favored the Government candidates. He also opposed the salaries received by the deputies in the National Assembly, arguing that they were more than they needed or earned.[3] He then criticized the general lack of knowledge of some of the deputies which further affirmed his point that they were paid too much. In reporting the conversation to Washington, Wood maintained that Lê Si Ngạc represented the elite professionals in Saigon who were close to the Saigon Government but not actively involved in politics. The inference was that these Saigon intellectuals believed that the National Assembly was not functioning as a true organization of the Republic and that many of its members, loyal to the Government, were benefiting from their salaries without improving the overall situation in South Vietnam.

Another Vietnamese point of view was delivered by Elting a week later. On July 13, he had a dinner conversation with Độ Mặn Quát, leader of the Minority Bloc in the National Assembly and chairman of the Judiciary Committee.[4] Độ Mặn Quát was one of the few experienced lawyers who served in the National Assembly and considered by Elting to be a reasonable man. He asserted that the 1959 election laws had some significant changes in it that troubled him, including the elimination of the twelve deputy seats for refugees and the four seats for the Montagnards. He argued that the deletion of the former also removed any legitimate representation and voice of the North Vietnamese who had fled between 1954 and 1955.[5] While Độ Mặn Quát did not have anxiety about the 1959 elections, he did show some concern for the role of the National Assembly in the Republic. The National Assembly never approved of the bill that defined their status and had only approved bills sponsored by the Government's representatives. The conversation was not one that elicited concern though it was representative of a trend of embassy-supplied information about the National Assembly that would cause concern for one who looked for it.

Another critic of the 1959 National Assembly election laws and procedures was Phan Quang Đán, who had been vocal in his opposition to some of Saigon's policies in the past.[6] Phan Quang Đán published an article under an assumed name on July 19 in *Tự do*. Because he was a leader in the opposition to Ngô Đình Diệm's National Revolutionary Movement, his criticism was republished in other newspapers. Phan Quang Đán argued that Saigon-Cholon was underrepresented in the National Assembly. Because Saigon-Cholon held one-sixth of the total population of the Republic of Vietnam, he argued that it should have the equivalent in delegates. Instead of twenty, which would have been the proportioned number, it possessed only nine. His point was that the greatest opposition to Ngô Đình Diệm came from the capital and by underrepresenting Saigon-Cholon in the National Assembly, the government made sure that it would diminish the opposition. He also questioned the wisdom of allowing civil servants and the military to vote wherever they were on Election Day if they could not return to their home district, which allowed the possibility of multiple voting. Finally, he called on a more stringent procedure for counting and checking votes to include striking a name from a voting list once that individual had voted as was done in 1956. Phan Quang Đán offered other observations and criticisms, all of which helped to undermine Colegrove's earlier assertions that there was no discussion or debate in Ngô Đình Diệm's Vietnam. These were the points that were being examined by the House of Representatives and the Senate.

On August 4, the candidates for the National Assembly were posted and the voter cards distributed on August 5.[7] On August 10, *Lê Sống* reported that 6,738,922 voters were eligible to cast a ballot in the August 30 election and that there were 625 candidates vying for the 123 delegate seats, though the list would not be finalized until August 14.[8] During the period preceding the campaign season there was much discussion in Saigon about the National Assembly and the candidates. While criticism and concern about the elections was reported through the Embassy to Washington, there were some who defended the system. On August 11, Madame Ngô Đình Nhu gave a speech at a meeting of the Vietnamese Women's Association in which she answered critics of the National Assembly.[9] She specifically discussed the rationale behind the delegate salaries as a ward against temptation for bribery and continued to stress the importance of women serving in the National Assembly as well as in places of prominence within the government. In reporting the speech to Washington, Joseph Mendenhall, who was now the Counselor of the American Embassy in Saigon for Political Affairs, argued that it was more effective in its appeal to women to use the ballot to affirm their power in society than as a counter to the criticisms leveled against the National Assembly. *Chuông Mai* reminded the Vietnamese people that the outside world was watching the election to determine how far Vietnam had come in its democracy. Additionally, sabotage, directed from Hanoi, was surely planned to disrupt the elections.[10] The ability of the Saigon Government to counter these moves would also indicate how secure Vietnam was at the end of the decade.

As the election campaigning commenced, there were incidents that threatened to undermine the showcase of democracy that Saigon wished to project. Not all eligible voters were able to receive their cards, which caused *Tin Mới* to plead to the government to make the process easier, while *Tiếng Chuông* (Bell Toll) reported on a rash of violence within the second district of Saigon during a campaign rally.[11] *Buổi sang* complained that some candidates were using "empty words and promises" in their speeches and called for a revised tone or new candidates. *Tiếng Chuông* echoed this sentiment.[12] There were other incidents that caused concern for both those supporting and opposed to Ngô Đình Diệm's continued rule.

Two independent candidates, Bùi An Tuấn and Trần Thế Xương, were fined 5,000 piasters ($70.00) for campaigning before the date set by the election law, while Nguyễn Văn Cẩn was fined 6,000 piasters ($83.00) for giving a false home address.[13] Other candidates also received fines for violating the election laws or illegally raising money for campaigning.[14] Phan Quang Đán voiced his discontent in an open letter published by *Buổi sang* on August 22. He reported two instances where his representatives were attacked during a campaigning session. On August 18, a member in the crowd tried to pull away the microphone in use by one of his representatives and, on August 20, an assailant hit the man standing next to him in the nose.

Phan Quang Đán also protested over the six-minute time limit to give speeches, which did not allow for questions or substance.[15] On August 20, Phan Quang Đán and Hoàng Cơ Thụy filed suit against Ngô Sách Vinh, who represented the National Revolutionary Movement, for threatening voters. A countersuit was also filed by Ngô Sách Vinh, alleging violations in the electoral law.[16] Other candidate names were stricken from the ballot for a variety of reasons, not all universally accepted.[17] These types of actions did nothing to help the image of Vietnam as a democracy, though they were no worse than what was happening in the Jim Crow South in the United States.

There was a worry that the Việt Cộng might disrupt the Election Day process, though if it was one of its objectives it did not succeed. Ngô Đình Diệm did inform Williams of a few incidents leading up to August 30, though Williams conveyed to Durbrow that he did not think these occurrences were directly connected to the election.[18] Ngô Đình Diệm maintained that his forces had been active in rounding up individuals who might disrupt the process for most of the summer months. Durbrow reported to Washington that during the months of July and August, the Việt Cộng had stepped up its activities to sabotage the election by killing, wounding, or kidnaping Vietnamese associated with the government, which was met with resistance. The result was thirty-six Việt Cộng dead, nine arrested and a significant amount of guns, ammunition, equipment, and documents seized.[19] Durbrow concluded that the elections proceeded without serious incident and in perfect order.

The total number of votes cast represented about eighty-five percent of the electorate. Of the 123 delegate seats available, the National Revolutionary Movement won seventy-eight while independent candidates won thirty-six. The remaining seats went to the Vietnamese Socialist (four), National Restoration (two), and Social Democrats (three). Fifty incumbents regained their seats and nine women were elected to the National Assembly.[20] The election results were boosted during the last week of campaigning when the Saigon Government decided to permit candidates who had been stricken from the ballot because they had violated the election laws to run. While some of these candidates, including Phan Quang Đán, won their election bid, it was unclear whether they would be allowed to take their seat in the National Assembly when it convened. These delegates, if denied their seats, could appeal any lower court judgment to the Court of Cassation and then to the National Assembly if needed. On September 30, the Court of Cassation rejected Phan Quang Đán's appeal against a conviction of bribing voters, which made a by-election necessary.[21]

On the second day of the National Assembly, October 6, Phan Khắc Sửu, a member of the opposition, asked why Phan Quang Đán and Nguyễn Trân, who defeated the National Revolutionary Movement's candidate in Saigon's first district, were not present. When he was told that they had no right to be in the Assembly, he remarked that, "In that case, we have no real independence in this country."[22] The uncertainty caused by the decision to allow individuals who violated the election law but still run as a candidate and win their seat would cause tension within the Saigon intelligentsia and the American Embassy for months to come. It would be one of the major obstacles placed between Ngô Đình Diệm and Durbrow when it increasingly became important for the two to work together during the critical year 1960.

Ngô Đình Diệm was satisfied with the National Elections even though his National Revolutionary Movement party lost seats. He considered that loss a healthy sign for the Republic of Vietnam.[23] Those seats went to independent delegates for the most part because, as Ngô Đình Diệm described it, of a lack of trust by the Vietnamese people in organized political parties other than his National Revolutionary Movement. Ngô Đình Diệm also told

Williams that he thought the caliber of those independents elected was strong, citing three well-educated individuals. Many of the September 1 editorials in the Vietnamese dailies shared Ngô Đình Diệm's opinion about the electoral process as well as urging the candidates who won to live up to their campaign promises.[24] *Lê Sống* argued that the National Assembly elections were a "'triumphant success' for the republic and at the same time a bitter failure for the communists."[25] The daily newspaper maintained that the success of the election would increase the people's confidence in the government.

In his September 1 weekly press conference, Minister of Information Trần Chánh Thành argued that the process went smoothly and freely even though there were persistent rumors that sought to discredit the elections, such as servicemen being forced to vote for a particular candidate or candidates suing one another for violating the election laws.[26] *Chuông Mai* asserted that the success of the election was seen in the variety of delegates elected who represented every part of Vietnamese society.[27] While both positive and negative aspects of the elections were discussed in the Vietnamese press, personnel in the American Embassy focused on the negative aspects in their reporting to Washington.

The American embassy in Saigon became involved in the domestic controversy surrounding whether Phan Quang Đán and Nguyễn Trân should be allowed their seats in the National Assembly after the Court of Cassation rejected the appeal. The denial by the courts meant that the National Assembly, when it convened on October 5, would decide their future.[28] The National Assembly was expected to choose its twenty-five member credentials committee, which would then validate the uncontested results within a week and the contested results within two weeks.[29] Durbrow did not think that either candidate would be seated in the National Assembly though he did think it possible that the Saigon Government could use its influence to ensure that their election results were validated. *Lê Sống* examined the controversy and concluded that electoral law 19/50 did not address the issue, though it maintained that the next step was to use French law that had been promulgated in Indochina to do so.[30] It cited an April 14, 1914, law to conclude that neither candidate would be eligible to take their seats. This line of logic was not convincing to many of the Saigon intellectuals who opposed Ngô Đình Diệm, nor was it enough for the Americans in Saigon who supported Phan Quang Đán.

This led Durbrow to discuss the matter on September 11 at a small dinner party which included Nguyễn Ngọc Thơ, Nguyễn Đình Thuần, Director of General Foreign Aid Vũ Văn Thái, and Gardiner.[31] Durbrow brought up the issue of Phan Quang Đán, as he had done earlier with Nguyễn Đình Thuần and Trần Chánh Thành, and argued that he needed to be allowed to take his seat in the National Assembly. He maintained that Phan Quang Đán would not pose a serious threat to the Saigon Government's policies, though his participation in the National Assembly as a vocal opponent would lend prestige to the Republic of Vietnam's experiment in democracy as well as counter propaganda originating from Hanoi. Nguyễn Ngọc Thơ countered that while he did not like the idea of denying Phan Quang Đán his seat, he believed Ngô Đình Diệm would not harbor it. Ngô Đình Diệm wanted to have an independent, loyal, and responsible opposition and he did not think that Phan Quang Đán represented that option. Nguyễn Ngọc Thơ also argued that Phan Quang Đán's opposition within the National Assembly would be used by the North Vietnamese in their propaganda efforts.

While Durbrow attempted to show his Vietnamese hosts that denying Phan Quang Đán the seat would only further Hanoi's propaganda, he also pointed out that Phan Quang Đán would most likely make even more inflammatory remarks if he was denied his seat. Durbrow made some rational and reasonable points in the conversation but he also indicated quite forcefully to these members of the upper echelon in the Saigon Government that the United States was indirectly interfering in the internal politics of the Republic of Vietnam. This one event was innocuous, but when coupled with the continued interference emanating from the American Embassy in Saigon over the next year, it would cause a serious strain in relations.

Ngô Đình Diệm's rejection of Phan Quang Đán was more than just wanting to have a loyal opposition in the National Assembly, as Nguyễn Ngọc Thơ had told Durbrow. When Ngô Đình Diệm and Williams met on September 30, primarily to discuss the situation in Laos and the possibility of having Vietnamese train Laotian Army officers and NCOs, the question of Phan Quang Đán arose.[32] Ngô Đình Diệm told Williams that many Americans, the implication included Durbrow, believed that a healthy opposition was good but Ngô Đình Diệm characterized Phan Quang Đán as a traitor who was a manipulator and playing a dangerous game with the French. He then relayed his experiences with Phan Quang Đán from the end of the Second World War to the formation of the Republic. The portrayal of Phan Quang Đán was extremely negative and included questionable actions during the Bảo Đại reign after the war, a sizable amount of money he received as Minister of Information under the Emperor, and questionable activities with the Cao Đài after he returned to Vietnam in 1955. The accuracy of these stories was certainly based on perspective and unproven allegations, but they did give a real sense that the Saigon Government would not work to allow Phan Quang Đán into the National Assembly. In William's memorandum to Durbrow, he did not include any of the discussion of Phan Quang Đán.[33]

The credential committee met on October 15 and examined and validated the election of 121 of the 123 delegates. As expected, Phan Quang Đán and Nguyễn Trân were not confirmed as deputies. The National Assembly elected their officers on October 21, with Trương Vĩnh Lê as president, Trương Công Cửu as first vice president, Lại Tử as second vice president, and Nguyễn Phương Thiệp as secretary general. Only Trương Công Cửu did not belong to the National Revolutionary Movement. Trương Vĩnh Lê announced on October 22 that the National Assembly would organize into two groups, titled the Personalist Community and the Social Alliance, which replaced the majority and minor groups in the previous National Assembly. Both groups were expected to support the Saigon Government.[34] This new organization did not go as far as the United States would have liked and helped to justify some of Phan Quang Đán's criticism in 1960.

While election politics and their consequences where discussed and debated in Saigon and Washington, the situation between Vietnam and Cambodia took a turn for the worse in September. Earlier, on August 31, there was an assassination attempt on the lives of Cambodia King Norodom Suramarit and Queen Sisowath Kossamak. When queried about it during a September 2 meeting that focused primarily on the situation in Laos, Ngô Đình Diệm told Williams that he believed the attempt was not politically motivated and that the main target was the Queen.[35] Because of her immense wealth and holdings as well as how her business interests manipulated financial institutions, Ngô Đình Diệm maintained that her attacker was most likely a disgruntled Chinese. The bomb meant for the Royal family came in a parcel from Hong Kong. It was prematurely detonated by Prince Norodom Vakrivan, who had opened the box just as the King and Queen had left the room in which it was located.[36]

The Prince was killed, though the King and Queen remained safe. Ngô Đình Diệm reiterated to Williams that the assassination was not motivated by internal Royal family intrigue and that Sihanouk was not involved. In mentioning Sihanouk, Ngô Đình Diệm argued that if he "were to take over he would work at the task from four to six months but would eventually lose interest and want to spend three to four months on the Riviera to compensate for the hardships of being King."[37] It did not help the two countries' relationship when a Vietnamese, who had been associated with the controversial Ngô Trọng Hiếu, was arrested for delivering the bomb to the Royal Palace.[38]

The attempt on the Royal Family's lives and the continued broadcasting of the Free Khmer Movement justified Sihanouk's decision to reevaluate Cambodia's relationship with the Republic of Vietnam. When three members of the Free Khmer Movement were captured, Cambodian Security Forces took their confession that they had been trained in sabotage at a school in South Vietnam. Another ten Vietnamese were captured in Cambodian territory and confessed to being associated with the movement as well.[39] Sihanouk continued to maintain that the broadcast originated from South Vietnam even as Vietnamese denied that allegation and instead asserted that the radio transmitters were in Cambodian territory near the border. When questioned about the broadcasts, Vũ Văn Mẫu told Durbrow that he had offered the Cambodians assistance to eliminate the broadcasts. He argued that it was not in his country but, rather, on the border in a forested area north of Saigon and that it was guarded by at least 400 personnel. Durbrow interrupted Vũ Văn Mẫu to inform him that he had seen Ngô Đình Diệm, under instructions, and was quite firm about the broadcasts originating from Vietnam and that if he desired it, the United States would locate the transmitter for the Vietnamese.[40] Durbrow claimed that Vũ Văn Mẫu put on an act of being surprised and then reaffirmed his position that the transmitter was in Cambodia. When Parsons met with Nguyễn Đình Thuần in Washington, he restated what Durbrow had told Vũ Văn Mẫu, with similar results.[41]

As the month of September progressed, the rhetoric originating from Phnom Penh, and specifically from Sihanouk, intensified. Sihanouk discussed the bomb plot on several occasions and made reference to the support the would-be assassin must have received from foreign interests.[42] The renewed deterioration in relations between Cambodia and Vietnam as a result of the attempted assassination and radio broadcasts, which were highly critical of Sihanouk, prompted Durbrow to further action to force Ngô Đình Diệm to desist in aiding the Free Khmer Movement. When Durbrow learned on October 12 that Parkes had informed Lalouette of Durbrow's first démarche to Ngô Đình Diệm on his country's position toward Cambodia, he recommended that Trimble inform Sihanouk of Durbrow's efforts to influence the Vietnamese. The implication was that Sihanouk would appreciate that the Americans were working on Ngô Đình Diệm and they did not believe the Vietnamese to be innocent. Durbrow commented in his report to Washington that the Voice of Khmer Freedom Movement's broadcasts had ceased after Durbrow's efforts.[43]

Secretary of State Christian Herter, through J. Graham Parson, responded to Durbrow's suggestion in the negative. Washington did not think it advisable to inform Sihanouk of Durbrow's actions until they could be sure that those actions were effective in stemming the tide of the Voice of Khmer Freedom Movement.[44] Durbrow disagreed with this point of view and also protested the decision to give the Cambodians Radio Detection Finder (RDF) units to locate the origin of the radio broadcasts. In his démarche to Ngô Đình Diệm earlier, Durbrow informed the president that the United States already knew the exact location of broadcasts. To give the Cambodians the equipment would be, "pouring unnecessary salt into [the] wound."[45] Trimble agreed with Durbrow that he should be authorized to inform Sihanouk of the démarche if only to prevent Sihanouk thinking that it was his pressure on Trimble that resulted in the encounter.[46]

Herter, however, believed it was advisable to inform Ngô Đình Diệm about the RDF units. If Ngô Đình Diệm became angered about it, Herter instructed Durbrow to remind Ngô Đình Diệm that the United States had given similar equipment to the Vietnamese while a refusal to provide the same to the Cambodians might cause Sihanouk to think the United States rejected the request to cover up a Vietnamese clandestine operation aimed against Cambodia.[47] Trimble concurred with the added caveat that if the United States refused Cambodia the equipment, he believed Sihanouk would ask the Chinese Communists for it.[48] When the Cambodians made the request on October 21, Trimble was more adamant. Failure to provide the necessary RDF equipment would confirm, in Sihanouk's mind, that the United States was plotting with the Republic of Vietnam against Cambodia.[49] Trimble understood the situation that Durbrow faced in Saigon though he did argue that the silence of the transmitter located in Vietnam, which had been absent since September 29, would most likely remain so when the Cambodians possessed the RDF units.[50]

While Durbrow informed Ngô Đình Diệm about the equipment, Trimble had yet to receive authorization to do so with Sihanouk. On October 29, he requested that he be able to do so before he was told as it would enhance the American position. Trimble also asked to be able to inform Sihanouk of Durbrow's démarche to Ngô Đình Diệm so that he understood that the United States was acting firm in Saigon.[51] Herter, through Parsons, agreed to both requests as Sihanouk had probably already been informed about the démarche, and he wanted to make sure that Sihanouk understood that the equipment represented the United States desire to counter the Voice of the Free Khmer Movement broadcasts.[52] With the RDF equipment on its way, the silence of the anti–Sihanouk broadcasts, and an impending Sihanouk trip to Egypt, the level of tension within Phnom Penh decreased to the point Trimble could confidently report that the situation was as relaxed as it had been during the Ngô Đình Diệm-Sihanouk talks.[53] Sihanouk had attended an October 26 celebration event marking the anniversary of the Republic of Vietnam while the Cambodian newspapers continued to restrain themselves when reporting on issues related to Vietnam and the border.

The National Assembly election and Cambodia both served as a backdrop for the renewed tension between the American Embassy and Ngô Đình Diệm. The election, which should have been a milestone in the Republic of Vietnam's movement towards a democracy was, instead, mired in the case of Phan Quang Đán, who the Americans admired and Ngô Đình Diệm detested. Cambodia represented a situation in which the Americans refused to accept or even acknowledge the degree to which Ngô Đình Diệm distrusted Sihanouk and his brand of neutrality and saw his removal as an improvement for Southeast Asia in its struggle against Communism. Under these and other emerging issues in Saigon, the American Embassy staff continued to report on Ngô

Đình Diệm in increasingly negative ways, even when he was purportedly praised. Mendenhall sent a despatch to Washington on October 15 enumerating the many inspection trips Ngô Đình Diệm had taken since July 4, 1958, within the Republic of Vietnam. Given the state of Vietnam at the time and the demands on the president, the nearly sixty trips was impressive but Mendenhall could not help but invoke imagery in his despatch that connected Ngô Đình Diệm with an aloof Emperor as he discussed how Ngô Đình Diệm had "left his walled grounds" to "grace a Saigon exhibition or to tour foreign ships paying calls in the port."[54] Mendenhall, newly arrived in at the Embassy in Saigon but familiar with Durbrow's position regarding Ngô Đình Diệm through their relationship while he was on the Vietnam Desk in the State Department, would continue a campaign that involved passive complaint against Ngô Đình Diệm during his tenure in Saigon.

Another source of unnecessary tension was the impending visit of a Congressional group headed by John Pilcher (D–Georgia), which was a result of the hearings in the House and Senate over the Colegrove articles. The official visit challenged Durbrow and his staff in early November.[55] While the hear-

Ngô Đình Diệm (second from left) with Gardiner (left) and others on an inspection trip along Route 14, September 4, 1960. Arthur Z. Gardiner Papers (2014-1561) (Harry S. Truman Library & Museum).

ings had found nothing wrong with the American aid program in Vietnam, the group was dispatched to confirm those findings. It was designated with the task of examining the American side of the program and had no interest or authority to review the Saigon Government or its expenditure of American aid. Nonetheless, the Congressional group caused tension in Saigon. Durbrow visited Ngô Đình Diệm on November 3 to discuss the group and its role as well as stave off a diplomatic slight that seemed to be in the making.[56]

Durbrow was concerned that Ngô Đình Diệm had failed to organize a dinner for the group and that Saigon Government officials had refused a dinner invitation that Durbrow was planning to host. Ngô Đình Diệm had been congenial to American visitors in the past, which made the snub all the more obvious. The implication was that Ngô Đình Diệm was purposely insulting the Congressional group because he resented their being sent to Saigon to investigate the Vietnamese government and its use of American aid. This had been reported in Scripps-Howard editorials and articles when the trip was announced. Rumors were also being spread around Saigon by individuals who had been the source for much of Colegrove's articles, including Frank Gondor.[57]

Frank Gonder had earned a reputation in Saigon as a questionable businessman who dabbled in Saigon politics and allegedly had a tendency to stir up trouble by starting rumors and instigating instability. He was not well liked by the American embassy staff, nor was he admired by the Vietnamese Government. According to James Lucas, a special correspondent for Scripps-Howard, who was in Saigon to follow up on the Colegrove articles, Gonder was a "congenital liar" who was experiencing business failure and attempted to control Lucas's actions upon his arrival in Saigon.[58] Gondor had reportedly told members of the Pilcher group, while they were in Saigon, that formal hearings were needed, which Lucas maintained was improper.

When Durbrow tried to explain all of this to Ngô Đình Diệm, though he did not discuss Gondor, his response was that it was tradition in Vietnam not to socialize with members of an investigating committee because it might embarrass the group and could be interpreted as an attempt to sway their findings. Durbrow persisted with the needs to fulfill the diplomatic niceties involved with the visit, concluding that if Ngô Đình Diệm and his cabinet continued to resist meeting with Pilcher's group, only Vietnam would suffer. Ngô Đình Diệm finally agreed to hold the meeting though no formal dinner was organized while he continued to maintain his position about Vietnamese tradition. There was no question that Ngô Đình Diệm was insulted not only by the Colegrove articles but also by hearings and subsequent Congressional visit. Even if Vietnam was one of fifteen countries that Pilcher's team planned to visit, it still personally affected Ngô Đình Diệm more than it should have given the nature of the trip.

The failure of Ngô Đình Diệm to offer a dinner did result in some repercussions for the Vietnamese. When the group met with Ngô Đình Diệm on November 5, Pilcher did not attend in response to the way he believed Ngô Đình Diệm had treated him. Even though Pilcher was absent, the meeting was deemed successful by the American embassy with the Congressional group commenting on Ngô Đình Diệm's sincerity and determination in leading his country's struggle against Communism.[59] Nonetheless, there was enough concern in American circles about Pilcher's refusal to attend the meeting with Ngô Đình Diệm that Wolf Ladejinsky, who was attending a conference of the American Friends of Vietnam in the United States, cut short his trip to return to Saigon to reassure Ngô Đình Diệm about the commitment of the United States to the Republic of Vietnam.[60]

Another source for the Colegrove articles was USOM officer Austin Menzies. *Time-Life* correspondent James Wilde confirmed that Menzies arranged a clandestine meeting between Lucas and Phan Quang Đán while Menzies also met privately with Senator Hickenlooper, who had travelled to Vietnam to inspect how American aid was being handled in Vietnam. Durbrow maintained to Parsons that Menzies was a "sick man with a warped mind who will continue to spread false information as long as he is allowed to stay here."[61] When Lucas and Durbrow met at the end of November with Vice Admiral H.D. Riley, who was Chief of Staff, CINCPAC, the three discussed the Colegrove affair.[62] Lucas confirmed that he had been sent by Scripps-Howard to follow up on Colegrove's leads and had met with the latter's informers but had not been able to confirm any of the major criticisms that had appeared in the articles. Lucas complained that he was tired of the assignment and had begun to avoid Colegrove and the USOM informants who fed him false leads and questionable facts.

The aftermath of the Colegrove article and the subsequent United States action overshadowed events in Saigon. When coupled with the American involvement in the Phan Quang Đán situation and the frustration surrounding the Voice of the Khmer Freedom Movement, it should not be surprising that the relationship between Durbrow and Ngô Đình Diệm was at an all-time low. Neither man believed himself to be the instigator in their troubles while both viewed the other with suspicion and a degree of scorn. As Vietnam entered a critical time in its young life as a Republic, the split between these two significant men would have lasting repercussions.

12
The Struggles of a Young Republic

There was a sense of a progress in Vietnam despite the poor relationship with Cambodia and the controversy surrounding the National Assembly election and the future of Phan Quang Đán and Nguyễn Thân. There was a rise in assassinations, kidnappings, and sabotage, but the Việt Cộng had failed to disrupt the elections. However, not all Americans were convinced that the National Assembly elections fulfilled the democratic expectations imposed by the United States model. In a December 7 despatch, Mendenhall argued rather forcefully that despite the election results, Vietnam remained under authoritarian rule.[1] Other members of the Country Team warned of the possibility of the troubles over rising expectations with Vietnam. As stability surfaced and endured in the urban areas, the ability to criticize the government increased. The attention and energy that had been devoted to other concerns would refocus itself against the Saigon Government. This criticism, generally led by the Saigon intelligentsia, could make itself problematic for Ngô Đình Diệm depending upon how he dealt with this vocal group.[2]

In some respects, this line of thinking about the rise in expectations was false. There were continuous instances of armed attacks against the Vietnamese, even if the urban centers appeared to be safe. On December 6, a clash involving Vietnamese troops and the Việt Cộng resulted in five insurgent deaths in Cái Nước District, An Xuyên Province. Another engagement, on December 11 in Đức Lập village, Long An Province resulted in the deaths of three Việt Cộng and the seizure of many weapons and documents. Several other attacks in Long An Province signaled that the Việt Cộng were not complacent in the countryside while its targets for assassination were selected to discredit the ability of the Saigon Government to extend its rule outside of the urban centers. This policy of *Trụ Giãn* (targeted assassinations) would

135

ensure some level of instability in the countryside despite any successes achieved by the Vietnamese military or other forces.[3]

Nonetheless, the rise-in-expectations argument explained urban dissent against Ngô Đình Diệm and helped to justify American response and action emerging from an embassy that was turning decidedly against the Vietnamese president's rule. Ngô Đình Diệm was characterized as obstinate and aloof by members of the Country Team, with the exception of Williams. This line of thinking was seen in a December 7, 1959, Country Team assessment titled, "Role of the Military in Less-developed Countries: Vietnam, a Country Team Assessment."[4] Mendenhall was the principle author of the report, though he was aided in its development by Political Officer and First Secretary for the Embassy in Vietnam William E. Colby.[5] The assessment delineated the Embassy's position as it related to Ngô Đình Diệm and American assistance to the Republic of Vietnam. It also explored the conflicting opinion within the Country Team. The assessment, which was approved by Durbrow, established the divisions within the Country Team with Mendenhall and Durbrow on the side that reflected a negative position toward Ngô Đình Diệm and his rule and Colby and Williams who advocated a more conciliatory approach in dealing with the Vietnamese.

The assessment argued that Ngô Đình Diệm had become more authoritarian in his efforts to subdue the countryside as his government moved away from a more American model of democracy towards one that followed a uniquely Vietnamese perspective. Mendenhall's influence in the assessment on this line of thinking asserted that this strict rule was troublesome given the lack of a unified threat against Saigon, that is, Ngô Đình Diệm was using the threat in the countryside to strong-arm his people and opposition into line. Mendenhall saw no evidence of a possible military inspired coup d'état, which might have justified such a move, implying that Ngô Đình Diệm acted as he did because of his need for complete control. Colby attempted to challenge that assertion by examining the nature of Ngô Đình Diệm's political philosophy, which had its foundations in Vietnamese tradition rather than an American model. This reasonable approach was overwhelmed by the forces against Ngô Đình Diệm.

Ngô Đình Diệm saw himself as a modern-day Gia Long. This former Nguyễn dynasty emperor established the law that served as a foundation for Vietnamese self-rule at the beginning of the 19th Century and worked to unite the Vietnamese people before French colonialism asserted itself toward the end of the century.[6] As such, Ngô Đình Diệm wanted American aid to help his country become economically stable and secure but he believed that this aid should not come with conditions or a price. Ngô Đình Diệm maintained that he knew what was best for his people, as did the Vietnamese emperors of the past, and Americans coming to Vietnam for a temporary period, regardless of their position in the hierarchy, needed to defer to him on issues for which he was more familiar. Williams had been able to overcome this attitude with some success because he brought with him credentials that Ngô Đình Diệm respected while he tended to speak with, rather than speak at, the Vietnamese president when the two met.

Where Ngô Đình Diệm advocated strict discipline of his people in their efforts to achieve independence and prosperity, the Country Team assessment argued that this attitude explained Ngô Đình Diệm's authoritarian rule and his weak attempts that created a "democratic façade" which offered little chance for political evolution without significant change.[7] This was why the Saigon Intelligentsia protested against Ngô Đình Diệm and why members of the National Assembly lamented their inability to make effective policy that would balance the politics in the Republic of Vietnam. These same critics argued that a minority of the National Revolutionary Movement delegation held the real power in the National Assembly and they answered to the Ngô family.[8] The assessment concluded that a failure to make the necessary adjustments might result in a political crisis that would potentially threatened the democratic experiment as well as give an advantage to the communist threat from the North. Press coverage of the first session of the National Assembly suggested an opposite perspective though this was rarely commented upon by the embassy.[9]

Coverage of the National Assembly within the Vietnamese press was extensive and not always supportive of the Saigon Government position. While some dailies, like *Buổi sang*, praised the National Assembly for not blindly supporting the government, others took a more direct approach in highlighting some of the serious issues within the Republic of Vietnam not caused by the insurgency.[10] During the course of the debate over the budget, deputies of the National Assembly also voiced their protest over what they considered recurring problems in Vietnam. During the December 19 debate on the section of the budget for the Department of Interior related to political training centers and reeducation centers for political detainees, Assemblyman Bùi Quang Ngô asked how individuals in these centers were being treated and then called for Ngô Đình Diệm to grant amnesty, or a reduced sentence, to some of the detainees. Within the debate was the implied criticism that there were detainees who had been suspected of political subversive but had not been charged.[11] Phan Khắc Sửu joined the debate and argued that the Saigon Government should adopt a policy of clemency rather than hold individuals based on suspicion while Huỳnh Thành Vị and Nguyễn Văn Liên asserted that members of the police force were using torture to acquire oral or written confessions.[12] This opposition position eventually led Ngô Đình Diệm to create the position of Directorate General for Political Re-education Centers on January 13, 1960, headed by the former commander of the Fifth

Military Region, Colonel Nguyễn Văn Y.[13] This type of action suggests that Ngô Đình Diệm was not entirely dismissive of the National Assembly efforts to help shape the future of the country.

Despite these examples of a young Republic attempting to work its way to improve the political situation, members of the Country Team opposed to Ngô Đình Diệm continued to minimize this positive process. It did not acknowledge the role of the National Assembly and dismissed Ngô Đình Diệm's style of leadership as one which was not interested in seriously attempting any experiments in democracy.[14] Anti–Ngô Đình Diệm members of the Country Team maintained that he based his actions on the inexperience of his government in politics, the consequences of French colonialism, and the need for security and discipline because of the Việt Cộng. Ngô Đình Diệm argued on several occasions that his country lacked trained cadres in both politics and the military, which required his total supervision. While Ngô Đình Diệm saw this as his Mandarin responsibility, those Americans who were prone to oppose him equated it with the beginnings of despotism. It did not help that Durbrow, Mendenhall, and others wary of Ngô Đình Diệm relied more on the urban intelligentsia for their information than those connected to Ngô Đình Diệm. This made the job of Williams more difficult and also placed him into a political arena for which he was not supported or prepared. It also gave the anti–Ngô Đình Diệm factions in Saigon an avenue to the American embassy that allowed them to help disrupt the Vietnamese-American relations in the coming year.

The Saigon Government was not without blame, however. One continuing source of concern was the role of the 20,000-member Cần Lao Party, which was closely connected to Ngô Đình Diệm. The Country Team examined the Cần Lao Party in its assessment and expressed apprehension on its actions, such as spying and intimidation, which were counter to the ideals of a democracy.[15] The assessment did acknowledge, however, that the Cần Lao Party served the purpose of keeping the country together at a difficult time. The assessment did not report the many humanitarian and social program sponsored or organized by the Party. The Cần Lao Party had also infiltrated the Vietnamese military to the point that the Country Team concluded that those without party affiliation held very little political influence in the Saigon Government. This became significant when the Country Team enumerated the possible replacements or alternatives for Ngô Đình Diệm with the end of his presidency. The team had little hope of a constitutional linkage as vice president Nguyễn Ngọc Thơ, though competent, did not share the trust of all the powerful factions in Vietnam. There were other options, including anyone in the Ngô family or a military figure in the event of a coup d'état. These discussions became relevant when it was announced that the presidential election would take place in April 1961.

12. The Struggles of a Young Republic

With all of the Country Team's discussion of accession, political intrigue, and problems plaguing the current Vietnamese government, it did conclude that the best option for the United States was continued support for Ngô Đình Diệm. While its assessment lamented that the Saigon Government might never achieve a Western style of democracy, America's continued support of it was the most likely avenue to stop the Communist encroachment in the region. Over the course of Durbrow's remaining time in Vietnam, he would cautiously at first, and then with more vigor, erode support for this part of the assessment. Durbrow became convinced that Ngô Đình Diệm would not adjust his policies to adhere to a more Western-style Human Rights position nor did he think that the August 1959 National Assembly elections boded well for the future experiment in democracy in Vietnam. The failure to support Phan Quang Đán and Nguyễn Thân in their attempt to retain the seats they won in the election because of personality conflicts—though Ngô Đình Diệm would have deemed the differences in a more serious way—was used by Durbrow to question the seriousness of the Vietnamese efforts to achieve a free Republic. Both Phan Quang Đán and Nguyễn Thân would play a central role in the growing intelligentsia opposition to Ngô Đình Diệm in Saigon and would become the source of anti–Ngô stories relayed to the United States embassy over the next year.

Durbrow and most of his staff believed that the intelligentsia needed to play a more important role in the Saigon Government and that their participation would make the Republic stronger. This belief was reinforced by the Country Team's recommendation that Ngô Đình Diệm be encouraged to include this group in deliberations about Vietnam's future even though he had made it clear that he could not work with Phan Quang Đán. It did not escape Ngô Đình Diệm's attention that should he be forcibly replaced, Phan Quang Đán also represented a possible leader. Phan Quang Đán epitomized a Vietnam that Ngô Đình Diệm did not want; efforts to persuade the Vietnamese president to include him in governance would only serve as a source of significant discomfort in future conversations between Ngô Đình Diệm and the Americans. While Ngô Đình Diệm had made some progress in the development of the Republic of Vietnam, Durbrow and some members of the Country Team did not believe it had been enough.

One of the areas that Durbrow wanted to see greater improvement was in economic development. He had been wary of Ngô Đình Diệm in the past of focusing too much of his attention and resources on the military rather than the economy, which Durbrow maintained was detrimental for the future success of Vietnam. Ngô Đình Diệm believed that the creation of economic infrastructure was tied to his democracy but he argued it would not be successful until after the countryside was secure. One effort to achieve this was land redistribution and the further development of the Civil Guard and Self-

Defense Forces. Ngô Đình Diệm also had a near myopic fixation on the development of roads and other lines of communication, which he had pressed upon Durbrow, Williams, and any American visitor to his country.[16] For Ngô Đình Diệm, improved roads meant greater communication, a stronger economy, and improved internal security.

Ngô Đình Diệm acknowledged that much was left to be done in the Republic of Vietnam, despite many advances. When he became chief of state in 1954, the Vietnamese people had seen conflict of one nature or another for most of their adult lives. French rule after the end of World War II had not meant an improvement in the day-to-day lives of the Vietnamese and in most cases had resulted in a worsening condition. Even after the French colonial experiment had ended, Ngô Đình Diệm was tasked with the difficult job of building a nation that lacked political and economic infrastructure, a homogeneous people, or a seasoned military. While, at times, it appeared to Durbrow and his American supporters that the Vietnamese were not doing enough, this position caused many on the Vietnamese side to take umbrage with this attitude.

Vice president Nguyễn Ngọc Thơ expressed this frustration to Durbrow during a December 11 meeting in which he observed a certain duplicity in the way Americans reported their impressions while visiting Vietnam. He referred to a recent visit to Vietnam by Senator Al Gore (D–Tennessee) who had praised the Vietnamese while in the country but then gave an account to the press that was less than flattering.[17] Senators Gore and Gale McGee (D–Wyoming) arrived in Vietnam on December 6 for a five-day visit to study American Aid to Vietnam. After meeting with Ngô Đình Diệm, Nguyễn Ngọc Thơ, and Nguyễn Đình Thuận, Gore criticized the policies of Ngô Đình Diệm to the press.[18] His remarks offended the Vietnamese who had accomplished much since 1955 with American assistance. Nguyễn Ngọc Thơ warned Durbrow that Gore's remarks only helped the Communists and were not representative of an ally whose aid was critical at a significant point in its development.

The year 1959 ended with a few questions left unanswered about the status of the experiment of the Republic that Ngô Đình Diệm was trying to construct and the Americans were working to advance. In his New Year's message, Ngô Đình Diệm praised his people for their efforts in developing Vietnam's infrastructure after so many years of French colonial rule.[19] With this praise came also a call to continue to work towards the future of a more modern state despite the recurring obstacles of the insurgency, political intrigue, and former French colonial activities in the region. Ngô Đình Diệm asked the Vietnamese people to put aside their differences for the sake of the Republic.[20] He did not mention United States economic and military aid in his speech, which caused some consternation within American circles, though it was clear that this aid was beneficial in the continuing success of the Vietnamese economy.[21]

The seriousness of the growing division between Ngô Đình Diệm and Durbrow made itself known when Secretary of the Army Wilber M. Brucker visited Saigon from January 6 to January 8, 1960.[22] Brucker and Ngô Đình Diệm met on January 7 with Durbrow, Williams and Nguyễn Đình Thuận. Because Brucker had been in Vietnam in 1955, the conversation was more relaxed than with first-time visitors. Ngô Đình Diệm expanded upon the security threat as a result of increased Việt Cộng activity over the previous eighteen months and continued on in a friendly tone until Brucker commented that the Vietnamese needed better airports.[23] Durbrow reported that Brucker had justified the statement because jet-capable airstrips were necessary should the United States enter into a conflict with the North Vietnamese. Durbrow took exception to this statement and, according to Williams, told Brucker he could not make such a statement. Williams described Durbrow's language as unfitting and unprofessional, as it occurred in front of Ngô Đình Diệm and Nguyễn Đình Thuận. While the exact words were not revealed, the tone was enough that Brucker walked out of the conference.[24] This clash was the forerunner of many more to come in 1960 as the Department of State and Department of Defense vied for control over the United States policy in Vietnam. Each sought to control the story generated from Saigon.

While the confrontation was most likely embarrassing for both Ngô Đình Diệm and Nguyễn Đình Thuận, it was telling how the Department of State viewed the incident. On January 25, Chalmers B. Wood, the Officer in Charge of Vietnam Affairs in the Department of State who had also worked for Durbrow in the embassy, defended the ambassador's actions and argued that Ngô Đình Diệm had caused the situation to escalate in order to divide the Americans over his policy.[25] Wood, who was not present for the exchange, had no basis for this assessment other than his already predisposed position against Ngô Đình Diệm.

Later in the evening, Nguyễn Đình Thuận telephoned Williams to ask if he and Brucker would return to the Presidential Palace without Durbrow. While Brucker accepted, Williams declined. He had no desire to be caught between Brucker and Durbrow and his presence would only exacerbate the strained relationship the general had with the ambassador. In their evening session Brucker and Ngô Đình Diệm discussed raising the number of American personnel beyond what was allowed in the 1954 Geneva Agreements. The United States was limited to 342 personnel thought it added an additional 350 with the Temporary Equipment Recovery Mission (TERM). TERM personnel were tasked with recovering Mutual Defense Assistant Program equipment though they also worked to improve the logistical capabilities of the South Vietnamese Armed Forces.[26]

During the course of the conversation, Brucker learned from Nguyễn Đình Thuần that Durbrow and Williams had approved a deadline to remove the TERM personnel by 1960. This was the opposite of what Brucker had wanted to see happen and asked for confirmation at which time Nguyễn Đình Thuần repeated that Durbrow had supported this action with Williams' consent. However, Williams had never given his consent. Durbrow had used Williams' name to reinforce his recommendation that the TERM personnel needed to be withdrawn.[27] While there was no one reason why Durbrow did this, it was possible that he knew the decision would not be favored by the Vietnamese. By adding Williams' approval to the recommendation, it might be accepted more readily.[28] Regardless, both Williams and Durbrow offered two very different versions of the Brucker meeting.[29]

Brucker left the meeting with a promise to Ngô Đình Diệm to work towards maintaining the level of American personnel in Vietnam and later reflected on the role of Durbrow as the principle American representative to Vietnam, concluding that the ambassador was not doing enough.[30] The Brucker incident reinforced the tension that existed in Saigon among the Americans stationed there to assist their Vietnamese ally. As the year 1960 progressed, the level of tension would only increase to the point where American policy decision-making originating from Saigon was divided and harmful to the continued rule of Ngô Đình Diệm. The episode also established a precedent. It reinforced the notion for Ngô Đình Diệm that there were still some in Washington would wished to continue assistance toward Vietnam despite what Durbrow had recommended. It also exposed the level of distrust between personnel from the Department of State and Department of Defense. Ngô Đình Diệm reaffirmed that he had an ally in Williams though he was less sanguine about Durbrow's role. As 1960 continued, that confidence would continue to erode though other events would take center stage.

On January 26, approximately 200 Việt Cộng attacked the 32nd Regiment, 21st ARVN Division camp in Trảng Sụp, Tây Ninh province.[31] The hour long battle by the four companies resulted in sixty-six ARVN soldiers killed, which was approximately one-fourth of the defender's force.[32] The regimental headquarters was also destroyed while a large number of weapons and ammunition was lost. Trảng Sụp was near the Cambodian border, which rekindled the long running Vietnamese concern about Cambodia's complicity with insurgents using its country as a safe haven. The attack was a sound defeat for the ARVN and reinforced William's concern about its level of preparedness.

Two weeks earlier Williams and Ngô Đình Diệm met, during which time Williams enumerated the deficiencies within the ARVN.[33] He argued that the military leadership in Vietnam was too lax because it expected the United States to intervene should the North Vietnamese attack. Ngô Đình Diệm disagreed but he did concede that the Vietnamese General Staff did not challenge their men to work hard. Williams was also concerned that the ARVN was under-strength, with some units having only 130 of the 150 men required while less than half of the planned 15,000 reservists had been trained. The Country Team had used these low numbers to justify recommendations that would stop any increase in the Armed Forces. Durbrow even argued that the reservists should be included in the 150,000 ARVN in order to divert American aid to economic development.[34] One of the explanations of the Việt Cộng success at Trảng Sụp was that the ARVN was too spread out along the border.[35] The ARVN defeat reaffirmed the concern of Williams but it also reinforced what Durbrow proposed. The ARVN needed to be better trained, equipped, and expanded in order to secure Vietnam's border but this would come at the expense of economic development. This was something Durbrow was not willing to concede.

The Trảng Sụp attack allowed for a review of tactics employed by the ARVN and gave Williams a chance to convey his concerns about the state of the Vietnamese army to Ngô Đình Diệm.[36] The Việt Cộng attacked at 2:30 a.m. after the troops had been celebrating the New Year. There were not enough sentries posted, which allowed the attackers to gain the element of surprise. He also criticized the policy of allowing the families of married personnel to stay with them while out in the field and questioned the practice of locking up weapons rather than allowing them to be accessible at all times. Williams also defended the colonel commanding the 21st ARVN Division, who had purportedly been replaced because of the attack, but had really been removed because he clashed with his commanding officer. Williams argued that the removal of a trusted commander for political reasons was bad for morale. It did not make sense to remove an officer who had the support of MAAG just to save the reputation of a commanding general who should ultimately assume the blame for the failure. The 21st ARVN Division's relief column did not arrive until after 3:00 p.m., even though the attack had taken place twelve hours earlier. This was not the fault of the local leader. Ngô Đình Diệm agreed but still believed he had to make the change in order to keep the peace.

The Trảng Sụp incident was one of, if not the largest, attack during the month of January that signaled increased Việt Cộng activity. In Long An province, twenty-six people were killed in targeted assassinations. The Việt Cộng assassinated several others, including hamlet leaders in Bình Dương and Kiến Hòa province, as part of a larger plan to throw the countryside into turmoil.[37] This increased Việt Cộng activity forced the Saigon Government to respond while Ngô Đình Diệm stepped up his inspection visits to the countryside to make sure that the people knew the government was present.[38] Rather than conduct himself in an aloof manner, as was reported by some in the American embassy, Ngô Đình Diệm made himself visible in a time of crisis. This might not have been reported by the embassy, but the evidence was available in the Saigon newspapers.[39]

The increased Việt Cộng activity in the countryside was just one of the many battlefields of Vietnam. Ngô Đình Diệm continued to pressure the United States for a greater military budget for the next fiscal year.[40] MAAG believed it would be operating at a budget of $169.3 million, which was less than the $185 million requested from Congress. Durbrow reduced the allocation by another $4.3 million with the justification that the ARVN would not be operating at full strength.

Durbrow argued that the difference between the original proposed sum and what was allocated could be bridged with customs receipts collected on Defense Support aid and other available Vietnamese resources. He believed this alternative would help to make the Vietnamese more self-sufficient.[41] While this may have been true, it came at a difficult time for the Vietnamese with the increased Việt Cộng activity. Ngô Đình Diệm asserted to Williams that the reduction in aid would show the North Vietnamese and Việt Cộng that the United States was not fully committed to Saigon.[42] Ever cognizant of the propaganda war, Ngô Đình Diệm asked for a public announcement of increased aid instead of a decrease to reaffirm the confidence of the people. However, when Ngô Đình Diệm met Durbrow on February 12, 1960, he did not bring up the proposed reduction, even after Durbrow hinted that he would be willing to discuss it. Instead, he offered some insight as to how the ARVN could counter the increased Việt Cộng activity.[43] Durbrow expected a fight, but instead received a dissertation on the flaws in ARVN organization and a lamentation on the inability to use the Civil Guard to combat this threat because it was tied down with staff or specialist duties or employed in static defensive positions.[44] In reporting the exchange, Durbrow complained that Ngô Đình Diệm did not let him enter into the conversation though he did note his surprise that the budget issue was not brought up.

One item that Ngô Đình Diệm did mention was the use of former NCOs and other enlisted personnel who had been demobilized. He argued that they needed to be recalled to help strengthen existing Civil Guard and ARVN units.[45] Durbrow did not support the plan and asserted that it was an attempt by Ngô Đình Diệm to increase American military assistance for the 1960 fiscal year. Where Durbrow focused on the budget and its ability to control the Vietnamese, Ngô Đình Diệm seemed more concerned about the security threat from the insurgency.

It was this lack of communication, and even the failure to communicate that would hamper the Durbrow–Ngô Đình Diệm relationship. The Brucker episode also reinforced the need that Durbrow had of controlling the situation in Saigon, just as he had tried to do earlier with the Cambodian crisis. Durbrow was dismayed with the 1959 election, concerned about the increased Việt Cộng activity, and frustrated by the Vietnamese president. Ngô Đình Diệm, for his part, was equally frustrated that the American ambassador seemed more interested in being an obstacle rather than helping to facilitate solutions to the many problems in his country. As a result, 1960 promised to be a difficult year for both sides as the situation in Vietnam deteriorated.

13

American Lines Divide Over Vietnam

Williams and Durbrow clashed on the methodology the Americans needed to use in advising Ngô Đình Diệm. For Williams, who found an ally in Lansdale, the American role was one of advisor who treated his ally firmly but with respect. Williams engaged in several long conversations with Ngô Đình Diệm since the two first met. There was never a moment when he complained about Ngô Đình Diệm dominating the conversation and Williams spoke freely when he conversed with, and not at, Ngô Đình Diệm. Durbrow, on the other hand, maintained that Ngô Đình Diệm needed to follow American advice in order to succeed. Durbrow, joined by Mendenhall and others from the Country Team, often complained of Ngô Đình Diệm's monologues and had a tendency to talk at, rather than talk with, the Vietnamese president. The distinction might not have seemed important, but for Ngô Đình Diệm, who was the leader of a country under threat, it was significant.

Lansdale had been involved with Vietnam since 1954 when he headed the Saigon Military Mission.[1] He took a more holistic approach as he viewed the obstacles facing the country. While he had been away from Vietnam for a few years, save for some letters to Williams, Lansdale refocused his attention in February. In a letter to Deputy Secretary of Defense, C. Douglas Dillon, Lansdale maintained that Vietnam faced both a political and military problem.[2] Lansdale was a proponent of Ngô Đình Diệm, whom he believed a strong leader, and argued that the United States needed to work with him rather than offer veiled threats of financial manipulation to achieve its goals in the region. This conflicted with Durbrow, which set up a clash between the two before the year was out.

One contested subject was how American Army Special Forces should train the Civil Guard.[3] Durbrow advocated anti-guerrilla instruction; Lansdale suggested counter-guerrilla training. Lansdale wanted the Civil Guard to conduct operations against the Việt Cộng rather than hold in static defensive positions as Durbrow had envisioned. Because the Communist insurgents could be anywhere and at any time, the only possible solution was taking the battle to them.[4] This was also Ngô Đình Diệm's position, which broadened the schism between Durbrow and Lansdale as the two vied for the Vietnamese president's influence. The political jockeying for power and influence was not limited to the Americans. Several Vietnamese had approached the Americans in Saigon about the rule of Ngô Đình Diệm since he first assumed power. The complaints had not changed since then though the recipient Americans had.

Minister of Agriculture Lê Văn Đông conveyed to Wolf Ladejinsky his worry about how Ngô Đình Diệm dealt with the Vietnamese peasants.[5] He complained that government officials were forcing policy without consulting local leaders. The implied assumption was that Ngô Đình Diệm approved, and even encouraged, this method. While Lê Văn Đông had a legitimate concern in the former, it was difficult to blame Ngô Đình Diệm for the acts of local government officials beyond the traditional argument that he was responsible for all of their actions as their president. Lê Văn Đông also commented on the failing morale within the ARVN officer corps because many had been passed over for promotion. He argued that political alignment was more important than military prowess. While Lê Văn Đông had grounds to complain about agricultural policy in Vietnam, his position vis-à-vis the military was less convincing. Lê Văn Đông offered second-hand information that he believed important but he had no reliable facts to back up his assertions other than the recent setbacks at the beginning of the year.[6] Ladejinsky passed along Lê Văn Đông's concerns, which he believed were genuine, and offered the warning that something needed to be done soon before it affected Ngô Đình Diệm's rule, though Durbrow interpreted the complaint as one that resulted from Lê Văn Đông's friends being passed over for promotion.[7]

Another Vietnamese who added his name to the list of Ngô Đình Diệm's critics was his private secretariat, Võ Văn Hải, who told Ladejinsky that the Cần Lao Party was involved in corruption.[8] He did not implicate Ngô Đình Diệm though it was clear that a solution needed to come from the top and it was not possible for this to happen. Both Ladejinsky and Durbrow recognized that members within the Saigon Government were reluctant to bring these issues up to Ngô Đình Diệm because they often involved members of his extended family.[9] Durbrow maintained that Ngô Đình Diệm's inner core of advisors told him what they thought he wanted to hear, which resulted in an unrealistic appraisal of the internal security situation. This may have been true though he offered no evidence that this was the case. Durbrow argued that Ngô Đình Diệm's request for a separate force to combat the Việt Cộng was based on faulty assumptions. He failed to acknowledge Williams' role in formulating the strategy or his attempts to influence Ngô Đình Diệm towards the American approach.

While Durbrow questioned Ngô Đình Diệm's position, he focused in on Ngô Đình Nhu as the principle culprit to the misinformation being disseminated in the Palace. Durbrow did credit Nguyễn Ngọc Thơ for trying to get an accurate accounting of the countryside to Ngô Đình Diệm.[10] As such, Durbrow recommended that Ngô Đình Nhu be eased out as an advisor to his brother so that others with a more realistic view of the situation could be in a better position to influence Ngô Đình Diệm. This included Nguyễn Ngọc Thơ and Durbrow, at the expense of Ngô Đình Nhu and the Cần Lao Party. While this might have been a sensible strategy from Durbrow's perspective, its implementation was too close to the old French Colonial method of manipulating the local leaders. Ngô Đình Diệm was aware of this, which further aided the growing rift between the president and ambassador. Heavner also provided negative reports on members of Ngô Đình Diệm's family. In a conversation with Phạm Ngọc Vinh, who had been the president of the Thừa Thiên Citizen's Rally, he learned that Ngô Đình Cẩn lived in near isolation and surrounded himself with only those who agreed with his decisions, regardless of their rationality.[11] Even though the two had had a long history, Phạm Ngọc Vinh was refused a meeting when he wanted to remove himself from Cần Lao Party activities, though this was not suggested as the reason for the negative assessment.

While Durbrow and the Country Team were concerned about Ngô Đình Diệm's family, Durbrow still offered mixed reports on the president himself. In noting the declining security within the countryside, Durbrow commended Ngô Đình Diệm for recognizing the seriousness of the situation.[12] However, Durbrow was still concerned about the fate of the National Assembly and worried over the freedom of the press when *Tự do* and *Buổi sang* were suspended for reporting too many Việt Cộng atrocities.[13] Durbrow saw this issue as a question of freedom of the press and ignored the suggestion that the papers were suspended for not verifying their facts rather than the nature of their stories.[14] Despite Ngô Đình Diệm's awareness of the situation, Durbrow argued that it was his policies and the increased Việt Cộng activity that accounted for the seriousness of the threat in the countryside. It was important to note that Durbrow did not report any of the positives originating from South Vietnam, such as the mass rallies for the Government or the ceremonies that marked defections from the North or the insurgency.[15]

When Ngô Đình Diệm offered a theory as to why the Việt Cộng had increased its activities, Durbrow dismissed it. Ngô Đình Diệm believed that the rising number of assassinations and kidnappings were designed to disrupt his Agroville Program.[16] The first Agroville at Vị Thanh and Hỏa Lựu in Phong Dinh Province was inaugurated during the week of March 12. The program was designed to gather up Vietnamese in the countryside who were vulnerable to the Việt Cộng and relocate them into protected areas while at the same time provide for them with the benefits of the modern world. Durbrow believed that the Agroville Program was the main reason why the people were unhappy. The source of the discontent was the need for volunteers, or corvée labor, which required people to neglect their own livelihood for the good of the community. The coercive nature of the program made the people fear and despise the local officials and served as useful recruiting propaganda for the Việt Cộng.[17]

The Agroville Program did have this and other shortcomings that Durbrow observed and Ngô Đình Diệm acknowledged. Ngô Đình Diệm started the process of fixing the program, though it would eventually be abandoned for another effort in 1962.[18] However, there were some successful Agrovilles. The Agrovilles at Vị Thanh and Hỏa Lựu in Phong Dinh Province were often mentioned as model Garden Cities, as Ngô Đình Diệm referred to them. On March 15, during a conversation about the program, Ngô Đình Diệm explained to Williams all of the improvements that had been made since the two Agrovilles had started.[19] Williams let Ngô Đình Diệm detail its benefits before letting him know that he had also visited the same Agrovilles and was also very impressed. Rather than cut him short, as Durbrow might have done, Williams allowed the president his laurels and then affirmed his support. That was the difference between Williams and Durbrow. Williams understood Ngô Đình Diệm and was willing to relinquish control of a conversation when his host was enthusiastic; Durbrow was not.

In addition to the Agroville Program, Ngô Đình Diệm also sought to counter the increased Việt Cộng activity with a 10,000-man commando unit. This force would deal with the newer strategy employed by the Việt Cộng, which now operated in larger groups and attacked more prominent targets, such as the one at Trảng Sụp.[20] The commando force would be divided into 131 companies. Durbrow did not think that the force was militarily necessary, arguing this point to Nguyễn Đình Thuận on March 3.[21] The combined strength of ARVN, the Civil Guard, and the Self-Defense Corps was approximately 230,000 personnel. This, he believed, was more than enough for the current threat level. Rather than diminish the effectiveness of the ARVN units by removing select personnel to create the Commando companies, Durbrow recommended rotating troops from training missions to meet the threat. Ngô Đình Diệm's plan had called for retired NCOs to return to duty with the commando companies rather than dilute ARVN, which addressed one of Durbrow's concerns though Williams, who was also opposed to the idea, shared Durbrow's concern regardless of Ngô Đình Diệm's assurances. He also worried that the force might not be equipped to do the specific job for which it was created.[22] In addition, funding was an issue which continued to frustrate

(*Left to right*) Tôn Thất Đính, Nguyễn Đình Thuận, Linh Quang Viên, and Nguyễn Cao Kỳ, 1959. Arthur Z. Gardiner Papers (2014-1587) (Harry S. Truman Library & Museum).

Ngô Đình Diệm, as the USOM held back money for projects until Ngô adhered to their plans. This was true for the commandos as it had been for the Civil Guard.[23] Even as Williams opposed the idea, he was willing to work with Ngô Đình Diệm to find a better compromise and still represented the military needs of the Vietnamese in a way to maximize the American assistance program.[24]

Williams and Lansdale were most concerned with the extent to which Ngô Đình Diệm controlled the military. Williams criticized Ngô Đình Diệm's handling of selecting the military leadership in Vietnam but he did it in a way that was respectful and self-reflective.[25] This was a trait that Durbrow might have had when he first arrived in Saigon but had lost along the way. Williams questioned the individual military control of some of the Province Chiefs who had no military background, which had led to poor decisions, or in some case indecision, during a critical stage in an operation. Ngô Đình Diệm accepted the criticism and informed Williams that the Mekong Delta region, a principle area of concern, was to come under the military control of Colonel Nguyễn Khánh, who had earlier replaced Colonel Nguyễn Văn Y as commander of the Fifth Military Region.[26] This was good news to Williams, who was concerned about the Delta. He believed Nguyễn Khánh, if given a free hand in operations, would turn the situation to the positive.[27]

Because internal security became the predominant topic in early 1960, it seemed inevitable that Williams and Durbrow would clash. The two men had different ideas on how American assistance to Vietnam should be distributed and they shared conflicting views on the ability of Ngô Đình Diệm to lead the country. Williams had already confided in Ngô Đình Diệm that Durbrow was working against him as it related to the level of the military aid package for Vietnam and that members of the Country Team were reluctant to use American dollars to help fund the commando companies.[28] If the commando companies were created, Durbrow would count them within the 150,000-man ceiling for ARVN that would be funded by the Department of Defense. In telling Ngô Đình Diệm this, Williams confirmed the Vietnamese president's fears that Durbrow was working against him and doing so in a disreputable way. In confiding to Ngô Đình Diệm, Williams was also exposing his split with Durbrow as this type of admission about the ambassador would only serve to harm the fragile relationship that Ngô Đình Diệm and Durbrow held. Before the Williams-Durbrow conflict, Durbrow and Ngô Đình Diệm would clash.

On March 10, Durbrow and Ngô Đình Diệm met before the president's departure for a state visit to Malaya.[29] Ngô Đình Diệm informed Durbrow that he had already gathered 4,500 commando volunteers for the new companies. Durbrow renewed his disapproval of the plan, only to be countered with another dissertation on the internal security threat in the Mekong Delta. After more pleas for better weapons to fight the Việt Cộng and a generally negative air about the meeting, Durbrow reported to Washington that Ngô Đình Diệm was using the commando scheme to get more military aid to exceed the 150,000-personnel ceiling. After the meeting, Durbrow aggressively pushed for economic, political, and military reforms to win the allegiance of the Vietnamese people and improve internal security, which countered Ngô Đình Diệm's plan to defeat the Việt Cộng militarily before enacting economic or political reform. While both men wanted to see Vietnam free from subversion, they held different plans on how to accomplish it. As the months progressed, Durbrow's point of view seeped into the political and military discussions about the future of Vietnam.[30]

Another plan to deal with the internal security threat that originated from the American embassy came from Chalmers Wood. He suggested that either Malaya or the Philippines be asked to send personnel to advise the Ministers of Defense and Interior, as well as placing advisors at the Province level.[31] Malayan advisors were preferred given their recent success against a Communist insurgency. There were a number of problems associated with this idea, as Lansdale would communicate to Williams, that demonstrated a disconnect between the Americans in Saigon and the Vietnamese.[32] First, and most significant, the Malayan affair was a colonial experience and the idea of transferring one colonial experiment to a country that had just rid itself of the French was inadvisable. Second, the two countries had very different insurgent histories and the suggestion that triumph in Vietnam was assured because there had been the same in Malaya seemed fallacious. Lansdale also argued that there were Americans in Vietnam advising the Vietnamese already who could do the same job as the Malayans without the tint of a colonial past. It made little sense to him to complicate the situation further with Wood's proposal.

While both Lansdale and Williams would point out the cultural insensitivities of these types of plans, they continued to gain ground in Washington as the United States grappled with the ongoing threat in Vietnam. The Vietnamese shared this concern, but had a hard time reconciling the commitment of the United States to see the problem through to its successful conclusion with the shrinking financial contributions at a time when American aid and support was most needed. In early April, Nguyễn Đình Thuận traveled to the United States to discuss these issues. With Vietnamese ambassador Trần Văn Chương, he met with Parsons and other State Department officials on April 4.[33] Nguyễn Đình Thuận focused the conversation on American aid, which had declined 38 percent since 1956 and enumerated the consequences the diminishing budget had on programs that counter the Việt Cộng, such as the Agrovilles and Republican Youth Movement. American aid was paramount in Nguyễn Đình Thuận's thinking and the real purpose for his visit to Washington. For Parsons, the American agenda included internal security, Cambodia, and the value of foreign exchange. Regarding Cambodia, Parsons suggested that the Vietnamese compromise with the Cambodians, though he was quick to point out that the United States did not want to dictate to the Vietnamese what they should do. He offered similar remarks as it related to foreign currency. In true diplomatic fashion, Parsons used a feint to reluctantly mention uncomfortable topics for the Vietnamese in an apologetic way in an effort to seek resolution favorable to U.S. policy in Southeast Asia.

Nguyễn Đình Thuận was not fooled by the move, nor was he comfortable with the direction of the conversation. He dismissed the topic of foreign exchange, as that was not a part of his expertise; this was something Parsons should have known. Regarding Cambodia, Nguyễn Đình Thuận maintained that the Vietnamese would send a delegation to that country after Ngô Đình Diệm's state visit to Malaya. Nguyễn Đình Thuận did remark that he could not go to Cambodia because he was in Washington and could not be in two places at once, which suggested either frustration at the broaching of the subject or an attempt to diplomatically respond to Parsons.[34] It was clear that Nguyễn Đình Thuận's primary concern, the decline of military aid, was not the most important issue for the Americans at the meeting, which must have caused some concern for the Vietnamese delegation.

Nguyễn Đình Thuận met with Parsons again before he left. When he brought up the military contributions topic again, Parsons informed him that the situation would not be altered until two other issues were resolved. Ngô Đình Diệm had to deal with the corruption with the Cần Lao Party and the Vietnamese president needed to improve his relationship with his people.[35] Parsons informed Nguyễn Đình Thuận that Durbrow had already passed along these concerns to Ngô Đình Diệm while Nguyễn Đình Thuận had been traveling and that he needed to speak with Durbrow upon his return. Nguyễn Đình Thuận did address these issues but the tone of the conversation suggested that Durbrow was the primary point of contact on all matters related to Vietnam. Nguyễn Đình Thuận would need to wait until he returned to Vietnam to address these, and other, issues. When Nguyễn Đình Thuận met with Durbrow on April 21, they did not discuss the military budget. Durbrow reported that Nguyễn Đình Thuận was pleased but alluded to his frustration in communicating Vietnam's needs to Parsons.[36] The positive tone of the meeting may have been true, or it might have been Durbrow's description of what was a downward-spiraling relationship with the Vietnamese.

The meeting between Durbrow and Ngô Đình Diệm, to which Parsons referred, took place on April 7. Durbrow asked for the meeting to discuss the possibility of an additional $4.6 million allocation, but he used the time to outline reports of alleged Cần Lao corruption. Durbrow warned that American aid would be lost if the Cần Lao Party was not reformed.[37] Durbrow, who claimed to be speaking as a friend, told Ngô Đình Diệm that he had evidence of criminal behavior but refused to provide the documentation when Ngô Đình Diệm asked for it. Ngô Đình Diệm also argued that the source of Durbrow's evidence might be his opposition, which should make it suspect. Most likely he was correct, as Durbrow did not want to reveal his sources. There was no way to gauge what Ngô Đình Diệm thought of the conversation, though an ally who threatened to withdraw additional aid because of alleged corruption, of which he had evidence he refused to share, must have rankled the president.

Later, in the conversation, Durbrow agreed that the evidence might not be accurate but he was concerned about its persistence and he did eventually outline some of the consequences of the activities. If the abundance, rather than accuracy, of the allegations was the litmus test for Durbrow, then Ngô Đình Diệm had no chance with the ambassador when faced with an intelligentsia opposed to him and a propaganda organization in Hanoi that far surpassed the one in Saigon. Durbrow would also repeat his concerns to Nguyễn Ngọc Thơ and Nguyễn Đình Thuận and believed that both men were sympathetic to his argument but unable to do anything about it because of fear of reprisals from Ngô Đình Diệm or his brothers.[38]

Ladejinsky informed Durbrow that Ngô Đình Diệm had discussed the allegations with him after the meeting. Durbrow concluded that he had made his point and asserted that the Vietnamese president was concerned now that the Americans knew of the illicit dealings of the Cần Lao Party or would start to investigate it more seriously.[39] He did not consider the possibility that Ngô Đình Diệm was angered and confused by Durbrow's refusal to provide the evidence so that the problems could be addressed, and neither did he acknowledge the response to a threat to withhold additional aid if that problem was not corrected.[40] Just as the relationship between Ngô Đình Diệm and Durbrow was beginning to show signs of strain, so was the rapport between the ambassador and Williams. During Durbrow's tenure, it was clear that Williams had a better relationship with Ngô Đình Diệm, which might have annoyed the ambassador. With the internal security threat on the rise within the first few months of 1960 and the clash with Ngô Đình Diệm fresh on his mind, Durbrow turned against Williams and accused him of offering conflicting advice and guidance to ARVN.

In an April 19 letter to Parsons, Durbrow criticized Williams for advocating conventional training for ARVN rather than focusing on anti-guerrilla warfare.[41] He based this assumption on an exchange between army attaché Colonel Richard Comstock and Colonel Nguyễn Ngọc Khôi, who served as the Chief of Staff to the Deputy Secretary of State for National Defense, Trần Trung Dũng. Nguyễn Ngọc Khôi maintained that MAAG wanted ARVN to move away from anti-guerrilla training in two letters dated July 14 and November 10, 1958, which Williams had sent to the ARVN Chief of Staff. In what seemed a contradiction, Williams also provided Durbrow with a plan that called for commando training in Nhà Trắng and widespread anti-guerrilla training. This proposal was dated September 7, 1958. With Comstock present and Williams not informed about the nature of the meeting, Durbrow confronted Williams about the inconsistencies on April 12. The meeting did not go well. Durbrow may have been genuinely concerned about these events from 1958 though he might have also been pushing for this confrontation to discredit Williams, with whom he was less than cordial. Regardless, the meeting confirmed that the two were at odds. After the exchange, Durbrow sent Williams a memorandum that he also forwarded to Parsons.[42] The document, which was highly critical of Williams, was most likely for Parsons, as Durbrow placed the blame for Vietnam's military failure on the MAAG.

When Williams met with Ngô Đình Diệm on April 13, the Comstock–Nguyễn Ngọc Khôi exchange was reviewed.[43] Ngô Đình Diệm immediately called for his aide to find Nguyễn Ngọc Khôi and Trần Trung Dũng so that they could explain themselves. Ngô Đình Diệm was not as easily persuaded about the alleged inconsistency as had been Durbrow. While they waited, Ngô Đình Diệm offered a possible reason for the misunderstanding, suggesting that Nguyễn Ngọc Khôi had most likely misunderstood Trần Trung

Dũng. Ngô Đình Diệm was clearly bothered by how upset Williams was and was looking for a way to assuage the concerned Williams. Ngô Đình Diệm vowed that the two men would explain themselves, though Williams thought it better that they clear up the matter with Durbrow. Just as Ngô Đình Diệm had an ally in Williams, Williams possessed the same with Ngô Đình Diệm. Both began to see Durbrow as another obstacle in Vietnam.

While the conflict within American circles affected Ngô Đình Diệm, it paled in comparison to the other event that occurred in April. On April 26, The Bloc for Liberty and Progress met in the Caravelle Hotel in Saigon and published a document, later referred to as the Caravelle Manifesto, which was highly critical of Ngô Đình Diệm. The eighteen members of the group, all prominent Saigon businessmen, community leaders, or politicians, demanded that Ngô Đình Diệm reform his government or allow other politicians an opportunity to do so. The Caravelle Manifesto questioned Ngô Đình Diệm's early record in defending Vietnam against French Colonial rule and in some ways paralleled the Communist propaganda emanating from Hanoi.[44] It was a direct challenge to Ngô Đình Diệm from the Saigon intelligentsia, most of whom had ties to the former emperor Bảo Đại or had been involved with the Cao Đài, Hòa Hảo, or Bình Xuyên.[45] While members of the Caravelle Manifesto claimed that the document was a call for Ngô Đình Diệm to act and that they supported the continued progression of the Republic of Vietnam, it was clearly an attempt to make him react and thus lose credibility with the people of Saigon and the United States. It outlined all of the problems in Vietnam's political arena, including corruption, intimidation, and non-democratic practices. The Caravelle Manifesto called on Ngô Đình Diệm to fix these problems, end the Agroville Program, and reform the Cần Lao Party.

Ngô Đình Diệm did not take the bait to react. During the political life of the Caravelle Manifesto, he chose to ignore it, which did not sit well with Durbrow and some members of the Country Team, even after they learned the entire history behind the movement. Ngô Đình Diệm did not believe the authors of the Caravelle Manifesto were legitimate and refused to accept that they represented anything more than a group of failed politicians who wanted to have their voice heard. They offered no solutions but only highlighted what they believed to be problems. Ngô Đình Diệm had other, more significant, concerns to deal with at this time.

Interestingly, the Country Team was aware of the Caravelle Manifesto before its release. Comstock, who had been involved in the earlier Williams-Durbrow controversy, was contacted by Gonder, who had been discredited in the Colegrove article dispute. In their March 15 conversation, Gonder informed Comstock that the former Minister of National Economy under Bảo Đại, Trần Văn Văn, and the Vice-Chairman of the Vietnamese Red Cross, Dr. Hồ Văn Nhựt. had formed a group in opposition to Ngô Đình Diệm.[46]

The group planned to provide Ngô Đình Diệm with their document in early April. Comstock learned all of this from Gonder, who had assumed the unofficial role as liaison between the Embassy and the opposition group. The two would meet several more times before the Manifesto was released, during which time Gonder relayed the message that the group wanted Ngô Đình Diệm removed from office by peaceful means if possible or by force if necessary. On April 11, Gonder handed Comstock a copy of the Manifesto, a full two weeks before it was released. Mendenhall then reported its contents to Washington, and he and Durbrow kept the information to themselves before the final release of the Manifesto on April 26.

While neither Mendenhall nor Durbrow held much confidence in Gonder, they did not share the document with Ngô Đình Diệm. Both would echo the complaints listed in the Caravelle Manifesto in the months to come, even as Durbrow maintained that the group was harmless.[47] It was for this reason that Durbrow chose not to inform Ngô Đình Diệm. While this may have been true, it was also possible that Durbrow withheld the information so that its release would have a greater impact on Ngô Đình Diệm. The document paralleled Durbrow's thinking and he must have seen the benefits of a Vietnamese voice added to his own to try to compel Ngô Đình Diệm to reform his government. The Caravelle Manifesto was affirmation that he had correctly interpreted the situation. Durbrow developed a strategy to deal with Ngô Đình Diệm if the Vietnamese president questioned him about knowledge of the document before it was released. That eventuality was possible.[48] Rather than acknowledge that this significant information had been withheld, Durbrow suggested informing Ngô Đình Diệm that the United States Embassy had already issued multiple warnings to Ngô Đình Diệm that this type of action was inevitable and confirmed the need for reform. This begs the question, if the group's message was harmless and thus not worth informing Ngô Đình Diệm about it in advance, why did the ambassador use it to reaffirm his stance that Ngô Đình Diệm needed to initiate reforms? Durbrow was playing a dangerous diplomatic game.

The Williams-Durbrow clash signaled an open break in how the United States would work with Vietnam in 1960. Underlying tension had been evident earlier but the nature of the public conflict and its significance was not lost on Ngô Đình Diệm. The release of the Caravelle Manifesto, the internal American conflict, and Durbrow's handling of Ngô Đình Diệm resulted in the possibility of an even greater disaster as frayed nerves, domestic bickering, and mixed loyalties all contributed to the deepening divide within Vietnam.

14

The Vietnam Triangle: Durbrow, Lansdale and Williams

Any long-term significance for the Caravelle Manifesto had diminished within a few months. The Bloc for Liberty and Progress failed to elicit a response from Ngô Đình Diệm, which meant it also never gained the legitimacy it needed to be a viable opposition to the Vietnamese president. While the group did not gain support within Saigon, Durbrow reported that news and acceptance of its Manifesto had spread rapidly around the capital. This might have been a misinterpretation caused by the individuals who approached American Embassy personnel to gauge their reaction about the group and document.[1] Ngô Đình Diệm never acknowledge the significance of the group and told Williams that it was less important than Durbrow had suggested.[2] The Bloc for Liberty and Progress had failed to organize the people of Saigon for its April 30 rally and was further frustrated by Ngô Đình Nhu, who convinced the trade unions to hold their May 1 rallies inside rather than in the streets so that they would not be connected to the group. Because the group lacked leadership and was disorganized, it slowly faded away from the political scene.[3] It certainly did not have the support of the Saigon dailies.[4]

While the Caravelle Manifesto was nothing more than a minor irritant for Ngô Đình Diệm, the way that Durbrow handled the affair was more significant. He withheld information from Ngô Đình Diệm about the document which allowed for the maximum possible effect when it was released. While the proclamation of the Caravelle Manifesto failed to gain ground in the opposition's attempt to discredit the Vietnamese president, it did reaffirm to Ngô Đình Diệm that his list of friends and allies in the United States embassy was growing shorter. Durbrow had made it clear to Ngô Đình Diệm that he represented an American approach to solving Vietnam's problems and would confront any threats or obstacles to that approach, even other Americans, if it meant success for Vietnam.

In the midst of the Caravelle Manifesto, another controversy was brewing. This time it was in Washington and involved Edward Lansdale. Nguyễn Duy Liên, who served as the counselor in the Vietnamese embassy in Washington, met with Deputy Director of the Office of Southeast Asian Affairs, Richard Usher, and the Officer in Charge of Cambodian Affairs, Laurin Askew. During the course of the meeting, Nguyễn Duy Liên passed along a request from Ngô Đình Diệm to have Lansdale travel to Vietnam and offer advice to solve the internal security issue.[5] Durbrow rejected the idea.[6] Not only should have the request come through him, but he also suspected that the move was designed to either diminish his influence in Saigon or strengthen Williams' faction in Vietnam. Durbrow framed his rejection of the proposal in more diplomatic terms.

He argued that a visit by Lansdale would provide too much propaganda fodder for the North Vietnamese, and would outweigh any benefits. He also questioned Lansdale's expertise on anti-guerrilla operations and suggested that his involvement was redundant at best, given the recent arrival of three British experts from Malaya. Nonetheless, Durbrow was savvy enough to realize that some indulgence was needed with Ngô Đình Diệm's request so he suggested bringing American experts in on a temporary basis. This, he concluded, should satisfy Ngô Đình Diệm and was a much better option than Lansdale.[7] Lansdale entered this fray on April 25 with a memorandum on Vietnam's internal security that he sent to secretary to the General Staff of the United States Army, Major General Charles H. Bonesteel.[8] In it, he criticized Durbrow's counterinsurgency strategy, suggesting that the introduction of British officers, who had gained their expertise in a colonial environment, might not be the best choice for a country experiencing the same problems but recently rid of its colonial past. It was true that Ngô Đình Diệm had requested three British officers after his recent trip to Malaya, but Lansdale maintained that the British model in Malaya would not work in Vietnam. He also argued that Vietnamese officers who had traveled to Malaya had been treated as colonials by the British, even if Ngô Đình Diệm had had a more pleasant reception.

Like Ngô Đình Diệm, Williams was anxious to get Lansdale to Vietnam. He recognized the importance of surrounding the Vietnamese president with Americans he could trust and welcomed an ally against Durbrow. Williams was also growing tired of the political struggle between himself and Durbrow as the latter vied for a position of power in their relationship. The two corresponded at the end of April, with Lansdale requesting Williams' help in getting the invitation approved and Williams confirming that Lansdale represented a threat to Durbrow.[9] When Williams met with Ngô Đình Diệm on May 9, they discussed the Lansdale situation and the reasons the invitation had been rejected by Durbrow.[10] Ngô Đình Diệm understood the political division among his American allies and sought to dispel the growing tension. During a visit of the former commander-in-chief, Pacific Admiral Felix B. Stump, Ngô Đình Diệm requested that he intervene and told Stump that Durbrow and his staff, "were out to get General Williams."[11] Durbrow still held the upper hand, however, and his allies in Washington possessed more influence on the situation in Vietnam than those of Williams and Lansdale.

Durbrow understood that he stood opposed to Williams and Ngô Đình Diệm and during the early days of May, he reconstituted criticisms against the Vietnamese president. Durbrow enumerated the problems with Ngô Đình Diệm's rule in a May 3 telegram, which highlights included support for the Movement of the Free Khmers and their broadcasts and the Vietnamese response to the contested islands in the Gulf of Thailand.[12] Durbrow also continued to report on the alleged corruption of the Cần Lao Party. While he placed most of the blame for these developments on Ngô Đình Nhu, he complained of Ngô Đình Diệm's failure to control his brother.[13] With the Caravelle Manifesto and Lansdale controversies hanging over Saigon, Durbrow proposed a more drastic move against Ngô Đình Diệm in order to force the Vietnamese president to reform and improve the American position in Southeast Asia.[14] It was Durbrow's intention to be authorized to tell Ngô Đình Diệm that the United States would withhold American aid unless he reformed the Cần Lao Party and ceased in assisting the Free Khmer Movement. Durbrow maintained that this was the only way to make Ngô Đình Diệm realize the seriousness of the situation and accept that something needed to be done.

Durbrow's former Second Secretary and Political Officer, Chalmers B. Wood, who was now the Officer in Charge of Vietnam Affairs in the State Department, provided a response.[15] Joined by the Director of the Office of Southeast Asian Affairs Daniel Anderson, the two authorized Durbrow to do what he thought necessary to save the situation. The document, however, needed to be approved by the Office of the Assistant Secretary of Defense (International Security Affairs), which meant that Lansdale had an opportunity to reject this plan. It also signaled that the Durbrow-Williams dispute was now extended to Washington as the Departments of State and Defense supported their principle representatives in Saigon.[16]

Wood continued to advocate the Durbrow line in Washington. On May 5, he joined Deputy Assistant Secretary of Defense for International Security Affairs Robert Knight and Lieutenant Colonel Joseph Flesch, who represented the Far East Region for International Security Affairs, in recommending that the United States withhold emergency military equipment from the Republic of Vietnam, though Knight stood as the representative of Lansdale and offered the consequences to such a move.[17] Wood used Durbrow's false claim that the recommendation was Williams' and argued that it was necessary to make the move even though it might put Ngô Đình Diệm at a disadvantage in his fight against the Việt Cộng. As Wood advocated for Durbrow in Washington, Durbrow was hard at work gathering allies among the diplomatic corps in Saigon. He found a willing partner in Lalouette, who had always been wary of Ngô Đình Diệm, and support from the Federal Republic of Germany ambassador, Baron Von Wendland, who bemoaned the influence of the Cần Lao Party, which was interfering with Germany's attempts to exploit the lumber industry in Vietnam.[18]

Durbrow received an answer to his request to use aid as a leverage to affect policy change on May 9, though it was different than the original response that had been drafted by Wood.[19] Durbrow was instructed to inform Ngô Đình Diệm about the concerns raised in his original telegram to Washington but he was not allowed to issue the threat of withholding additional aid. He met with Ngô Đình Diệm on May 13, though an earlier meeting between Durbrow, Williams, Ladejinsky, and Ngô Đình Diệm had predetermined the tone for the May 13 confrontation.[20] During the earlier May 11 meeting, Ngô Đình Diệm singled out Williams for praise and was supposedly critical of Durbrow in a show of support for the general, who Ngô Đình Diệm believed was being eased out of Saigon.[21] Durbrow entered the meeting in a disadvantageous position, having failed to get his desired instructions from Washington and having his adversarial position versus Williams exposed. During the meeting, Ngô Đình Diệm had his secretary, Võ Văn Hải, provide a series of transcripts of questionable press messages related to a May 2, 1960, incident along the Vietnamese-Cambodia border and asserted that Durbrow had been their source. After some conversation that Major John Dolan, who was responsible for transcribing the meeting, noted could not be heard by the other participants, Durbrow appeared to have admitted his role. This may have been a moral victory for Ngô Đình Diệm, though it did not mean that Durbrow had altered his position.

After this exchange, Durbrow read, in French, the list of concerns that the United States had about Vietnam, suggesting that this apprehension was shared by many in Washington. While Durbrow believed that Ngô Đình Diệm acknowledged the list, he reported that the Vietnamese president responded forcefully to the allegation that the Cần Lao Party was corrupt.[22] The Vietnamese did not offer an official reply to Durbrow's written instructions until June 20. On that day, ambassador Trần Văn Chương shared with the State Department Ngô Đình Diệm's resentment of the allegations.[23] Ngô Đình Diệm could not control all of the inner workings of the Cần Lao Party and he was making an attempt to stabilize relations with Cambodia, though Sihanouk was not making it easy. While there was evidence that members of the Cần Lao Party engaged in questionable acts, which Ngô Đình Diệm did not support, Durbrow used this issue as a rallying point to put pressure on him. This caused Ngô Đình Diệm anxiety not only because he and Durbrow agreed on the need for eliminating corrupt practices, but also because Durbrow had refused to provide specific information about corrupt individuals when the Vietnamese president had asked. Ngô Đình Diệm wanted to filter rumors and stories of corruption from actual acts that negatively impacted the Republic. He wanted to use Durbrow as an ally while Durbrow seemed to want to use the issue as a political point to force additional reforms.

While Durbrow may not have seen the desired results in his meeting with Ngô Đình Diệm, he was having more success in his efforts to deny Lansdale's visit to Saigon. Deputy Assistant Secretary of State for Far East Affairs John Steeves met with Deputy Secretary of Defense James Dillon, Knight, and Wood on May 13 to renew the discussion.[24] Steeves represented the Durbrow position and maintained that Lansdale had a reputation for not following the plan. He referred to Lansdale's time with the Saigon Military Mission, citing old reports. In reality, Steeves did not want Lansdale in Saigon because he would serve as a conduit to Ngô Đình Diệm that might bypass Durbrow. It would be difficult for Durbrow to exert pressure on Ngô Đình Diệm to reform if Lansdale was available as an alternative or liaison to the ambassador. This was a dangerous proposition as Trần Văn Chương explained to Dillon earlier. Lansdale was available to Ngô Đình Diệm during a critical time in 1954. In many ways, 1960 paralleled those earlier times and denying Lansdale a presence would signal to the Vietnamese president that the United States either did not understand the significance of the current situation or was less of an ally than it had been six years earlier.[25] Durbrow's role in blocking the visit for which Ngô Đình Diệm must have been aware did nothing to improve their relationship.

One result of the Steeves-Dillon meeting was an agreement to allow Lansdale a 60-day temporary duty assignment to Vietnam under Durbrow's supervision. Durbrow accepted this though he continued to question the value of the mission.[26] He argued that Lansdale's knowledge of Vietnam was outdated and asserted that he needed to be the one to brief him. He also required that Lansdale provide him with complete and accurate reporting of his conversations with Ngô Đình Diệm and follow his specific instructions. Durbrow might not have known that Lansdale had already been in contact with Williams, or he had offered these conditions as a direct insult to the MAAG general, who he had come to accept as another adversary.[27]

While the situation in Washington was slowly beginning to resolve itself, Durbrow continued to create conditions in Saigon that were designed to discredit Ngô Đình Diệm. During a May 17 Country Team meeting, Durbrow announced that members of the diplomatic corps had asked him if the United States was looking to replace Ngô Đình Diệm, with the suggestion that information his confrontations with Ngô had been publicized.[28] Williams, who was well aware that this conversation would reach Vietnamese in Saigon who opposed Ngô Đình Diệm, wondered why Durbrow would initiate it. He was also surprised when Durbrow asked him if ARVN commander Dương Văn Minh might replace Ngô Đình Diệm.[29] Williams, who could not believe Durbrow posed the question at the Country Team meeting, asked him to repeat it. Such a statement would be the natural source for rumors within Saigon and could only provide those who were already opposed to Ngô Đình Diệm the false sense that the Americans in Saigon were sympathetic to their plight.

The question of whether Lansdale would be allowed to travel to Saigon was resolved on May 19. Parsons and Knight agreed that the request should be denied because it would diminish Durbrow's stature at a time when the United States needed him to apply pressure on Ngô Đình Diệm for reform.[30] Allowing Lansdale to go to Vietnam, Parsons maintained, would be a reward for Ngô Đình Diệm that he had not earned. While Knight, representing the Department of Defense, had been an advocate for Lansdale, he informed Parsons that the Pentagon would not pursue the matter if the Department of State was wholly opposed to it.[31] Durbrow may have lost the battle to get instructions from Washington to threaten to withhold aid from Ngô Đình Diệm without a plan to reform, but he won in the fight to keep Ngô Đình Diệm isolated from Americans who were sympathetic to him.

By the end of the Lansdale affair, Williams and Durbrow were at opposite ends of how to work and treat their Vietnamese allies. Durbrow had the upper hand in the relationship as Williams was occupied by inquiries from Senator Mike Mansfield (Montana–D) on MAAG organization and its use of personnel through the Temporary Equipment Recovery Mission. While attempting to deflect allegations that TERM personnel constituted a violation of the 1954 Geneva Agreements, Williams was also involved in finishing a memorandum on ARVN training that Durbrow had requested earlier.[32] There was little time to spar politically with the ambassador even if Williams had any desire to do so. Williams' time in Vietnam was near its end as the MAAG chief was scheduled to leave in a few months. While the Department of Defense failed to consult the Department of State on Williams' replacement, it was in a position of strength in Vietnam that would allow for its way of thinking to prevail. When Williams' replacement, Lieutenant General Lionel C. McGarr, was announced, Parsons schemed to make sure that he was briefed in a way that would help Durbrow rather than continue the Williams line of thinking.[33] Parsons wanted McGarr to be malleable regarding the Department of States' stance on Vietnam.

Lansdale had other ideas, however. Aware of the unwanted influences directed toward McGarr, he asked Williams to return to Washington to help with the fight against the Department of State and also consider extending his time in Vietnam beyond his retirement date.[34] Williams, however, was not ready for this political struggle and, in addition to conceding that the

Department of State had the upper hand in Vietnam, informed Lansdale that he did not want to become a political sacrifice in this losing battle. Williams had been in Vietnam since October 1955 and was completing a military career that started in 1916. The fight in Washington was more than he was willing to take on. Durbrow may have won the battle against Williams, but his struggle against Ngô Đình Diệm was far from over.

The months of April and May were difficult for Ngô Đình Diệm. He found few allies in Saigon and even fewer in Washington. Lansdale may have been denied him but he still had Williams, even though the General was due to leave soon. On June 2, the two met to discuss internal security, though domestic politics did make an appearance.[35] Ngô Đình Diệm admitted that there was criticism of his actions from members of his cabinet but he rejected opposition from outside the formal government as coming from war profiteers. These individuals were making more money than his government appointees and he thought it ironic that they would complain of corruption when they were the principle instigators of such practices. As with many of his conversations with Williams, Ngô Đình Diệm expressed his frustrations at a double standard in a way that he could not with Durbrow. Ngô Đình Diệm did not acknowledge, however, that any alleged corruption in the

General Samuel T. Williams (center), October 1959. Arthur Z. Gardiner Papers (2014-1511) (Harry S. Truman Library & Museum).

Saigon Government discredited it, regardless of where the allegations originated. This would remain one of Durbrow's most effective means to question Ngô Đình Diệm's continued rule.

Ngô Đình Diệm was aware of the discussions among the Americans, Vietnamese, and members of the diplomatic corps who deliberated his fate and possible replacement. Williams was correct in assuming that such rumors would eventually make their way to the Palace. On June 10, Ngô Đình Diệm informed Ladejinsky that he was concerned with the American stance toward the Caravelle Group.[36] Ngô Đình Diệm maintained that Frank Gonder, as the liaison between the Embassy and the Americans, was the principle troublemaker, and claimed that he was supported by members of the Embassy. Ladejinsky denied this assertion, which most likely reassured him, but it did not put him at complete ease. There were still Americans in Saigon who actively worked to discredit him. Theodore Heavner, as the consul in Huế, continued to write reports that reaffirmed the questionable actions of Ngô Đình Cẩn and his rule in Central Vietnam.[37] Heavner had been critical of all members of the Ngô family and was quick to report any observations that confirmed his position.

In addition to the Heavner reports, Durbrow was persistent in informing Washington of the divisions among the Vietnamese in Saigon. He reported that Nguyễn Ngọc Thơ had shied away from discussions with Americans because of Ngô Đình Diệm and the fear that any such talks would be a mark against the vice president.[38] In the atmosphere of distrust associated with the Caravelle Manifesto, Durbrow argued that Nguyễn Ngọc Thơ did not want to be seen as collaborating with Ngô Đình Diệm's adversaries. This may have been true but it also reflected poorly on Durbrow and his Country Team, who allowed such conditions to develop. Some criticisms of Ngô Đình Diệm's actions were easy to report even if their political significance was suspect, such as the passage of laws 3/60 and 4/60, which fixed a tax on beer and soft drinks. Durbrow had no trouble finding individuals opposed to these laws among the urban intelligentsia.[39] There were other criticisms, however, that were seen as much more important in Washington. One such voice came from Professor Joseph Zasloff, whose negative report on the Agroville at Tân Lược in Vĩnh Long province was significant.[40] Zasloff maintained that the Agroville used forced unpaid labor that negated any benefits of the project.[41] Another dispatch accompanied the July 14 one on Zasloff and the Agroville Program that discussed the potential role for Ngô Đình Luyện, the Vietnamese ambassador to the United Kingdom and Ngô Đình Diệm's younger brother.[42] While Durbrow's assessment of Ngô Đình Luyện was positive, his suggestion that he replace Ngô Đình Nhu as Ngô Đình Diệm's principle advisor harkened back to the French colonial days.

Even as Durbrow and his Country Team jockeyed for position in Saigon,

Ngô Đình Diệm seemed more focused on the threat to the internal security of his country. He met with Williams on July 25 to discuss his summer and fall strategy.[43] He hoped it would be boosted by the creation of the National Security Council to coordinate Vietnamese intelligence agencies and the reorganization of the 1st and 5th Military Regions, which meant that General Nguyễn Khánh, who oversaw the new area, would be given additional responsibilities. Williams agreed but also cautioned Ngô Đình Diệm that he needed to strengthen the officer corps and improve on the high failure rate of his commando units. Durbrow's concern about the commandos was that they raised the Vietnamese troop levels above the 150,000 limit established by American aid. He was also concerned by the high number of Civil Guard personnel that exceeded the 50,000 limit.[44]

It was important to note that the events that affected Vietnam in 1960 were not isolated in a Saigon vacuum, though most of the American reporting originated from there. Ngô Đình Diệm had made continuous calls for both Americans and Vietnamese in Saigon to get a sense of what was transpiring in the countryside by visiting strategic locations throughout the country. A firsthand examination was better than relying on reports. This lack of perspective applied to many of the American groups that did fact-finding tours and offered significant policy recommendations, but only visited Saigon or another large urban center for a few days. It also applied to many Vietnamese in Saigon. Ngô Đình Diệm urged National Assembly members to visit the countryside as did some of the Saigon dailies.[45] Those who did so were usually praised by the Government leadership, but it was never enough.[46]

While not all Vietnamese leaders would heed Ngô Đình Diệm's advice, many would find their way to the Americans to voice their position on the political situation. Not all of the dialogue was negative, however, though how the Americans chose to view the positives was revealing. During a trip to Washington in early August, president of the National Assembly Trương Vĩnh Lê and five other National Assembly delegates met with Wood and Parsons.[47] Trương Vĩnh Lê highlighted the significant advances that the Saigon Government had made in the countryside with a special acknowledgment for the Agroville Program though he did confirm that it had started off poorly. There was data from the USOM Public Safety Division that collaborated this assessment, though Durbrow was not convinced.[48] He was more swayed by the observations of the Bloc for Freedom and Progress leaders Phan Khắc Sửu and Trần Văn Văn, who called for an end to the program because of its unsavory tactics it employed with the peasants to create the Agrovilles.[49] Durbrow also focused on the criticisms of Phan Quang Đán and tended to offer his counter observations to Ngô Đình Diệm's explanations whenever it seemed necessary.[50]

Durbrow was not alone in finding fault with Ngô Đình Diệm and, even though he required his staff to distance themselves from high-profile critics to avoid the allegation that the Americans were taking sides, members of the Country Team continued the practice. On August 17, Mendenhall met with the Secretary General of the National Assembly Nguyễn Phương Thiệp, who complained about the political atmosphere in Vietnam, while Wood saw former Secretary of State for Land Reform, Nguyễn Văn Thời, on September 1, and reported his observations that the Vietnamese people were unhappy with Ngô Đình Diệm's rule.[51] He also had willing allies in the French who continually affirmed Durbrow's views or offered an assessment of their own that supported his position.[52]

Durbrow reported to Washington that Ngô Đình Diệm faced two real threats.[53] The first was from the Communist insurgency, while the second was from the trade unions.[54] Durbrow feared that the former would exploit the discontent of the latter in a way that was similar to the failed effort on August 21. To avoid this possibility, Durbrow recommended that Ngô Đình Nhu and Madame Nhu have their influence over Ngô Đình Diệm diminished and that the head of the secret intelligence service, Trần Kim Tuyến, be removed.[55] For Durbrow, not only was the reorganization of Ngô Đình Diệm's cabinet necessary, but he also desired the end of the Cần Lao Party and a greater role for the National Assembly. In this way, he echoed the French desire to see a significant change in Saigon.

Lansdale, again, served as a counter to Durbrow in Washington.[56] While he did agree with Durbrow's idea of moving Nguyễn Ngọc Thơ to the Ministry of the Interior and inserting Nguyễn Đình Thuận as Minister of Defense, he was not in favor of replacing Ngô Đình Nhu and getting rid of Trần Kim Tuyến. Lansdale was not supportive of Durbrow's other initiatives when one considered Vietnamese politics holistically. He knew that Ngô Đình Diệm did not trust Durbrow and questioned the ambassador's ability to connect with him at any significant level. Even if Lansdale was denied access to Ngô Đình Diệm by traveling to Saigon, he still believed that he could be useful to him and Williams by pointing out what he thought was the obvious. Ngô Đình Diệm needed an American ambassador that he could both trust and respect. He did not need one who worked against his continued rule.

Durbrow's attempts to isolate Ngô Đình Diệm from Americans who were sympathetic to his rule was an attempt to gain the upper hand not only in Saigon, but also in Washington. Lansdale and Williams represented the greatest threats. With his successful campaign to deny Lansdale's entry into Saigon and the pending recall of Williams back to the United States at the end of his tour in Vietnam, Durbrow had accomplished much. He was still hampered by elements within the Department of Defense though he also had many allies in his embassy, the diplomatic corps in Saigon, and the State Department. Ngô Đình Diệm was aware of Durbrow's actions, though he had little power to stop them. He recognized that he was being isolated and that his main American protagonist, Durbrow, was still present and powerful. This meant that the two sides could either compromise or clash. The next steps would be significant for the diplomatic career of Durbrow and the political life of Ngô Đình Diệm.

15

Influencing Ngô Đình Diệm and the Abortive November 1960 Coup d'état

The departure of Williams from Vietnam at the end of August and the arrival of his replacement, General Lionel McGarr, did not defuse the tension over Vietnam policy that had existed between the Departments of State and Defense in Washington or Saigon. Both Durbrow and Lansdale wanted to brief McGarr on the situation in Vietnam to ensure that he was sympathetic to their position. Lansdale was also busy responding to an August 23 Special National Intelligence Estimate (SNIE 63.1–60) titled, "Short-Term Trends in South Vietnam."[1] The rather bleak assessment of the conditions in Vietnam and the negativity directed at Ngô Đình Diệm for his role in the deteriorating conditions caused Lansdale to counter that a more reasoned and objective assessment was needed.[2] Lansdale questioned the reporting from Saigon and Huế, which he argued was steeped in emotional bias. While it was true that Lansdale believed a crisis was looming in Vietnam and his inability to visit Saigon because of Durbrow might have influenced his judgment, he offered a more critical assessment of the ability and strategies of the Việt Cộng.[3]

Lansdale forwarded his concerns about SNIE 63.1–60 and other data to McGarr on August 11.[4] While Lansdale's principle point in doing so was to better inform the General on the real situation in Vietnam, he also cautioned McGarr not to be mired in the political intrigue that infused Saigon. McGarr was more prepared for his assignment in Saigon than either Lansdale or Durbrow realized. Upon the request from the Joint Chiefs of Staff for a list of recommendations to improve the Vietnamese position, McGarr forwarded a position paper that reaffirmed several items that either Williams or Ngô Đình Diệm had requested in the previous year.[5] Durbrow was not pleased to receive the position paper on September 2, arguing that it was counter to the policies he had tried to establish since arriving in Vietnam; he did agree to send it to the Country Team for review.[6] Even as this was being done, Durbrow informed Parsons of the MAAG move and justified the attempted change of course in Vietnam as existing frustration that was being released by long-term military personnel in Vietnam.

Durbrow did not think McGarr's recommendations reflected the Vietnamese military situation; neither did he believe that McGarr was responsible for the position paper. In fact, Durbrow argued that the request for an additional 20,000 men was a result of Williams' failure. He maintained that MAAG should have been more diligent in training the ARVN troops before the crisis that gripped the countryside in 1960.[7] However, Durbrow did believe that McGarr was much more reasonable than Williams, though it was not clear whether this was because he thought that McGarr could be manipulated, where Williams could not, or a genuine reflection.[8] Durbrow did expect McGarr to back him in putting pressure on Ngô Đình Diệm to reform if the Vietnamese expected further American aid.

Durbrow continued to rally the diplomatic corps against Ngô Đình Diệm. After the president's speech opening the National Assembly on October 3, Durbrow discussed it with Lalouette and the British ambassador to the Republic of Vietnam, Henry Hohler.[9] They agreed that the speech failed to address the political aspects of the Việt Cộng problem; all three expressed concern that Ngô Đình Diệm had failed to mention the importance of foreign aid in Vietnam's many accomplishments. In reporting his observations about the speech to Washington, Durbrow made sure that it was clear that his views were shared by the French and British. He used this joint approach in his continuing request to have another frank talk with Ngô Đình Diệm.[10] Durbrow was encouraged in this effort by both Ladejinsky and Nguyễn Ngọc Thơ.[11] Nguyễn Ngọc Thơ was keen on seeing the diminished influence of Ngô Đình Nhu, Madame Nhu and Trần Kim Tuyến, while all three wanted steps taken to reduce or eliminate corrupt practices in Vietnam. Durbrow also pushed his proposal to increase the power of the National Assembly.[12]

Durbrow employed a strategy that offered both praise and concern in order to sway Ngô Đình Diệm to his way of thinking. It was a strategy not unfamiliar with Ngô Đình Diệm who saw it used by the Việt Cộng, albeit in a much more extreme way, in their dealings with the Vietnamese people. On October 14, Durbrow met with Ngô Đình Diệm and Nguyễn Đình Thuận to discuss the release of a letter by Eisenhower after Ngô Đình Diệm gave his October 26 speech commemorating the anniversary of the Republic. This perceived reward, along with another that saw an increase in the Civil Guard, was designed to offer Durbrow's renewal of the need for political reforms, which would be delivered in the strongest terms.[13] While reading from the fourteen-page document that he had worked on with the Department of State, Durbrow offered an apology when he got to the section that called for the removal of

Ngô Đình Nhu, Madame Nhu, and Trần Kim Tuyến. It seems reasonable that Ngô Đình Diệm recognized the apology for what it really was, given his knowledge that Durbrow wanted the three out. Diplomatic niceties had diminished under the current atmosphere in Saigon. Durbrow's explanation that they needed to be removed whether or not the allegations against them were true surely failed to strengthen Ngô Đình Diệm's confidence in his American ally.[14] Durbrow reported that the Vietnamese president remained quiet for most of the reading of the document, though he did mention that it was difficult to find qualified individuals to fill important government positions. Durbrow was under instructions not to offer recommendations, though he did have some in mind, even if they were not palatable.

While Ngô Đình Diệm held back his retort during the Durbrow interview, he did show his displeasure at Durbrow's suggestions by not reforming his cabinet as Durbrow had advised. When meeting with Parsons on October 18, Ngô Đình Diệm criticized the opposition for only speaking against the Republic when they needed to act to help it.[15] Ngô Đình Diệm refused to legitimize the opposition for not assisting in the countryside as the Government had requested; they did not deserve acceptance while others took risks for Vietnam. Instead of agreeing to dismiss the Ngô Đình Nhu, Madame Nhu, and Trần Kim Tuyến issue, Ngô Đình Diệm spent most of his time with Parsons discussing Ngô Đình Nhu's value to the Republic. Again, Durbrow's reply to this justification confirmed that he was not Ngô Đình Diệm's ally.

Durbrow argued that it did not matter how important Ngô Đình Nhu was to the Republic if there were rumors circulating around him that pointed to corruption. As more people repeated these rumors, Ngô Đình Nhu's value diminished.[16] Ngô Đình Diệm was not willing to accept the logic of acting on rumors, most likely started, in his mind, by an opposition that wanted to replace Ngô Đình Nhu and his influence with the president. On this matter, Ngô Đình Diệm and Durbrow were at a standoff. Even so, Durbrow believed he had made his point. On October 18, Ngô Đình Diệm made three significant cabinet changes that fell into line with Durbrow's thinking.[17]

The French reaction to Ngô Đình Diệm's moves was that it was too little, too late.[18] This opinion was corroborated by three conversations that took place between Vietnamese and the American Vice Consul in Huế, Thomas Barnes. Barnes passed along the conversations with individuals who had reason to be critical of Ngô Đình Diệm: one had been denied promotion in the military on numerous occasions, one was a member of the 1954–1955 exodus from North Vietnam because of his family's connections with the French, and the final one was more comfortable speaking in French than in Vietnamese. Nonetheless, as the Consulate in Huế had done on more than one occasion, these conversations were taken to represent the state of the Vietnamese people in relation to Ngô Đình Diệm.

There was much to counter these Vietnamese voices. On October 26, Ngô Đình Diệm delivered his National Day address on the occasion of the fifth anniversary of the Republic.[19] He praised the Vietnamese people, condemned the Việt Cộng, and outlined his plans to counter the communist insurgency. Celebrations marked National Day both in Vietnam and in Vietnamese communities in Cambodia and Laos. A few days later, Trần Văn Chương finalized a U.S. $17,500,000 loan from the Development Loan Fund to improve Saigon's water supply.[20] This was a much needed improvement for the growing city. In addition, and counter to the Vietnamese critics, the National Assembly introduced three pieces of significant legislation on the freedom of the press that belied the notion that it answered only to the Palace.[21] The National Assembly also adopted resolution 7/60 in order to more effectively fight the Communist insurgency, which prompt thousands of Vietnamese to protest the Việt Cộng.[22]

By November, it was clear that the Communist insurgency was now a significant threat to the Republic. Ngô Đình Diệm and Durbrow did not agree on how best to combat the danger and constantly clashed as two dominant egos vied for control. Durbrow continued to push for more frank talks so that he could apply pressure on the Vietnamese to reform and conform to American advice while Ngô Đình Diệm struggled to find an American ally to replace Williams. Domestically, Saigon seemed stable though the underlying tension that had manifested itself with the Caravelle Manifesto was about to erupt in the greatest challenge to date in Ngô Đình Diệm's tenure as president.

In the early hours of November 11, several Vietnamese airborne battalions began a coup d'état against Ngô Đình Diệm.[23] While the attempt would ultimately fail, American reaction during and after it would significantly affect how Ngô Đình Diệm saw his principle allies and dictate Durbrow's role in Vietnam until he was replaced in 1961. No one in the United States embassy expected the action, though the CIA Station Chief, and officially the Political Officer and First Secretary to the United States Embassy, William Colby, reported the event to Durbrow soon after it began and correctly speculated that it was a coup attempt.[24] The leaders targeted the ARVN headquarters, Tân Sơn Nhứt Airbase, the Saigon radio station, Presidential Palace, National Assembly building, and police and Sûreté headquarters. They also hoped to cut the roads leading into Saigon.[25] However, the attempt did not proceed as planned.[26]

The initial attack in Saigon lasted an hour, though there was continued sporadic firing throughout the morning.[27] In the opening minutes of the attempt a small group attacked the Presidential Palace guard, but they were repelled when General Nguyễn Khánh arrived on the scene and took over.[28] Durbrow learned that Lieutenant Colonel Vương Văn Đông was in charge and his source, *Time* correspondence James Wilde, informed him that the attackers had taken the airport, Presidential Palace, and radio station in addition to other key objectives. This proved not to be true. Vương Văn Đông was involved but not in control, and Ngô Đình Diệm still held the palace as of 6:20 a.m.[29]

Nguyễn Đình Thuận telephoned the American Embassy later in the morning to inform the ambassador that he had escaped the attackers.[30] He confirmed that the Palace held, though Tân Sơn Nhứt and the military radio system had not. Radio Saigon, however, was still in Government hands and started broadcasting a message by Ngô Đình Diệm for loyal troops to come to his assistance.[31] He also sent an urgent request at some point before 10:00 a.m., through the Belgium Rev. Raymond J. De Jaeger, to the Embassy, asking American Marines to protect their citizens and property, and to secure the airport from the rebels.[32] Durbrow received the message after the coup d'état forces had secured Tân Sơn Nhứt and decided to ignore the request.[33] This was a clear signal to Ngô Đình Diệm, though Durbrow would justify his position by arguing that the United States could not take sides as long as Americans were not threatened.

Fighting continued to be heavy around the Presidential Palace, with the rebel troops in the guard houses and loyal troops attempting to dislodge them.[34] While the addition of two armored units helped to stabilize the situation around 7:30 a.m., the Palace guards were still outnumbered and the final results were as of yet unknown.[35] Near this time, Colby was informed by Saigon lawyer Hoàng Cơ Thụy, the uncle of Lieutenant Colonel Vương Văn Đông, that the coup d'état was mostly successful and would be over as soon as the Palace fell.[36] This would not take place, as Ngô Đình Diệm developed a strategy to maintain his position while also calling in loyal forces to outnumber the attackers.

However, as the morning continued and forces loyal to Ngô Đình Diệm were still far from the city, the situation remained fluid. The Vietnamese Marines were divided between the two sides with two companies joining the Palace Guard to protect Ngô Đình Diệm and another two joining the rebels. The Vietnamese Navy was observed patrolling the Saigon River but did not enter into the fray.[37] It was the opinion of United States Embassy Air Attaché Lieutenant Colonel Butler Toland that the attack had gone very well. While the Presidential Palace was still being contested, Toland believed that Ngô Đình Diệm would either surrender or take his own life.[38] He also reported that the people of Saigon had maintained their normal routine and the general sense was that the coup d'état attempt would be successful.[39] By 10:30 a.m., this seemed true as loyal forces were still not in sight and some ARVN troops who had been sent to the Palace to defend it had joined the rebels instead. Believing that they had the upper hand, the leaders of the coup gave Ngô Đình Diệm until 11:00 a.m. to surrender.[40]

15. The Abortive November 1960 Coup d'état 173

By mid-morning, it appeared that the coup d'état had been successful. Durbrow informed Washington that they had occupied the Palace and were in negotiations with Ngô Đình Diệm for his surrender, while broadcasts issued an "Order of the day of the Revolutionary Council" that proclaimed victory.[41] Neither interpretation was correct. The Revolutionary Council called for the Vietnamese people to remain calm and unite under new leadership to finish the work in establishing the Republic and fighting the Communist insurgency.[42] By the early afternoon, Durbrow, who still maintained that the rebels did not want to harm Ngô Đình Diệm and only desired to see the Republic whole, thought that Ngô Đình Diệm would surrender. If he managed to escape the situation and retain power, Durbrow also believed the November 11 events would be a warning to Ngô Đình Diệm that Durbrow could use as leverage.[43]

When Durbrow finally arrived at the Embassy around 12:00 p.m., there was still confusion on what exactly was happening in Saigon. Many different reports filtered into the Embassy from American personnel around the city but also from Vietnamese and members of the foreign diplomatic corps. However, when Durbrow first had an opportunity to speak with Ngô Đình Diệm around 2:00 p.m., it must have been clear that the coup d'état had not been the success reported, and that the people of Saigon were not united behind the event. Durbrow maintained that he had no recollection of his conversation with Ngô Đình Diệm and no transcript was available, though both Mendenhall and Colby remembered it.[44] Mendenhall remembered that Durbrow failed to offer support for Ngô Đình Diệm and, instead, advised him to accept a compromise so that the fight against the communist insurgency would not be jeopardized.[45]

While there was no written record to explain this position, it seemed clear that Durbrow believed that the rebels had the upper hand and did not want to interfere with the natural course of events. Mendenhall supported Durbrow in this position but he also recalled that the telephone conversation was the beginning of the end of Durbrow's working relationship with Ngô Đình Diệm. Colby also recalled Durbrow offering no support or encouragement but went further than Mendenhall in asserting that the call signaled the break between the ambassador and Vietnamese president. While Ngô Đình Diệm's reaction to the conversation was not recorded, his action in the days following the coup d'état confirm that he held little trust for most Americans in Saigon.

Soon after the conversation ended, word reached the Embassy that troops loyal to Ngô Đình Diệm were approaching the city and would arrive before any surrender might take place. Trần Thiện Khiêm brought seven battalions with him from the Cần Thơ region, while Major Lâm Quang Thơ had organized armored units from Mỹ Tho and was near Cholon. More loyal units were on their way after hearing Ngô Đình Diệm's radio appeal.[46] Around 2:00 p.m., Durbrow learned of negotiations between Ngô Đình Diệm and the Revolutionary Committee.[47] Ngô Đình Diệm was offered the honorary position of Supreme Adviser. While Ngô Đình Diệm would never accept such an offer, Durbrow encouraged the move, using the argument that a united front against the Việt Cộng was the most important thing to consider. Durbrow received much of his information that afternoon from Nguyễn Đình Thuận, who served as the conduit between the Embassy and the Palace.[48]

Through him, he continued to press for compromise and promised to pass along any information or demands he received from the rebels. This did not take long to happen. McGarr telephoned the Embassy at 3:00 p.m. to let Durbrow know that Revolutionary Committee representatives and members of the press were at his home.[49] True to his word, Durbrow directed McGarr to maintain a position of non-interference, though he also called for the retention of Ngô Đình Diệm in the government in some capacity. As this was something the Revolutionary Committee had already suggested, Durbrow's request was not too extreme. However, while these conversations were taking place, troops loyal to Ngô Đình Diệm were converging on Saigon.

The 2nd Armored Regiment entered the city and took up a defensive position around the Presidential Palace, and was joined by another two companies of Marines soon thereafter.[50] With these forces in place, the Palace was no longer an easy target. Most of the fighting had ceased by 5:00 p.m. as the two sides paused for the next action. These delays had been the strategy of Ngô Đình Diệm. He kept the Revolutionary Committee waiting for his answer as troops loyal to him gathered in Saigon. Ngô Đình Diệm knew that all he needed to do was buy extra time. The strategy was successful. Ngô Đình Diệm correctly assessed that the rebel leadership was not united. Some wanted him removed from power while others were willing to compromise. Ngô Đình Diệm skillfully played one side off of the other as he prolonged the negotiations. At 5:30 p.m., Radio Saigon broadcast a Revolutionary Committee announcement that proclaimed the surrender of Ngô Đình Diệm and support of all of the Vietnamese generals. The reality of the situation was different, as more loyal troops arrived throughout the evening.[51]

A CIA assessment came in at 10:30 p.m., which concluded that the Revolutionary Committee had Ngô Đình Diệm's agreement on a compromise that would see him assume the role as Head of State if his family received safe conduct out of the country.[52] This was a part of the stalling plan though the Americans were not aware of it. Radio Saigon broadcast a loop from 10:30 p.m. to 11:15 p.m. that outlined the new agreement, which gave credence to the CIA's claim.[53] This was followed by another Radio Saigon broadcast calling for a rally outside the Presidential Palace to celebrate the new regime in Saigon.[54] One would take place but it would be far different than the one called for by the Revolutionary Committee. Ngô Đình Diệm survived the night, still in power, and emboldened by the arrival of fresh troops loyal to him. In the early morning hours, the tide would shift as the rebels bickered and Trần Thiện Khiêm organized the new force to assault the troops surrounding the Palace.[55]

In the early hours of November 12, General Lê Văn Nghiệm added elements of his 7th ARVN Division to the forces loyal to Ngô Đình Diệm.[56] Before their assault against the rebels, Ngô Đình Diệm sent one last broadcast to delay and confuse the rebels. In a tape recorded message, he requested the establishment of a provisional government to serve as interim rule until he and the Revolutionary Committee formed a coalition government. Ngô Đình Diệm also ordered a ceasefire.[57] This might have seemed surprising to some, but McGarr learned that the loyal troops were getting into their final position and would have the rebels surrounded in minutes.[58] Rather than a broadcast of surrender, Ngô Đình Diệm was lulling his foes into complacency.

The final battle of the attempted coup d'état began just before 6:30 a.m. on November 12 resulting in the surrender of three Airborne Companies to elements of the 5th ARVN troops loyal to Ngô Đình Diệm. Durbrow and members of the Country Team were still under the impression that Ngô Đình Diệm had surrendered.[59] Durbrow learned of the negotiations that placed Ngô Đình Diệm as a Head of State with no real power less than a half hour later; it seemed to him that the coup d'état had been successful.[60] A radio broadcast by Phan Quang Đán half an hour later did nothing to alter Durbrow's thinking. His speech was intended to rally the people against Ngô Đình Diệm though, at the time, the rebels were about to be overwhelmed by loyal forces.[61] The planned rally organized by the Revolutionary Committee did take place in front of the Palace despite the recent setback for the rebels.[62] However, as Durbrow feared, it turned violent as Palace defenders open fired on the group.[63] This effectively ended the anti–Government rally, but it also made the decision for Durbrow to confront Ngô Đình Diệm necessary. Soon after the 8:35 a.m. incident, Durbrow called Ngô Đình Diệm and expressed his concern at the renewed fighting and events that took place during the rally. He warned Ngô Đình Diệm not to allow the failure of the coup d'état to end in a bloodbath that would benefit only the Việt Cộng.[64]

While Ngô Đình Diệm's actual response was unknown, it was fair to assume that his feelings at that moment were mixed. He had survived the coup d'état but the inaction of his closest allies must have been some cause for animosity. Durbrow's angst about the rebels seemed to be more prevalent than his concern for Ngô Đình Diệm and his family. His distress at Ngô Đình Diệm breaking his word with the Revolutionary Committee, which would have seen an end to his rule, did nothing to ease the Vietnamese president's anxiety.[65] Ngô Đình Diệm did defend the actions of his troops, but he finally agreed not to seek retribution against the rebels.

With the upper hand against the rebels, Ngô Đình Diệm could have issued any order to see the end of the coup d'état. Durbrow's worries were misplaced. Ngô Đình Diệm knew that the troops following the Revolutionary Committee had been tricked into attacking the Presidential Palace. He was not going to destroy these forces.[66] Before Trần Thiện Khiêm led elements of the 21st ARVN Division against the rebels, he ordered an L-17 transport to drop pamphlets over the scene of the earlier battles calling for common sense and an end to the fighting. It offered forgiveness rather than threats and was persuasive.[67] By 11:20 a.m., ARVN troops had recaptured Radio Vietnam, the Office of the Police and Sûreté, the Great Market, the Tea Dan Gardens, and the Central Police.[68] McGarr toured the scene of the earlier heavy fighting and noted that the situation appeared calm, with the intermingling of the one-time adversaries; he also reported that Tân Sơn Nhứt would reopen November 13.[69]

McGarr confirmed that there was no evidence that a bloodbath would follow the failed coup. Ngô Đình Diệm was more interested in detaining the officers who had led the movements and had tricked their men into action.[70] This did not prevent the creation of plans by the United States to deal with possible retributions.[71] When reprisals did not occur, Durbrow congratulated Ngô Đình Diệm on his restraint, though Ngô Đình Diệm was focused on detaining the coup's leaders rather than a general reprisal. However, before they could be dealt with, Captain Phan Phụng Tiên, the commander of the 1st Transportation Squadron stationed at Tân Sơn Nhứt, took off in a C-47 aircraft heading west, presumably toward Phnom Penh.[72] Aboard the aircraft were Colonel Nguyễn Chánh Thi, Lieutenant Colonel Vương Văn Đông, and Major Ngô Xuân Soạn though it was later discovered that Ngô Xuân Soạn, commander of the 5th Airborne Battalion, was murdered when he refused to join the coup.[73] General Thái Quang Hoàng, who had been taken as a hostage, was aboard.[74] While these officers escaped, others who had supported the coup d'état politically were arrested. This list included the civilians Trần Văn Văn, Trần Văn Đỗ, Phan Khắc Sửu and Phan Huy Quát, all of whom had voiced their opposition to Ngô Đình Diệm's rule.[75]

On the evening of November 12, Ngô Đình Diệm did announce that military personnel who were involved in the attempted coup d'état would be exonerated.[76] He also broadcast a radio message that Colonels Nguyễn Chánh Thi, Vương Văn Đông, and Major Ngô Xuân Soạn had attempted to trick their paratroopers into overthrowing him; Ngô Đình Diệm was not aware, at this time, of Ngô Xuân Soạn's loyalty to him.[77] With the attempted coup d'état over, it was now time to deal with how the other principle actors in the event behaved. It would be a difficult period for Durbrow and his Country Team.

Durbrow, and many of his staff at the embassy, had assumed that the attempted coup would be successful and that it would be vigorously supported by the people of Saigon. Much of the reporting from the embassy over the past several months suggested that this would be the case. Durbrow kept the Americans out of the conflict, which was the proper thing to do, though his inaction and his less than supportive advice marked the end of any productive relationship he would have with Ngô Đình Diệm. Durbrow's moves in the days that immediately followed only made the situation worse.

On November 14, Durbrow met with Ngô Đình Diệm to offer him congratulations on the outcome of the earlier events, though he had a more pressing issue to discuss.[78] Despite Ngô Đình Diệm's earlier guarantees, Durbrow again brought up the inadvisability of retribution against the rebels. He argued that such action would be harmful to the larger fight against the Việt Cộng, especially since the rebels were not associated with the Communist movement. Restraint, Durbrow maintained, would increase Ngô Đình Diệm's reputation. Ngô Đình Diệm reaffirmed that he had no intention on punishing the troops, though he did see it necessary to take action against the leadership.[79] Neither Vương Văn Đông nor Nguyễn Chánh Thi deserved leniency and both had poor military records that did not warrant exceptions.[80] Ngô Đình Diệm's reaction to Durbrow's priority in the meeting was not evident though his, and Ngô Đình Nhu's, actions afterwards suggested that the United States would not escape blame for its inactivity during the attempted coup.

The first formal Government action after the end of the fighting was to organize its own mass demonstration. The November 13 event would be a march from the National Assembly to the Presidential Palace. A much larger, more organized crowd than the anti–Ngô Đình Diệm rally gathered in the morning to walk the route and listen to speeches praising the ARVN troops and Ngô Đình Diệm.[81] As the Vietnamese celebrated the averted crisis, the two adversaries, the Department of State and Defense, resumed their debate on America's Vietnam policy and its relationship with Ngô Đình Diệm. On November 15, Lansdale forwarded a memorandum to Deputy Secretary of Defense James H. Douglas in which he asserted that the failure of the United States to act in support of Ngô Đình Diệm would lead the Vietnamese president to conclude that Durbrow was too influenced by those opposed to him.[82] There would be consequences for the United States-Vietnamese relations as a result.

Lansdale's assessment was close to the mark. Ngô Đình Diệm already had his concerns about the Country Team which he had shared earlier with Williams; Williams had voiced these concerns to Lansdale in private communications. Lansdale requested that Douglas use his influence to have those involved in American policy in Vietnam take the time to understand the Vietnamese people, their history, culture, and personalities. Too many Americans involved, he believed, did not. Jerome T. French, an officer in the Office of Special Operations under Lansdale, toured South Vietnam between November 14 and November 17 and confirmed that rumors were surfacing that held the Americans were involved with the Revolutionary Committee.[83]

The manifestation of the backlash to the attempted coup organized into the People's Committee Against Communists and Rebels. This new committee took over from the People's Counter-Coup d'état Committee, which had been active on November 11–12.[84] The stated goal of the new group was to strengthen relations between Saigon residents and the ARVN. It also sought to improve morale. However, the committee would soon turn its attention to the role of the Americans during the crisis, which threatened to damage the already fragile relationship. Its first leaflet, titled "People's Committee Against Rebels and Communists," suggested that the United States, Britain, and France were involved in the attempted coup d'état. It implied that colonialists and imperialists were at work to discredit Ngô Đình Diệm and see his replacement at the head of the Republic.[85]

It was not surprising that Durbrow found this document troublesome, though he suggested that the real purpose of it was to divert attention away from the flawed leadership of Ngô Đình Diệm rather than a real condemnation of the United States. He also conjectured that the leaflet was an attempt to thwart continued American pressure for him to reform his government.[86] Durbrow, however, did concede that the document might have been an attempt by the Vietnamese to emphasize their anger with the United States for not coming to his aid. Another difficulty arising from the events of November 11–12 was the presence of American personnel at the rebel headquarters. Given the tension of the week, it was reasonable for members of the Ngô family to speculate on their motives.[87]

The People's Committee Against Communists and Rebels targeted not only the United States, Britain, and France. It focused attention on those Saigon newspapers that reported favorably toward the rebels during the attempted coup d'état.[88] The offices of *Dân chúng* and *Tin Mới* were ransacked, while *Chuông Mai*, *Buổi sang*, and *Sài Gòn Mới* received lesser damage.[89] This type of action was what Durbrow was trying to avoid. He believed the Communists would take advantage of any additional domestic fallout after November 11. However, there was duplicity in Durbrow's actions. Durbrow and McGarr spoke about the recent events with American reporters on November 14.[90] Durbrow offered the obligatory statement that he was glad Ngô Đình Diệm was safe and the Republic secure after the attempted coup d'état. There was nothing surprising in the conference until Durbrow insisted that a portion of it be off the record.

During this time, Durbrow discussed the failed strategy of the rebels and questioned how they could not have succeeded when they held the upper hand in the early hours of November 11. At several points, Durbrow seemed to almost lament the mistakes in their strategy.⁹¹ Durbrow also questioned the notion that the paratroopers had been tricked into starting the attempted coup, which was confirmed by journalist Stanley Karnow. Karnow, however, had received this confirmation from the officers in charge rather than the paratroopers themselves so it was of questionable value. Durbrow, however, concurred, which reaffirmed his position vis-à-vis Ngô Đình Diệm.⁹² The press conference evolved into an exchange of ideas about why the rebels failed and the level of real support for Ngô Đình Diệm. All in attendance, save McGarr, were of the same mind. If Ngô Đình Diệm needed to worry about the American press in Saigon, he only would have to have read a transcript of the off-record portion of the press conference.

Even as the Embassy continued to collect accounts of anti–Ngô Đình Diệm sentiment, Durbrow struggled to counter the allegations that the United States was involved in the events of November 11. On November 16, he met with Nguyễn Đình Thuận on the issue and stressed that blaming external forces was not productive, as the real motivations for the attacks was internal.⁹³ While Nguyễn Đình Thuận disagreed with Durbrow, he acknowledged that some reforms were necessary. Durbrow was not persuaded by Nguyễn Đình Thuận's dissent against his position and chose to blame Cần Lao party members who deflected the actual reasons that the abortive coup took place.⁹⁴ For Durbrow, Ngô Đình Diệm was the source of the real problems for Vietnam. One of the reasons Durbrow met with Nguyễn Đình Thuận was to discuss the press conference scheduled for the next day between Nguyễn Đình Thuận and members of the international press corps.⁹⁵ While Nguyễn Đình Thuận declared that no foreign government was involved in the attempted coup d'état, it seemed clear that the level of animosity between the Vietnamese and the Americans was at an all-time high.⁹⁶ When reporters pressed the issue and produced a "People's Committee against the Communists and Rebels" leaflet which mentioned the United States, France, and Britain, Nguyễn Đình Thuận hinted that the Saigon Government was aware of how foreign governments had repeated some Vietnamese claims against Ngô Đình Diệm without legitimate verification, suggesting that the press was culpable for the recent loss of life and property.⁹⁷ He ended the press conference by thanking only the British and French press corps for their attempts at objectivity toward the Vietnamese. American reporters were not included.

A meeting between McGarr and Ngô Đình Diệm right after the press conference helped to clarify the direction of the Vietnamese ire. Ngô Đình Diệm assured McGarr that he appreciated the support he had received from MAAG in the past and that he held the United States in high regard. The suggestion, however, was that the same could not be true for other Americans in Vietnam.⁹⁸ Ngô Đình Diệm lamented the rumors he had heard that suggested some Americans regretted the coup d'état failed and continued to encourage dissent among Vietnamese. He requested McGarr's assistance in countering such forces. He had cause to be concerned, as he did not have the full support of Durbrow or the non-military members of the Country Team.[99]

Things were not any better for the Vietnamese in Washington. Parsons met with Trần Văn Chương on November 18 during which time he questioned the ambassador about the People's Committee leaflet.[100] Parsons maintained that Washington did not think the group represented the Saigon Government; he did express concern about the alleged connections that members of the committee had with the Ngô family. Parsons denied the idea that the United States had been involved in a campaign of disparagement, as expressed in Nguyễn Đình Thuận's remarks, and assured his guest that any complaints American representatives had with Vietnamese policy was also made privately to the parties concerned.[101] Trần Văn Chương did not have an official reply, though he would be hard pressed to find a way to agree to such a sentiment when the evidence available presented an alternative perspective.

The first attempt at reconciliation came with a proposed draft congratulatory message from Eisenhower to Ngô Đình Diệm that highlighted his actions during the attempted coup d'état and offered continued American support.[102] Durbrow refused to approve it and argued that Eisenhower needed to distance himself from Ngô Đình Diệm until he initiated reforms which had been confirmed as necessary based on the events of November 11–12. Durbrow did not think the message proper until after the People's Committee's leaflet had been denounced by the Saigon Government but, more importantly, he did not want praise for the Vietnamese president while he was garnering pressure against him. In addition to trying to hold the line in Washington, Durbrow worked with the various chief diplomats in Saigon to present a unified force to call for reforms.[103] Durbrow knew he had angered Ngô Đình Diệm and Ngô Đình Nhu by his actions and that they were distressed by stories originating from the American press in Saigon. He suggested that the United States lessen its direct pressure against him, but also be prepared to deliver a stronger ultimatum if Ngô Đình Diệm did not initiate the much-needed reforms.[104]

The attempted coup d'état and the Vietnamese reaction to alleged American involvement helped to deepen the rift that had developed in Washington between the Departments of Defense and State. While Williams was no longer involved in the debate, McGarr and Lansdale still championed the Vietnamese president's position. The Department of Defense was firmly behind it as well. This was seen in a November 18 meeting involving members of the State Department and the Joint Chiefs of Staff.[105] The Chief of Staff of the Army, General Lyman Louis Lemnitzer, expressed concern with Durbrow's observations during the crisis and the idea that the United States should stand in the way of Ngô Đình Diệm when his life had been threatened. Trying to restrain Ngô Đình Diệm when he needed to act decisively was not the role of an ally. Lemnitzer was not advocating a bloodbath, as Durbrow had feared, but rather the idea that you could not handcuff Ngô Đình Diệm with threats when he needed to deal with those who had tried to topple the Republic. Durbrow was defended by Deputy Under Secretary of State for Political Affairs Livingston Merchant, who argued that it was not Durbrow's intention to weaken Ngô Đình Diệm's position.

The two sides were set up for another clash when the Department of Defense again made the recommendation that Lansdale visit Vietnam. Lansdale and McGarr had corresponded since the General's arrival in Saigon.[106] Durbrow, however, conceded that a visit was in order even if Hanoi would protest it. However, he stipulated that Lansdale would need to cooperate with Durbrow and follow Department of State instructions. He also expected Lansdale to fully and accurately report all conversations that he had with Ngô Đình Diệm.[107] Durbrow expected Lansdale to support his calls for reform and maintain the pressure on Ngô Đình Diệm. These would be conditions that Lansdale would accept though he would not necessarily follow them.[108] While Durbrow compromised on the Lansdale visit, he held his ground elsewhere.

Durbrow continued to counter the Department of Defense in its attempts to allegedly undermine him as he worked on furthering his plan in Saigon. He finally met with Ngô Đình Diệm on November 26 after his earlier attempts had been thwarted.[109] Ngô Đình Diệm stressed the importance of self-reliance in the villages and the need to send the best young Vietnamese into the countryside to offer guidance. He noted that his critics offered no actions but only voiced their complaints. These were common themes for Ngô Đình Diệm, and Durbrow did not have much to offer. He was more concerned about the movement of Civil Guard activities from the Ministry of the Interior to the Ministry of Defense. Durbrow maintained that any continued connection with the Ministry of the Interior would hamper United States efforts to support the Civil Guard. Durbrow did walk away from the meeting more confident while the November 22 promulgation of Decision No 272-NV, which temporarily placed the Civil Guard under the Ministry of Defense, was encouraging.[110]

With the resolution of the attempted coup d'état and its aftermath, Durbrow and Ngô Đình Diệm could once again focus on the immediate problems for the Republic. The most pressing matter for Ngô Đình Diệm was the 20,000 personnel increased in the Vietnamese military. This had been a priority for some time though Durbrow continued to use the request as a means to extract concessions from Ngô Đình Diệm. Durbrow wanted Ngô Đình Diệm to liberalize Vietnamese society and reform the Saigon government and pressed him when an opportunity arose.[111] This only resulted in frustrating Ngô Đình

Diệm who grew increasingly convinced that Durbrow did not understand, or want to understand, Vietnam. Durbrow chose to interpret that frustration as a sign that Ngô Đình Diệm was not serious about creating a Republic, nor did he have any intention of relinquishing the power that had accumulated since his ascendancy to the Presidency. This failure to communicate and resolve the clash of perceptions would have serious repercussions in the years to come.

While Ngô Đình Diệm did not find a willing ally in Durbrow, he still shared a confidence with MAAG that had been established by Williams earlier. Right before the attempted coup d'état, MAAG released a study that addressed the Vietnamese military and the strategy it needed to employ against the Việt Cộng.[112] It served as one of the points of disagreement between the Departments of Defense and State until all attention was diverted to the events of November 11–12. With that situation calmed, discussion of the MAAG study resumed with each side firmly entrenched in their position on what to do in Vietnam. It called for an increase in the Civil Guard, improved intelligence gathering at the local level, and an emphasis on psychological warfare. MAAG also supported the 20,000-man increase and a permanent reorganization of the Civil Guard under the Ministry of Defense.

Before the attempted coup d'état, Durbrow offered his thoughts on the study. He agreed with most of it, though he did not believe the increase in personnel was warranted, nor did he think the Vietnamese would be able to use the extra force efficiently.[113] Durbrow countered with two alternatives to the extra personnel. He maintained that if ARVN reorganized from a Corps model to smaller units, it would be better suited to fight the Việt Cộng. He also recommended that the Civil Guard be trained, advised, and equipped by the United States to take over the static duties of the ARVN.[114] McGarr was not able to respond to Durbrow's points until after the attempted coup d'état. When he did, McGarr defended the 20,000-man increase.[115] It was necessary to allow for better troop rotation to give units time to rest or train. It would also allow for greater coverage of Vietnam's long borders and difficult terrain. There was no substitute for additional forces to do these two things. McGarr did agree with a few of the minor points Durbrow offered, such as eliminating Military Region and the Field Command headquarters, though the number of personnel it might free up was insignificant. He, however, held firm against the idea of using the increase as a way to leverage reforms. The situation was too critical.

McGarr handed the differences in opinion that he had with Durbrow over to the Department of Defense. He hoped that Admiral Felt would be in a better position to counter the Department of State actions.[116] McGarr did warn Felt that Ngô Đình Diệm was likely to proceed in increasing his military plan regardless of the United States decision and that American support for it would allow MAAG to guide the Vietnamese rather than deal with decisions made outside of their influence. Durbrow used Parsons as his Washington champion and provided his insight on the MAAG comments on November 30.[117] He continued to think that the reforms initiated by the Saigon Government did not justify American support for the increase in military personnel. Durbrow was clear that the United States needed to use the 20,000-man increase request as a reward for appropriate reforms as he saw fit. Only reforms would bring about the successful conclusion of the American objectives in Vietnam. The extra military forces would not make a significant difference. Durbrow knew that this ran counter to Ngô Đình Diệm, who valued American support for this project. That Durbrow chose to use it for bargaining rather than acknowledge Ngô Đình Diệm's real need would not have sat well with the Vietnamese president.[118]

Ngô Đình Diệm's objections to the way the American embassy was dealing with the Vietnamese were well known. On November 28, he and Ngô Đình Nhu met with Hohler and complained that the Americans in Saigon misunderstood them.[119] This was especially true of the American press. Both brothers knew that Hohler would pass this information on to Durbrow so it allowed them to voice their opinions without directly embarrassing, or confronting, the American ambassador. Tensions ran high in Saigon. When Nguyễn Đình Thuận met with Gardiner to discuss a temporary end to conscription, Gardiner told him the Vietnamese would have to pay the cost. Nguyễn Đình Thuận relayed the conversation to Ngô Đình Diệm with the added comment that, "this was the first time we have ever received authorization to spend our own money."[120] While not all American relations with members of the Saigon Government were strained, the Country Team members seemed to be the focal point for much of the animosity.

If events during the attempted coup d'état strained the United States–Vietnamese relationship, the days that followed brought it to the brink of failure. Neither Ngô Đình Diệm nor Ngô Đình Nhu trusted Durbrow, and their general feeling was shared by others within the Saigon Government. This did not mean that all Vietnamese supported Ngô Đình Diệm, and the American embassy was quick to report that opposition. The attempted coup was the culmination of a year of frustration, failed opportunities, and dissent for both the United States and Republic of Vietnam. Neither Durbrow nor Ngô Đình Diệm would recover. Durbrow would be out of Vietnam within six months, while Ngô Đình Diệm started his long, final downward journey that would end with his assassination three years later.

16
Durbrow's Last Days in Vietnam

By the third week after the attempted coup d'état, even Durbrow had to admit that Ngô Đình Diệm was not going to initiate reprisal attacks against those who had sought his overthrow. Việt Cộng activity was on the decline though Durbrow maintained it was the calm before the storm and reforms to the Saigon Government were on their way. Still, Durbrow did not believe Ngô Đình Diệm needed to be rewarded with a 20,000-man increase to his military.[1] He seemed to take Ngô Đình Diệm and Ngô Đình Nhu's resentment for his actions during November 11–12 personally and refused to acknowledge any potential benefits or explanations for their success. Instead, Durbrow argued that the morale of the military was low while the potential leadership of the loyal opposition had been caught up in the post-coup consequences. There was a particular concern for Phan Quang Đán, Dr. Phan Huy Quát, and Phan Khắc Sửu.[2] All three had been arrested. Phan Khắc Sửu and Phan Huy Quát were released, but the status of Phan Quang Đán was unknown.[3] Both Durbrow and Mendenhall justified their anxiety about Ngô Đình Diệm's rule with the criticism expressed by the Saigon intelligentsia over the Phan Quang Đán situation.[4] To the end of the year, Durbrow and Mendenhall set several messages that highlighted the internal dissent in Saigon.[5] Both men worked in concert to gather evidence against Ngô Đình Diệm and block future attempts at rewarding him with additional support to allow the 20,000-man increase.

Durbrow continued to assert that another coup d'état was probable if Ngô Đình Diệm failed to rectify the domestic situation in Saigon. He maintained that Ngô Đình Diệm had no incentive to initiate any changes so long as he was emboldened by groups like the People's Committee Against Rebels and Communists and not countered by American pressure to reform. On December 9, Durbrow was again thwarted in his attempts to connect reforms with a troop increase.[6] Herter, through Parsons, instructed Durbrow to inform Ngô Đình Diệm that the increase was under consideration so that the Vietnamese did not attempt to fulfill their needs by themselves. The Department of State directives suggested that Durbrow's position against Ngô Đình Diệm was waning, though the fight was far from over.

Both the Director of the Office of Southeast Asian Affairs in the Department of State, Daniel Anderson, and Undersecretary of State for Political Affairs, Livingston Merchant, championed Durbrow's side. They argued that Ngô Đình Diệm was either not willing or able to initiate reforms and thought the American position to encourage the troop increase was a reward that Ngô Đình Diệm had not earned.[7] They recommended, instead, that the United States focus any resources marked for the increase to better train the Civil Guard and Self-Defense Corps; this was a position that Durbrow found acceptable.[8] Durbrow was also supported by Chalmers B. Wood, who was now the Officer in Charge of Vietnam Affairs in the Department of State. Wood questioned why Ngô Đình Diệm resented Americans after November 11 though he acknowledged that the lack of support during the crisis was probably the cause.[9] Wood argued against sending a message of support to Ngô Đình Diệm. His position, which also echoed that of Durbrow, was one in which a lack of understanding of the Vietnamese mind and culture was evident. After the attempted coup d'état, the failure to make a serious effort to show support for Ngô Đình Diệm was equivalent to confirming that the United States was not a trusted ally.

Durbrow and Ngô Đình Diệm met on December 14, during which time Ngô Đình Diệm presented his case for additional forces to prepare for the increased military activity from North Vietnam and the urgent need to give the Civil Guard time to train and equip itself for the challenge.[10] Durbrow, confined by his instructions from Washington, did not dissent but observed that it would take time for the troops to get into place before they would be effective. Durbrow's plan to pressure Ngô Đình Diệm for additional reforms received a setback on December 16 when the acting Secretary of State John M. Steeves, who served as the Deputy Assistant Secretary for Far East Affairs, directed Durbrow to focus on finalizing Ngô Đình Diệm's liberalization policies already in motion rather than call for new reforms.[11] The Department of State maintained that the completion of these items before moving on to other reforms would help to smooth relations between Ngô Đình Diệm and the Americans. Steeves was sympathetic to Durbrow's point of view, however.[12] In a December 20 letter to the ambassador, he reaffirmed his support for Durbrow and his strategies in Vietnam. He did not think the 20,000-man increase was necessary and agreed that a more responsive Saigon Government was more important as part of a holistic solution to the Việt Cộng threat. They were joined in this position by Parsons, who had long agreed with Durbrow's methods.

When Durbrow met with Ngô Đình Diệm on December 23 to discuss the possible troop increase, he found the Vietnamese president to be distant in their conversation.¹³ Durbrow followed instructions, even if they were not as stringent as he had hoped, and tried to lessen the negative impact of the American position by reminding Ngô Đình Diệm of the other recent contributions by the United States. Ngô Đình Diệm, however, concentrated on the possibility of the additional troops and the problems with the foreign press. There was a sense of Ngô Đình Diệm's frustration with the lack of support by the non-military elements within the American community in Saigon and their influence on the Vietnamese and other foreign groups opposed to his rule.

After the meeting, and as McGarr had predicted, Ngô Đình Diệm decided to act without United States support. He called up reservists and former ARVN soldiers to serve in the Armed Forces and increased the size of the Civil Guard by 10,000.¹⁴ Upon learning of this, Durbrow found out that Ngô Đình Diệm wanted to contain the Việt Cộng threat before initiating any of the liberalization policy that had already been announced. The meeting with Ngô Đình Diệm and his subsequent announcement pushed Durbrow to the limit. This became evident in Durbrow's end-of-the-year report.¹⁵

Durbrow warned of difficult times in Vietnam based on his assessment of the climate of dissatisfaction that permeated Saigon. He believed it possible that Ngô Đình Diệm's rule would be short-lived and, as a result, the United States needed to consider who might replace him. Given the recent events and Vietnamese reaction to them Durbrow might have been overly pessimistic, though those in the Department of State did not think so. Parsons praised Durbrow and his Country Team though he requested that they ease the pressure for liberalization and warned that discussions on Ngô Đình Diệm's replacement be kept secret.¹⁶ Durbrow's position, however, was emboldened by a recent CIA report that argued for the same thought process in selecting a new leader, given the political climate in Saigon.¹⁷ While there were several options as a replacement for Ngô Đình Diệm, the CIA warned that any new leadership would not be as strong as the current one.¹⁸ Such an attempt would also result in an internal struggle that would only help the Việt Cộng.

While Durbrow searched for alternatives to an uncooperative Ngô Đình Diệm, McGarr countered with a telegram to Admiral Felt in which he argued that the United States needed to provide Ngô Đình Diệm with the resources he needed in order to be successful. The situation in Laos continued to be worrisome while the Việt Cộng gave every indication that its activities would intensify.¹⁹ The combined pressure from McGarr, Ngô Đình Diệm, and Washington eventually convinced Durbrow that the United States needed to support the additional troop request. He acknowledged the current crisis in Southeast Asia and the reality that Ngô Đình Diệm was not going to change his mind, though Durbrow still advocated pressuring the Vietnamese president to reform and liberalize his government.

With the New Year, Durbrow made a concerted effort to mend relations with Ngô Đình Diệm, though repairing the damage done in the previous month, and strained relations since Durbrow's arrival in Vietnam, would take time.[20] There would still be challenging obstacles ahead, as Lansdale would visit Saigon and the presidential elections were scheduled for April 1961. Durbrow had been opposed to Lansdale's visit for a number of reasons but conceded his approval so long as certain conditions were met. He wanted to control Lansdale just as he had been trying to control Ngô Đình Diệm.

Parsons and Durbrow shared this perspective. Parsons wanted to use it as a way to strengthen Durbrow's position with Ngô Đình Diệm so that the Vietnamese president would be more malleable to the ambassador's advice.[21] The Department of Defense, however, had different ideas. Lansdale's visit to Saigon was an opportunity to gather information on the country's internal security and reconnect with Ngô Đình Diệm, in order to heal some of the damage inflicted from the previous year.[22] Because Lansdale had a positive history with Ngô Đình Diệm, it was believed he had the best opportunity to accomplish this mission. This fell more in line with Lansdale's goals for the trip.[23] When he eventually arrived in Vietnam on January 2, Lansdale found a Vietnam in need of change, encouragement, and a realistic assessment of the situation.

Upon his return from Vietnam after his thirteen-day trip, Lansdale submitted his findings, which elicited much discussion and debate in Washington.[24] He warned of the increased Việt Cộng threat and the real possibility that it might not be stopped unless the United States moved quickly, though he also cautioned that future American moves needed to acknowledge Vietnamese strategy and needs. A loss in Vietnam would have repercussions throughout the world and significantly affect the United States' position in the postcolonial regions. However, Lansdale affirmed his support for Ngô Đình Diệm as the most likely leader to be successful in achieving Vietnamese and American objectives. He warned of the possibility of another coup d'état, perhaps in reference to the CIA and Durbrow messages, as a real threat to Vietnam. There were too many factions in Saigon vying for power that would not be able to wield it should Ngô Đình Diệm fall. As such, Ngô Đình Diệm was the best solution to the current crisis and Lansdale stressed the necessity to make sure the Vietnamese president understood that he had the full confidence of all Americans.

Lansdale also criticized some of the Americans in Saigon with the observation that they were entangled in the political intrigue in that city. This caused a rift with Ngô Đình Diệm, who was generally the target of their attacks. Lansdale named no specific individuals, though there was an implied sense that Durbrow and Mendenhall were at the top of his list. He asserted that these individuals were doing more harm to American efforts than good.

He did recommend that Durbrow's time in Vietnam should be near its end, maintaining that he was tired and had lost focus on the ultimate United States' objectives for Southeast Asia.[25] He also wanted to see USOM Director Arthur Gardiner relieved as well. Lansdale offered a list of qualifications for the next ambassador who would see Vietnam towards its goal of a democracy, with veiled criticisms of how Durbrow had behaved towards Ngô Đình Diệm during his tenure.[26] He commented on the events since November 11 and how it had affected Ngô Đình Diệm, with the suggestion that a new ambassador would need to work with the Vietnamese president rather than browbeat him into initiating unwanted reforms.

While Lansdale was in Vietnam, a long anticipated study titled *Basic Counterinsurgency Plan for Viet Nam* was released.[27] The January 4 draft of the report, which was overseen by Mendenhall, who chaired the committee responsible for its development, highlighted the negative effects of Ngô Đình Diệm, Ngô Đình Nhu, and Madame Nhu though it acknowledged that Ngô Đình Diệm was the best leader available. Both Lansdale's trip report and the *Basic Counterinsurgency Plan for Viet Nam* were discussed at the White House on January 28 with Lansdale and Parsons championing each one respectively.[28] John F. Kennedy, who had been recently sworn in as the United States president on January 20, questioned the value of additional troops, given that they would not be available for at least one year, as well as why additional troops were necessary when the Vietnamese Armed Forces outnumbered the Việt Cộng 17 to 1. Kennedy was not a novice on Vietnamese matters having taken an interest in the country as a member of the American Friends of Vietnam while serving as the junior Senator from Massachusetts.[29]

He agreed to send a note of confidence to Ngô Đình Diệm after Lansdale reviewed his findings that pointed to the current poor relations being a result of the American Embassy in Saigon rather than the American military personnel stationed there. A letter had already been drafted by the new Secretary of State, Dean Rusk, in response to the letter of congratulations sent by Ngô Đình Diệm after Kennedy's victory in November. Rusk defended Durbrow's performance in Vietnam, given the difficult nature of the job but also agreed that Durbrow needed to be rotated out of Vietnam. Throughout the meeting, Lansdale seemed to have the upper hand and was even allowed to brief Kennedy on what needed to be done to win in Vietnam.[30] One point of emphasis for Lansdale was that Ngô Đình Diệm had lost confidence in the United States Embassy staff and that their opportunity to influence his future actions had been forfeited.

After the meeting, Parsons worked to counter Lansdale's assessment. He met with Rusk later in the day after Rusk asked for further information on Vietnam and Lansdale.[31] Parsons argued that Lansdale was not working as a member of the American foreign policy team but rather as a lone wolf. He suggested that part of Lansdale's assessment was based on his dislike for the Country Team rather than the actual situation in Saigon. It focused too much on United States actions rather than what the Vietnamese needed to do though this assessment falls into line with what Lansdale had argued even if Parsons did not see it. The United States needed to act to assist Vietnam rather than have Vietnam respond to American requirements. Parsons was highly complementary of Durbrow, who he argued had saved Ngô Đình Diệm during the attempted coup d'état, even though there was no evidence to suggest such an action. He also asserted that Ngô Đình Diệm was an unpopular leader whose effectiveness was waning. In the end, Kennedy agreed to authorize the funds to increase the Vietnamese military by 20,000 personnel, as well as dedicate additional assistance to improve the Civil Guard.[32]

On January 30, Lansdale sent Ngô Đình Diệm a note of thanks for the kindness shown him during the visit to Vietnam though he also offered some advice that did not go through the Department of State channels.[33] He urged Ngô Đình Diệm to reorganize his cabinet and decentralize control of significant responsibilities. He also suggested a conference to reappraise the military situation and that it include McGarr and Colby. Lansdale did not mention Durbrow or other members of the Country Team. Finally, he called on Ngô Đình Diệm to work with the opposition and include them in the country's governance. Not only would this counter American concerns but it would rally individuals to the Republic.[34]

While Lansdale seemed to have the advantage after the January 28 meeting, Durbrow continued to push his agenda.[35] He agreed with Lansdale that the United States needed to show its support for Ngô Đình Diệm but he worried that anything originating from Washington before the presidential elections in April would signal American backing of Ngô Đình Diệm and discourage opposition candidates from running. He also maintained that a letter of support would counter his instructions of pushing for liberalization. Any pressure that Durbrow had managed to achieve would be lost. He argued that the United States needed to continue to apply pressure while guiding the Vietnamese towards a more liberal Republic. He did not agree that a two-party system would work, as Lansdale had advocated, until the opposition became more sophisticated and Ngô Đình Diệm more willing to allow it to function. Interestingly, Durbrow worried that another coup d'état attempt would allow Ngô Đình Diệm to distance himself from American advice, even as he continued to lament the failure of the last attempt.

Ngô Đình Diệm began to implement Lansdale's advice on February 6 when he gave his first press conference to foreign correspondents.[36] During the conference, Ngô Đình Diệm was affable and informative, responding to questions about the reorganization plans in his government and his strategies to defeat the Việt Cộng.[37] Ngô Đình Diệm's press conference even impressed and encouraged Durbrow.[38] In reporting the event, Durbrow expressed confidence that Ngô Đình Diệm's reforms were more than he had expected while his call for decentralization was promising. For the first time in a while, Durbrow was encouraged by what he saw in Ngô Đình Diệm.

Durbrow's cause for encouragement did not mitigate the desire to initiate reforms. Within the new Kennedy administration, he found a supporter in Under Secretary of State Chester Bowles. Bowles met with Trần Văn Chương on January 25 to discuss the Vietnam situation.[39] He focused on the need for land redistribution either neglecting or not knowing about the extensive redistribution program that had already been accomplished in Vietnam. Bowles thought that Vietnam needed an aggressive program similar to the Thailand or Japanese model. Trần Văn Chương diplomatically reminded Bowles of the North Vietnamese failure in their land redistribution scheme because it moved too fast, though he did not remind Bowles that neither Japan nor Thailand had to deal with an insurgency while conducting such a scheme. Trần Văn Chương also did not correct Bowles on Vietnam's history of land redistribution, though it might have been frustrating to have a member of the new administration recommend a plan that had already been in operation for some time.

It might also have been disconcerting for Trần Văn Chương that Bowles made an analogy between Vietnam's current alliance with the United States and the earlier American alliance with Britain in the 19th century that allowed the United States to flourish. Connecting the benefits of working with a colonial country was probably not what Bowles advocated though the link was evident. In addition to Bowles, Wood continued to advocate Durbrow's position, meeting with the British Minister in the United States Viscount Samuel Hood and his staff to review Durbrow's attempts to initiate liberalization in Vietnam and *Basic Counterinsurgency Plan for Viet Nam*.[40] Wood shared Durbrow's encouraging observations that Ngô Đình Diệm's recent actions indicated a move toward liberalization with which Lord Hood agreed.

The Vietnamese response to the *Basic Counterinsurgency Plan for Viet Nam*, provided by Nguyễn Đình Thuận at the end of February, was also encouraging.[41] The response came quicker than Durbrow had predicted and supported most of the American concepts. Nguyễn Đình Thuận was concerned with the plan to create a zone along the Cambodian border because it would force the removal of many people living in that area, though the issue of how to pay for the 20,000-man increase had been resolved. The Saigon Government did raise concerns about the idea to give the National Assembly a greater role in serving as the ombudsman over Ministry operating expenses and appointing members of the opposition to the cabinet. Nguyễn Đình Thuận also indicated that Ngô Đình Diệm was willing to discuss further reforms and a change in status of the Cần Lao Party.[42]

All of these announcements demonstrated that Ngô Đình Diệm was moving in the right direction. Whether these moves had been pushed along because of Durbrow's pressure or as part of the evolution of the Republic was debatable. Durbrow had been in Saigon for nearly four years and, after the events of November and the Washington meetings in January, it was clear that his time was up in Vietnam. His replacement, Frederick E. Nolting, Jr., was endorsed by the Vietnamese on February 20, though he would not arrive in country until May.[43] Nolting was a bit of an unknown in Saigon, though his work under the Department of State had gained him experience in service at the North Atlantic Treaty Organization and North Atlantic Council in Paris. Before Nolting arrived, however, Durbrow still had work to do to finalize his legacy in Vietnam.

On March 1, Rusk instructed Durbrow to begin implementing the *Basic Counterinsurgency Plan for Viet Nam* with or without Ngô Đình Diệm's approval.[44] The Kennedy administration was eager to appear to be winning in Vietnam in order to demonstrate its commitment to the Free World as well as signal to the Soviet Union that the policy of Containment was still active.[45] Specifically, Rusk wanted Durbrow to initiate the sections that improved the quality of MAAG personnel and introduce British advisors into ARVN despite the earlier objections of MAAG and Lansdale. Rusk also indicated the need to implement the part of the *Basic Counterinsurgency Plan for Viet Nam* which reorganized the ARVN to be better suited to counter the Việt Cộng. Durbrow was eager to comply and expressed his concern over the inability of Ngô Đình Diệm and Nguyễn Đình Thuận to endorse the plan, suggesting that the delay was a product of Ngô Đình Diệm's refusal to diminish his power.[46] Even if Durbrow was correct, it was reasonable to understand his inaction based on the events of 1960. If Ngô Đình Diệm showed signs of weakness, the various opposition groups would be more interested in assuming power than sharing it.

Another concern with Rusk's instructions was the implied consent to move quickly rather than allow the *Basic Counterinsurgency Plan for Viet Nam* to develop naturally. McGarr was particularly worried about this aspect of Rusk's directive and argued that it would impede the progress that had already been achieved.[47] McGarr recognized that if the Vietnamese were told what to do rather than advised in their actions, the response would be to shut out the Americans. This was similar to what Williams and Lansdale had warned, though the new Administration did not have that institutional knowledge.

Durbrow discussed the *Basic Counterinsurgency Plan for Viet Nam* with Nguyễn Đình Thuận on March 11.[48] The first problem was funding the plan. The Vietnamese were seeking a VN $1,500,000,000 loan but could not find a bank willing to fund military projects exclusively rather than combining it with economic development. Nguyễn Đình Thuận also repeated his concerns about bringing the opposition into the Cabinet though Durbrow insisted that the loyal opposition needed to be included. It was not clear that the two sides agreed on the definition of loyalty, and Ngô Đình Diệm certainly had a right to be skeptical after November 11. Nguyễn Đình Thuận also balked at relinquishing oversight power to the National Assembly as required in the *Basic Counterinsurgency Plan for Viet Nam* though he indicated that Ngô Đình Diệm would allow the press to attend National Assembly hearings and report on them. This positive move, in Durbrow's mind, was countered by the failure to either reform or dismantle the Cần Lao Party.

McGarr, who had been confident that Ngô Đình Diệm would accept the *Basic Counterinsurgency Plan for Viet Nam* when he met with him on March 6, was less assured after the Durbrow-Ngô Đình Diệm conversation.[49] In a letter to Nguyễn Đình Thuận, McGarr warned that the military plan needed to be fully approved and funded before it began. A piecemeal approach, as it appeared to be, was less guaranteed to be successful.[50] When Durbrow met again with Ngô Đình Diệm on March 16, he informed him that he would be seeing Rusk in Bangkok and would need to provide an update on the plan's status.[51] He essentially gave Ngô Đình Diệm a ten-day period to identify military and civilian personnel to meet with their American counterparts to finalize the plan. Ngô Đình Diệm still resisted, despite the logic behind the argument, including admitting the opposition into his cabinet so soon after November 11. He was not willing to disband the Cần Lao Party when it was significant to his continued rule and a necessary part for the improvement of the Republic.[52]

Nguyễn Đình Thuận met with the Country Team to discuss the plan, resolving a number of the military issues, and had another conversation with Rusk and Durbrow on March 27 when all three were at the SEATO Council meeting in Bangkok.[53] Nguyễn Đình Thuận explained to Rusk why Ngô Đình Diệm had yet to enact the liberalization policies that Durbrow and the Department of State had pushed, citing the insurgency and cost involved in both building infrastructure and defending the Vietnamese people. Rusk informed Nguyễn Đình Thuận that Kennedy personally approved the Basic Counterinsurgency Plan and acknowledged Vietnam's financial difficulties. The cost of the new strategy remained an obstacle for the Vietnamese that played a role in their delay of accepting the entire plan. When Trần Văn Chương met with the Acting Assistant Secretary for Far Easter Affairs John M. Steeves on April 8, he made a strong request for additional aid beyond the U.S. $41,000,000 offer that was tied to a VN $1,500,000,000 Vietnamese contribution that was detailed in the plan.[54] With the National election looming, there seemed little chance that the Basic Counterinsurgency Plan would be finalized.

Rostow's intent was to have Ngô Đình Diệm authorize it after the April

9 election and recommended that McGarr return to Washington to brief Nolting before his arrival. The two could then return to Vietnam together and represent a united front with the objective of finalizing the Basic Counterinsurgency Plan. Rostow required action rather than discussion to resolve the Vietnam problem. He wanted greater use of the American military equipment already in country, and a change of attitude that held back nothing to achieve the end objective of a free, democratic Vietnam void of a Communist threat.[55] With the election near, he would not have to wait long before the United States could take a more active stance.

The election for president and vice president of the Republic of Vietnam was an important milestone for the young Republic. There was some controversy surrounding the election law though it was compiled by an interparliamentary committee that had broad representation.[56] Members of the opposition also believed that their ability to have a voice during the campaigning was greatly diminished.[57] One advantage that Ngô Đình Diệm did have as the incumbent was the ability to make appearances in his role as president that also served as campaigning. This was done before the other candidates in the election were even allowed to declare their intent to run.[58] However, it was difficult to distinguish actual presidential duties from campaigning, and Ngô Đình Diệm would have been criticized for inactivity had he refrained from his normal routine of inspection trips. In addition, as an obvious candidate, Ngô Đình Diệm received hundreds of endorsements before the filing deadline. This allowed his name to appear in the Vietnamese press as a candidate, thus building his momentum for a re-election bid, well before others had a chance to participate in the process.

Groups and organizations such as the faculty and staff of the Schools of Liberal Arts, Law, Science, Pedagogy, and Advanced Architecture, Ex-Servicemen's Association, National Revolutionary Movement, Women's Association, Association for the Study of Confucius, Buddhist Association, and Vietnamese Confederation of Christian Workers supported his cause early. They were followed by hundreds of petitions, rallies, and notes of support from within the country.[59] These endorsements and rallies were not recounted by the Embassy to Washington, though Durbrow would observe how impressed he was with Ngô Đình Diệm when the official campaigning began. Ngô Đình Diệm and vice presidential candidate Nguyễn Ngọc Thơ formed the first slate of candidates when the list became available on February 7.[60] Slate II included presidential candidate Nguyễn Đình Quát and his running mate, Nguyễn Thành Phương. Hồ Nhật Tân headed Slate III with Nguyễn Thế Truyền.[61] The three slates were validated by the National Assembly.

Though all three slates offered unique positions and solutions to the challenges facing the Republic of Vietnam, it was clear that Slate I had an advantage not only as being the incumbent but also relied on a practiced political strategy that offered the best chances for success. This was seen in something as simple as the Slate emblem, for which Slate I chose portraits of themselves, while the other two Slates selected a buffalo and lotus flower. The latter two choices were symbolic to Vietnam, but in this modern political campaign image recognition was significant.[62]

The campaign season would last for twenty-five days with strict rules on everything from how many posters and flyers a candidate could put up to a schedule of when and where candidates or their representatives would speak.[63] This was designed to make the individual candidates' exposure as equal as possible though Ngô Đình Diệm still had the advantage as he needed to continue his role and responsibilities as president. However, Ngô Đình Diệm made sure not to become involved in the organization of the process and left the logistics to the Central Presidential Election Campaign Committee.[64] There were nearly seven million eligible voters in the Republic of Vietnam with ten percent residing in Saigon.[65] Slate II and Slate III needed to actively campaign outside the capital if they wanted to be competitive. The campaigning period made that difficult as did the familiarity of Ngô Đình Diệm with the Vietnamese people. Ngô Đình Diệm did not commit much time to campaigning because the other two Slates had failed to make an impact. As his representatives upheld the accomplishments of Slate I, Ngô Đình Diệm focused on the Basic Counterinsurgency Plan for Viet Nam, the departure of Durbrow, and the arrival of a new ambassador.

There was not much reporting of the campaigning originating from the United States embassy in Saigon other than possible instances of potential election fraud. John Helble, Third Secretary of the Embassy, reported on a conversation he had with the Directorate General of Customs, Hoàng Huy. Hoàng Huy alleged that the Saigon Government had issued secret orders to have all government employees advocate for Slate I as they provided an explanation of the electoral process.[66] The plan was to publicize the fact that the employees were helping individuals understand how democracy worked while privately recording how each family planned to vote. Implied in the accusation was that Ngô Đình Diệm was developing a reprisals list for after the election. There was no evidence that Helble or anyone else in the Embassy had a copy of the secret message, though it was allegedly handed out to thousands of government employees. Helble, like many within the Embassy, did not need physical evidence to pass along the allegation.

The election campaign had its share of tense moments but nothing to seriously impede the process. By the time a siren sounded at 7:00 a.m. on April 9, the three Slates had been able to deliver their message to the people, even if those messages varied in effectiveness and relevance. Despite concerns about election-day disruptions, voters turned out in heavy numbers, with long lines and a generally pleasant atmosphere.[67] The night before the election a grenade exploded near the Xóm Côi School, in the eighth district where polling booths had been set up, but otherwise Saigon remained calm.[68] All around Vietnam, every indication pointed to heavy voter turnout and few problems.[69]

There was never a doubt about the election results. Ngô Đình Diệm had greater name recognition throughout Vietnam, was the incumbent, and had a much stronger political organization to back up his re-election campaign. After the results were released and the National Assembly certified the final vote on April 15, Durbrow sent a somewhat sterile note of congratulations.[70] He praised Ngô Đình Diệm's courage and determination and then reminded him that he would be leaving Saigon soon. Once the election was over, Durbrow began his farewell visits. He was honored at dinners hosted by Vũ Văn Mẫu and the Saigon Lion's Club.[71] His days in Vietnam were numbered, as Nolting planned to arrive shortly to assume the position as ambassador.[72] Durbrow's final public appearance occurred on April 29 during the inauguration of Ngô Đình Diệm.[73] Durbrow delivered Kennedy's note of congratulations but did not make any public comments. On April 30, Durbrow and Ngô Đình Diệm held their final meeting and then he left on May 3, marking the end of his fifty-month tour as the United States ambassador to the Republic of Vietnam.

Conclusion

Much had occurred during Durbrow's tenure in Vietnam that would affect United States–Vietnamese relations, though this has been obscured for the most part by historians of the war who chose to focus on the critical years of 1962 and 1963. Durbrow's time in Vietnam was one that established a foundation of mistrust and frustration between the Republic of Vietnam and its principle ally. The Vietnamese needed the United States if they were to have any chance of surviving the early years in the formation of the Republic but it also required the United States to allow Vietnam to grow and make mistakes as it fashioned its own form of democracy.

Durbrow was either not willing or unable to allow this to happen. His intentions may have been honorable, but his actions in the last year of his ambassadorship cast a veil of frustration over the relationship that neither Nolting nor Ngô Đình Diệm could completely remove. By the time Ambassador Henry Cabot Lodge arrived in Vietnam in August 1963, the once fruitful relationship that had existed with Durbrow in 1957 and Williams and McGarr through the late 1950s and into 1960 had vanished. It was replaced by a real concern on the side of Ngô Đình Diệm that the United States no longer served his best interests. The inevitable path that led to the November 1963 assassination of Ngô Đình Diệm and Ngô Đình Nhu began in the early years of Durbrow's tenure.

In many ways, Durbrow was responsible for the narrative of that path, as he controlled what was reported to Washington and thus provided the data that the State Department used to formulate American foreign policy in Southeast Asia. Filled with hope and determination upon his arrival in 1957, Durbrow set about on the task to aid the Republic of Vietnam and its leader, Ngô Đình Diệm. Over the years that followed, he turned away from the Vietnamese president, as well as his American and Vietnamese supporters. In this shift of perspective, he was aided, if not encouraged, by American career diplomats in Washington, Saigon, and Huế, who believed they knew better than Ngô Đình Diệm how to govern in Vietnam and what was best for the Vietnamese people. The American ambassador, between 1957 and 1961, shaped the narrative coming from Vietnam in the final years of the Eisenhower administration and provided the foundation for State Department policy in Vietnam for the Kennedy administration, which would ultimately abandon Ngô Đình Diệm and assume the primary responsibility for the survival of the country. While Durbrow was not responsible for the tragedy that ensued in Vietnam in the 1960s and 1970s, his actions marked his role in what the country would experience in the years following his departure.

Chapter Notes

Chapter 1

1. Anderson to the Department of State, Telegram 2663, March 2, 1957, Folder 751G.00 (W)/11-357, Box 3344, Central Decimal Files (CDF) 751G, Record Group (RG) 59, National Archives and Records Administration (NARA), College Park, MD. All documents from the CDF that cited, hereafter, without specific additional reference are located in RG 59. See also Anderson to the Department of State, Despatch 252, "Attempted Assassination of President Diem," March 6, 1957, Folder 751G.1/7-855, Box 3346, 751G.

2. Anderson to the Department of State, Despatch 252, "Attempted Assassination of President Diem," March 6, 1957, Folder 751G.1/7-855, Box 3346, 751G. See also Nguyễn Công Luận, *Nationalist in the Viet Nam Wars*, 164.

3. Anderson to the Department of State, Telegram 2713, March 6, 1957, Folder 751G.1/7-855, Box 3346, 751G.

4. Anderson to the Department of State, Despatch 256, "Recent Anti-government Activity in the Cao Dai," March 14, 1957, Folder 751G.00/3-157, Box 3339, 751G, RG 59, NARA.

5. In November, the Voice of the National Salvation Movement, a clandestine broadcast from the Dai Viet, maintained that Phùng had been tortured and then killed while under custody, though no other evidence exists to confirm this assertion. See "Attempts Against Diem's Life Probable," *Voice of the National Salvation Movement*, November 11, 1957, *Foreign Broadcast Information Service* (FBIS), F3, November 13, 1957, Record Group 263: Records of the Central Intelligence Agency, NARA.

6. Ngô Đình Nhu received his education at the University of Paris and the École Nationale des Langues Orientales Vivantes and was the first Vietnamese to attend the École Nationale des Chartes. He was trained as an archivist and, after his return to Vietnam in 1938, served as the Director of Archives and Libraries of Indochina. Ngô Đình Nhu was thought of as a pure intellectual who could write in Greek, Latin, and French. These skills served his brother well, though he was criticized by many of the Saigon intelligentsia, which would lead to his undoing in the early 1960s. See William J. Sebald to the Secretary of State, "Call by Brother of President of Vietnam," March 28, 1957, Folder, "Ngo Dinh Nhu Visit 030.50," Box 1, Entry 5155, "Bureau of East Asian Affairs, Vietnam Desk, Vietnam Subject Files, 1955–1962," RG 59, NARA; and, Lâm Quang Thi, *The Twenty-Five Year Century*, 92.

7. Anderson to the Department of State, Telegram 2732, March 8, 1957, Folder 751G.1/7-855, Box 3346, 751G.

8. Memorandum of Conversation with Ngô Đình Nhu and Trần Văn Chương, "Ngo Dinh Nhu's Views on Vietnamese Affairs," March 25, 1957, Folder 751G.00/3-157, Box 3339, 751G, RG 59, NARA; Eric Kocher to Walter Robertson, "Call by Ngo Dinh Nhu," March 26, 1957, Folder, "Ngo Dinh Nhu Visit 030.50," Box 1, Entry 5155, "Bureau of East Asian Affairs, Vietnam Desk, Vietnam Subject Files, 1955–1962," RG 59, NARA; and, Memorandum of Conversation between Eisenhower, Ngô Đình Nhu, and Trần Văn Chương, "Radio Facilities in Vietnam," March 28, 1957, Folder, "Ngo Dinh Nhu Visit 030.50," Box 1, Entry 5155, "Bureau of East Asian Affairs, Vietnam Desk, Vietnam Subject Files, 1955–1962," RG 59, NARA.

9. Commander in Chief, Pacific, Admiral Felix Stump, to the Chief of the Military Assistance Advisory Group, Vietnam, Samuel Williams, Telegram 192359Z (Navy message), March 20, 1957, *Foreign Relations of the United States* (FRUS), *1955–1957: Volume I: Vietnam*, 766.

10. Williams to Secretary of State, Telegram MAGCH-CH 5515, 210309Z (Navy message),

March 22, 1957, Folder 751G.1/7-855, Box 3346, 751G.

11. Williams to Stump, Telegram MAGCTE-CH 552 (Navy message), March 22, 1957, *FRUS, 1955–1957: Volume I: Vietnam*, 766–768; and, Anderson to the Department of State, Telegram 3116, April 13, 1957, Folder 751G.11/4-357, Box 3346, 751G, RG 59, NARA.

12. Memorandum of Conversation, Ngô Đình Nhu and Trần Văn Chương, and Director of International Cooperation Agency John B. Hollister, "Economic Aid to Viet-Nam," April 4, 1957, Folder 751G.5-MSP/1-357, Box 3351, 751G RG 59, NARA.

13. Memorandum of Conversation, Ngô Đình Nhu and Trần Văn Chương, and, Director of International Cooperation Agency John B. Hollister, "Economic Aid to Viet-Nam," April 4, 1957, Folder 751G.5-MSP/1-357, Box 3351, 751G RG 59, NARA. Ngô Đình Nhu used as his example the question of triangular franc aid and other triangular currency aid asking that the Saigon Government be informed of decisions before the aid was disseminated.

14. Memorandum of Conversation, Ngô Đình Nhu and Trần Văn Chương, and Director of International Cooperation Agency John B. Hollister, "Economic Aid to Viet-Nam," April 4, 1957, Folder 751G.5-MSP/1-357, Box 3351, 751G RG 59, NARA; and, Memorandum for the Record, Assistant Secretary of the United States Army General Staff, Lieutenant Colonel E. B. Roberts, "Report of Chief of Staff's Trip to the Far East Southeast Asia, and Pacific Areas, 16 March–12 April 1957," *FRUS, 1955–1957: Volume I: Vietnam*, 783–787.

15. Memorandum of Conversation, Ngô Đình Nhu and Trần Văn Chương, and Assistant Secretary of Defense Mansfield D. Sprague, "Military Aid for Viet-Nam," April 5, 1957, Folder 751G.5-MSP/1-357, Box 3351, 751G RG 59, NARA.

16. Anderson to the Department of State, Telegram 2957, March 30, 1957, Folder 751G.00/3-157, Box 3339, 751G, RG 59, NARA.

17. Anderson to the Department of State, Despatch 267, "Communist Tract," March 21, 1957, Folder 751G.00/3-157, Box 3339, 751G, RG 59, NARA.

18. An April 7 United States assessment listed the total force at 146,756 with 137,856 in the Army of the Republic of Vietnam, 4,802 in the Navy of the Republic of Vietnam, and 4,098 in the Air Force of the Republic of Vietnam. Anderson to the Department of State, Telegram 3037, April 7, 1957, Folder 751G.00(W)/11-357, Box 3344, CDF; and, Memorandum of Conversation, Ngô Đình Nhu and Trần Văn Chương, and, Assistant Secretary of Defense Mansfield D. Sprague, "Military Aid for Viet-Nam," April 5, 1957, Folder 751G.5-MSP/1-357, Box 3351, 751G RG 59, NARA.

19. Memorandum of Conversation, Ngô Đình Nhu and Trần Văn Chương, and, Director of International Cooperation Agency John B. Hollister, "Economic Aid to Viet-Nam," April 4, 1957, Folder 751G.5-MSP/1-357, Box 3351, 751G RG 59, NARA; and, Memorandum for the Record, Assistant Secretary of the United States Army General Staff, Lieutenant Colonel E. B. Roberts, "Report of Chief of Staff's Trip to the Far East Southeast Asia, and Pacific Areas, 16 March–12 April 1957," *FRUS, 1955–1957: Volume I: Vietnam*, 783–787.

20. Geoffrey Shaw, *The Lost Mandate of Heaven: The American Betrayal of Ngo Dinh Diem, President of Vietnam* (San Francisco: Ignatius Press, 2013).

21. Memorandum of Conversation, Ngô Đình Nhu and Trần Văn Chương, and, Director of International Cooperation Agency John B. Hollister, "Economic Aid to Viet-Nam," April 4, 1957, Folder 751G.5-MSP/1-357, Box 3351, 751G RG 59, NARA; Howard P. Jones to Kenneth Young, "Vietnamese Land Reform Program," April 8, 1957, Folder 503.1 Vietnamese Land Reform Program," Box 3, Decimal File, Entry UD51 Records of the Office of Southeast Asian Affairs (Cambodia and Vietnam), 1953–1958; and, Memorandum of Conversation, "General Conversation with President Ngo Dinh Diem," April 26, 1957, Folder 751G.11/4-357, Box 3346, 751G; and, Durbrow to the Department of State, Telegram 3292, April 30, 1957, Folder 751G.11/4-357, Box 3346, 751G.

22. See Jacobs, *Cold War Mandarin*, 104–105; and, Catton, *Diem's Final Failure*, 58.

23. Anderson to the Department of State, Telegram 3032, April 6, 1957, Folder 751G.11/4-357, Box 3346, 751G.

24. Anderson to the Department of State, Despatch 291, "First Week of National Assembly's Spring Session," April 2, 1957, Folder 751G.21/3-455, Box 3347, 751G. Official English Translation of the Speech Delivered by Trần Văn Lắm, President of the National Assembly, Opening the Assembly's First Regular Session of 1957 is attached.

25. Lloyd C. Gardner, *Approaching Vietnam: From World War II through Dienbienphu* (New York: W. W. Norton & Company, 1988), 21–53.

26. Ronald B. Frankum, Jr., *Operation Passage to Freedom: The United States Navy in Vietnam, 1954–1955*. Lubbock: Texas Tech University Press, 2007.

27. Jessica M. Chapman, *Cauldron of Resistance: Ngo Dinh Diem, the United States, and 1950s Southern Vietnam* (Ithaca, NY: Cornell University Press, 2013).

Chapter 2

1. Durbrow navigated through diplomatic immunity, a Vietnamese and Canadian-led investigation, and the question of whether Embassy personnel should cooperate with the investigation. See Saigon to Secretary of State, Telegram 3118, April 13, 1957, Folder 751G.00 (W)/11-357, Box 3344, 751G; Saigon to Secretary of State, Telegram 3142, April 16, 1957, Folder 751G.00/4-157, Box 3339, 751G, RG 59, NARA; Dulles to American Embassy, Saigon, April 19, 1957, Folder 751G.00/4-157, Box 3339, 751G, RG 59, NARA; and, Saigon to the Department of State, Telegram 3197, April 21, 1957, Folder 751G.00/4-157, Box 3339, 751G, RG 59, NARA. See also Anderson to the Department of State, Despatch 32, "Interrogation of Embassy Employees in Connection with the Cannon Murder Case," July 23, 1957, CDF751G.00/7-2357; and, Anderson to the Department of State, Despatch 61, "The Cannon Murder Case: Fingerprinting of Embassy American Employees," August 13, 1957, CDF 751G.00/8-1357; Saigon to the Department of State, Telegram 3255, April 26, 1957, Folder 751G.00/4-157, Box 3339, 751G, RG 59, NARA; Saigon to the Department of State, Telegram 3257, April 27, 1957, Folder 751G.00/4-157, Box 3339, 751G, RG 59, NARA; and, Saigon to the Department of State, Telegram 3294, April 30, 1957, Folder 751G.00/4-157, Box 3339, 751G, RG 59, NARA.
2. Chapman to Durbrow through Anderson, "Your Call on President Diem Regarding Proposed Schedule of His Visit," Folder 361.1 "Chief Executive President Diem's Visit to Washington," Box 1, Entry 3340B-Vietnam, Saigon Embassy, General Records, 1956–1963, RG 84 Records of the Foreign Service Posts of the Department of State, NARA.
3. Ngô Đình Diệm had spent two years at the Maryknoll Seminaries between 1951 and 1953.
4. Durbrow to the Department of State, Telegram 3185, April 20, 1957, Folder 751G.11/4-357, Box 3346, 751G, RG 59, NARA.
5. Chapman to Durbrow, "Tentative List of Presidential Party," April 20, 1957, Folder 361.1 "Chief Executive President Diem's Visit to Washington," Box 1, Entry 3340B, RG 84, NARA; and, Anderson to the Department of State, "Biographies of Members of President Diem's Party," April 30, 1957, Folder 751G.521-MSP/3-1457, Box 3353, 751G, RG 59, NARA. Ngô Đình Diệm was joined in the trip by Secretary of State at the Presidency and Secretary of State ad interim for Internal Affairs, Nguyễn Hữu Châu, the son-in-law of Trần Văn Chương, the current Vietnamese ambassador to the United States, though he was separated from his wife, the sister to Madame Ngô Đình Nhu. The Americans considered Nguyễn Hữu Châu the most important member of Ngô Đình Diệm's party. See Anderson to the Department of State, Telegram 3352, May 5, 1957, Folder 751G.521-MSP/3-1457, Box 3353, 751G, RG 59, NARA. Anderson maintained that Nguyễn Hữu Châu was second only in influence to Nhu and argued that Nguyễn Hữu Châu saw himself as Ngô Đình Diệm's successor. Secretary of State for Public Works and Communications, Trần Lê Quang, and the Chief of Staff of the Vietnamese Armed Forces and acting senior aide de camp Major General Trần Văn Đôn were also members of the official party. In addition to these three senior officials, Ngô Đình Diệm had also included the Director General of Planning, Huỳnh Văn Điểm, the Administrator General of Foreign Aid, Vũ Văn Thái, the Chief of the President's Personal Staff and Private Secretary, Võ Văn Hải, the Chief of the Presidential Press and Information Service, Tôn Thất Thiện, the Assistant to the Chief of the Internal Services Office at the Presidency, Nguyễn Đình Gia, and Trần Văn An, an employee at the Internal Services Office.
6. Durbrow to the Department of State, Telegram 3292, April 30, 1957, Folder 751G.11/4-357, Box 3346, 751G, RG 59, NARA; and, Durbrow to the Department of State, Telegram 3293, April 30, 1957, Folder 751G.11/4-357, Box 3346, 751G, RG 59, NARA.
7. The Civil Guard was officially established by Ngô Đình Diệm in April 1955 and was organized as a paramilitary organization to assist the ARVN. It had units in nearly every district of each province and was responsible for internal security. The Self-Defense Corps was similar though it operated only at the district level. Both the Civil Guard and the Self-Defense Corps were generally poorly trained and equipped. Their purpose was to patrol the countryside and keep the insurgents off balance. The Republican Youth was also a paramilitary organization designed to recruit the youth toward supporting the Republic of Vietnam and Ngô Đình Diệm.
8. Durbrow to the Department of State, Telegram 3293, April 30, 1957, Folder 751G.11/4-357, Box 3346, 751G, RG 59, NARA.
9. Anderson to Country Team, Vietnam, "GVN's Agenda for Washington's Talks with President Diem," May 3, 1957, Folder 361.1 "Chief Executive President Diem's Visit to Washington," Box 1, Entry 3340B-Vietnam, Saigon Embassy, General Records, 1956–1963, RG 84, NARA.
10. Memorandum of Conversation with President Ngô Đình Diệm, May 3, 1957, Folder 361.1 "Chief Executive President Diem's Visit

to Washington," Box 1, Entry 3340B-Vietnam, Saigon Embassy, General Records, 1956–1963, RG 84, NARA; Anderson to the Department of State, Telegram 3348, May 5, 1957, Folder 751G.00(W)/5-457, Box 3344, 751G, RG 59, NARA; Anderson to the Department of State, Telegram 3358 (in two sections), May 6, 1957, Folder 751G.11/5-157, Box 3346, 751G, RG 59, NARA; and, Director of the Office of Southeast Asian Affairs Kenneth T. Young, Jr., to Assistant Secretary of State for Far Eastern Affairs Walter Robertson, "Points Ngo Dinh Diem will probably raise in talk with President," May 9, 1957, Folder 751G.11/5-157, Box 3346, 751G, RG 59, NARA.

11. Also present in the meeting were C. Hoyt Price, Officer-Charge, Cambodian Affairs, Frederick Bunting, Chief, Cambodia, Laos, and Vietnam Division, International Cooperation Agency (ICA), and Mary Joan Fox, acting Desk Officer, Vietnam, ICA. See Memorandum of Conversation, "Economic Aid in Viet-Nam," May 7, 1957, Folder 751G.5-MSP/5-757, Box 3351, 751G.

12. Memorandum of Conversation, "General Discussion of Situation in North Viet-Nam by President Ngo Dinh Diem," May 9, 1957, *FRUS, 1955–1957: Volume I: Vietnam*, 794–799. Also present at the meeting were Nguyễn Hữu Châu, ambassador Trần Văn Chương, John Foster Dulles, Walter Robertson, and the interpreter Charles Sedgwick.

13. On May 10, Ngô Đình Diệm met with Deputy Secretary of State Donald A. Quarles and the other with Dulles and State Department staff; Durbrow attended both meetings. See "Meeting Between President Diem and Deputy Secretary Quarles," May 10, 1957, Folder 751G.11/5-1557, Box 3346, 751G, RG 59, NARA; and, Memorandum of Conversation, "Economic Aid Problems in Viet-Nam," Folder 751G.5-MSP/5-757, Box 3351, 751G, RG 59, NARA. Ngô Đình Diệm argued that the communist Chinese were training and equipping the communist insurgents in the Southeast Asia. He also expressed concern for the security of Laos, which was central to the defense of Vietnam.

14. Memorandum of Conversation, "Military Aid and Force Levels," May 9, 1957, *FRUS, 1955–1957: Volume I: Vietnam*, 799–801.

15. Memorandum of Conversation, "The Situation in Laos," May 9, 1957, *FRUS, 1955–1957: Volume I: Vietnam*, 801–802; and, Memorandum of Conversation, "Chinese Minority Problem," May 9, 1957, *FRUS, 1955–1957: Volume I: Vietnam*, 803–806. Walter Robertson's version of the Chinese discussion is located in the document, Memorandum of Conversation, "Chinese Minority Problem," May 9, 1957, Folder 751G.08/9-656, Box 3346, 751G, RG 59, NARA.

16. Memorandum of Conversation, "Chinese Minority Problem," May 9, 1957, Folder 751G.08/9-656, Box 3346, 751G, RG 59, NARA; Department of State to the American Embassy, Taipei, Telegram 876, May 17, 1957, Folder 751G.08/9-656, Box 3346, 751G, RG 59, NARA; and, Department of State to the American Embassy, Taipei, Telegram 886, May 21, 1957, Folder 751G.08/9-656, Box 3346, 751G, RG 59, NARA.

17. One instance of this assessment came on the long flight to Los Angeles during which Trần Văn Chương and Durbrow reviewed Ngô Đình Diệm's speech for in that city. Ngô Đình Diệm was a nearly silent observer in the conversation. See Memorandum of Conversation, "Doubtful SEATO and American aid in case of armed hostilities in Vietnam," May 17, 1957, *FRUS, 1955–1957: Volume I: Vietnam*, 820–822; and, Durbrow to the Department of State, Despatch 383, "Transmittal of Memoranda of Conversations Regarding the Defense of Viet Nam," June 11, 1957, CDF 751G.5/6-1157. The conversation centered around Trần Văn Chương's assertion that the Vietnamese people feared that the United States would not come to their aid in some circumstances of a northern invasion, nor would the United States employ an atomic or hydrogen bomb to defend the Republic of Vietnam. Durbrow listened to Trần Văn Chương and reported his remarks to Washington and Commander-in-Chief, Pacific Admiral Felix B. Stump, whom Ngô Đình Diệm was scheduled to meet on May 20. Stump made it a point to reassure Ngô Đình Diệm of America's intention of honoring its commitments as well as its flexibility in using atomic weapons depending upon the circumstances, though he made no reference to the Durbrow–Trần Văn Chương exchange or even indicated that Durbrow had briefed him. See Memorandum of Conversation, "Summary of Talk Between Admiral Stump and President Ngo Dinh Diem at Honolulu," May 20, 1957, *FRUS, 1955–1957*: Volume I: Vietnam, 822–823. The episode demonstrated to Ngô Đình Diệm that Durbrow listened to his counterpart and respected his opinion enough to report it to his superiors.

18. Department of State to the United States Embassy in Paris, Telegram 6059, May 28, 1957, Folder 751G.5/5-2456, Box 3347, 751G, RG 59, NARA.

19. Durbrow to the Department of State, Telegram 3517, May 24, 1957, Folder 751G.11/5-2157, Box 3346, 751G; and, Durbrow to the Department of State, Telegram 3526, May 25, 1957, Folder 751G.00(W)/5-457, Box 3344, 751G, RG 59, NARA.

20. Department of State to the United States Embassy, Saigon, May 24, 1957, Folder 751G.11/5-257, Box 3346, 751G, RG 59, NARA; Correspondence and the actual exchange is located in Folder 361.1 Chief Executive President Diem's Visit to Washington, Box 1, Entry 3340B-Vietnam, Saigon Embassy, General Records, 1956–1963, RG 84 Records of the Foreign Service Posts of the Department of State, NARA.

21. Operation Exodus was the Vietnamese name for their role in assisting the 810,000 individuals who chose to move South during the 300-day period between 1954 and 1955 that was outlined in the 1954 Geneva Agreements.

22. Durbrow to the Department of State, Telegram 3548, May 29, 1957, Folder 751G.08/9-656, Box 3346, 751G, RG 59, NARA.

Chapter 3

1. Durbrow to the Department of State, Despatch 386, "Reactions of President Ngo Dinh Diem to State Visit to the United States," June 15, 1957, CDF 751G.11/6-1557.

2. Durbrow to the Department of State, Telegram 3570 (Corrected), June 1, 1957, CDF 751G.00(W)/6-157.

3. Durbrow to the Department of State, Telegram 3616, June 8, 1957, CDF 751G.00(W)/6-857.

4. The note was mentioned in the Saigon-Cholon Press Review for August 2. The paper that reported the event was *Công nhân*. See FBIS, G1, August 5, 1957. Lê Quang Vinh, better known as Ba Cụt, was a military commander in the Hòa Hảo who was involved in the 1955 attempt to remove Ngô Đình Diệm from power. In 1956, he was captured and publically beheaded. See also Dommen, *The Indochinese Experience of the French and Americans*, 281, 299.

5. Central Intelligence Agency Current Intelligence Weekly Summary, OCI No. 3959/57, August 15, 1957, 7. See also Strom to the Department of State, Telegram 171, August 16, 1957, CDF 651G.51H/8-1657. A longer history of the tension was reported in "Geographic Intelligence Review," Central Intelligence Agency, Office of Research and Reports, CIA/RR-MR-53, October 1957, Declassified Documents, NARA.

6. Strom to the Department of State, Telegram 136, August 8, 1957, CDF 651G.51H/8-857.

7. Corcoran to the Department of State, Telegram 99, August 12, 1957, CDF 651G.51/8-857.

8. Durbrow to the Department of State, Telegram 329, August 14, 1957, CDF 651G.51H/8-1457.

9. Durbrow to the Department of State, Telegram 637, September 24, 1957, CDF 651G.51H/9-2457.

10. Strom to the Department of State, Telegram 209, August 24, 1957, CDF 651G.51H/8-2457. Norodom Sihanouk, the son of King Norodom Suramarit and Queen Sisowath Kossamak, became king in September 1941 after the death of his maternal father, Chea Sim, on 23 April 1941. Sihanouk was anti-colonial and advocated an end to French rule in Indochina. On 2 March 1955, Sihanouk abdicated the throne to his father, Norodom Suramarit, and took the position of prime minister. In 1960 after his father died, Sihanouk became Cambodian head of state. His rule in Cambodia was characterized by an anti–Vietnamese, anti–Ngô Đình Diệm position that helped to maintain a tense relationship between Cambodia and the Republic of Vietnam.

11. Kellogg to the Department of State, Despatch 72, "Cambodian negotiations with Vietnam, North and South," August 28, 1957, CDF 651G.51/8-2857. Kellogg also noted that Ngô Trọng Hiếu was known for being overly optimistic.

12. Strom to the Department of State, Telegram 266, September 8, 1957, CDF 651G.51H/9-357.

13. Memorandum of Conversation between Durbrow and Ngô Đình Diệm, September 11, 1957, CDF 751G.11/9-957.

14. Alfred E. Wellons, First Secretary of the United States Embassy in New Delhi to the Department of State, Despatch 330, "Cambodian complaint against South Viet Nam," September 25, 1957, CDF 651G.51H/9-2557. See also United States ambassador to India, Ellsworth Bunker, to the Department of State Telegram 860, October 2, 1957, CDF 651G.51H/10-157.

15. Durbrow reported two days later to Washington that MAAG had seen no attempt by the Vietnamese to build up troop strength near the border. He also recommended not bringing pressure to Ngô Đình Diệm to settle the issue before his trip to the Republic of Korea. See Durbrow to the Department of State, Telegram 556, September 13, 1957, CDF 651G.51H/9-1357.

16. Strom to the Department of State, Telegram 272, September 11, 1957, CDF 651G.51H/9-1157.

17. Bowie to the Department of State, Despatch 80, "Fanatic Sect Appears in Southwest Viet Nam," August 20, 1957, CDF 751G.00/9-357.

18. American Embassy, Saigon to the Department of State, Despatch 78, "September 2, 1957, Weekly Economic Review," September 3, 1957, CDF 851G.00/9-357.

19. Durbrow to the Department of State, Despatch 106, "Conversation with President Ngo dinh Diem, September 16, 1957," September 26, 1957, CDF 751G.00/9-2657. The memorandum of conversation is attached.

20. The need to increase the armed forces by 20,000 was continually pressed by the Vietnamese. On October 29, Ngô Đình Diệm met with Assistant Secretary of Defense for International Security Affairs Mansfield Sprague and reiterated the need for a 170,000-man army. See "Record of Conversation between the President and Honorable M. D. Sprague, Ass't Sec. Def/ISA," October 29, 1957, Folder 2, "Ngo-Dinh-Diem-Conferences, October-December 1957," Box 13, Papers of Samuel T. Williams (Williams Papers), Hoover Institute, Stanford University, Palo Alto, Calif. Ngô Đình Diệm again brought up the need during his debriefing to Durbrow of his conversation with Prime Minister of India and Minister for External Affairs and Commonwealth Relations Jawaharlal Nehru. He visited India in early November. See Memorandum of Conversation "President Ngo dinh Diem's Visit to India," November 11, 1957, Folder 751G.11/9-957, Box 3346, CDF.

21. Ngô Đình Diệm was aided by his Ministers, such as Secretary of State for Information Trần Chánh Thành, who traveled to Malaya at the end of June to coordinate the exchange of diplomatic representatives and build up cultural exchanges. See Durbrow to the Department of State, Telegram 22, July 6, 1957, CDF 751G.00(W)/7-657.

22. Durbrow to the Department of State, Despatch 48, "Official Visit of President Ngo dinh Diem to Thailand, August 15 to 19, 1957," August 1, 1957, CDF 751G.11/8-157. See also, Durbrow to the Department of State, Telegram 241, August 3, 1957, CDF751G.11/8-357.

23. Katay was not able to form a government and Bong Souvannavong was designated by the Crown Prince Savang Vatthana to form one in late June. See "Bong Souvannavong Issues Policy Statement," *Laotian Home Service*, June 25, 1957, FBIS, I1, June 26, 1957. When he failed to accomplish this, Katay was requested to try again. He failed. It was not until August 9 that Souvanna Phouma was able to form a cabinet acceptable to the Laotian National Assembly. See "Laos Assembly Approves New Government," FBIS, I1, August 9, 1957.

24. Durbrow to the Department of State, Despatch 107, "President DIEM's Remarks to Senator SPARKMAN Concerning Laos and Cambodia," September 26, 1957, CDF 751G.11/9-2657. The Memorandum of Conversation is attached.

25. Counselor of the Embassy in Laos Leonard Bacon outlined three dangers of continued United States–Loatian relations which included their negotiations with the Pathet Lao, the subversion in the provinces and the irregular use of aid funds. See Bacon to the Department of State, Telegram 463, September 26, 1957, CDF 651G.51J/9-2657.

26. Durbrow to the Department of State, Telegram 3616, June 8, 1957, CDF 751G.00(W)/6-857. See also Durbrow to the Department of State, Telegram 3570 (Corrected), June 1, 1957, CDF 751G.00(W)/6-157.

27. Durbrow to the Secretary of State, Telegram 3583, June 4, 1957, CDF 751G.00/6-457.

28. Durbrow to the Department of State, Despatch 413, "Withdrawal of French Air and Naval Training Missions," June 27, 1957, CDF 751G.58/6-2757.

29. *Tự do* Editorial, June 4, 1974, FBIS, G1, June 5, 9157. See also, "Exiles form National Salvation Movement," *Tự do*, June 4, 1957, FBIS, G2, June 7, 1957. Tự do was established by a group of journalists who fled the Democratic Republic of Vietnam during the 300 days following the 1954 Geneva Agreements. It was funded, in part, by the Saigon Government and American investors. See Nguyễn Thái, "South Vietnam" in *The Asian Newspapers' Reluctant Revolution*, 243.

30. "Change in SVN Government Prognosticated," *Sống chung*, June 7, 1954, FBIS, H1, June 28, 1957.

31. Durbrow to the Department of State, Despatch 1, "President Ngo dinh Diem's Views on Recent Malicious Rumor Campaign," July 1, 1957, CDF 751G.00/7-157.

32. Durbrow to the Department of State, Despatch 1, "President Ngo dinh Diem's Views on Recent Malicious Rumor Campaign," July 1, 1957, CDF 751G.00/7-157.

33. Phan Quang Đán, "We Protest Against the Clearing of the Chuong Duong Quay," *Thời luân*, June 30, 1957, FBIS, G6, July 9,1957. See also, Phan Quang Đán interview in *Troi Nam*, July 3, 1957, FBIS, G3–G6, July 9, 1957. Second part of the interview is located in FBIS, G4–G5, July 10, 1957.

34. Phan Quang Đán, "The Saigon-Bien Hoa Highway," *Thời luân*, August 4, 1957, FBIS, G6, August 6, 1957.

35. "Letter from a group of Chinese merchants in Cholon," *Thời luân*, August 25, 1957, FBIS, G4, August 28, 1957. See also "Soldiers Ask Why Discharges Are Delayed," *Thời luân*, August 25, 1957, FBIS, G4–G5, August 30, 1957; and, Phan Quang Đán, "Consequences of Ordinance No. 53," *Thời luân*, June 16, 1957, FBIS, G2, June 26, 1957.

36. Bowie to the Department of State, Despatch 82, "Trial of Twenty-Three Binh Xuyen

Rebels," September 6, 1967, CDF 751G.00/9-657. See also, Phan Quang Đán, "On the Occasion of the Recent Political Trials," *Thời luận*, September 1, 1957, FBIS, G1, September 4, 1957.

37. Bowie cited the Vietnamese journalists Nguyễn Ngọc Liên, a leader among the Saigon intelligentsia, and Lê Quang Luật, who had been Minister of Information in one of Ngô Đình Diệm's earlier cabinets. The final source was Chương Văn Dīnh, the Chief of Protocol in the Foreign Office. See Bowie to the Department of State, Despatch 82, "Trial of Twenty-Three Binh Xuyen Rebels," September 6, 1967, CDF 751G.00/9-657.

38. Durbrow to the Department of State, Telegram 559, September 15, 1957, CDF 751G.00(W)/9-1557.

39. For *Ngôn luận*'s position, see FBIS, G2, September 11, 1957.

40. Durbrow to the Department of State, Telegram 610, September 21, 1957, CDF 751G.00(W)/9-2157.

41. See Saigon-Cholon Press Review for September 5, 1957, FBIS, G1, September 5, 1957; and, *Cách mạng Quốc gia* editorial on September 5, 1957, FBIS, G2, September 5, 1957. *Lê Sống* also published a critical piece on Phan Quang Đán. *Đan Nguyên* echoed the ideas of *Ngôn luận*. See Saigon-Cholon Press Review for September 7, 1957, DBIS, G1, September 9, 1957. *Cách mạng Quốc gia* was published by the Movement for National Revolution and was decidedly pro–Ngô Đình Diệm. See Nguyễn Thái, "South Vietnam" in The Asian Newspapers' Reluctant Revolution, 243.

42. "Restoration Party Leader Counter Dan," *Tự do*, September 3, 1957, DBIS G2, September 6, 1957. An October 4 editorial in *Tự do* stated that *Thời luận*'s survival was necessary, despite its shortcomings, for the promotion of Democracy. See Press Review for October 4, FBIS, G4, October 4, 1957; and, "Don't Kill Thoi Luan," *Tự do*, October 4, 1957, FBIS, G3–G5, October 4, 1957.

43. Press Review for September 9, 1957, FBIS, G2, September 9, 1957.

44. "Mobs Reported to have Attacked Thoi Luan," *Sun Wun Jinh Pao*, September 8, 1957, FBIS, G3, September 9 1957; and, "Police Investigating," *Yuan Thun Jinh Pao*, September 10, 1957, FBIS, G1, September 10, 1957. See also "Report by Eyewitness," *May Jin Luan Zan*, September 10, 1957, FBIS, G2, September 10, 1957.

45. "More Details on Raids," *Vietnam Press*, September 8, 1957, FBIS, G4, September 10, 1957.

46. Durbrow to the Department of State, Despatch 112, "Conversation with President Ngo dinh Diem, September 27, 1957," October 3, 1957, CDF 751G.11/10-357. The memorandum of conversation is attached. See also a similar memorandum of conversation, October 17, 1957, Box 3340, Folder 751G.009-1257.

47. Record of Conversation with President Diem, June 18, 1957, Folder 1, "Ngo-Dinh-Diem-Conferences, January–September 1957," Box 13, Williams Papers.

48. The strategic importance of the Central Highlands and Durbrow's involvement in that area is explored in Harris, *Vietnam's High Ground*, 37, 44, and 46.

49. Memorandum of Conversation between Ngô Đình Diệm and Williams, August 27, 1957, Folder 1, "Ngo-Dinh-Diem-Conferences, January–September 1957," Box 13, Williams Papers.

50. Ngô Đình Diệm questioned the USOM practice of over planning for the perfect road when all that was needed was scraping to make the roads passable. While it would not last as long, it did require less planning, resources, and execution. See Record of Conversation with President Ngô Đình Diệm, June 27, 1957, Folder 1, "Ngo-Dinh-Diem-Conferences, January–September 1957," Box 13, Williams Papers; Durbrow to the Department of State, Despatch 17, "Conversation with the President," July 16, 1957, CDF 751G.11/7-1657; Memorandum of Conversation between Ngô Đình Diệm and Williams, August 27, 1957, Folder 1, "Ngo-Dinh-Diem-Conferences, January–September 1957," Box 13, Williams Papers. See also Williams to Durbrow and Barrows, "Conference with President Ngô Đình Diệm, 27 August," August 28, 1957, Folder 1, "Ngo-Dinh-Diem-Conferences, January–September 1957," Box 13, Williams Papers. When Vice Admiral George Anderson visited Vietnam on July 22, Ngô Đình Diệm used their meeting as an opportunity to get additional ships to stop the increased Viet Cong infiltration by sea. See Memorandum of Conversation "Meeting at Presidential Palace, 22 July 1957," Folder 1, "Ngo-Dinh-Diem-Conferences, January–September 1957," Box 13, Williams Papers.

51. "President Ngo Dinh Diem's Speech on Third Anniversary of Accession to Office, July 7, 1957, folder 7, box 15, Douglas Pike Collection, Unit 6-Democratic Republic of Vietnam, The Vietnam Archive, Texas Tech University.

52. Memorandum of Conversation between Ngô Đình Diệm and Durbrow, July 23, 1957, CDF 751G.11/5-2157. See also Durbrow to the Department of State, "Conversation with President Ngo dinh Diem, July 23, 1957," July 30, 1957, CDF 751G.11/7-3057.

53. Barbour to the Department of State, Despatch 3, "Contacts, abortive an Otherwise, with the Ngo Family at Hue," August 30, 1957,

CDF 751G.11/8-3057. The United States Consulate opened on July 29, 1957. See also Dommen, *The Indochinese Experience of the French and Americans*, 301–302.

54. Barbour to the Department of State. Telegram 5, September 9, 1957, CDF 751G.00/9-957.

55. Jelley defined "mandarin mentality" as being aristocratic, bureaucratic, and authoritarian. See Memorandum of Conversation between Robert E. Jelley and Nguyễn Văn Báu, "Comments by Nguyen Van Bau on Current VN Affairs," September 18, 1957, CDF 751G.009-1857. Apparently, Nguyễn Văn Báu was making the rounds because he had a similar conversation with Thomas Bowie, Counselor of the United States Embassy for Political Affairs. See also Bowie to the Department of State, Despatch 139, "Conversation with Nguyen van Bau, National Assembly Deputy," October 24, 1957, CDF 751G.00/10-2457.

Chapter 4

1. Durbrow to the Department of State, Despatch 115, "Conversation with President Ngo dinh Diem on October 1, 1957," October 8, 1957, CDF 751G.00/10-857. The memorandum of conversation is attached.

2. Memorandum of Conversation of the same meeting recorded by Williams, October 1, 1957, Folder 2, "Ngo-Dinh-Diem-Conferences, October–December 1957," Box 13, Williams Papers. William's transcript of the meeting was much more exact than the one provided by Durbrow.

3. Durbrow to the Department of State, Despatch 115, "Conversation with President Ngo dinh Diem on October 1, 1957," October 8, 1957, CDF 751G.00/10-857. See also Durbrow to the Department of State, Telegram 902, October 28, 1957, CDF 751G.5 MSP/10-2857.

4. Durbrow to the Department of State, Telegram 1269, December 16, 1957, CDF 751G.5 MSP/12-1657.

5. Ngô Đình Diệm was referring to a May 13, 1957 *Life* Magazine article by John Osborne that labeled him the "Tough Miracle Man of Vietnam." See "The Tough Miracle Man of Vietnam," *Life* Magazine, May 13, 1957, 156–158. The article was part of a larger public relations campaign that occurred in connection with Ngô Đình Diệm's trip to the United States during that same month. See also Jacobs, "America's *Miracle Man in Vietnam*," 221.

6. "Record of Conversation between President Ngo Dinh Diem and General Williams," October 5, 1957, Folder 2, "Ngo-Dinh-Diem-Conferences, October–December 1957," Box 13, Williams Papers. See also Williams to Durbrow, "Conference with President—4 October 1957," October 5, 1957, Folder 2, "Ngo-Dinh-Diem-Conferences, October–December 1957," Box 13, Williams Papers.

7. Durbrow to the Department of State, Despatch 162, "Conversation with Nguyen huu CHAU on Subject of Financial Aid to the Self-Defense Corps," November 5, 1957, CDF 751G.5/11-557.

8. The two met again on November 7, while Ngô Đình Diệm was in India, to discuss budgetary matters. Durbrow again questioned the value of the Self-Defense Force and reported that Nguyễn Hữu Châu appeared to be unable to answer the same questions he had asked on their previous visit. It was clear that Durbrow had established his position and reported it as such to Washington. See Memorandum of Conversation between Nguyễn Hữu Châu and Durbrow, "Economic Aid Problems, Civil Guard, and Self-Defense Force," November 7, 1957, Folder "751G.5-MSP/10-257," Box 3351, RG 59. NARA. See Also Durbrow to the Department of State. Despatch 180, "Memorandum of Conversation Between Ambassador Durbrow and Nguyen huu Chau," November 21, 1957, CDF 751G.5 MSP/11-2157. The Country Team in Vietnam consisted of representatives of the Military Assistance and Advisory Group, United States Operations Mission, United States Information Service and, Office of the Special Assistant to the ambassador in Vietnam, and the United States Embassy in Saigon.

9. Memorandum of Conversation, "Conversation between General Williams and President 3 December 1957," December 3, 1957, Folder 2, "Ngo-Dinh-Diem-Conferences, October–December 1957," Box 13, Williams Papers.

10. "General Williams–President Diem Conversation 20 December 1957," Folder 2, "Ngo-Dinh-Diem-Conferences, October–December 1957," Box 13, Williams Papers.

11. "General Williams–President Diem Conversation 20 December 1957," Folder 2, "Ngo-Dinh-Diem-Conferences, October–December 1957," Box 13, Williams Papers, 1.

12. Ngô Đình Diệm needed the tents because he had no place to stay when he visited Pleiku and Kontom. He had stayed at the house of the Province Chief in Pleiku but it was small and when he did stay there, the family had to move out. Ngô Đình Diệm did not want to disturb them. See "General Williams' Visit to President Diem 27 December 1957," Folder 2, "Ngo-Dinh-Diem-Conferences, October–December 1957," Box 13, Williams Papers, 4–5.

13. Durbrow to the Department of State,

Despatch 237, "Highlights of Trips through Countryside with President Ngo dinh DIEM," January 6, 1958, CDF 751G.11/1-658.

14. Durbrow to Official Americans in Saigon, October 4, 1957, Folder "CDF 751G.00/9-1257," Box 3340, RG 59, NARA.

15. Durbrow to the Department of State, Despatch 121, "Possible Terrorist Campaign Against Americans in Viet Nam," October 10, 1957, CDF 751G.00/10-1057. See also "Record of Conversation between President Ngo Dinh Diem and General Williams," October 5, 1957, Folder 2, "Ngo-Dinh-Diem-Conferences, October–December 1957," Box 13, Williams Papers. See also Williams to Durbrow, "Conference with President—4 October 1957," October 5, 1957, Folder 2, "Ngo-Dinh-Diem-Conferences, October–December 1957," Box 13, Williams Papers.

16. Durbrow to the Department of State, Telegram 843, October 22, 1957, CDF 751G.00/10-2257. Earlier, on October 14, two unexploded grenades with their pins pulled were found on the eaves of an apartment on Gia Long Street in Saigon. While there was no indication that they were directed towards Americans, the grenades were designed to cause damage and destruction for all around had they detonated. See Ðan Nguyên, October 16, 1957, FBIS, G8, October 17, 1957. See also Mann, *A Grand Delusion*, 212–213.

17. Durbrow to the Department of State, Telegram 848, October 22, 1957, CDF 751G.00/10-2257.

18. *Tự do* published an editorial that asserted the attacks were designed to thwart the Colombo Plan conference that was going on in Saigon. See Saigon-Cholon Press Review for October 24, 1957, FBIS, G1, October 24, 1957. See also, "Communists' Warlike Tactics Scored," *Tự do*, October 23, 1957, FBIS, G7-G8, October 24, 1957. On October 10, 1958, Ngô Ðình Diệm informed Durbrow that the Communist agent responsible for the three bombings had been captured.

19. Durbrow to the Department of State, Telegram 868, October 24, 1957, CDF 651G.51H/10-2457.

20. "Record of Conversation between the President and General Williams," October 24, 1957, Folder 2, "Ngo-Dinh-Diem-Conferences, October–December 1957," Box 13, Williams Papers.

21. "U.S. Suffers Bombings for Backing Diem," *Voice of the National Salvation Movement*, October 23, 1957, FBIS, F1-F2, October 28, 1957. See also "Diem Police Cannot Maintain Security," *Voice of the National Salvation Movement*, October 25, 1957, FBIS, F3-F4, October 28, 1957.

22. Durbrow to the Department of State, Telegram 944, November 2, 1957, CDF 751G.00(W)/11-257.

23. Saigon-Cholon Press Review for October 28, 1957, FBIS, G1, October 28, 1957.

24. "7. Security Situation in South Vietnam," November 8, 1957, Central Intelligence Agency, Office of Current Intelligence, Current Intelligence Bulletin, November 8, 1957, Declassified Documents, NARA.

25. "Labor Confederation Writes President," *May Jih Luan Zan*, November 15, 1957, FBIS, G2, November 15, 1957.

26. "Paper Scores Raid on Border Residents," *Sống chung*, October 15, 1957, FBIS, H1, October 22, 1957. On November 6, the French-language *Agence Khmer Presse* reported of an additional skirmish on October 6 and denied that Cambodians had been driven out of South Vietnam as *Công nhân* and *Lê Sống* had reported on October 14. See "Statement on Border Clashes Issued, *Agence Khmer Presse*, October 20, 1957, FBIS, H1, November 6, 1957.

27. One of the issues with this cross border skirmishes was whether or not the Vietnamese involved were military personnel or groups of insurgents or bandits. The Cambodian press reported the skirmishes with armed Vietnamese without making the distinction most of the time, though often the forces being engaged were the same ones that Ngô Ðình Diệm was trying to eliminate. See Strom to the Department of State, Telegram 610, December 3, 1957, CDF 651G.51H/12-357.

28. Dulles to the American Embassy in Saigon, Telegram 708, October 12, 1957, CDF 651G.51H/10-1257.

29. Durbrow to the Department of State, Telegram 773, October 11, 1957, CDF 651G.51H/10-1157.

30. "Record of Conversation between the President, General Williams, and General Myers," October 13, 1957, Folder 2, "Ngo-Dinh-Diem-Conferences, October–December 1957," Box 13, Williams Papers.

31. Strom to the Department of State, Telegram 415, October 15, 1957, CDF 651G.51H/10-1557.

32. Durbrow to the Department of State, Telegram 804, October 16, 1957, CDF 651G.51H/10-1657. Durbrow included the United States embassy in Phnom Penh in this telegram and it seems written for Strom than Washington.

33. Durbrow to the Department of State, Telegram 820, October 18, 1957, CDF 651G.51H/10-1857.

34. Southeast Asian Affairs Director Eric Kocher to Assistant Secretary of State for Far Eastern Affairs, Walter Robertson, "Recent

Negotiations Between the Cambodians and the Viet-Minh," November 15, 1957, CDF 651G.51H/11-1557.

35. Durbrow to the Department of State, Telegram 808, October 17, 1957, CDF 651G.51H/10-1757. See also Durbrow to the Department of State, Despatch 167, "Conversation with President Diem on October 17, 1957," CDF 751G.00/11-1257.

36. Durbrow to the Department of State, Telegram 863, October 23, 1957, CDF 651G.51H/10-2357.

37. Durbrow to the Department of State, Telegram 876, October 24, 1957, CDF 651G.51H/10-2457.

38. Strom to the Department of State, Telegram 503, November 4, 1957, CDF 61G.51H/11-457.

39. Durbrow to the Department of State, Telegram 918, October 29, 1957, CDF 651G.51H/10-2957.

40. Kellogg to the Department of State, Telegram 466, October 29, 1957, CDF651G.51H/10-3057.

41. Williams to Stump, October 18, 1957, Folder 2, "Ngo-Dinh-Diem-Conferences, October–December 1957," Box 13, Williams Papers. The *Voice of the National Salvation Movement* offered the same assessment in its October 25 broadcast. See FBIS, F3-F4, October 28, 1957.

42. Kellogg to the Department of State, Telegram 435, October 22, 1957, CDF 651G.51H/10-2257.

43. Durbrow to the Department of State, Telegram 951, November 3, 1957, CDF 651G.51/11-357.

44. "Military Pact with Pathet Lao Announced," *Laotian Home Service*, November 13, 1957, FBIS, I1, November 15, 1957. See also "Political Pact with Pathet Lao Signed," *Laotian Home Service*, November 14, 1957, FBIS, I1, November 18, 1957. The official ceremony of the handover of the San Neua took place on December 8. See "Ceremony Marks Transfer of Pathet Lao," *Laotian Home Service*, December 11, 1957, FBIS, I1, December 12, 1957. Phong Saly was turned over in a December 18 ceremony. See "Phong Saly Administration Transferred," *Laotian Home Service*, December 21, 1957, FBIS, I1, December 23, 1957.

45. "7. Laotian Government Acts to Check Subversion," November 30, 1957, *Current Intelligence Bulletin*, Office of Current Intelligence, Central Intelligence Agency, Declassified Documents, NARA.

46. Memorandum of Conversation, "Conversation between General Williams and President 3 December 1957," December 3, 1957, Folder 2, "Ngo-Dinh-Diem-Conferences, October–December 1957," Box 13, Williams Papers.

47. Saigon-Cholon Press Review, December 5, FBIS, G1, December 5, 1957.

48. "Activities of Mr. L. of the OSS Organization in Vietnam," Ðan Nguyên, September 28, 1957, FBIS, G4, October 1, 1957.

49. "Dan Nguyen Demands Answers from Dr. Dan," Ðan Nguyên, October 3, 1957, FBIS, G6, October 4, 1957.

50. "Our Answer to the Slanders Against Dr. Phan Quang Dan," Thời luận, September 29, 1957, FBIS, G4-G7, October 3, 1957.

51. "Postponement Granted in Thoi Luan Trial," *Times of Vietnam*, October 4, 1957, FBIS, G3, October 7, 1957.

52. "Don't Kill Thoi Luan," Tự do, October 4, 1957, FBIS, G3-G5, October 4, 1957.

53. "State Should Reimburse Ransacked Papers," Thời luận, October 13, 1957, FBIS, G4-6, October 15, 1957; Chinh Nghia, "To Comply with the People's Wishes," Thời luận, October 13, 1957, FBIS, G5-G6, October 15, 1957; and, Nghiem, Xuan Thien, "Building Democracy in the South," Thời luận, October 13, 1957, FBIS, G7-G8, October 15, 1957.

54. "Indictment Against Thoi Luan Dismissed," Ngôn luận, October 12, 1957, FBIS, G9, October 15, 1957. On November 21, Phan Quang Ðán was acquitted in a different defamation suit brought forth by Phục Quốc Hội (Cao Ðài Political Party). Thời luận was convicted of two other charges of defamation; one against the Economic Control Service for which it was fined 20,000 piasters and another against the Armed Forces for 10,000 piasters. It was acquitted of a defamation charge against the police and Sûreté. See Durbrow to the Department of State, Telegram 1105, November 24, 1957, CDF 751G.00(W)/11-2457.

55. "Press Must Unite to Fight Intimidation," Dân chúng, November 19, 1957, FBIS, G6, November 20, 1957.

56. "Corrupt Officials Impede Labor Movement," Thời luận, November 9, 1957, FBIS, G1, November 22, 1957.

57. Saigon-Cholon Press Review for November 22–25, 1957, FBIS, G2, November 25, 1957.

58. Saigon-Cholon Press Review for November 27, 1957, FBIS, G1, November 27, 1957. See also Durbrow to the Department of State, Telegram 1210, December 6, 1957, CDF 751G.00(W)/12-657.

59. Durbrow to the Department of State, Telegram 1122, November 26, 1957, CDF 751G.5 MSP/11-2557.

60. Durbrow to the Department of State, Telegram 1122, November 26, 1957, CDF 751G.5 MSP/11-2557. See also, Memorandum of Con-

versation, "FY 1958 Aid Levels for Viet-Nam," November 25, 1957, CDF 751G.5-MSP/11-2557.

61. Memorandum of Conversation between Ngô Đình Diệm and Durbrow, November 27, 1957, Folder "751G.5-MSP/10-257," Box 3351, CDF. See also, Memorandum of Conversation, Despatch 202, "Conversation with President Ngo dinh DIEM, November 27, 1957," CDF 751G.5 MSP/12-1057.

62. Memorandum of Conversation, "Conversation between General Williams and President 3 December 1957," December 3, 1957, Folder 2, "Ngo-Dinh-Diem-Conferences, October–December 1957," Box 13, Williams Papers.

63. "Budget Conference with the President of Vietnam 29 Nov 57 as recorded by Lt Col Foster, MAAG," November 30, 1957, Folder 2, "Ngo-Dinh-Diem-Conferences, October–December 1957," Box 13, Williams Papers. See also Durbrow to the Department of State, Telegram 1161, November 30, 751G.5 MSP/11-3057.

64. See also Durbrow to the Department of State, Telegram 1161, November 30, 751G.5 MSP/11-3057.

65. "Budget Conference with the President of Vietnam 29 Nov 57 as recorded by Lt Col Foster, MAAG," November 30, 1957, Folder 2, "Ngo-Dinh-Diem-Conferences, October–December 1957," Box 13, Williams Papers.

66. Durbrow to the Department of State, Telegram 1161, November 30, 1957, CDF 751G.5 MSP/11-3057.

67. Confidential Note, December 2, 1957, Folder 751G.5-MSP/10-257, Box 3351, CDF. See also Durbrow to the Department of State, Telegram 1269, December 16, 1957, CDF 751G.5 MSP/12-1657.

68. "General Williams Visit to President Diem—13 December 1957," Folder 2, "Ngo-Dinh-Diem-Conferences, October–December 1957," Box 13, Williams Papers.

69. "General Williams Visit to President Diem—13 December 1957," Folder 2, "Ngo-Dinh-Diem-Conferences, October–December 1957," Box 13, Williams Papers.

70. "General Williams Visit to President Diem—13 December 1957," Folder 2, "Ngo-Dinh-Diem-Conferences, October–December 1957," Box 13, Williams Papers, 6.

71. The Saigon-Cholon Press Review for December 26 has Ngô Đình Diệm visiting the Prech Tong resettlement center, which was about fifty kilometers from Tây Ninh. See Saigon-Colon Press Review, December 26, 1957, FBIS, G1, December 27, 1957.

72. See Strom to the Department of State, Telegram 662, December 21, 1957, CDF 651G. 51H3/12-2157; and, Kellogg to the Department of State, Despatch 192, "Cambodian Plans to Make Landings on Poulo Panjang Island," CDF 651G/51H3/12-23-57.

73. Bowie to the Department of State, Despatch 294, "Peripatetic President," February 17, 1958, CDF 751G.00/2-1758.

Chapter 5

1. It was estimated that the number of attackers was near 500 while the *Times of Vietnam* speculated that the group came from the Cao Đài dissidents that operated in the area. See Durbrow to the Department of State, Telegram 1442, January 11, 1958, CDF 751G.00(W)/1-1158. See also "Armed Gang Attacks French Plantation," *Times of Vietnam*, January 7, 1958, FBIS, G2-G2, January 7, 1958.

2. Personalism, as adopted by Ngô Đình Diệm, derived from the French personalist philosophy as enumerated by Emmanuel Mounier during the interwar period. See Chapman, *Cauldron of Resistance*, 121–124.

3. Durbrow to the Department of State, Despatch 263, "Conversation with Bishop Ngo dinh THUC of Vinh-Long Province Concerning Personalism," January 20, 1958, CDF 751G. 11/1-2058. A memorandum of conversation between the two is attached.

4. Barbour to the Department of State, Telegram 10, January 30, 1958, CDF 751G.00/1-3058.

5. Saigon-Cholon Press Review, January 24, 1958, FBIS, G1, January 24, 1958.

6. Barbour to the Department of State, Despatch 15, "A Distorted Denunciation Campaign in Quang Nam Province," February 20, 1958, CDF 751G.00/2-2058.

7. "Dai Loc Notables Appeal for Justice," *Tự do*, January 20, 1958, FBIS, G3–G5, January 24, 1958.

8. "Dai Loc Notables Appeal for Justice," *Tự do*, January 20, 1958, FBIS, G4, January 24, 1958. See also, "Dai Loc Anticommunist Issue Report," *Tự do*, January 22, 1958, FBIS, G2–G4, January 28, 1958; and, "Dai Loc Anticommunist Issue Report," *Tự do*, January 25, FBIS, G2–G4, January 28, 1958.

9. Barbour to the Department of State, Despatch 16, "Meeting with Ngo dinh Can," February 25, 1958, CDF 751G.11/2-2558.

10. Barbour to the Department of State, Despatch 16, "Meeting with Ngo dinh Can," February 25, 1958, CDF 751G.11/2-2558. Throughout his dispatch, Barbour words and tone are more of a novelist than a diplomat.

11. Bowie to the Department of State, Despatch 297, "Conversation with French Political Counselor," February 22, 1958, CDF 751G.00/2-2258.

12. In the transcript of the conversation, the

word never is emphasized. See "General Williams–President Diem Conversation 8 January 1958," Folder 3, "Ngo-Dinh-Diem-Conferences, January–March 1958," Box 13, Williams Papers.

13. Durbrow to the Department of State, Telegram 1469, January 15, 1958, CDF 651G.51H/1-1558. Another controversy brewed when *Công nhân* published a January 15 article that claimed Prince Nordom Sihanouk absolved all of the Communists in his country of their crimes. *Pracheaserey* published a denial on January 22. See "Khmer Still Neutral Despite SVN Paper," *Sống chung*, January 29, 1958, FBIS, H1, February 5, 1958.

14. Dulles to the American Embassy in Saigon, Telegram 1263, January 16, 1958, CDF 651G.51H/1-1558. See also Strom to the Department of State, Telegram 757, January 16, 1958, CDF 651G.51H/1-1658; and, Strom to the Department of State, Telegram 753, January 16, 1958, CDF 651G.51H/1-1658.

15. United States ambassador to France, Armory Houghton, to the Department of State, Telegram 3674, February 7, 1958, CDF 651G.51H/2-758; and, Under Secretary of State Christine Herter to the American Embassy (Saigon), Telegram 1432, February 7, 1958, CDF 651G.51H/2-758. See also Strom to the Department of State, Telegram 839, February 10, 1958, CDF 651G.51H/2-1058.

16. Strom to the Department of State, Despatch 258, "Cambodian Claims Against South Vietnam and Thailand," February 21, 1958, CDF 651G.51H/2-2158.

17. Memorandum of Conversation, "General Williams Visit to President Diem 23 January 1958," Folder 3, "Ngo-Dinh-Diem-Conferences, January–March 1958," Box 13, Williams Papers, 3–4.

18. Memorandum of Conversation, Despatch 289, "Conversation of Ambassador Durbrow and Mr. Elting with Ngo dinh NHU," February 10, 1958, 751G.00/2-1053.

19. Durbrow to the Department of State, Telegram 1689, February 13, 1958, CDF 651G.51H/2-1358.

20. Strom to the Department of State, Telegram 880, February 25, 1958, CDF 651G.51H/2-2558.

21. Strom to the Department of State, Telegram 884, February 27, 1958, CDF 651G.51H/2-2758. Durbrow later learned that the French government was indifferent to the talks and that the French in Cambodia had been instructed to only take part in the meetings if all parties agreed. They only relented to attend when the Cambodians pressed them. See Durbrow to the Department of State, Telegram 71, July 10, 1958, CDF 651G.51H/7-1058.

22. Durbrow to the Department of State, Despatch 305, "Conversation with President DIEM and Mr. CHAU," March 5, 1958, CDF 751G.11/3-558. A Memorandum of Conversation is attached.

23. Memorandum of Conversation, "General Williams Visit to President Diem 23 January 1958," Folder 3, "Ngo-Dinh-Diem-Conferences, January–March 1958," Box 13, Williams Papers, 2.

24. When Williams and Ngô Đình Diệm met again on February 25, Ngô Đình Diệm expressed a real and immediate concern for the Central Highland regions and the need for additional roads to offset the Communist insurgent infiltration into the region. See "General William's Visit to President Diem 25 February 1958," Folder 3, "Ngo-Dinh-Diem-Conferences, January–March 1958," Box 13, Williams Papers. The Vietnamese worried about how influential the Communist insurgents had become with the Montagnard people. Ngô Đình Diệm used a recent reconnaissance mission and evidence of Việt Minh activity to once again request road equipment. Williams encouraged the Vietnamese president to speak again with Durbrow while he gathered information about a surplus auction in Japan that might yield the desired road building equipment. At one point during the hour long conversation in which Ngô Đình Diệm spoke in English and seemed pressed for time, he indicated that he might have to go to the French for assistance even if the cost was more if the USOM did not act quicker. Ngô Đình Diệm would offer Durbrow the same reasoning and justification on February 27. See Durbrow to the Department of State, Telegram 1770, February 27, 1958, CDF 751G.5 MSP/2-2758.

25. Memorandum of Conversation, "General Williams Visit to President Diem 23 January 1958," Folder 3, "Ngo-Dinh-Diem-Conferences, January–March 1958," Box 13, Williams Papers, 4–5.

26. Memorandum of Conversation, "General Williams Visit to President Diem 23 January 1958," Folder 3, "Ngo-Dinh-Diem-Conferences, January–March 1958," Box 13, Williams Papers, 7.

27. "General Williams' Conference with President Diem-29 March 1958," Folder 3, "Ngo-Dinh-Diem-Conferences, January–March 1958," Box 13, Williams Papers.

28. Durbrow to the Department of State, Telegram 1653 (in two sections), February 8, 1958, CDF 751G.5-MSP/2-858. See also Durbrow to the Department of State, Despatch 293, "Memorandum of Conversation between President Diem and Ambassador Durbrow," February 13, 1958, CDF 751G.5 MSP/2-1358.

29. When Williams and Ngô Đình Diệm

met on February 16, Williams pressed the President on the issue. The Americans had offered an agreement to fund 43,500 Self-Defense Force personnel but Williams could not release the money until the Vietnamese signed a letter accepting caveats from the Country Team. This had been given to the Vietnamese in November 1957. After some discussion, Ngô Đình Diệm agreed to have Nguyễn Hữu Châu sign the letter. See "General Williams Visit to President Diem 16, February 1958" Folder 3, "Ngo-Dinh-Diem-Conferences, January–March 1958," Box 13, Williams Papers. One of Ngô Đình Diệm's concerns was the ability of companies and agencies to pay Tet bonuses. These bonuses helped to stimulate the economy and without them there would be a financial stress. It also led to strikes such as the one taken at a French printing company. See Saigon-Cholon Press Review, February 5, 1958, FBIS, G1, February 5, 1958. If economic programs were canceled or the threat of such cancelations resulted in the elimination or delay of bonuses, more Vietnamese could strike.

30. Durbrow to the Department of State, Telegram 1658, February 8, 1958, CDF 751G.5 MSP/2-858.

31. Durbrow to the Department of State, Telegram 1658, February 8, 1958, CDF 751G.5 MSP/2-858.

32. Elting to the Department of State, Despatch 304, "The Civil Guard," March 1, 1958, CDF 751G.5 MSP/3-158. A copy of Durbrow's letter is attached.

33. Durbrow to the Department of State, Despatch 305, "Conversation with President DIEM and Mr. CHAU," March 5, 1958, CDF 751G.11/3-558. A Memorandum of Conversation is attached.

34. "Civil Guard Meeting with President Diem 5 March 1958," Folder 3, "Ngo-Dinh-Diem-Conferences, January–March 1958," Box 13, Williams Papers. Elting provided a timeline of events from March 5 to March 10. See Elting to the Department of State, Telegram 1848, Mach 11, 1958, CDF 751G.5-MSP/3-1158.

35. "Civil Guard Meeting with President Diem 5 March 1958," Folder 3, "Ngo-Dinh-Diem-Conferences, January–March 1958," Box 13, Williams Papers, 2.

36. How the number increased from 50,000 to 55,000 in the week that passed is not clearly explained though the increase of 5,000 matching the Gendarmerie numbers seems the closest answer.

37. Elting to the Department of State, Despatch 353, "Country Team's Civil Guard Study and GVN Counter-Proposals," April 1, 1958, CDF 751G.5-MSP/4-158.

38. Memorandum of Conversation between Durbrow and Ngô Đình Diệm, March 7, 1958, Folder "751.G.5-MSP/1-1158, Box 3352, CDF.

39. Memorandum of Conversation between Durbrow and Ngô Đình Diệm, March 7, 1958, Folder "751.G.5-MSP/1-1158, Box 3352, CDF.

40. Williams to Colonel Edward G. Lansdale, March 20, 1958, Folder 2, "General K-Y," Box 12, Series "Military Assistance Advisory Group (MAAG), Vietnam, October 1955–August 1960," Williams Papers.

41. Memorandum of Conversation between Elting and Nguyễn Hữu Châu, "Civil Guard," March 10, 1958, Folder 751.G.5-MSP/1-1158, Box 3352, CDF.

42. Elting to the Department of State, Telegram 1848, Mach 11, 1958, CDF 751G.5-MSP/3-1158.

43. Memorandum of Conversation between Roderick Parkes and Howard Elting, "Civil Guard," March 9, 1958, Folder 751.G.5-MSP/1-1158, Box 3352, CDF.

44. While not called by name, Ngô Đình Diệm most likely was referring to Durbrow and Barrows' argument that placing the Civil Guard under the Ministry of Interior would facilitate Congressional approval for additional equipment. This conversation took place before the revised Vietnamese TO&E was submitted.

45. Memorandum of Conversation between Roderick Parkes and Howard Elting, "Civil Guard," March 9, 1958, Folder 751.G.5-MSP/1-1158, Box 3352, CDF. See also Williams to Lansdale, March 20, 1958, Folder 2, "General K-Y," Box 12, Series "Military Assistance Advisory Group (MAAG), Vietnam, October 1955–August 1960," Williams Papers.

46. "Meeting of General Williams and Mr. Chau on 12 March 1958," Folder 3, "Ngo-Dinh-Diem-Conferences, January–March 1958," Box 13, Williams Papers.

47. Elting to Williams, Arthur Gardiner, Bowie, and Nicholas A. Natsios, "Memorandum on Civil Guard," March 12, Folder 751. G.5-MSP/1-1158, Box 3352, CDF.

48. "General Williams Visit to President Diem 26 March 1958," Folder 3, "Ngo-Dinh-Diem-Conferences, January–March 1958," Box 13, Williams Papers.

49. Miller, *Misalliance*, 193–194.

50. Elting to the Department of State, Telegram 2007, March 30, 1958, CDF 751G.13/3-3058. See also Elting to the Department of State, Telegram 2308, May 16, 1958, CDF 751G.00 (W)/5-1458.

51. Elting to the Department of State, Telegram 2276, May 10, 1958, CDF 751G.00(W)/5-1058. See also, "Presidential Secretary," *Yuan Tung Jih Pao*, May 8, 1958, FBIS, G4, May 14, 1958.

Chapter 6

1. "Thoi Luan Issue Seized," FBIS, G2, March 4, 1958. There are some later references that suggest that it was the March 2 issue that was seized though this does not make much sense.
2. "Thoi Luan Publisher Defends His Paper," Ngôn luận, March 7, 1958, FBIS, G3, March 11, 1958.
3. Saigon-Cholon Press Review, March 8, 1958, FBIS, G1, March 10, 1958.
4. Saigon-Cholon Press Review, March 8, 1958, FBIS, G1, March 10, 1958.
5. Saigon-Cholon Press Review, March 12, 1958, FBIS, G1, March 12, 1958.
6. Saigon-Cholon Press Review, March 13, 1958, FBIS, G1, March 13, 1958.
7. "Thoi Luan Publisher Served Summons," Yuan Tung Jih Pao, March 10, 1958, FBIS, G2, March 12, 1958. Yuan Tung Jih Pao also claimed that Phan Quang Đán was served as well but Tự do only lists Nghiêm Xuân Thiện.
8. "Court Forbids Publishing of Thoi Luan," Paris AFP, March 13, 1958, FBIS, G4, March 13, 1958. See also Elting to the Department of State, Telegram 1887, March 15, 1958, CDF 751G.00(W)/3-1558.
9. Saigon-Cholon Press Review, March 14, 1958, FBIS, G1, March 14, 1958.
10. Elting to the Department of State, Telegram 1946, March 22, 1958, CDF 751G.00(W)/3-2258.
11. "Thoi Luan Publisher," FBIS, G4, March 21, 1958.
12. Press Review for March 24, FBIS, G3, March 24, 1957.
13. "Journalists Accused," Saigon-Cholon Press Review, March 25, 1958, FBIS, G3, March 25, 1958. Sài Gòn Mới was a commercial newspaper that did not receive funding from the Saigon Government. It was one of the best-selling Saigon dailies. See Nguyễn Thái, "South Vietnam" in The Asian Newspapers' Reluctant Revolution, 243.
14. "USIS Journalist Arrested," Saigon-Cholon Press Review, March 27, 1958, FBIS, G5, March 27, 1958.
15. "Bubonic Plague," Saigon-Cholon Press Review, March 27, 1958, FBIS, G5, March 27, 1958. The Vietnamese Ministry of Health issued a communiqué on March 27 confirming that the plague had been eliminated in the Long Điền area, "Bubonic Plague," Ah Chau Jih Pao, FBIS, G5, April 2, 1958.
16. Saigon-Cholon Press Review, April 2, 1958, FBIS, G1, April 2, 1958.
17. "We Ask for Release of Phi Van," Dân chúng, April 2, 1958, FBIS, G2-G4, April 7, 1958.
18. Elting to the Department of State, Telegram 2047, April 6, 1958, CDF 751G.00(W)/4-658.
19. Elting to the Department of State, Telegram 2087, April 12, 1958, CDF 751G.00(W)/4-1258. See also, "New Publication," Ngôn luận, April 15, 1958, FBIS, G1, April 18, 1958.
20. "Political Party Legalized," Tự do, April 10, 1958, Saigon-Cholon Press Review, April 15, FBIS, G2, April 15, 1958. See also Phan Quang Đán's April 17 letter to the publisher of Tự do, FBIS, G2-G4, April 21, 1958.
21. "Democratic Party Split," Tự do, April 14, 1958, FBIS, G1, April 18, 1958.
22. "Free Democratic Party," Thôi Quốc, April 29, 1958, FBIS, G2, May 8, 1958. The new party was referred to as the Free or New Democratic Party in some publications. See also Colby, Lost Victory, 63–64.
23. "Interior Official Admonishes Press," Vietnam Press Agency, April 20, 1958, FBIS, G5, April 23, 1958.
24. "A Disciplinary Council for the Press," Ngôn luận, April 21, 1958, FBIS, G2, April 24, 1958.
25. Press Review for April 25, FBIS, G3, April 25, 1958.
26. "Press Disciplinary Council," Dân chúng, April 21, 1958, FBIS, G10, April 25, 1958.
27. Elting to the Department of State, Telegram 2189, April 26, 1958, CDF 751G.00(W)/4-2658.
28. "General Williams–President Diem Conversation-24 May 1958," Folder 4, "Ngo-Dinh-Diem-Conferences, May-August 1958," Box 13, Williams Papers.
29. Elting to the Department of State, Telegram 2357, May 24, 1958, CDF 751G.00(W)/5-2458.
30. Elting to the Department of State, Telegram 2523, June 19, 1958, CDF 751G.00(W)/6-1958; and, Saigon-Cholon Press Review, June 2, 1958, FBIS, G1, June 3, 1958. See also, "Cong Nhan Publication," May Jih Luan Zan, May 19, 1958, FBIS, G4, June 2, 1958.
31. Elting to the Department of State, Despatch 352, "Transmittal of Memorandum of Conversation with President Ngo Dinh DIEM," April 5, 1958, CDF 851G.2612/4-558.
32. "General Williams Visit to President Diem 26 March 1958," Folder 3, "Ngo-Dinh-Diem-Conferences, January–March 1958," Box 13, Williams Papers.
33. Memorandum of Conversation between Ngô Đình Diệm, Trần Lê Quang, Gardiner, and Elting, March 28, 1958. Attached to Elting to the Department of State, Despatch 352, "Transmittal of Memorandum of Conversation with President Ngo Dinh DIEM," April 5, 1958, CDF 851G.2612/4-558.
34. Barbour to the Department of State,

Despatch 19, "Cracks in the Citadel Wall–Central Viet Nam's Disenchanted Intellectuals," April 10, 1958, CDF 751G.00/4-1058.

35. Barbour to the Department of State, Despatch 19, "Cracks in the Citadel Wall–Central Viet Nam's Disenchanted Intellectuals," April 10, 1958, CDF 751G.00/4-1058, 2.

36. Bowie to the Department of State, Despatch 368, "Views of Two Vietnamese Officials on How the Regime Should be Strengthened," April 15, 1958, CDF 751G.00/4-1558.

37. Bowie to the Department of State, Despatch 368, "Views of Two Vietnamese Officials on How the Regime Should be Strengthened," April 15, 1958, CDF 751G.00/4-1558, 3.

38. Bowie forwarded another dispatch on June 13 that relayed a conversation the Second Secretary to the Embassy, Alan Campbell, had had with the Định Tường Province Chief, Nguyễn Trân. See Bowie to the Department of State, Despatch 452, "Conversation with Chief of Dinh Tuong Province," June 13, 1958, CDF 751G.00/6-1358. A memorandum of conversation between Campbell and Nguyễn Trân is attached. The Vietnamese complained over the inability of the government to extend its influence to the South, asserting that it was too top heavy. Nguyễn Trân, a northerner, blamed the poor security in his province on bad administrators. He asserted that the Civil Guard and Self-Defense Corps were overpaid and maintained that he could hired five times the number of personnel than he paid for them and attain his objectives quicker. Nguyễn Trân advocated using American aid for economic infrastructure rather than to build up the military. Essentially, he argued as the Americans under Durbrow had and was another justification for American objections to the rule of Ngô Đình Diệm. Bowie, in reporting the conversation, did admit that Nguyễn Trân was also frustrated because the Civil Action personnel in his province did not answer to him; that is, he was not given a free hand. While this complaint may have been justified, the conflict in Định Tường was really just one battle in a larger war in the Republic of Vietnam. Nguyễn Trân's observation, however, helped to solidify the growing case against Ngô Đình Diệm.

39. "Logistics Briefing for President Diem—29 May 1958," Folder 4, "Ngo-Dinh-Diem-Conferences, May-August 1958," Box 13, Williams Papers.

40. American Embassy, Saigon to the Department of State, Despatch 446, "Weekly Economic Review, May 27–June 2, 1958," CDF 851G.00/6-1058. A transcript of the interview is located in "Ngo Dinh Nhu on Relations with France," *Le Journal D'Extreme-Orient*, June 3, 1958, FBIS, G5, June 5.

41. Elting to the Department of State, Telegram 2492, June 15, 1958, CDF 751G.00(W)/6-1558.

42. "U.S. Specialists Disregard Vietnamese," *Người Việt Tự Do, June 11, 1958*, FBIS, G2–G3, June 12, 1958.

43. This was not an uncommon observation. See Colby, *Lost Victory*, 71.

44. Kellogg, "Issues between Cambodia and Vietnam," attached to Memorandum of Conversation between Kellogg, Chalmers Wood, Cambodian Representative in Saigon, Siem Hieng, and the Chief of the Political Section in the Vietnamese Ministry of Foreign Affairs, Nguyễn Chí, May 21, 1958, CDF 751G.00/5-2158. See also Press Review for June 5, *Cách mạng Quốc gia*, FBIS, G3, June 5, 1958.

45. Strom to the Department of State, Despatch 366, "Cambodian-South Vietnamese Relations," June 5, 1958, 651.51H/6-558. See also Elting to the Department of State, Telegram 2523, June 19, 1958, CDF 751G.00(W)/6-1958.

46. Robertson to the American Embassy, Saigon, Telegram 2145, June 5, CDF 651G.51H/6-658. See also CIA Daily Brief, "Relations Between Cambodia and South Vietnam Deteriorating," *Central Intelligence Bulletin*, Central Intelligence Agency, Office of Current Intelligence, Declassified Documents, NARA, 7.

47. Strom to the Department of State, Telegram 1269, June 11, 1958, CDF 651G.51H/6-1158.

48. Elting to the Department of State, Telegram 2481, June 12, 1958, CDF 651G.51H/6-1258. On June 21 Vũ Văn Mẫu handed Durbrow a note titled, "Note Concerning Incidents on the Vietnamese-Cambodian Frontier Provoked by the Cambodians" that enumerated the numerous violations and the Cambodian intransigence in working with the Vietnamese. See Bowie to the Department of State, Despatch 475, "Vietnamese Note Concerning Incidents on the Vietnamese-Cambodian Frontier," June 27, 1958, CDF 651G.51H/6-2758.

49. Robertson to the American Embassy, Saigon, Telegram 2202, June 13, 1958, CDF 651G.51H/6-1358.

50. Durbrow to the Department of State, Telegram 2497, June 16, 1958, CDF 651G.51H/6-1658. The financial settlement from the Paris Accords was one of many issues that needed to be resolved after the dissolution of the French Union in Southeast Asia. See Deputy Director of the Office of Southeast Asian Affairs Eric Kocher to Chief of the Division of Research and Analysis, Bureau of Intelligence and Research William Magistretti, "The Paris Accords: one of the Bones of Contention between Cambodia and Vietnam," August 4, 1958, CDF 651G.51H/8-458.

51. Strom to the Department of State,

Telegram 1298, June 18, 1958, CDF 651G.51H/6-1958. Vietnamization would take on a new meaning during the Nixon Administration's Vietnam policy.

52. Strom to the Department of State, Telegram 1301, June 18, 1958, CDF 651G.51H/6-1858. See also Durbrow to the Department of State, Telegram 2530, June 20, 1958, CDF 651G.51H/6-2058.

53. Strom to the Department of State, 1334, June 25, 1958, CDF 651G.51H/6-2558. See also "Vietnamese Troops Reported in Cambodia," Paris, AFP, June 25, 1958, FBIS, H1, June 25, 1958.

54. Strom to the Department of State, Telegram 1335, June 25, 1958, CDF 651G.51H/6-2558. See also "Cambodia to Seek Non–U.S. Aid if Forced," *Paris Agence France-Presse*, June 25, 1958, FBIS, H1, June 26, 1958.

55. Strom to the Department of State, Telegram 1337, June 25, 1958, CDF 651G.51H/6-2558. See also CIA Daily Brief, "Cambodia Charges South Vietnam Invasion," June 26, 1958, *Central Intelligence Bulletin*, Central Intelligence Agency, Office of Current Intelligence, Declassified Documents, NARA, 6. A copy of the proclamation is located in Strom to the Department of State, Telegram 43, July 8, 1958, CDF 651G.51H/7-858.

56. Strom to the Department of State, Telegram 1338, June 25, 1958, CDF 651G.51H/6-2558.

57. Durbrow to the Department of State, Telegram 2567, June 26, 1958, CDF 651G.51H/6-2658.

58. Durbrow to the Department of State, Telegram 2567, June 26, 1958, CDF 651G.51H/6-2658, 1–2.

59. Durbrow to the Department of State, Telegram 2568, June 26, 1958, CDF 651G.51H/6-2658.

60. Durbrow to the Department of State, Telegram 2579, June 26, 1958, CDF 651G.51H/6-2658.

61. Durbrow to the Department of State, Telegram 2580, June 26, 1958, CDF 651G.51H/6-2858.

62. Durbrow to the Department of State, Telegram 2580, June 26, 1958, CDF 651G.51H/6-2858.

63. Storm to the Department of State, Telegram 1341, June 26, 1958, CDF 651G.51H/6-2658.

64. Durbrow to the Department of State, Telegram 2585, June 27, 1958, CDF 651G.51H/6-2758.

65. Durbrow to the Department of State, Telegram 2590, June 27, 1958, CDF 651G.51H/6-2758.

66. Durbrow to the Department of State, Telegram 2604, June 27, 1958, CDF 651G.51H/6-2758. Ngô Đình Diệm and Williams discussed the movement of Cambodian troops on July 1 with the same conclusion. See "Interview Between General Williams and President Diem on 1 July 1959," Folder 4, "Ngo-Dinh-Diem-Conferences, May-August 1958," Box 13, Williams Papers.

67. Durbrow to the Department of State, Despatch 7, "Alleged GVN Invasion of Cambodia," July 8, 1958, CDF 651G.51H/7-858.

68. Strom to the Department of State, Telegram 1348 (Section One), June 27, 1958, CDF 651G.51H/6-2758.

69. Strom to the Department of State, Telegram 1348 (Section Two), June 27, 1958, CDF 651G.51H/6-2758.

70. Strom to the Department of state, Telegram 1356, June 28, 1958, CDF 651G.51H/6-2858.

71. Strom to the Department of State, Telegram 1348 (Section Three), June 27, 1958, CDF 651G.51H/6-2758.

72. Saigon-Cholon Press Review, June 27, 1958, FBIS, G1, June 27, 1958. See also Saigon-Cholon Press Review, June 28, 1958, FBIS, G1–G4, June 28, 1958; and, "Cambodia-SVN Border Issue Clarified," *Vietnam Press*, June 26, 1958, FBIS, G3–G4, June 27, 1958. Durbrow reported the press restraint to Washington. See Durbrow to the Department of State, Telegram 5, July 1, 1958, CDF 651G.51H/7-158.

73. "Interview Between General Williams and President Diem on 1 July 1959," Folder 4, "Ngo-Dinh-Diem-Conferences, May-August 1958," Box 13, Williams Papers.

74. Durbrow to the Department of State, Telegram 192, August 2, 1958, CDF 651G.51H/8-258.

Chapter 7

1. Elting to the Department of State, Despatch 28, "Lt. General John W. O'Daniel's report on his visit to Viet-Nam May 19–June 17," July 26, 1958, CDF 751G.00/7-2658.

2. Durbrow to the Department of State, Telegram 428, September 4, 1958, CDF 651G.51H/9-458.

3. Durbrow to the Department of State, Telegram 432, September 5, 1958, CDF 651G.51H/9-558.

4. Chalmers Wood, Second Secretary of the Embassy, to the Department of State, Despatch 38, "The Unification of the National Revolutionary Movement and the Citizens Rally," August 2, 1958, CDF 751G.00/8-258. The merging of chapters for each group occurred over several weeks in the provinces. See "Political Merger," *Vietnam Press*, September 9, 1958, FBIS, G5, September 15, 1958.

5. Daily Briefing, "Souvanna Phouma Fails

in Bid to Form Government in Laos," August 8, 1958, Current Intelligence Bulletin, Central Intelligence Agency, Office of Current Intelligence, Declassified Documents, NARA. See also "Souvanna Phouma Unable to Form Cabinet," *Laotian Home Service*, August 6, 1958, FBIS, I1, August 8, 1958.

6. "Meeting Between Gen Williams and President Diem on 1 September 1958 at 1500 Hours," September 1, 1958, Folder 5, "Ngo-Dinh-Diem-Conferences, September–December 1958," Box 13, Williams Papers.

7. "Phoui Declares Opposition to Communism," Maritime Press Service (Manila), September 2, 1958, FBIS, I1, September 3, 1958.

8. Durbrow to the Department of State, Telegram 1048, December 2, 1958, CDF 651G.51J/12/258.

9. United States ambassador to Laos Horace Smith to the Department of State, Telegram 1079, December 20, 1958, CDF 651G.51J/12-2058.

10. Daily Briefing, "Communist Economic Sabotage in South Vietnam" August 16, 1958, Current Intelligence Bulletin, Central Intelligence Agency, Office of Current Intelligence, Declassified Documents, NARA. See also Saigon-Cholon Press Review, August 14, 1958, FBIS, G1, August 14, 1958.

11. American Embassy, Saigon to the Department of State, Despatch 61, "Weekly Economic Review, August 5–11, 1958," August 19, 1958, CDF 851G.00/8-1858.

12. Memorandum for the Record, "Interview between President Ngo Dinh Diem and Lt Gen S. T. Williams, Chief MAAG, between the hours of 1100 and 1305, 14 August 1958," Folder 4, "Ngo-Dinh-Diem-Conferences, May–August 1958," Box 13, Williams Papers.

13. Memorandum for the Record, "Interview between President Ngo Dinh Diem and Lt General S. T. Williams, Chief MAAG, during the period, 211500 August and 211706 August 1958," Folder 4, "Ngo-Dinh-Diem-Conferences, May–August 1958," Box 13, Williams Papers.

14. "Rubber Plant Damaged," FBIS, G4, October 2, 1958.

15. "Meeting Between Secretary of the Army Honorable Wilber Brucker and President Ngo Dinh Diem of Vietnam—3 September 1958 at 1700 Hours," September 3, 1958, Folder 5, "Ngo-Dinh-Diem-Conferences, September–December 1958," Box 13, Williams Papers.

16. "Meeting Between Secretary of the Army Honorable Wilber Brucker and President Ngo Dinh Diem of Vietnam—3 September 1958 at 1700 Hours," September 3, 1958, Folder 5, "Ngo-Dinh-Diem-Conferences, September–December 1958," Box 13, Williams Papers, 2.

17. The conversation switched to communication and propaganda; Ngô Đình Diệm complained that the Vietnamese equipment was poor and that he relied on Voice of America in the Philippines as the source for Vietnamese propaganda. When Durbrow commented that this solution was temporary, Williams offered the handwritten comment that according to USIS, it was not. While Williams did not contradict Durbrow in the meeting, he noted these and other inconsistencies.

18. "Meeting between the President Ngo Dinh Diem and General Williams on 10 September 1958 at 0900 Hours," Folder 5, "Ngo-Dinh-Diem-Conferences, September-December 1958," Box 13, Williams Papers.

19. "Meeting Between General Williams and President Diem on 23 September 1958 at 1700 Hours," September 23, 1958, Folder 5, "Ngo-Dinh-Diem-Conferences, September–December 1958," Box 13, Williams Papers.

20. Williams to Durbrow, "Visit to President 23 September," September 24, 1958, Folder 5, "Ngo-Dinh-Diem-Conferences, September–December 1958," Box 13, Williams Papers.

21. Daily Briefing, "Discontent in South Vietnam," October 1, 1958, Current Intelligence Bulletin, Central Intelligence Agency, Office of Current Intelligence, Declassified Documents, NARA.

22. Wood to the Department of State, Despatch 132, "Cambodian-Vietnamese Relations: Conversation with Vietnamese Representative, October 8, 1958, CDF 651G.51H/10-858. A memorandum of conversation is attached.

23. Counselor of the Embassy, Randolph Kidder to the Department of State, Despatch 763, "New Vietnamese Dissident Materials," October 28, 1958, CDF751.00/10-2858.

24. Kidder to the Department of State, Despatch 798, "Comments of Quai d'Orsay Official on Vietnam," November 3, 1958, CDF 751.00/11-358. A memorandum of conversation is attached.

25. Kidder to the Department of State, Despatch 798, "Comments of Quai d'Orsay Official on Vietnam," November 3, 1958, CDF 751.00/11-358. A memorandum of conversation is attached.

26. "Meeting Between General Williams and President Ngo Dinh Diem on 30 October 1958," Folder 5, "Ngo-Dinh-Diem-Conferences, September–December 1958," Box 13, Williams Papers.

27. Memorandum of Conversation between Takehiko Nishiyama and R. E. Jelley, December 2, 1958, Folder "500 Aid to Vietnam, 1956–1958," Box 2, Entry 3340B-Vietnam, Saigon Embassy, General Records, 1956–1963, RG 84, NARA.

28. Heavner to the Department of State, Despatch 6, "Hue's Intellectuals," December 12, 1958, CDF 751G.00/12-1258.
29. American Embassy, Paris to the Department of State, January 16, 1959, CDF 751G.00/1-1659.
30. Burgess to the Department of State, Telegram G-1048, February 4, 1959, CDF 751G.00/2-459.
31. Wood to the Department of State, Despatch 256, "Personal Views of the Secretary General of the National Assembly," February 5, 1959, CDF 751G.00/2-559.
32. "Meeting Between General Williams and President Diem on 13 November 1958 at 0900," Folder 5, "Ngo-Dinh-Diem-Conferences, September–December 1958," Box 13, Williams Papers.
33. "Meeting Between Mr. Shuff and President Diem on 14 November 1958," Folder 5, "Ngo-Dinh-Diem-Conferences, September–December 1958," Box 13, Williams Papers.
34. "Meeting Between General Williams, General Lampert and President Diem on 8 December 1958," Folder 5, "Ngo-Dinh-Diem-Conferences, September–December 1958," Box 13, Williams Papers.
35. "Meeting between General Williams and President Diem on 5 January 1959," Folder 6, "Ngo-Dinh-Diem-Conferences, January–August 1959," Box 13, Williams Papers, 3.
36. Saigon-Cholon Press Review, December 2, 1958, FBIS, G1, December 2, 1958.

Chapter 8

1. Durbrow to the Department of State, Telegram 1278, January 3, 1958, CDF 751G.00(W)/1-359.
2. Robertson to Dillon, "Proposed Civil Guard Program for Viet-Nam," January 8, 1959, Folder "Civil Guard," Box 1 Entry 5155, "Asian Affairs, Vietnam Desk, Vietnam Subject Files, 1955–1962," RG 59, NARA.
3. Secretary of State John Foster Dulles, who had been battling cancer, resigned on April 22. During his illness, Christian Herter, who would replace him, signed off on most of the cable traffic to Saigon, Vientiane, and Phnom Penh.
4. Smith to the Department of State, Telegram 1134, January 1, 1959, CDF 651G.51J/1-159. See also "Diplomatic Representation Elevated," Vietnam Press, December 16, 1958, FBIS, G3, December 17, 1958; and, "May Ask U.N. Intervention," Vietnam Press, January 7, 1959, FBIS, I1, January 8, 1959.
5. "DRV Troops Enter Laos in Major Force," Australian Overseas Service, January 4, 1959, FBIS, I1, January 5, 1959. An editor's note marks the first revision two hours after the initial report. DRV stands for the Democratic Republic of Vietnam (North Vietnam).
6. Daily Briefing, "Laos to Protest Border Incursion by North Vietnam," January 3, 1959, Current Intelligence Bulletin, Central Intelligence Agency, Office of Current Intelligence, Declassified Documents, NARA.
7. "Government Release Denies Coup Rumors," Le Journal D'Extreme Orient, January 3, 1959, FBIS, I1, January 5, 1959.
8. Counselor of the United States Embassy in Laos, Leonard Bacon, to the Department of State, Telegram 1155, January 5, 1959, CDF 651G.51J/1-559. See also "Laotian Note Calls DRV Charges False," Laotian Home Service, January 5, 1959, FBIS, I1, January 6, 1959.
9. Bacon to the Department of State, Telegram 1157, January 5, 1959, CDF 651G.51J/1-559.
10. "Pathet Lao Charges of Misuse Denied," Laotian Home Service, January 12, 1959, FBIS, I1, January 13, 1959. This type of charge was repeatedly offered by the Pathet Lao and the Peoples Republic of China. See "Paper Exposes Persecution of Pathet Lao," Peking NCNA, February 6, 1959, FBIS, I2, February 9, 1959.
11. Durbrow to the Department of State, Telegram 1313, January 7, 1959, CDF 651J.51J.1-759.
12. Dulles to the American Embassy in Vientiane, Telegram 806, January 7, 1959, CDF 651G.51J/1-759.
13. Dulles to the American Embassy, Vientiane, Telegram 839, January 9, 1958, CDF651G.51J/1-959.
14. Durbrow to the Department of State Telegram 1324, January 8, 1958, CDF 651G.51J/1-859.
15. Saigon-Cholon Press Review, January 9, 1959, FBIS, G1, January 9, 1959.
16. "Times of Vietnam on Threat to Laos," Times of Vietnam, January 8, 1959, FBIS, G2, January 9, 1959.
17. "Meeting Between President Diem, General Williams, Ambassador Durbrow, and Mr. Gardiner on January 10, 1959," Folder 6, "Ngo-Dinh-Diem-Conferences, January–August 1959," Box 13, Williams Papers.
18. In Durbrow's version of the conversation, Ngô Đình Diệm also mentioned SEATO though Williams's memorandum of conversation for the meeting has Durbrow mentioning SEATO, not Ngô Đình Diệm. See Durbrow to the Department of State, Despatch 237, "Conversation between President Ngo Dinh Diem and Ambassador Durbrow January 10, 1959," January 21, 1959, CDF 751G.11/1-2159.
19. Durbrow to the Department of State, Telegram 1340, January 11, 1959, CDF 651G.5J/1-1159.

20. Durbrow to the Department of State, Telegram 1364, January 14, 1959, CDF 651G.51H/1-1459.
21. Bacon to the Department of State, Telegram 1229, January 13, 1959, CDF 651G.51J/1-1359.
22. Saigon-Cholon Press Review, January 10, 1959, FBIS, G2, January 12, 1959.
23. Memorandum of Conversation between French Embassy Counselor Pierre Landy, Director of the Office of Southeast Asian Affairs Eric Kocher, and Corcoran, "Lao Communication to UN on Vietnamese Communist Border Violation," January 13, 1959, CDF 651G.51J/1-1359.
24. Dulles to the American Embassy, Vientiane, Telegram 847, January 13, 1959, CDF 651G.51J/1-1359.
25. The Vietnamese press, however, did give cause for some anxiety. While Ngô Đình Diệm privately told Durbrow that Vietnam would not intensify its role in the crisis, some Vietnamese newspapers continued to press for action that did not suit the United States. *Cách mạng Quốc gia* continued its call for a stronger SEATO that would reinforce the Laotians while *Tự do* maintained that Laos could not be defended without SEATO checking the Communists. See Saigon-Cholon Press Review, January 13, 1959, FBIS, G1, January 13, 1959. Both papers included Cambodia with Laos in their reporting. On January 14, *Cách mạng Quốc gia* took it a step further by calling for political and military intervention by the Free World in Laos. It argued, "SEATO must understand that its defense must be based on a good offense. If the communist promote war, SEATO's duty was to hold the line and simultaneously move against the enemy's rear." *Tin Mới* (New Reports) also joined the conversation and agreed with the positions of *Cách mạng Quốc gia* and *Tự do*. Another underlying thread in the Vietnamese newspapers was the concern that the North Vietnamese action was designed to put pressure on the Republic of Vietnam without having to openly fight. Negotiating from a position of strength, for either side, was an alluring proposition. See Saigon-Cholon Press Review, January 14, 1959, FBIS, G1, January 14, 1959; and, Saigon-Cholon Press Review, January 16, 1959, FBIS, G1, January 16, 1959.
26. Cook to the Department of State, Telegram 547, January 15, 1959, CDF 651G.51J/1-1559.
27. Executive Director to the United States Mission to the United Nations, Albert Watson to the Department of State, Despatch 704, "Communication to the SYG-UN from the Permanent Representative of Laos to the UN," January 21, 1959, CDF 651G.51J/1-2159. A translated copy of the document is attached.

28. Daily Briefing, "Laos," January 17, 1959, Current Intelligence Bulletin, Central Intelligence Agency, Office of Current Intelligence, Declassified Documents, NARA.
29. Smith to the Department of State, Telegram 1268, January 21, 1959, CDF 651G.51J/1-2159.
30. "Laotian Legation Denies DRV Charges," *Vietnam Press*, January 20, 1959, FBIS, G1, January 21, 1959.
31. "New Cabinet Announced by Government," *Laotian Home Services*, January 24, 1959, FBIS, I1, January 26, 1959. See also correction issued in FBIS, I1, January 27, 1959.
32. Daily Briefing, "Laos," February 7, 1959, Current Intelligence Bulletin, Central Intelligence Agency, Office of Current Intelligence, Declassified Documents, NARA.
33. "Geneva Terms Now Invalid-Sananikone," *Laotian Home Service*, February 11, 1959, FBIS, I1-I2, February 12, 1959. See also Daily Briefing, "Laos Repudiates 1954 Geneva Agreements," February 12, 1959, Current Intelligence Bulletin, Central Intelligence Agency, Office of Current Intelligence, Declassified Documents, NARA, 5.
34. Saigon-Cholon Press Review, February 14, 1959, FBIS, G1, February 17, 1959.
35. Press Review for February 16, 1959, FBIS, G2, February 17, 1959.
36. Acting Secretary of State C. Douglas Dillon to the American Embassy, Vientiane, Telegram 967, February 11, 1959, CDF 651G.51J/2-1159.
37. Smith to the Department of State, Telegram 1401, February 13, 1959, CDF 651G.51J/2-1359.
38. Dillon to the American Embassy, Vientiane, Telegram 983, February 13, 1959, CDF 651G.51J.2-1359.
39. Smith to the Department of State, Telegram 1419, February 16, 1959, CDF 651G.51J/2-1659. Smith gathered this information as Phoui Sananikone explained his answers given to British ambassador to Laos Anthony Lincoln earlier.
40. Smith to the Department of State, Despatch 88, "Suggested Points for Public Statement by Royal Lao Government," February 17, 1959, CDF 651G.51J3/2-1759. See also Smith to the Department of State, Telegram 1425, February 19, 1959, CDF 651G.51J3/2-1859.
41. Lyon to the Department of State, Telegram 2994, February 16, 1959, CDF 651G.51J3/2-1659. See also Daily Briefing, "Laos Under Pressure to Retreat Denunciation of Geneva Accords," February 18, 1959, Current Intelligence Bulletin, Central Intelligence Agency, Office of Current Intelligence, Declassified Documents, NARA.

42. "Laos Affirms Its Peaceful Intentions," *Laotian Home Service*, February 18, 1959, FBIs, I1-I2, February 19, 1959.

43. "Protocol Call on President Diem by Admiral Felt and General Williams on 16 February 1959," Folder 6, "Ngo-Dinh-Diem-Conferences, January–August 1959," Box 13, Williams Papers.

44. Smith to the Department of State, Telegram 1513, March 3, 1959, CDF 651G.51J/3-359.

45. Durbrow to the Department of State, telegram 1886, March 10, 1959, CDF 651G.51J/3-1059.

46. Smith to the Department of State, Telegram 1437, February 19, 1959, CDF 651G.51J3/2-1959.

47. Herter to the American Embassy, Vientiane, Telegram 1027, February 20, 1959, CDF 651G.51J3/2-1959.

48. Hammarskjold informed Lodge of this possibility on February 19. See Counselor to the United States Mission to the United Nations James Barco to the Department of State, Telegram 684, February 19, 1959, CDF 651G.51J3/2-1959.

49. Herter to the United States Mission to the United Nation, Telegraph 694 (repeated to the American Embassy, Vientiane, Telegram 1021), February 19, 1959, CDF 651G.51J3/2-1959.

50. Herter to the American Embassy, Vientiane, Telegram 1020, February 19, 1959, CDF 651G.51J3/2-1959. See also United States Representative to the United Nations Henry Cabot Lodge to the Department of State, Telegram 695, February 20, 1959, CDF 651G.51J3/2-2059.

51. Smith to the Department of State, Telegram 1464, February 21, 1959, CDF 651G.51J3/2-2159.

52. Lodge to the Department of State, Telegram 696, February 21, 1959, CDF 651G.51J3/2-2159. See also Herter to the American Embassy, Vientiane, Telegram 1061, February 26, 1959, CDF 651G.51J3/2-2459.

53. As quoted in Herter to the American Embassy, Vientiane, Telegram 1055, February 26, 1959, CDF 651G.51J3/2-2659. See also Lodge to the Department of State, Telegram 700, February 24, 1959, CDF 651G.51J3/2-2459; and, Lodge to the Department of State, Telegram 704, February 24, 1959, CDF 651G.51J3/2-2459.

54. "Suppression of Neo Lao Hak Xat Denied," *Laotian Home Service*, March 1, 1959, FBIS, I1, March 5, 1959.

55. "Paper Urges Resumption of ISCC in Laos," *Voice of Vietnam* (Hanoi), March 9, 1959, FIBS, I1, March 12, 1959.

56. Kellogg to the Department of State, Telegram 1224, March 17, 1959, CDF 651G.51J/3-1759.

57. Smith to the Department of State, Telegram 1620, March 23, 1959, CDF 651G.51J3/3-2359.

58. Robert Ballantyne to the Department of State, Telegram G-877, April 4, 1959, CDF 651G.51J3/4-459. It was previously reported that the conversation took place with Prime Minister of India and Minister for External Affairs and Commonwealth Relations Jawaharlal Nehru though that was corrected in early May. See United States ambassador to the United Kingdom, John Hay Whitney to the American Embassy, London, Telegram G-969, May 4, 1959, CDF 651G.51J3/5-359.

59. Lodge to the Department of State, Telegram 910, April 21, 1959, CDF 651G.51J/4-2159. Lodge learned of the Desai approach from the Canadian Member Secretariat.

60. Smith to the Department of State, Telegram 1701, April 6, 1959, CDF 651G.51J3/4-659.

61. Herter to the American Embassy, Vientiane, Telegram 1286, April 25, 1959, CDF 651G.51J/4-2159.

62. "Communique on Danger of Pathet Lao," *Laotian Home Service*, May 17, 1959, FBIS, I1-I3, May 18, 1959; and, "State Firm on Pathet Lao Integration, *Laotian Home Service*, May 21, FBIS, I1, May 22, 1959. See also Daily Briefing, "Laos," May 20, 1959, Current Intelligence Bulletin, Central Intelligence Agency, Office of Current Intelligence, Declassified Documents, NARA.

63. Saigon-Cholon Press Review, May 20, 1959, FBIS, G1, May 20, 1959; and, Saigon-Cholon Press Review, May 22, 1959, FBIS, G1, May 22, 1959. *Cách mạng Quốc gia* would later call for the dissolution of the Neo Lao Hak Xat Party because of the defections. See Saigon-Cholon Press Review, May 30, FBIS, G1, June 1, 1959.

64. Durbrow to the Department of State, Telegram 2448, May 20, 1959, CDF 651G.51H/5-2059.

65. Daily Briefing, "USSR-Laos," June 4, 1959, Current Intelligence Bulletin, Central Intelligence Agency, Office of Current Intelligence, Declassified Documents, NARA.

66. Daily Briefing, "Laos," June 8, 1959, Current Intelligence Bulletin, Central Intelligence Agency, Office of Current Intelligence, Declassified Documents, NARA.

67. "Pathet Lao Incident Considered Closed," *Laotian Home Service*, June 6, 1959, FBIS, I1, June 10, 1959.

Chapter 9

1. "Meeting Between General Williams and President Ngo Dinh Diem at 2000 Hours,

on 2 February 1959," Folder 6, "Ngo-Dinh-Diem-Conferences, January–August 1959," Box 13, Williams Papers.

2. Sihanouk had made statements during his visit to Djakarta that the Vietnamese representative to Cambodia, Ngô Trọng Hiếu, was the ringleader in a plot to overthrow him. See "Sihanouk: SEATO Meddles in Cambodia," *NCNA*, February 16, 1959, FBIS, H1, February 17, 1959; and, Durbrow to the Department of State, Telegram 1761, February 24, 1959, CDF 651G.51H3/2-2159.

3. Sam Sary had once served as Sihanouk's deputy prime minister in the 1950s but fell out of favor and turned against him. Sihanouk accused him of plotting against him in 1959 and he remained a figure of controversy until his disappearance in the early 1960s.

4. "Sihanouk on Neutrality, Conspiracy," *New China News Agency*, February 4, 1959, FBIS, H1, February 5, 1959.

5. Strom to the Department of State, Telegram 1005, February 12, 1959, CDF 651G.51H/2-1229. In the military court trial of September 30, 1959, the brother of Dap Chhuon, Slat Peou, testified that Ngô Trọng Hiếu gave Dap Chhuon approximately $30 million worth of gold and that Victor Matsui, in the American Embassy in Phnom Penh, gave Slat Peou a receiving and transmitting radio set. Matsui was allegedly a CIA operative working in Cambodia. See "Military Court Tries Dap Chhuon Case," *Le Dépêche du Cambodge*, October 1, 1959, FBIS, H1, October 8, 1959. See also Dommen, *The Indochinese Experience of the French and Americans*, 354–355.

6. Durbrow to the Department of State, Telegram 1761, February 24, 1959, CDF 651G.51H3/2-2159.

7. Durbrow to the Department of State, Telegram 1799, March 1, 1959, CDF 751G.00(W)/3-159.

8. Durbrow to the Department of State, Telegram 1745, February 21, 1959, CDF 751G.00(W)/2-2159.

9. Dap Chhuon had once been an ally of Sihanouk's until he turned against him in 1957.

10. "Dap Chhuon Mochulpich Arrest Ordered," *Cambodian Home Service*, February 23, 1959, FBIS, H1, February 24, 1959. See also Durbrow to the Department of State, Telegram 1799, March 1, 1959, CDF 751G.00(W)/3-159; and, Daily Briefing, "Cambodia-South Vietnam" March 3, 1959, Current Intelligence Bulletin, Central Intelligence Agency, Office of Current Intelligence, Declassified Documents, NARA.

11. Durbrow to the Department of State, Telegram 1752, February 24, 1959, CDF 651G.51H/2-2459.

12. Durbrow to the Department of State, Telegram 1756, February 24, 1959, CDF 651G.51H/2-2459.

13. "Meeting Between President Diem, General Williams, Mr. Gardiner, and Mr. Thuan on Tuesday 17 Mach at 1600 Hours," Folder 6, "Ngo-Dinh-Diem-Conferences, January–August 1959," Box 13, Williams Papers.

14. "Plot Against Royal Government Denied," *Vietnam Press*, February 24, 1959, FBIS, G1, February 25, 1959.

15. "Let Cambodia Not Go Beyond Its Right," *Cách mạng Quốc gia*, February 26, 1959, FBIS, G3-G4, March 3, 1959. *Sài Gòn Mới* followed by publishing three letters from the Vietnamese legation in Phnom Penh to the Cambodian Foreign Ministry that enumerated hostile acts by Cambodian troops against Vietnamese or the refuge of communist insurgents across the Cambodian border. *Tin Mới* reinforced the notion that Dap Chhuon and Sam Sary were allies of Sihanouk during the French struggle and could never betray their country and Prince for ten million French francs.

16. "Sihanouk Reports on Foreign Plotting," *Cambodian Home Service*, February 27, 1959, FBIS, H1, March 2, 1959. The theme of Judas was repeated in subsequent communications. See "Provinces Hail the Death of Dap Chhuon," *Cambodian Home Service*, March 6, 1959, FBIS, H1, March 6, 1959.

17. "Where Are the Responsible People," *Le Depeché du Cambodge*, February 26, 1959, FBIS, H1, March 4, 1959.

18. Deputy Chief of Mission for the United States Embassy in France, Cecil Lyon to the Department of State, Telegram 3082, February 25, 1959, CDF 651G.51H/2-2559.

19. Lyon to the Department of State, Telegram 3132, February 27, 1959, CDF 651G.51H/2-2759.

20. Daily Briefing, "France May Increase Unilateral Activity in Indochina" March 23, 1959, Current Intelligence Bulletin, Central Intelligence Agency, Office of Current Intelligence, Declassified Documents, NARA.

21. Durbrow to the Department of State, Telegram 1804, March 2, 1959, CDF 651G.51H/3-259.

22. "Envoy to Cambodia Is Brought Home," *Cambodian Home Service*, March 1, 1959, FBIS, G3, March 2, 1959. The Vietnamese Press argued that the recall request, which had been accepted, did not implicate him in any plot. See Saigon-Cholon Press Review, March 4, 1959, FBIS, G1, March 4, 1959.

23. Durbrow to the Department of State, Telegram 1809, March 2, 1959, CDF 651G.51H/3-259.

24. Strom to the Department of State, Tele-

gram 1153, March 2, 1959, CDF 651G.51H/3-259.

25. "Envoy to Cambodia Recalled by Decree," FBIS, G2, 1959, March 6, 1959.

26. Strom to the Department of State, Telegram 1164, March 4, 1959, CDF 651G.51H/3-459.

27. "Welcome to Ambassador Trimble," *Réalités Cambodgiennes*, April 11, 1959, FBIS, H1, April 15, 1959.

28. Lyon to the Department of State, Telegram 3185, March 4, 1959, CDF 651G.51H/3-459.

29. Herter to the American Embassy, Phnom Penh, Telegram 784, March 4, 1959, CDF 651G.51H/3-459.

30. Durbrow to the Department of State, Telegram 1837, March 5, 1959, CDF 651G.51H/3-559. See also "Gen. Dap Chhuon's Death, *Chuông Mai*, March 9, 1959, FBIS, G2, March 10, 1959.

31. Daily Briefing, "Cambodia Claims Dap Chhuon Made 'Revelations,'" March 7, 1959, *Current Intelligence Bulletin*, Central Intelligence Agency, Office of Current Intelligence, Declassified Documents, NARA. See also "Dap Chhuon Makes Important Confession," *Cambodian Home Service*, March 5, 1959, FBIS, H1, March 5, 1959; and, "Dropped Papers Show Treachery," *Cambodian Home Service*, March 5, 1959, FBIS, H1, March 5, 1959.

32. Durbrow to the Department of State, Telegram 1859, March 6, 1959, CDF 651G.51H/3-659. Hamilton Fish Armstrong had a long career in diplomacy and served as the editor of *Foreign Affairs* magazine.

33. Sihanouk's March 4 speech to the Congress of the Royal Khmer Socialist Youth is a good example. See "Sihanouk Discusses Plot Against Kingdom," *Khmer Press Agency*, March 4, 1959, FBIS, H1–H4, FBIS, March 10, 1959.

34. Durbrow to the Department of State, Telegram 1858, March 6, 1959, CDF 651G.51H/3-659; and, Durbrow to the Department of State, Telegram 1859, March 6, 1959, CDF 651G.51H/3-659.

35. Durbrow to the Department of State, Telegram 1868 (Section One), March 7, 1959, CDF 651G.51H/3-759.

36. Durbrow to the Department of State, Telegram 1868 (Section One and Two), March 7, 1959, CDF 651G.51H/3-759.

37. Durbrow to the Department of State, Telegram 1873 (Section One and Two), March 7, 1959, CDF 651G.51H/3-759.

38. Elting to the Department of State, Despatch 289, "Transmitting Text of Vietnamese Aide-Memoire of March 7," March 9, 1959, CDF 651G.51H/3-959.

39. "Meeting Between General Williams and President Ngo Dinh Diem on 11 March 1959," Folder 6, "Ngo-Dinh-Diem-Conferences, January–August 1959," Box 13, Williams Papers.

40. "The Cambodian Crisis," *Cách mạng Quốc gia*, March 11, 1959, FBIS, G2, March 12, 1959.

41. Kellogg to the Department of State, Telegram 1202, March 12, 1959, CDF 651G.51H/3-1159.

42. Smith to the Department of State, Telegram 1550, March 11, 1959, CDF 651G.51H/3-1159.

43. Kellogg to the Department of State, Telegram 1215, March 14, 1959, CDF 651G.51H/3-1459.

44. Kellogg to the Department of State, Telegram 1209, March 13, 1959, CDF 651G.51H/3-1359.

45. Kellogg to the Department of State, Telegram G-135, March 17, 1959, CDF 651G.51H/3-1759. See also Durbrow to the Department of State, Telegram 1945, March 17, 1959, CDF 651G.51H/3-1759; and, "Sam Sary Men Arrested," *New China News Agency*, March 13, 1959, FBIS, H1, March 16, 1959.

46. "Traitor Reported Fleeing to America," *Cambodian Home Service*, March 16, 1959, FBIS, H1, March 16, 1959. See also "Khmer Issarak Leaders Under Arrest," *Cambodian Home Service*, march 13, 1959, FBIS, H2–H3, March 20, 1959.

47. Durbrow to the Department of State, Telegram 1994, March 22, 1959, CDF 751G.00 (W)/3-2259/.

48. "Cambodia Charged with False Accusation," *Đan Nguyên*, March 25, 1959, FBIS, G2, March 26, 1959.

49. Durbrow to the Department of State, Telegram 1929, March 14, 1959, CDF 751G.00 (W)/3-1459.

50. Durbrow to the Department of State, Telegram 1947, March 17, 1959, CDF 651G.51H/3-1759.

51. Kellogg to the Department of State, Telegram G-140, March 20, 1959, CDF 651H.00/3-2059.

52. "Letter Incriminates Ngo Trong Hieu," *VNA* (Hanoi), March 25, 1959, FBIS, H1, March 27, 1959.

53. Kellogg to the Department of State, Telegram 1239, March 20, 1959, CDF 651G.51H/3-2059.

54. "Meeting Between President Diem and General Williams on 25 March 1959," Folder 6, "Ngo-Dinh-Diem-Conferences, January–August 1959," Box 13, Williams Papers.

55. Kellogg to the Department of State, Telegram 1249, March 23, 1959, CDF 651G.51H/3-2359. Son Sann was a former cabinet member who was involved in the Sangkum Party.

56. "Declaration from the Government of the Republic of Vietnam concerning a recent communiqué by the Cambodian Royal Government," *Vietnam Press*, March 17, 1959, FBIS, G2-G3, March 18, 1959.

57. Durbrow to the Department of State, Telegram 2017, March 24, 1959, CDF 61G.51H/3-2459. See also Daily Briefing, "Cambodia-South Vietnam," March 24, 1959, *Current Intelligence Bulletin,* Central Intelligence Agency, Office of Current Intelligence, Declassified Documents, NARA.

58. "Cambodian Government Communique on the Republic of Vietnam's declaration proposing joint operations against armed gangs along the border," *Cambodian Home Service*, March 24, 1959, FBIS, H1–H2, March 25, 1959. See also Kellogg to the Department of State, Telegram 1257, March 24, 1959, CDF 651G.51H/3-2459; Kellogg to the Department of State, Telegram 1278, March 30, 1959, CDF 651G.51H/3-3059; and, "Saigon Urged to Accept Border Proposal," *Réalités Cambodgiennes*, March 28, 1959, FBIS, H3–H5, April 10, 1959.

59. Durbrow to the Department of State, Telegram 2025, March 25, 1959, CDF 651G.51H/3-2559.

60. Memorandum of Conversation between Vietnamese ambassador to the United States Trần Văn Chương, Parsons, and Mendenhall, "Call by the Vietnamese Ambassador," March 31, 1959, CDF 651G.51J/3-3159.

61. "Prince Sihanouk Departs for France," NCNA (Peking), March 31, FBIS, H8, April 1, 1959.

62. On March 30, *Cách mạng Quốc gia* published an editorial that lamented Cambodia's rejection of joint border control though it hoped that the Cambodians would come up with another idea rather than condemning them. See "Let Cambodia Provide Another Solution," *Cách mạng Quốc gia*, March 30, 1959, FBIS, G2-G3, April 1, 1959. For other examples of the tenuous truce see Bowie to the Department of State, Telegram 2192, April 17, 1959, CDF 651G.51H3/4-1759; Durbrow to the Department of State, Telegram 2246, April 24, 1959, CDF 651G.51H3/4-2459; Trimble to the Department of State, Telegram 1394, April 25, 1959, CDF 651G.51H/4-2559; and, Trimble to the Department of State, Telegram 1395, April 25, 1959, CDF 651G.51H/4-2559.

63. Second Secretary of Embassy Byron E. Byron to the Department of State, Despatch 406, "Son San restates Cambodian Foreign Policy: Speech at Vientiane, Laos, April 30, 1959," May 8, 1959, CDF 651H.00/5-859.

64. This was noted in a comment in the despatch sent by Byron.

65. Trimble to the Department of State, Telegram 1422, May 3, 1959, CDF 651G.51H/5-359.

66. A Royal Cambodian Government communiqué on May 13 reaffirmed its desire for a press truce and increased good will. See Trimble to the Department of State, Telegram 1470, May 14, 1959, CDF 651G.51H/5-1459.

67. Dillon to the American Embassy, Saigon, Telegram 1795, May 3, 1959, CDF 651G.51H/5-359.

68. Trimble to the Department of State, Telegram 1422, May 7, 1959, CDF 651G.51H3/5-759; and, Durbrow to the Department of State, Telegram 2366, May 9, 1959, CDF 651G.51H/5-959.

69. Trimble to the Department of State, Telegram 1458, May 12, 1959, CDF 651G.51H3/5-1259.

70. Trimble to the Department of State, Telegram 1472, May 14, 1959, CDF 651G.51H/5-1459.

71. Durbrow to the Department of State, Telegram 2402 (Section One), May 14, 1959, CDF 651G.51H/5-1459.

72. Durbrow to the Department of State, Telegram 2472, May 23, 1959, CDF 651G.51H/5-2359.

73. For issues related to the press, see Trimble to the Department of State, Telegram 1475, May 15, 1959, CDF 651G.51H/5-1559; and, Trimble to the Department of State, Telegram G-175, May 19, 1959, CDF 651G.51H/5-1959.

74. Durbrow to the Department of State, Telegram 2447 (Section Two), May 20, 1959, CDF 651G.51H/5-2059.

Chapter 10

1. "Meeting Between President Diem, Ambassador Durbrow and General Williams on 9 April 1959," Folder 6, "Ngo-Dinh-Diem-Conferences, January–August 1959," Box 13, Williams Papers. See also Daily Briefing, "South Vietnam Plans to Open Anti-Sihanouk Campaign," April 13, 1959, *Current Intelligence Bulletin*, Central Intelligence Agency, Office of Current Intelligence, Declassified Documents, NARA; and, Elting to the Department of State, Telegram 2525, May 29, 1959, Folder 6, "Ngo-Dinh-Diem-Conferences, January–August 1959," Box 13, Williams Papers.

2. Durbrow to the Department of State, Telegram 2135, April 10, 1959, CDF 651G.51H/4-1059.

3. Durbrow to the Department of State, Telegram 2143, April 11, 1959, CDF 751G.MSF/4-1159.

4. Durbrow to the Department of State,

Telegram 2143, April 11, 1959, CDF 751G.MSF/4-1159.

5. Durbrow to the Department of State, Telegram 2286, April 28, 1959, CDF 751G.001/4-2859.

6. Parsons to the Department of State, Telegram 588, May 5, 1959, CDF 651G.51H3/5-559.

7. Mandarin was misspelled in the original telegram though it is clear that it was the word meant.

8. Durbrow to the Department of State, Telegram 2371 (Section One), May 10, 1959, CDF 651G.51H/5-1059.

9. Durbrow to the Department of State, Telegram 2371 (Section One and Section Two), May 10, 1959, CDF 651G.51H/5-1059.

10. Lambert memorandum for Williams, May 9, 1959, Folder 6, "Ngo-Dinh-Diem-Conferences, January–August 1959," Box 13, Williams Papers.

11. Lambert put these words within a quotation though it clear from his previous sentence that they are a summation. Lambert memorandum for Williams, May 9, 1959, Folder 6, "Ngo-Dinh-Diem-Conferences, January–August 1959," Box 13, Williams Papers.

12. Colby would replace Natsios as the Central Intelligence Agency Station Chief in Saigon in June 1960. See Ahern, *House of Ngo*, 135.

13. Memorandum of Conversation between Vo Lang, Myriam Johnston, and Barbour, May 14, 1959 attached to Kidder to the Department of State, Despatch 2115, "Conversation with Mr. Vo Lang," May 15, 1959, CDF 751.00/5-1559.

14. Daily Briefing, "Communist Sabotage Campaign in South Vietnam," June 1, 1959, Current Intelligence Bulletin, Central Intelligence Agency, Office of Current Intelligence, Declassified Documents, NARA.

15. "Meeting between President Diem and General Williams on 4 June 1959 at 0900," Folder 6, "Ngo-Dinh-Diem-Conferences, January–August 1959," Box 13, Williams Papers. Attached is a summary of the meeting sent to Durbrow.

16. Lansdale to O'Donnell, "Vietnam," June 4, 1959, Folder "SP, Internal Security," Box 1, Entry 5155, "Asian Affairs, Vietnam Desk, Vietnam Subject Files, 1955–1962." Lansdale had a previous connection with Ngô Đình Diệm and Vietnam. After the 1954 Geneva Conference ended, the CIA sponsored the Saigon Military Mission under his leadership. One of his objectives was to conduct psychological warfare in North Vietnam to encourage Vietnamese to move to the South. The Saigon Military Mission also aided Ngô Đình Diệm in his consolidation of power in 1955.

17. Durbrow to the Department of State, Telegram 2554 (Section One), June 2, 1959, 651G/51H/6-259.

18. Deputy Under Secretary of State for Administration Loy Henderson to the American Embassy, Saigon, Telegram 1941, June 10, 1959, CDF 651G.51H/6-1059.

19. Durbrow to the Department of State, Telegram 2613, June 11, 1959, CDF 651G.51H/6-1159. The British Charge also agreed that preliminary talks were necessary for any Sihanouk–Ngô Đình Diệm conference to be successful. Durbrow to the Department of State, Telegram 2620 (Corrected), June 12, 1959, CDF 651G.51H/6-1259.

20. "Details of Border Fights with SVN Bandits," *Cambodian Home Service*, June 19, 1959, FBIS, H2, June 22, 1959.

21. Lê Quang Vinh (Ba Cụt) was a Hòa Hảo commander who opposed Ngô Đình Diệm during the 1955 Sect Crisis. See "Khmer Troops, Ba Cut Remnants Clash," *Tự do*, June 18, 1959, FBIS, G2, June 23, 1959.

22. Durbrow to the Department of State, Telegram 2620 (Corrected), June 12, 1959, CDF 651G.51H/6-1259. See also Dillon to the American Embassy, Saigon, Telegram 1955, June 12, 1959, CDF 651G.51H/6-1259.

23. Durbrow to the Department of State, Telegram 2642 (Section One), June 15, 1959, CDF 651G.51J/6-1559.

24. Durbrow to the Department of State, Telegram 2642 (Section Two), June 15, 1959, CDF 651G.51J/6-1559.

25. Lalouette informed Durbrow of this development during an after-dinner conversation on June 15. See Durbrow to the Department of State, Telegram 2647, June 16, 1959, CDF 651G.51H/6-1659.

26. Trimble to the Department of State, 1645, June 16, 1959, CDF 651G.51H/6-1659. This view was also shared by the British ambassador Frederic Garner.

27. Durbrow to the Department of State, Telegram 2673, June 18, 1959, CDF 651G.51H/6-1859.

28. Durbrow to the Department of State, Telegram 2673, June 18, 1959, CDF 651G.51H/6-1859.

29. Trimble to the Department of State, Telegram 1657 (Section One), June 18, 1959, CDF 651G.51H/6-1859.

30. Trimble to the Department of State, Telegram 1678, June 22, 1959, CDF 651G.51H/6-2259.

31. Durbrow to the Department of State, Telegram 2715, June 23, 1959, CDF 651G.51H/6-2359.

32. Trimble to the Department of State, Telegram 1690, June 24, 1959, CDF 651G.51H.6-2459; Trimble to the Department of State,

Telegram 1696, June 25, 1959, CDF 651G.51H/6-2559; and, Durbrow to the Department of State, Telegram 2738, June 26, 1959, CDF 651G.51H/6-2659.

33. Trimble to the Department of State, 1712, June 26, 1959, CDF 651G.51H/6-2659; Trimble to the Department of State, Telegram 1696, June 25, 1959, CDF 651G.51H/6-2559; and, Houghton to the Department of State, Telegram 4891, June 30, 1059, CDF 651G.51H/6-3059. The Eighth National Congress of the People's Socialist Community occurred between July 6 and July 9. See NCNA (Peking), July 4, 1959, FBIS, H2, July 6, 1959. For Son Sann's trip, see "Son Sann to Paris, FBIS, H2, July 10, 1959.".

34. Durbrow to the Department of State, Telegram 14, July 1, 1959, CDF 651G.51H/7-159.

35. Durbrow to the Department of State, Telegram 14, July 1, 1959, CDF 651G.51H/7-159.

36. Durbrow to the Department of State, Telegram 12, July 1, 1959, CDF 651G.51H/7-159.

37. Trimble to the Department of State, Telegram 32, July 7, 1959, CDF 651G.51H/7-759. There are dozens of transcripts of these highly anti–Sihanouk broadcasts located in the H section of the FBIS for 1959.

38. Durbrow to the Department of State, Telegram 66, July 8, 1959, CDF 651G.51H/7-859.

39. Durbrow to the Department of State, Telegram 67, July 9, 1959, CDF 751G.5 MSP/7-959.

40. Chester Opal to the United States Information Agency, Telegram 6, July 9, 1959, CDF 751G.5 MSP/7-859.

41. Trimble to the Department of State, Telegram 54, July 13, 1959, CDF 651G.51H/7-1359.

42. Lon Nol served concurrently as the Minister of Defense and Chief of Staff of the Royal Cambodian Armed Forces.

43. Durbrow to the Department of State, Telegram 205, July 24, 1959, CDF 651G.51H/7-2459; Houghton to the Department of State, Telegram 243, July 24, 1959, CDF 651G.51H/7-2459; and, Wood to the Department of State, Despatch 41 "Conversation between Ngo Dinh Nhu and the Ambassador on (1) Sihanouk Visit and (2) the Elections," July 30, 1959, CDF 651G.51H/7-3059.

44. Saigon-Cholon Press Review, August 1, 1959, FBIS, G6, August 3, 1959.

45. Houghton to the Department of State, Telegram 424, July 29, 1959, CDF 651G.51H/7-2959. The possible agenda was relayed by Gorce to Paris and transmitted to Houghton by the French.

46. See Sihanouk Press Statement on his arrive in Saigon on August 3, FBIS, G1–G2, August 4, 1959; and, Sihanouk declaration upon his return to Phnom Penh, August 6, *Cambodian Home Service*, August 6, FBIS, H1, August 7, 1959.

47. Joseph Mendenhall to the Department of State, Despatch 78, "GVN-RKG Talks During Prince Sihanouk's Visit to Saigon," August 28, 1959, CDF 651G.51H/8-2859.

48. Trimble to the Department of State, Telegram 151, August 5, 1959, CDF 651G.51H/8-559; and, Trimble to the Department of State, Telegram 161, August 5, 1959, CDF 651G.51H/8-559.

49. Second Secretary of Embassy (Phnom Penh) Daniel Arzac to the Department of State, Despatch 39, "Realities Summaries Results of Saigon Talks," August 12, 1959, CDF 651G.51H/8-1259; and, Arzac to the Department of State, Despatch 40, "Prince Norodom Sihanouk's Views on Peaceful Coexistence," August 12, 1959, CDF 651H.00/8-1259.

50. Elting to the Department of State, Telegram 448, August 12, 1959, CDF 651H/8-1259.

51. Dillon made this assessment during his meeting with Cambodian ambassador to the United States Nong Kimny on August 12. See Dillion to the American Embassy, Saigon, Telegram 278, August 13, 1959, CDF 651G.51H/8-1359.

52. The six articles were reprinted in hearings, 288–303. See also Dillion to the American Embassy, Saigon, Telegram 136, July 28, 1959, CDF 751G.5-MSP/7-2859. See also Mann, *A Grand Delusion*, 216–218. Additional hearings occurred in the House under the chairmanship of Clement Zablocki (D–Wisconsin). See Anderson, *Trapped by Success*, 180–182.

53. Transcripts for both of the hearings are available in Folder 4, Box 48, Douglas Pike Collection: Unit 3–Legal and Legislative, The Vietnam Archive, Texas Tech University, Lubbock, TX.

54. Durbrow to the Department of State, Telegram 215, July 24, 1959, CDF 751G.5-MSP/7-2459.

55. Heavner to the Department of State, "The 'Political Re-Education Center' at Quang Tri," August 20, 1959, CDF 751G.00/8-2059.

56. "Interview of Diem by Colegrove Released," *Vietnam Press*, July 28, 1959, FBIS, G1-G2, July 30, 1959; and, "Dear Mr. Colegrove," *Times of Vietnam*, July 29, 1959, FBIS, G1–G6, July 31, 1959.

57. Durbrow to the Department of State, Telegram 228, July 25, 1959, CDF 751G.5-MSP/7-2559.

58. "Tran Chanh Thanh Discusses Colegrove," July 31, 1959, FBIS, G1-G2, August 3, 1959.

59. Saigon-Cholon Press Review, August 6, 1959, FBIS, G1, August 6, 1959.

60. "Statement on Charges Against American Aid Program to Free Vietnam, Colegrove allegations," August 24, 1959, Folder 1, Box 11, Douglas Pike Collection: Other Manuscripts–American Friends of Vietnam, The Vietnam Archive, Texas Tech University. The American Friends of Vietnam, founded in 1955, supported the American efforts to aid Ngô Đình Diệm by providing information about the successes of Vietnam. See Joseph Morgan, *The Vietnam Lobby: The American Friends of Vietnam, 1955–1975*.

61. Durbrow to the Department of State, Telegram 251 (Section One), July 27, 1959, CDF 751G.5-MSP/7-2759. The Đại Việt Party was formed in the 1930s and was strongly nationalistic.

62. Durbrow to the Department of State, Telegram 251 (Section Two), July 27, 1959, CDF 751G.5-MSP/7-2759.

63. Deputy Director, International Cooperation Administration, L. J. Saccio to Director, ICA, James R. Riddleberger, "Vietnam Hearings before Senator Mansfield's Subcommittee," Folder, "Colegrove Articles (and Subsequent)–Miscellaneous Clippings," Box 1, Entry 3213, "Eastern Affairs, Office of Southeast Asian Affairs, Vietnam Files, 1959–1960," RG 59, NARA.

64. Durbrow returned on August 20. See "Local News," FBIS, G3, August 21, 1959.

65. Durbrow to the Department of State, Telegram 575, August 22, 1959, CDF 751G.5-MSP/8-2259.

66. "Summary of Meeting at the Presidency, 1600–1830 hours, 21 August 1959 (by Major Dolan), Folder 6, "Ngo-Dinh-Diem-Conferences, January–August 1959," Box 13, Williams Papers.

67. Durbrow to the Department of State, Telegram 635, August 27, 1959, CDF 751G.5-MSP/8-2959.

Chapter 11

1. Elting to the Department of State, Despatch 58, "Electoral Laws of 1959," August 10, 1959, CDF 751G.00/8-1059.

2. Wood to the Department of State, Despatch 12, "Views on Forthcoming Election," July 9, 1959, CDF 751G.00/7-959.

3. Lê Si Ngạc claimed he earned 400,000 piasters ($5,555) per year though the actual salary was 300,000 piasters ($4,166) per year.

4. Elting to the Department of State, Despatch 24, "The Forthcoming Elections and the National Assembly as Seen by the Leader of the Minority Bloc," July 18, 1959, CDF 751G.00/7-1959.

5. Elting to the Department of State, Despatch 58, "Electoral Laws of 1959," August 10, 1959, CDF 751G.00/8-1059.

6. Wood to the Department of State, Despatch 65, "Dr. Dan's Comments on the Electoral Laws," August 15, 1959, CDF 751G.00.8-1559. A translated copy of the *Tự do* article is attached.

7. "Domestic News," FBIS, G3, August 4, 1959.

8. Saigon-Cholon Press Review, August 10, 1959, FBIS, G5, August 11, 1959; and, Saigon-Cholon Press Review, August 13, 1959, FBIS, G5, August 13, 1959.

9. Mendenhall to the Department of State, Despatch 84, "Address of Madame Ngo Dinh NHU at the 'Women's Congress,' August 11, 1959," September 2, 1959, CDF 751.oo/9-259; and, "Mme Nhu Defends National Assembly," *Vietnam Press*, August 11, 1959, FBIS, G3-G4, August 13, 1959.

10. Saigon-Cholon Press Review, August 20, 1959, FBIS, G5, August 20, 1959.

11. Saigon-Cholon Press Review, August 21, 1959, FBIS, G5, August 21, 1959.

12. Saigon-Cholon Press Review, August 22, 1959, FBIS, G5, August 24, 1959.

13. Press Review for August 24, FBIS, G3, August 24, 1959.

14. Candidates Nguyễn Trân and Đặng Văn Sung were fined 4,000 ($55.00) and 5,000 ($70.00) piasters respectively for violating the campaign law while Nguyễn Văn Kim was sentenced to a one month suspended prison term for raising money from his friends to use for his campaign. See Saigon-Cholon Press Review, August 27, 1959, FBIS, G2, August 27, 1959.

15. "Hoodlums Wrecking Dr. Dan's Campaign," *Buổi sang*, August 22, 1959, FBIS, G2, August 25, 1959.

16. "Assembly Candidates Suing One Another," *Dân chúng*, August 22, 1959, FBIS, G3, August 27, 1959.

17. See "Newsman Barred from Assembly Candidacy," *Dân chúng*, August 27, 1959, FBIS, G2-G4, August 28, 1959.

18. "Summary of Meeting Between Lt. General S. T. Williams and President Ngo Dinh Diem, 0800–1040, 2 September 1959," Folder 7, "Ngo-Dinh-Diem-Conferences, September-December 1959," Box 13, Williams Papers. See also Williams to Durbrow, "Incidents," September 3, 1959, Folder 7, "Ngo-Dinh-Diem-Conferences, September-December 1959," Box 13, Williams Papers.

19. Durbrow to the Department of State, Telegram 697, September 2, 1959, CDF 751G.00/9-259.

20. Durbrow to the Department of State, Telegram 730, September 5, 1959, CDF 751G.00

(W)/9-559. See also Saigon-Cholon Press Review, "Domestic News," September 1, 1959, FBIS, G1, September 1, 1959. There were other controversies related to the National Assembly election, including allegations of intimidation and voting fraud by government officials and members of the National Revolutionary Movement members. See Nguyễn Tuyết Mai, "Electioneering: Vietnamese Style" *Asian Survey* 2, No. 9 (1962), 11–18; P. J. Honey, "The Problem of Democracy in Vietnam" *The World Today* 16, No. 2 (1960), 71–79; Robert G. Scigliano, "The Electoral Process in South Vietnam: Politics in an Underdeveloped State," *Midwest Journal of Political Science* 4, No. 2 (1960), 138–161; and, Robert G. Scigliano, "Political Parties in South Vietnam Under the Republic," *Pacific Affairs*, 33, No. 4 (1960), 327–346.

21. Durbrow to the Department of State, Telegram 1154, October 3, 1959, CDF 751G.00 (W)/10-359. These elections would take place on the first Sunday in January. Only candidates who lost in the first election and not been sued for violating the election laws were eligible to run for office. No new candidates were allowed. See Durbrow to the Department of State, Telegram 1647, November 14, CDF 751G.00(W)/11-1459; and, Saigon-Cholon Press Review, "Domestic News," November 12, 1959, FBIS, G1, November 13, 1959.

22. Durbrow to the Department of State, Telegram 1210, October 7, 1959, CDF 751G.00/10-759.

23. "Summary of Meeting Between Lt. General S. T. Williams and President Ngo Dinh Diem, 0800–1040, 2 September 1959, Folder 7, "Ngo-Dinh-Diem-Conferences, September-December 1959," Box 13, Williams Papers.

24. Saigon-Cholon Press Review, "Vietnamese Editorials," September 1, 1959, FBIS, G1, September 1, 1959.

25. Saigon-Cholon Press Review, "Vietnamese Editorials," September 2, 1959, FBIS, G1, September 2, 1959. *Buổi sang* and *Yuan Tung Jih Pao* offered a similar view. See Saigon-Cholon Press Review, September 3, 1959, FBIS, G1, September 3, 1959.

26. "Minister Recapitulates Election Results," *Tự do*, September 2, 1959, FBIS, G2, September 3, 1959.

27. Saigon-Cholon Press Review, "Editorial Report," September 4, 1959, FBIS, G1, September 8, 1959.

28. Durbrow to the Department of State, Telegram 906, September 19, 1959, CDF 751G.00(W)/9-1959.

29. "National Assembly to Check Membership," *Vietnam Press*, September 13, 1959, FBIS, G3, September 15, 1959.

30. "Legal Opinion on Whether or Not Candidates Tran and Dan Are Authorized to Run in By-Elections," *Lê Sống*, September 21, 1959, FBIS, G3-G4, September 25, 1959.

31. Durbrow to the Department of State, Telegram G-43, September 18, 1959, CDF 751G.00/9-1859.

32. "Conversation with President Diem (1100–1430 hours, 30 Sep 59," Folder 7, "Ngo-Dinh-Diem-Conferences, September-December 1959," Box 13, Williams Papers.

33. Williams to Durbrow, "Conference with President Diem, 30 September," Folder 7, "Ngo-Dinh-Diem-Conferences, September-December 1959," Box 13, Williams Papers.

34. Durbrow to the Department of State, Telegram 1458, October 24, 1959, CDF 751.00 (W)/10-2459.

35. "Summary of Meeting Between Lt General S. T. Williams and President Ngo Dinh Diem, 0800–1040 hours, 2 September 1959."

36. "King, Queen Escape as Bomb Explodes," *Cambodian Home Service*, September 1, 1959, FBIS, H1, September 1, 1959. See also "New Details Given on Bombing Plot," *Cambodian Home Service*, September 2, 1959, FBIS, H1, September 3, 1959.

37. "Summary of Meeting Between Lt General S. T. Williams and President Ngo Dinh Diem, 0800–1040 hours, 2 September 1959." The original memorandum of conversation includes a "(?)" after Sihanouk's name.

38. Daily Briefing, "Cambodian–South Vietnamese Relations," September 23, 1959, Current Intelligence Bulletin, Central Intelligence Agency, Office of Current Intelligence, Declassified Documents, NARA.

39. Daily Briefing, "Cambodian–South Vietnamese Relations," September 23, 1959, Current Intelligence Bulletin, Central Intelligence Agency, Office of Current Intelligence, Declassified Documents, NARA.

40. Durbrow to the Department of State, Telegram 999, September 26, 1959, CDF 651G.51H/9-2659.

41. Memorandum of Conversation between Nguyễn Đình Thuần, Parsons, Anderson, and Wood, "Vietnamese/Cambodian Relations," October 1, 1959, CDF 651G.51H/10-159.

42. "Sihanouk Relates Bombing Incident," *Cambodian Home Service*, September 3, 1959, FBIS, H1–H4, September 8, 1959.

43. The last broadcast occurred on September 29. See Durbrow to the Department of State, Telegram 1290, October 13, 1959, CDF 651G.51H/10-1359.

44. Herter to the American Embassy, Saigon, Telegram 710, October 13, 1959, CDF 651G.51H/10-1359.

45. Durbrow to the Department of State, Telegram 1345, October 16, 1959, CDF 651G.

51H/10-1659. See also Durbrow to the Department of State, Telegram 1374, October 19, 1959, CDF 651G.51H/10-1959.

46. Trimble to the Department of State, Telegram 505, October 16, 1959, CDF 651G. 51H/10-1659.

47. Herter to the American Embassy, Saigon, Telegram 771, October 19, 1959, CDF 651G. 51H/10-1959.

48. Trimble to the Department of State, Telegram 528, October 21, 1959, CDF 651G. 51H/10-2159.

49. Trimble to the Department of State, Telegram 531, October 21, 1959, CDF 651G.51H/1059.

50. Trimble to the Department of State, Telegram 553, October 23, 1959, CDF 651G. 51H/10-2359.

51. Trimble to the Department of State, Telegram 581, October 29, 1959, CDF 651G. 51H/10-2859.

52. Herter to the American Embassy, Phnom Penh, October 29, 1959, CDF 651G.51H/10-2959.

53. Trimble to the Department of State, Telegram 608, November 4, 1959, CDF 651G. 51H/11-459; and, Trimble to the Department of State, Telegram 619, November 6, 1959, CDF 651G.51H/11-659.

54. Mendenhall to the Department of State, Despatch 122, "Domestic Travels of President Ngo Dinh Diem between July 1, 1958 and September 30, 1959," October 15, 1959, CDF 751G. 00/10-1559.

55. Pilcher was joined by Senator Hiram Fong (Hawaii-R) and Representatives Marguerite Church (Illinois-R), Harris McDowell (Delaware-D), Thomas Curtis (Missouri-R), and Walter Judd (Minnesota-R).

56. Memorandum of Conversation between Ngô Đình Diệm and Durbrow, "Visit of Codel Filcher," November 3, 1959, CDF 751G.00/11-359.

57. As owner of the American Trading Company of Vietnam, Gonder had earned an anti–Ngô Đình Diệm reputation, blaming the Saigon Government for discriminating against the firms he represented who wanted to do business in Vietnam. It was Gonder who had supplied much of the alleged evidence of corruption and malpractice to Scripps-Howard correspondent Albert Colegrove and was involved with the Saigon intelligentsia who opposed Ngô Đình Diệm. See Dommen, *The Indochinese Experience of the French and Americans*, 411.

58. Mendenhall to Durbrow, "Of possible interest to the Ambassador," n.d. Document attached to Memorandum of Conversation between Durbrow and Lucas, "Colegrove Affair," November 10, 1959, Folder "Colegrove Articles (and Subsequent)—Miscellaneous Clippings," Box 1, Entry 3213, "Bureau of Far Eastern Affairs, Office of Southeast Asian Affairs, Vietnam Files, 1959–1960.

59. Mendenhall to the Department of State, Despatch 141, "Conversation Between President Diem, Codels Fong and Pilcher and Ambassador Durbrow," November 9, 1959, CDF 611.51G/11-959.

60. Parsons to the Under Secretary of State, "Mr. Ladejinsky's Call at 12:30 today," November 10, 1959, CDF 751G.00/11-1059.

61. Durbrow to Parsons, November 30, 1959, Folder "Colegrove Articles (and Subsequent)—Miscellaneous Clippings, Box 1, Entry 3213, Bureau of Far Eastern Affairs, Office of Southeast Asian Affairs, Vietnam Files, 1959–1960.

62. Memorandum of Conversation between Riley, Lucas, and Durbrow, reported December 1, 1959, Folder "Colegrove Articles (and Subsequent)—Miscellaneous Clippings," Box 1, Entry 3213, Bureau of Far Eastern Affairs, Office of Southeast Asian Affairs, Vietnam Files, 1959–1960.

Chapter 12

1. Elbridge Durbrow to the Department of State, Despatch 163, "Role of the Military in Less-developed Countries: Vietnam, a Country Team Assessment," December 7, 1959. *FRUS, 1958–1960: Volume I: Vietnam*, 260.

2. Durbrow to the Department of State, Despatch 163, "Role of the Military in Less-developed Countries: Vietnam, a Country Team Assessment," December 7, 1959. *FRUS, 1958–1960: Volume I: Vietnam*, 261.

3. See *Cách mạng Quốc gia*, December 6, 1959 and December 11, 1959, FBIS, G2, December 16, 1959; *Ngôn Luận*, December 14, 1959, FBIS December 16, 1959, G2; and, *Chuông Mai*, December 13, 1959, FBIS, G2, December 16, 1959.

4. Durbrow to the Department of State, Despatch 163, "Role of the Military in Less-developed Countries: Vietnam, a Country Team Assessment," December 7, 1959. *FRUS, 1958–1960: Volume I: Vietnam*, 255–271.

5. Colby would replace Natsios as the Central Intelligence Agency Station Chief in Saigon in June 1960. See Ahern, *House of Ngo*, 135.

6. Bernard Fall, *The Two Viet-Nams*, 237–238.

7. Durbrow to the Department of State, Despatch 163, "Role of the Military in Less-developed Countries: Vietnam, a Country Team Assessment," December 7, 1959. *FRUS, 1958–1960: Volume I: Vietnam*, 255.

8. Robert G. Scigliano, "The Electoral Process in South Vietnam," 138–161.

9. The exception to this lack of coverage in the embassy is Durbrow's correspondence with Senator Al Gore (D–Tennessee) who had visited the Republic of Vietnam in early December. Durbrow commented that the recent debates in the National Assembly included more participants than just the National Revolutionary Movement delegates. He maintained that the independent delegates raised concerns and criticisms expected of an opposition. See Durbrow to Gore, January 6, 1960, CDF 751K.00/1-660; Durbrow to the Department of State, Telegram 2165, January 17, 1960, CDF 751K.00/1-1860; and, Durbrow correspondence related to Gore's follow-up letter, CDF 751K.00/2-1760. See also Robert G. Scigliano, "The Electoral Process in South Vietnam," 138–161; and, P. J. Honey, "The Problem of Democracy in Vietnam," 71–79.

10. Buổi sang, December 21, 1959, FBIS, December 22, 1959, G4.

11. "Deputies Urge End to Police Brutality," Chuông Mai, December 22, 1959, FBIS, G1-G2, December 24, 1959.

12. Chuông Mai, December 22, 1959, FBIS, December 24, 1959, G1. Phan Khắc Sửu would also be one of the leading members of the April 1960 Caravelle Manifesto Group that openly opposed Ngô Đình Diệm and his rule.

13. Mendenhall to the Department of State, Despatch 233, "Establishment of Directorate General for Political Re-education Centers," February 4, 1960, CDF 751G.00/2-460.

14. Durbrow to the Department of State, Despatch 163, "Role of the Military in Less-developed Countries: Vietnam, a Country Team Assessment," December 7, 1959. FRUS, 1958–1960: Volume I: Vietnam, 258.

15. Durbrow to the Department of State, Despatch 163, "Role of the Military in Less-developed Countries: Vietnam, a Country Team Assessment," December 7, 1959. FRUS, 1958–1960: Volume I: Vietnam, 264.

16. Ngô Đình Diệm expounded upon these points during a December 8 press conference to a group of newspaper men and journalists touring the Far East. See "Press Interview Given by President Diem to CINCPAC Press Tour," December 22, 1959, Despatch 186, "Press Interview Given by President Diem to CINCPAC Press Tour," CDF 751G.11/12-2259. The transcript of the interview is attached.

17. Durbrow to the Department of State, Telegram 1932, December 11, 1959, CDF 751G.5/12-1159.

18. "Domestic News," Press Review for December 7, FBIS, G7, December 7, 1959.

19. Vietnam Press, January 27, 1960, FBIS, January 29, 1960, G1-G2. See also Mendenhall to the Department of State, Despatch 235, "President DIEM's Tet Message," February 4, 1960, CDF 751G.00/2-460, Box 1745; and, Memorandum of Conversation, February 9, 1960 and February 26, 1960. Both are located in Folder 1, Box 14, Williams Papers.

20. Vietnam Press, January 27, 1960, FBIS, January 29, 1960, G2.

21. A series of economic reports were published in the Vietnam Press highlighting the economic advances of the Republic of Vietnam. See "Viet Nam Rubber Exports Soar," Vietnam Press (Morning), October 4, 1960, H3; "Rubber Keeps First Place in Viet Nam Exports," Vietnam Press (Evening), October 5, 1960, H5; "Vietnamese Rice Production Increased by One Third," Vietnam Press (Evening), October 3, 1960, H23; "Viet Nam Exportable Rice Surplus Amounts to 400,000 Tons This Year," Vietnam Press (Morning), October 6, 1960, H6; 4. "Increased Vietnamese Rice Production and Exports Cited at International Rice Commission Meeting," Vietnam Press (Evening), November 16, 1960, H9–H12; "Rice Cultivation Development in Vietnam Topic of Discussion at IRC Session," Vietnam Press (Morning), November 18, 1960, H16–H18; "Viet Nam's Forestry and Farm Product Imports Top VN$1,278 Million," Vietnam Press (Morning), October 24, 1960, H6; "290,903 Tons of Fruit in 1959," Vietnam Press (Evening), October 6, 1960, H3; "Phuoc Tuy Produces 1,200 Tons of Peanuts," Vietnam Press (Single), October 30, 1960, H8; "Bến Cát Dairy Farm to Supply Saigon with Fresh Milk," Vietnam Press (Morning), December 1, 1960, H12; and, "Food Situation in Viet Nam," Vietnam Press (Morning), December 5, 1960, H10.

22. Durbrow to the Department of State, Telegram 2107, January 9, 2011, CDF 751K.00 (W)/1-960, RG 59.

23. Memorandum of Conversation, January 7, 1960, Folder 1, Box 14, Williams Papers.

24. Williams' handwritten notes on the Memorandum of Conversation, January 7, 1960, Folder 1, Box 14, Williams Papers. See also Williams' Memorandum for Record, March 1971, which refutes many of Durbrow's claims about the meeting in Folder 1, Box 14, Williams Papers. Durbrow offers no account of the heated visit in his weekly account to the Department of State; Durbrow to the Department of State, Telegram 2107, January 9, 2011, CDF 751K.00(W)/1-960.

25. "Secretary Brucker and the Geneva Agreements," January 25, 1960, CDF 751K.00/1-2560.

26. The second conversation was recorded as an addendum to the first Memorandum of

Conversation of January 7, 1960, Folder 1, Box 14, Williams Papers.

27. When Williams learned of this duplicity, he recorded his own memorandum for the record of the events surrounding the Brucker meeting and the TERM issue. See Memorandum for Record, March 1971, Folder 1, Box 14, Williams Papers.

28. On January 8, Durbrow sent Parsons a letter outline the course of events, which Williams believed was misleading and designed to protect himself should Brucker pursue the matter. Durbrow's January 8, 1960, letter, Parson's February 1, 1960, reply, and Williams' February 10, 1960, observation of the exchange are located in Folder 1, Box 14, Williams Papers. See also Williams' memory of the events in Williams' Memorandum for Record, March 1971, Folder 1, Box 14, Williams Papers.

29. Williams countered Durbrow's claim that both he and Williams had been asked not to come to the second meeting; Only Durbrow had been asked not to return. See Williams' Memorandum for Record, March 1971, Folder 1, Box 14, Williams Papers. Williams also maintained that Durbrow's January 8 summary failed to include information about the tone of his remarks to Brucker that caused the former to leave the first meeting. Durbrow never acknowledged that an embarrassing situation occurred. Williams would later assert that Durbrow was jealous of his relationship with Ngô Đình Diệm. See Memorandum of Conversation, January 7, 1960, Folder 1, Box 14, Williams Papers.

30. In February, Durbrow would push to have the Vietnamese request the MAAG ceiling raised to 685 rather than having the request come from the U.S. See Durbrow to the Department of State, Telegram 2430, February 16, 1960, CDF 751K.5-MSP/2-1660; Durbrow to the Department of State, Telegram 2443, February 18, 1960, CDF 751K.5-MSP/2-1860. Williams' analysis is found in Williams to the Secretary of State, Telegram MAGCC-OP 259, February 24, 1960, CDF 751K.5-MSP/2-2460.

31. *Vietnam Press*, January 31, 1960 and February 1, 1960, FBIS, February 2, 1960, G1. See also *Times of Vietnam*, February 3, 1960, FBIS, February 4, 1960, G1; and, *May Jih Luan Zan*, February 4, 1960, FBIS, February 4, 1960, G3.

32. Memorandum of Conversation, February 1, 1960, Folder 1, Box 14, Williams Papers.; and, Durbrow to the Department of State, Telegram 2337, February 6, 1960, CDF 751K.00 (W)/2-660. See also the press conference by Secretary of State for Information Trần Chánh Tranh and Secretary of State for the Presidency Nguyễn Đình Thuận as reported by *Tuan Tung Jih Pao*, February 2, 1960, FBIS, February 3, 1960, G1-G2. A.J. Langguth argued that three companies, or approximately 300 men attacked approximately 1,700 troops. See Langguth, *Our Vietnam*, 101. See also Spector, *Advice and Support*, 338–339. Spector correctly identifies the four companies and details Williams' conversation with Ngô Đình Diệm as a result of the failure of the 32nd Regiment.

33. "Conversation with President DIEM—1500–1800 hours 12 January 1960," Folder 1, "Ngo-Dinh-Diem-Conferences, January 1960," Box 14, Williams Papers.

34. Durbrow to the Department of State, Telegram 2431, February 16, 1960, CDF 751K.5-MSP/2-1660.

35. Memorandum of Conversation between Lieutenant Colonel Joseph A. Flesch OASD/ISA Far East Region and Chalmers B. Wood, officer in Charge of Vietnam Affairs in the Department of State, February 4, 1960, Folder 108 "VN 1960—National Defense Affairs (General)," Box 2, Entry 5155, Bureau of East Asian Affairs, Vietnam Desk, Vietnam Subject Files, 1955–1962.

36. Memorandum of Conversation, February 1, 1960, Folder 1, Box 14, Williams Papers.

37. *Tự do*, February 2, 1960, FBIS, February 2, 1960, G2. See also Race, *War Comes to Long An*, 113–115; Duiker, *Sacred War*, 124–126; and, Langguth, *Our Vietnam*, 105–107. See also Nguyễn Thị Định, *No Other Road to Take*, 17–18.

38. Mendenhall to the Department of State, Telegram 230, February 2, 1960. CDF 751G.00/1-2060.

39. There are several condemnations of the Viet Cong attacks in the Vietnamese press. See *Cách mạng Quốc gia*, February 5, 1960, FBIS, February 8, 1960, G2; February 9, 1960, FBIS, February 9, 1960, G3, and February 10, 1960, FBIS, February 10, 1960, and February 11, 1960, FBIS, February 11, 1960, G1; *Tự do*, February 8, 1960, FBIS, February 9, 1960, G1; *Ngôn Luận*, February 10, 1960, FBIS, February 10, 1960, G1, February 12, 1960, FBIS, and February 15, 1960, FBIS, February 17, 1960, G1-G3, February 12, 1960, G1; and, *Tiếng Chuông* on February 10, 1960, FBIS, February 10, 1960, G1.

40. Durbrow to the Department of State, Telegram 2014, December 24, 1959, *FRUS, 1958–1960: Volume I: Vietnam*, 276–278.

41. Durbrow to the Department of State, Telegram 2014, December 24, 1959, *FRUS, 1958–1960: Volume I: Vietnam*, 278.

42. Memorandum of Conversation, April 6, 1960, Folder 1, Box 14, Williams Papers.

43. Durbrow to the Department of State, Despatch 251, "Current Security Problems Facing the GVN," February 16, 1960, CDF 751K.5/2-1660. The memorandum of conversation

is attached. See also Durbrow to the Department of State, Telegram 2372, February 11, 1960, CDF 751K.11/2-1160; Durbrow to the Department of State, Telegram 2411, February 13, 1960, CDF 751K.11/2-1360.
44. Durbrow to the Department of State, Telegram 2519, February 27, 1960, CDF 751K.5-MSP/2-2760.
45. Memorandum of Conversation, February 1, 1960, Folder 1, Box 14, Williams Papers.; and, Memorandum of Conversation, February 20, 1960, Folder 1, Box 14, Williams Papers.

Chapter 13

1. Lansdale led the Saigon Military Mission in 1954–1955 and helped oversee psychological warfare and counterinsurgency efforts. Through this program, he interacted with Ngô Đình Diệm and became a confident as the Vietnamese leader rose to power.
2. Lansdale to Douglas, February 12, 1960, CDF 751K.5/3-460.
3. Memorandum from Lansdale to the Assistant Secretary of Defense for International Security Affairs, John N. Irwin II, "Counter-Guerrilla Training, Vietnam," February 19, 1960. *FRUS, 1958–1960: Volume I: Vietnam*, 288–289.
4. Memorandum from Lansdale to Irwin, "Counter-Guerrilla Training, Vietnam," February 19, 1960. *FRUS, 1958–1960: Volume I: Vietnam*, 289.
5. Memorandum of Conversation, "Internal Security Situation and Corruption," March 2, 1960, CDF 751K.00/3-260. See also Colby, *Lost Victory*, 70.
6. Memorandum of Conversation, "Internal Security Situation and Corruption," March 2, 1960, CDF 751K.00/3-260.
7. Memorandum of Conversation between Williams and Ngô Đình Diệm, January 12, 1960, Folder 1, Box 14, Williams Papers.
8. Memorandum of Conversation, "Internal Security Situation and Corruption," March 2, 1960, CDF 751K.00/3-260. See also Memorandum of a Conversation, "Conference on Internal Security in Viet-Nam and related Problem of Civil Administration," The Pentagon, March 18, 1960, *FRUS, 1958–1960: Volume I: Vietnam*, 340; and, Heavner to the Department of State, Despatch 14, "Comments on the Can Lao Party and Ngo Dinh Can by an 'Inactive' Party Member," February 8, 1960, CDF 751K.00/2-860.
9. Memorandum of Conversation, "Internal Security Situation and Corruption," March 2, 1960, CDF 751K.00/3-260.
10. Memorandum of Conversation, "Internal Security Situation and Corruption," March 2, 1960, CDF 751K.00/3-260.
11. Memorandum of Conversation, "The Can Lao Party and Ngo Dinh Can," February 8, 1960, CDF 751K.00/2-860. As President of Thừa Thiên Citizen's Rally, he oversaw the merger with the National Revolutionary Movement. Phạm Ngọc Vinh had supported Ngô Đình Diệm over Bảo Đại in 1955 and was most closely associated with Ngô Đình Cẩn.
12. Durbrow to the Department of State, Despatch 278," Special Report on Current Internal Security Situation," March 7, 1960, *FRUS, 1958–1960: Volume I: Vietnam*, 300. Much of Durbrow's comments come from a special report from the Country Team titled, "Special Report on Internal Security Situation in Viet-Nam" that was included as an enclosure to the Despatch and reprinted in *FRUS, 1958–1960: Volume I: Vietnam*, 303–320. See also Kahin, *Intervention*, 122.
13. "Security Anxiety in S. Viet Nam: Two Newspapers Suspended," *The London Times*, March 8, 1960. See also Robert Ballantyne, Second Secretary of the American Embassy in London to the Department of State, Despatch 2895, "Comment in London Press re Security Situation in South Vietnam," March 14, 1960, CDF 751K.00/3-1460; and, Durbrow to the Department of State, Telegram 2639, March 12, 1960, CDF 751K.00(W)/3-1260.
14. "'Tu Do' and 'Buoi Sang' are Suspended," *Vietnam Press*, March 8, 1960, FBIS, G1. *Tự do* was authorized to resume publishing in early April if they dismissed the two employees responsible for the stories. The publishers of the paper refused. See Durbrow to the Department of State, Telegram 2850, April 2, 1960, CDF 751K.00(W)/4-260.
15. FBIS, March 26, 1960, G3; and, "Former Communists Denounce Vietcong," March 28, 1960, FBIS, G4.
16. Durbrow to the Department of State, Despatch 278, "Special Report on Current Internal Security Situation," March 7, 1960, *FRUS, 1958–1960: Volume I: Vietnam*, 301. See Cunningham to the Department of State, Telegram 2692, March 19. 1960, CDF 751K.3-1960. See also Miller, *Misalliance*, 177–184.
17. Joseph J. Zasloff, "Rural Resettlement in South Viet Nam: The Agroville Program" *Pacific Affairs*, 35, No. 4 (Winter, 1962–1963), 327–340. See also Colby, *Lost Victory*, 69–70; and, Catton, *Diem's Final Failure*, 63–69.
18. Durbrow to the Department of State, Despatch 278, "Special Report on Current Internal Security Situation," March 7, 1960, *FRUS, 1958–1960: Volume I: Vietnam*, 302. The failure of the Agroville Program did not stop Ngô Đình Diệm from continuing his land redistribution efforts in Vietnam. By October 1960, 457,149 hectares of land had been redistributed

to 122,802 tenant families. Another 50,700 people were resettled on 101,500 reclaimed hectares. He believed this type of land redistribution assisted in the development of Vietnam. See Ngô Đình Diệm's State of the Union Message, October 3, 1960. Box 5, Folder "350 Internal Political Affairs: Vietnam, 1959–1961," Entry 3340B–Vietnam, Saigon Embassy, General Records, 1956–1963, RG 84, NARA.

19. Memorandum of Conversation between Williams and Ngô Đình Diệm, March 15, 1960, Folder 1, Box 14, Williams Papers. Durbrow's report of the conversation is located in Cunningham to the Department of State, Telegram 2691, March 19, 1960, CDF 751K.5/3-1960. See also Memorandum of Conversation between Williams and Ngô Đình Diệm, March 19, 1960, Folder 1, Box 14, Williams Papers.

20. Williams to Lansdale, March 10, 1960. *FRUS, 1958–1960: Volume I: Vietnam*, 320–324. See also Briefing Paper Prepared in the Department of Defense, undated. *FRUS, 1958–1960: Volume I: Vietnam*: 357; Durbrow to the Department of State, Telegram 2567, March 3, 1960, CDF 751K.00/3-360; and, Spector, *Advice and Support*, 349–355.

21. Telegram 2567, Durbrow to the Department of State, March 3, 1960, CDF 751K.00/3-360.

22. Williams complained to Assistant Deputy Chief of Army Staff for Logistics Lieutenant General Samuel L. Myers that the commando companies would take the best NCOs and privates from ARVN. Because of this, he worked to make sure the plan did not come to fruition. See Williams to Myers, March 20, 1960. *FRUS, 1958–1960: Volume I: Vietnam*, 343. See also Spector, *Advice and Support*, 349–355.

23. Memorandum of Conversation between Williams and Ngô Đình Diệm, March 7, 1960, Folder 1, Box 14, Williams Papers. In the case of the Civil Guard, the USOM claimed it would take $18 million to purchase the equipment it needed to be effective. With the support of the Michigan State University Group, the USOM wanted the Civil Guard to be a police force rather than an active military unit as Ngô Đình Diệm, Williams, and Lansdale. See also Memorandum of Conversation between Williams and Ngô Đình Diệm, March 15, 1960, and March 19. Both documents located in Folder 1, Box 14, Williams Papers.; and, Spector, *Advice and Support*, 335–336.

24. Memorandum of Conversation between Williams and Ngô Đình Diệm, March 19, 1960, Folder 1, Box 14, Williams Papers.

25. Several examples of the give-and-take between Ngô Đình Diệm and Williams are evident in their conversations. A few examples include the Memorandum of Conversations on January 12, February 1, and March 15 and 19, 1960, Folder 1, Box 14, Williams Papers. See also Memorandum from Lansdale to the Deputy Secretary of Defense, C. Douglas Dillon, "Security Situation in Vietnam," March 17, 1960. *FRUS, 1958–1960: Volume I: Vietnam*, 336–338; and, Memorandum of a Conversation, "Conference on Internal Security in Vietnam and Related Problem of Civil Administration," The Pentagon, March 18, 160, *FRUS, 1958–1960: Volume I: Vietnam*, 339–340.

26. See "Conversations with President Diem during Pleiku Area–Dalat Visit, 0715–2010 hours 22 January 1960," Folder 1, Box 14, Williams Papers. Ngô Đình Diệm would eventually promote Nguyễn Khánh to Brigadier General.

27. Telegram from Williams to Lansdale, March 10, 1960. *FRUS, 1958–1960: Volume I: Vietnam*, 324. For additional comments by Williams on Nguyễn Khánh see Williams to Myers, March 20, 1960. *FRUS, 1958–1960: Volume I: Vietnam*, 342.

28. Memorandum of Conversation, April 6, 1960, Folder 1, Box 14, Williams Papers.

29. Durbrow to the Department of State, Telegram 2622, March 10, 1960, CDF 751K.00/3-160.

30. A March 18 conference on internal security in Vietnam held at the Pentagon argued that the Civil Guard could not counter the Viet Cong. It called on Ngô Đình Diệm to relinquish more control of the military, and questioned the effectiveness of commando companies would strength of seventy-five men would be inferior to the larger Viet Cong groups roaming the countryside. It came to a conclusion that was similar to Durbrow's in that Ngô Đình Diệm wanted more military aid without having to justify it. See Memorandum of Conversation, "Conference on Internal Security in Vietnam and Related Problem of Civil Administration," March 18, 1960. *FRUS, 1958–1960: Volume I: Vietnam*, 339.

31. Memorandum of a Conversation, "Conference on Internal Security in Viet-Nam and Related Problem of Civil Administration" The Pentagon, March 18, 1960, *FRUS, 1958–1960: Volume I: Vietnam*, 339–341.

32. Lansdale to Williams, "Counter-Guerrilla Training in Vietnam," April 14, 1960. *FRUS, 1958–1960: Volume I: Vietnam*, 386–387.

33. Durbrow had already offered his position on the issue of money in his Telegram 2753, March 24, 1960, CDF 751K.5-MPS/3-2460 in which he had sought to resolve the matter before Nguyễn Đình Thuận's arrival in Washington to end his attempts to circumvent the process, that is, go through Durbrow for all of

the Vietnamese needs. A memorandum of conversation titled, "General Discussion of U.S. Aid to Viet-Nam, Internal Security Situation in Viet-Nam, and Vietnamese Relations with Cambodia," April 4, 1960, is located in CDF 751K.5-MSP/4-460. Nguyễn Đình Thuận also had an April 8 meeting with Wood, Deputy Director of the Central Intelligence Agency, General Charles P. Cabell, and CIA officers that covered Laos and its significance to the Vietnamese situation. See Memorandum of a Conversation, "Situation in Viet-Nam," April 8, 1960. *FRUS, 1958–1960: Volume I: Vietnam*, 383–384. The original document is located at CDF 751K.5-MSP/4-860.

34. Memorandum of a Conversation, "General Discussion of U.S. Aid to Viet-Nam, Internal Security Situation in Viet-Nam and Vietnamese Relations with Cambodia," April 4, 1960, CDF 751K.5-MSP/4-460. See also Parsons to the United States Embassy in Saigon, April 11, 1960, CDF 751G.00/4-1160.

35. Spector, *Advice and Support*, 344–347.

36. Durbrow to the Department of State, Despatch 391, "Conversation Between Ambassador Durbrow and Secretary of State for the Presidency Nguyen Dinh Thuan," May 17, 1960, CDF 751K.13/501760.

37. Durbrow to the State Department, Telegram 2884, April 7, 1960. CDF 751K.00/4-760. See Anderson, *Trapped by Success*, 183.

38. H. Francis Cunningham, Jr., Counselor of the Embassy to the Department of State, Despatch 364, "Rumored Corruption in the Government of South Viet-Nam," April 23, 1960, CDF 751K.00/4-2360. See also Durbrow to the Department of State, Despatch 371, "Can Lao Party Financial Activities as a Source of Unpopularity of the Diem Regime," April 28, 1960, CDF 751K.00/4-281960.

39. Durbrow to the State Department, Telegram 2884, April 7, 1960. CDF 751K.00/4-760. See also Durbrow to the Department of State, Despatch 348, "Morale of Vietnamese Armed Forces," April 15, 1960, CDF 751K.00/4-1560. The memorandum of conversation between Ladejinsky and Ngô Đình Diệm is attached to this document.

40. Later in the day on April 8, Durbrow reported to the Department of State that the Vietnamese had informed MAAG that the $165 million budget would only cover a force level of 135,000 instead of the projected 144,217. It needed an additional $3,781,512 to meet its financial obligations or an additional $6 million if the force level reached 148,000. Durbrow to the Department of State, Telegram 2893, April 8, 1960, CDF 751K.5/4-860.

41. Durbrow to Parson, April 19, 1960, CDF 751K.5-MSP/4-1960.

42. Durbrow to Williams, April 19, 1960, CDF 751K.5-MSP/4-1960.

43. Memorandum of Conversation, April 13, 1960, Folder 1, Box 14, Williams Papers. See also Williams to Durbrow listed as CINCPAC to the Secretary of State, Telegram 172145Z April (Navy Message), April 17, 1960, CDF 751K.022/4-1760.

44. Mendenhall to the Department of State, Despatch 358, "Reports of Opposition Activities," April 22, 1960, enclosure 4, CDF 751K.00/4-2260. A second version went out in Mendenhall to the Department of State, Despatch 400, "Transmittal of Documents Related to 'Opposition Group,'" May 14, 1960, CDF 751K.00/5-1460. For a similar version see Bernard Fall, *The Two Vietnams*, 435–438. See also Nguyễn Công Luận, *Nationalist in the Viet Nam Wars*, 188; and, Bradley, *Vietnam at War*, 88–89.

45. These three groups had presented a challenge to Ngô Đình Diệm in 1954–1955 and remained an obstacle to continued Vietnamese progress. They had the support of the French and were also closely connected to Americans who had served in Vietnam and had turned against Ngô Đình Diệm. See Karnow, *Vietnam: A History*, 235, Jacobs, *Cold War Mandarin*, 115; Kahin, *Intervention*, 122–123; and, Anderson, *Trapped by Success*, 183–184.

46. Mendenhall to the Department of State, Despatch 358, "Reports of Opposition Activities," April 22, 1960, enclosure 4, CDF 751K.00/4-2260. Other members of the group included Phan Khắc Sửu, who lead the Vietnamese Socialist Party, former Foreign Minister Trần Văn Đỗ, brother of ambassador Trần Văn Chương and uncle to Madame Ngô Đình Nhu, Saigon University professor Hồ Viết Điểu, Secretary of the Vietnamese Red Cross Trần Văn Hương, Lâm Văn Tết, and Đào Hưng Long.

47. Durbrow to the Department of State, Telegram 2981, April 19, 1960, *FRUS, 1958–1960: Volume I: Vietnam*, 404–406.

48. Durbrow to the Department of State, Telegram 2981, April 19, 1960, *FRUS, 1958–1960: Volume I: Vietnam*, 404–406.

Chapter 14

1. Mendenhall to the Department of State, Despatch 433, "Comments by Diplomatic Officials on Internal Political Situation in Viet-Nam," June 7, 1960, CDF 751K.00/6-760.

2. Memorandum of Conversation between Ngô Đình Diệm and Williams, May 19, 1960, Memorandum of Conversation, May 11, 1960, Folder 1, Box 14, Williams Papers.

3. Durbrow to the Department of State, Telegram 3185, May 12, 1960, CDF 751K.00/5-1260.

4. *Sài Gòn Mới* editorial, May 7, 1960, FBIS, May 11, 1960, G2; *Cách mạng Quốc gia* editorial, May 13, 1960, and *Sài Gòn Mới* editorial, May 13, 1960. Both located in FBIS, May 17, 1960, G6. See also *Cách mạng Quốc gia* editorial, May 17, 1960, FBIS, May 19, 1960, G1. These papers were already friendly to Ngô Đình Diệm so it was not surprising that they would condemn the Bloc for Liberty and Progress.

5. Memorandum of Conversation, "President Diem Requests Lansdale," between Nguyễn Duy Liên, Usher, and Askew, April 19, 1960, CDF 751K.58/4-1960.

6. Williams to Lansdale, May 9, 1960, *FRUS, 1958-1960: Volume I: Vietnam*, 443.

7. Durbrow to the Department of State, Telegram 3013, April 22, 1960, *FRUS, 1958-1960: Volume I: Vietnam*, 409.

8. Lansdale to Bonesteel, "'Third Country' Doctrine, Internal Security," April 25, 1960, *FRUS, 1958-1960: Volume I: Vietnam*, 410-411.

9. Lansdale letter to Williams, April 30, 1960, *FRUS, 1958-1960: Volume I: Vietnam*, 425-426. Williams to Lansdale, May 9, 1960, *FRUS, 1958-1960: Volume I: Vietnam*, 442-445. For example, Durbrow sent Williams a written reprimand for informing Ngô Đình Diệm that the United States had approved the transfer of 5,000 Thompson sub-machine guns to the Civil Guard. Durbrow had wanted to use the contribution at the right moment to gain a political or diplomatic advantage. The two also disagreed on the reduction of the military budget for the Republic of Vietnam, which would have seen the size of the Vietnamese military reduced by 7,000. See Williams to Mansfield, May 20, 1960, *FRUS, 1958-1960: Volume I: Vietnam*, 467-471.

10. Memorandum of Conversation between Williams and Ngô Đình Diệm, May 9, 1960, Folder 1, Box 14, Williams Papers. See also Anderson, *Trapped by Success*, 186.

11. "Resume of the Visit of Admiral Stump with President Ngo Dinh Diem at Dalat, 26-26 April 1960," April 30, 1960, Folder 1, Box 14, Williams Papers.

12. Durbrow to the Department of State, Telegram 3095, May 3, 1960, *FRUS, 1958-1960: Volume I: Vietnam*, 433-437. See Anderson, *Trapped by Success*, 187. Sam Sary had been a cabinet member in Norodom Sihanouk's government in the 1950s but turned against the government. He founded a newspaper and political organization that criticized the Phnom Penh Government and was generally a nuisance to Sihanouk. The Movement of the Free Khmer (Khmer Serei) was formed after the Second World War. It was opposed to continued French rule in Laos. In the late 1950s, leadership in the movement criticized Sihanouk for being too close to the Communists. See Dommen, *The Indochinese Experience of the French and Americans*, 352-353.

13. Durbrow to the Department of State, Telegram 3095, May 3, 1960, *FRUS, 1958-1960: Volume I: Vietnam*, 434.

14. Durbrow to the Department of State, Telegram 3095, May 3, 1960, *FRUS, 1958-1960: Volume I: Vietnam*, 435.

15. Draft Telegram from the Acting Secretary of State to the Embassy in Vietnam, May 3, 1960, *FRUS, 1958-1960: Volume I: Vietnam*, 437.

16. Parsons offered to visit Trần Văn Chương at the Vietnamese embassy to inform him of the State Department's position with the hope that it would shock him into action while Director of the Office of Southeast Asian Affairs, Kenneth Young worked on Nguyễn Đình Thuần. See Parsons to Durbrow, Telegram 2038, May 3, 1960, CDF 751K.00/5-360.

17. Memorandum of Conversation, "Question of Withholding Emergency Military Equipment from Viet-Nam," May 5, 1960, CDF 751K.00/5-51960.

18. Durbrow to the Department of State, Telegram 3133, May 6, 1960, CDF 751K.00/5-660. See also Durbrow to the Department of State, Despatch 403, "Political and Security Situation in Viet-Nam," May 16, 1960, CDF 751K.005-1660. See also Durbrow to the Department of State, Telegram 3272, May 23, 1060, CDF 751K.00/5-2360.

19. Herter to Durbrow, Telegram 2037, May 9, 1960, *FRUS, 1958-1960: Volume I: Vietnam*, 448-449. See also Anderson, *Trapped by Success*, 188.

20. Durbrow to the Department of State, Telegram 3196, May 13, 1960, *FRUS, 1958-1960: Volume I: Vietnam*, 453-457.

21. Memorandum of Conversation, May 11, 1960, Folder 1, Box 14, Williams Papers.

22. Williams reported from an observation by Nguyễn Đình Thuần that the meeting had Ngô Đình Diệm "white with anger," which was either not observed or reported by Durbrow. See Williams to Lansdale, May 17, 1960, *FRUS, 1958-1960: Volume I: Vietnam*, 464.

23. Department of State to the American Embassy in Saigon, Telegram 2277, June 21, CDF 751K.00/6-2160.

24. Memorandum of Conversation, "Possible TDY to Viet-Nam for Brigadier General Lansdale," May 13, 1960, *FRUS, 1958-1960: Volume I: Vietnam*, 457-458.

25. Memorandum of Conversation, "Possible TDY to Viet-Nam for Brigadier General Lansdale," May 13, 1960, *FRUS, 1958-1960: Volume I: Vietnam*, 457-458.

26. Durbrow to the Department of State, Telegram 3218, May 17, 1960, *FRUS, 1958–1960: Volume I: Vietnam*, 462.

27. Williams seemed to believe that Durbrow and the Country Team was not aware of his communications with Lansdale though their parallel arguments against Durbrow's actions would have made that a difficult proposition to believe. Williams to Lansdale, May 17, 1960, *FRUS, 1958–1960: Volume I: Vietnam*, 463–464.

28. Durbrow's question was based on a May 10 social gathering with the Indonesian Consul General who asked him if the United States was looking for another Diem. At the same party, other members of the diplomatic corps approached Durbrow with similar questions. See Durbrow to the Department of State, Telegram 3220, May 17, 1960, CDF 751K.00/5-1760. Another instance occurred later, suggesting the prolonged nature of these types of conversations. See Mendenhall to the Department of State, Despatch 450, "Conversation with Indian Official re Political Situation in Viet-Nam," June 17, 1960, CDF 751K.00/6-1760.

29. Williams to Lansdale, May 17, 1960, *FRUS, 1958–1960: Volume I: Vietnam*, 464.

30. Memorandum of a telephone conversation between Parsons and Knight, "Proposed Assignment of Brigadier General Lansdale as Adviser to President Diem," May 19, 1960, *FRUS, 1958–1960: Volume I: Vietnam*, 465.

31. Memorandum of a telephone conversation between Parsons and Knight, "Proposed Assignment of Brigadier General Lansdale as Adviser to President Diem," May 19, 1960, *FRUS, 1958–1960: Volume I: Vietnam*, 466.

32. Williams to Mansfield, May 20, 1960, *FRUS, 1958–1960: Volume I: Vietnam*, 467–471; and, Williams to Durbrow, "Training of the RVNAF (U)," June 1, 1960, *FRUS, 1958–1960: Volume I: Vietnam*, 471–483.

33. Parsons to Durbrow, June 9, 1960, *FRUS, 1958–1960: Volume I: Vietnam*, 492–493.

34. Lansdale to Williams, June 21, 1960, *FRUS, 1958–1960: Volume I: Vietnam*, 501–502.

35. "Summary of Conversation Between Lieutenant General Samuel T. Williams and President Ngo Dinh Diem, 1600–1945 Hours, 2 June 1960, June 2, 1960, Folder 2, "Ngo-Dinh-Diem-Conferences, February-August 1960," Box 14, Williams Papers.

36. Durbrow to the Department of State, Telegram 3430, June 11, 1960, CDF 751K.00/6-1160.

37. Heavner to the Department of State, Despatch 23, "Remarks by Nguyen Van Buu on Corruption and Communism in the Government of Vietnam," June 28, 1960, CDF 751K.00/6-2860. One such example was a report on a conversation with Nguyễn Văn Bưu, who was in the shrimp and cinnamon industry. Heavner believed Nguyễn Văn Bưu to be a significant source of credible information because he was the brother of the Quảng Trị Province Chief Nguyễn Văn Đông who was related to Ngô Đình Diệm by marriage. Nguyễn Văn Bưu criticized the internal security situation in Central Vietnam and Ngô Đình Nhu's Republican Youth, which he equated to Hitler's political thugs of 1930s Germany. Nguyễn Văn Bưu, however, was also in conflict with the Ngô brothers in Central Vietnam so it remains unclear whether his motives were out of real concern or as a way to gain credibility through the Americans.

38. Durbrow to the Department of State, "Uneasiness among GVN top officials," Airgram G-5, July 9, 1960, CDF 751K.00/7-960. See also Durbrow to the Department of State, Telegram 81, July 9, 1960, CDF 751K.5-MSP/7-960.

39. FBIS, July 7, 1960, G2.

40. Durbrow to the Department of State, Despatch 24, "Peasant Views on Tan Luoc Agroville, Vinh Long Province," July 14, 1960, CDF 751K.00/7-1460.

41. Zasloff continued to argue this point even though the second Agroville in Kiên Giang Province, which was completed in April 1960, was done with paid labor. Durbrow to the Department of State, Telegram 3369, June 4, 1960, CDF 751K.00(W)/6-460 HBS. See also Mann, *A Grand Delusion*, 218–219.

42. Durbrow to the Department of State, Despatch 22, "Conversation with Ngo Dinh Luyen about the Internal Situation in Viet-Nam, American Aid, and Relations with Cambodia," July 14, 1960, CDF 751K.00/7-1960.

43. Memorandum of Conversation between Williams and Ngô Đình Diệm, July 25, 1960, Folder 1, Box 14, Williams Papers.

44. Durbrow to the Department of State, July 1, 1960, CDF 751K.5/7-160.

45. FBIS, March 10, 1960, G3.

46. "New Province Functionaries Draw Advice," *Vietnam Press*, March 12, FBIS, G3–G4.

47. Memorandum of Conversation, "Situation in Viet-Nam" August 1, 1960, CDF 751K.00/8-160. See also memorandum of conversation, "U.S.–Vietnamese Relations," August 3, 1960, CDF 751K.5-MSP/8-360.

48. Durbrow to the Department of State, Airgram G-66, August 18, 1960, CDF 751K.00/8-1860.

49. Durbrow to the Department of State, "'Freedom and Progress Bloc' Petitions Diem re Agroville and GVN Responds," Airgram G-50, August 11, 1960, CDF 751K.00/8-1160. See also Mendenhall to the Department of State,

Despatch 63, "Freedom and Progress Bloc Petition re Agrovilles and GVN Response," August 17, 1960, CDF 751K.00/8-1760; and, Mendenhall to the Department of State, Despatch 62, "Phan Quang Dan Petition to President Diem for Institution Habeas Corpus," August 17, 1960, CDF 751K.00/8-1760.

50. Durbrow to the Department of State, "Phan Quan Dan Petitions re Habeas Corpus," Airgram G-52, August 12, 1960, CDF 751K.00/8-1260. This was especially true when Ngô Đình Diệm explained a planned coup d'état against him that was scheduled for August 21. Ngô Đình Diệm informed Durbrow that thirteen ringleaders from the trade union group had been arrested. He maintained that they planned to take advantage of student discontent after their baccalaureate examination results were published and taxicab drivers who were unhappy because of a recent gas price increase. See Durbrow to the Department of State, Telegram 432, August 22, 1960, CDF 751K.00/8-2260. See also Durbrow to the Department of State, Telegram 455, August 24, 1960, CDF 751K.00/8-2460; "Police Bar Anti-Government Demonstrations," London, Reuters, August 22, 1960, FBIS, August 23, 1960, G1; and, "Communist Adopt 'Nationalist' Disguise," *Chuông Mai*, August 23, 1960, FBIS, August 26, 1960, G5-G6. Durbrow was not convinced and reported to Washington that the coup d'état signaled a real problem with the Saigon Government. See Kahin, *Intervention*, 123.

51. Memorandum of Conversation, "Situation in Viet-Nam," September 1, 1960, CDF 751K.00/9-160. See also Mendenhall to the Department of State, Air Pouch 104, September 10, 1960, CDF 751K.00/9-1060. An August 17 memorandum of conversation, "Political Situation in South Viet-Nam" is attached to the document.

52. During a September 1 meeting between Lalouette, Durbrow, and British ambassador Henry Hohler, he informed them that Ngô Đình Diệm would not reorganize his government though he had planned to develop a National Security Council. Durbrow was also a proponent of such a reorganization. See Cunningham to the Department of State, Despatch 105, "Talk with French and British ambassadors on Internal Political Situation in Viet-Nam," September 10, 1960, CDF 751K.00/9-1060. A memorandum of conversation, titled "Internal Situation in Viet-Nam," September 1, 1960 is attached as enclosure 1. Houghton also received a warning from Etienne Manac'h that Ngô Đình Diệm was experiencing increased opposition from the Vietnamese people because of his actions. See Houghton to the Department of State, Telegram 964, September 7, 1960, CDF 751K.00/9-760. The French Indochina Section Chief of the Quai d'Orsay, Jean Brèthes, informed Houghton that the situation in the Mekong Delta was worsening on September 20. See Houghton to the Department of State, Airgram G-409, September 21, 1960, CDF 751K.00/9-2160.

53. Durbrow to the Department of State, Telegram 624, September 16, 1960, CDF 751K.00/9-1660. See also Colby, *Lost Victory*, 73-74; and, Anderson, *Trapped by Success*, 189.

54. In a September 5 telegram to Washington, Durbrow outline the possibility of a trade union move to overthrow Ngô Đình Diệm activities. While he also looked at other groups, the trade unions seemed the most likely candidate to lead such a move. See Durbrow to the Department of State, Telegram 538 (in two sections), September 5, 1960, CDF 751K.00/9-560.

55. Langguth, *Our Vietnam*, 104-105.

56. Lansdale to O'Donnell, "State Message, Saigon 624" September 20, 1960, *FRUS, 1958-1960: Volume I: Vietnam*, 579-585.

Chapter 15

1. Special National Intelligence Estimate 63.1-60, "Short-Term Trends in South Vietnam," August 23, 1960, *FRUS, 1958-1960: Volume I: Vietnam*, 536-541.

2. Lansdale to Kent, "Approaching Crisis in South Vietnam?" August 10, 1960, *FRUS, 1958-1960: Volume I: Vietnam*, 526-528. Kent had sent his memorandum to the Director of Central Intelligence on July 28.

3. Lansdale cautioned the Washington policymakers that the Việt Cộng knew how to exploit the discontent of the urban elite who opposed Ngô Đình Diệm and were masters at propaganda and creating an image of an unorganized but dedicated insurgency when they were, in fact, well trained and equipped to fight the Vietnamese military. Lansdale also asserted that accounts of those who had actually travelled to the Vietnamese countryside needed to be included in any United States position paper in order to get an accurate description of the situation and conditions in Vietnam. See Lansdale to Kent, "Approaching Crisis in South Vietnam?" August 10, 1960, *FRUS, 1958-1960: Volume I: Vietnam*, 526-528.

4. Lansdale to McGarr, "Vietnam," August 11, 1960, *FRUS, 1958-1960: Volume I: Vietnam*, 528-536.

5. The Joint Chiefs of Staff sent their request on September 2. McGarr responded by asking for an increase of the ARVN force levels by 20,000, putting the Civil Guard under the

Ministry of Defense, adding forty additional MAAG advisers to train the Civil Guard, and increasing the weapons and ammunition to that organization. McGarr also wanted an additional $20 million in aid. Parsons to Livingston T. Merchant, September 8, 1960; and, Durbrow to the Department of State, Airgram G-130, September 26, 1960. Both documents found in Entry 5155 Bureau of East Asian Affairs, Vietnam Desk, Vietnam Subject Files, 1955–1962, Box 2, Folder 102 VN 1960–Internal Security, RG 59, NARA. See also Durbrow to the Department of State, Telegram 539, September 5, 1960, CDF 751K.5-MSP/9-560.

6. The Country Team reviewed the document on September 4. See the paper prepared by the Military Assistance Advisory Group in Vietnam, "Actions to Strengthen Stability of Government of Vietnam," *FRUS, 1958–1960: Volume I: Vietnam* 550–556. This version is the copy as revised by the Country Team. The original document is located in Durbrow to Parsons, September 6, 1960, RG 59 Entry 5155 Bureau of East Asian Affairs, Vietnam Desk, Vietnam Subject Files, 1955–1962, Box 2, Folder 108 VN 1960—National Defense Affairs (General).

7. Durbrow to Parsons, September 6, 1960, RG 59 Entry 5155 Bureau of East Asian Affairs, Vietnam Desk, Vietnam Subject Files, 1955–1962, Box 2, Folder 108 VN 1960—National Defense Affairs (General). See also Durbrow to the Department of State, Despatch 145, "Conversation Between President Diem and General W. B. Palmer, September 29, 1960," October 5, 1960, CDF 751K.5-MSP/10-560 HBS. A memorandum of conversation is attached. Another memorandum of conversation which also included McGarr is located in Durbrow to the Department of State, Despatch 146, "Memorandum of Conversation with President Diem on September 30," October 6, 1960, CDF 751K.5-MSP/10-660.

8. Durbrow to Parsons, September 6, 1960, RG 59 Entry 5155 Bureau of East Asian Affairs, Vietnam Desk, Vietnam Subject Files, 1955–1962, Box 2, Folder 108 VN 1960—National Defense Affairs (General).

9. Durbrow to the Department of State, Airgram G-146, October 6, 1960, CDF 751K.00/10-660. For the Ngô Đình Diệm National Assembly speech see Ngô Đình Diệm's State of the Union Message, October 3, 1960. Box 5, Folder "350 Internal Political Affairs: Vietnam, 1959–1961," Entry 3340B–Vietnam, Saigon Embassy, General Records, 1956–1963, RG 84: Department of State Records, Foreign Service Post, NARA. A full copy of the text is located at, "President Open National Assembly's October Regular Session; Reviews National Achievements," *Vietnam Press* (Evening), October 3, 1960, H1–H22.

10. See Durbrow to the Department of State, Telegram 751, October 6, 1960, CDF 751K.00/10-660.

11. Durbrow to the Department of State, Telegram 751, October 6, 1960, CDF 751K.00/10-660.

12. Acting Secretary of State John Steeves to Durbrow, Telegram 581, October 7, 1960. *FRUS, 1958–1960: Volume I: Vietnam*, 593. See also Anderson, *Trapped by Success*, 189.

13. Memorandum from the Secretary of State to the President, October 20, 1960, CDF 751K.00/10-2060.

14. Mendenhall to the Department of State, Despatch 157, "Approach to President Diem on Suggested Political Action," October 15, 1960, CDF 751K.00/10-160. Enclosure 1 is the document titled, "English Text of Memorandum Handed to President Diem" that is referred to in Telegram 802. Durbrow handed a French-language version of this item to Ngô Đình Diệm during their October 14 meeting. Also attached is enclosure 2, titled, "English Text of Notes on Ngô Đình Nhu and Dr. Tran Kim Tuyen." See also Miller, *Misalliance*, 212–213.

15. Durbrow to the Department of State, Telegram 866, October 20, 1960, CDF 751K.00/10-2060. See also Anderson, *Trapped by Success*, 190.

16. Durbrow to Irwin, October 31, 1960. *FRUS, 1958–1960: Volume I: Vietnam*, 622.

17. Nguyễn Văn Lương replaced Secretary of State for Justice Nguyễn Văn Sỹ. Commissioner General for Land Development Bùi Văn Lương replaced Secretary of State for Interior Lam Lê Trinh while Nguyễn Đình Thuận added the position of Assistant Defense Secretary to his responsibilities that included Secretary of State to the Presidency when Trần Trung Dũng was reassigned. Ngô Đình Diệm also changed the Minister of Information into a Directorate General and filled the position with the former consul general of Vietnam to Rangoon Trần Văn Dĩnh. See "Cabinet Reshuffled; Information Minister Becomes Directorate General," *Vietnam Press* (Evening), October 18, 1960, H1; and, "Mr. Tran Van Dinh Appointed Information Director General," *Vietnam Press* (Evening), October 19, 1960, H3. The men replaced would be appointed to diplomatic posts abroad. See *Cách mạng Quốc gia* editorial, October 22, 1960, FBIS, October 25, 1960, G1. Durbrow's reaction is located in Durbrow to the Department of State, Telegram 852, October 19, 1960, CDF 751K.13/10-1960; and, Durbrow to the Department of State, Telegram 867, October 21, 1960, CDF 751K.13/10-2160.

18. Counselor for Political Affairs of the Embassy in France, Randolph Kidder, to the Department of State, Airgram G-683, November 6, 1960, CDF 751K.00/11-660.

19. "Presidential Message Delivered on National Day, October 26, 1960," *Vietnam Press* (Morning), October 26, 1960, H1–H3.

20. "US17.5 Million Loan To Improve Water Supply System in City," *Vietnam Press* (Morning), November 3, 1960, H5.

21. On November 5, Phan Khắc Sửu (Saigon Fourth Constituency), Lê Trọng Quát (Social Union Group), and Ngô Hữu Thời (Bình Lớn Second Constituency) submitted bills 7/11, 23/11 and 28/11 to the National Assembly Intercommittee for Information, Justice, and Internal Affairs. See Mendenhall to the Department of State, Despatch 184, "Socialist Bloc in National Assembly Announces Policy Goals," November 8, 1960, CDF 751K.00/11-860.

22. "Government Asked to Take 'Emergency Measures' to Check Red Subversion," *Vietnam Press* (Single), November 6, 1960, H1. See also "Explanation of Resolution," *Sài Gòn Mới*, November 7, 1960, FBIS, November 8, G1; and, "People Demonstrate Anti-Red Feelings," *Vietnam Press* (Morning), November 8, 1960, H13.

23. The coup attempt began around 3:00 a.m. See Toland to the Chief of Staff, United States Air Force Lieutenant General Isaac White, Telegram C-115, November 11, 1960. *FRUS, 1958–1960: Volume I: Vietnam*, 638; Durbrow to the Director of Naval Intelligence, Rear Adm. Vernon L. Lowrance, Folder 350 "Internal Political Affairs: Vietnam—November Coup d'etat," Box 5, Entry 3340B-Vietnam, Saigon Embassy, General Records, 1956–1963, RG 84, NARA; Durbrow to Department of State, Telegram 993, Folder 350 "Internal Political Affairs: Vietnam—November Coup d'etat," Box 5, Entry 3340B-Vietnam, Saigon Embassy, General Records, 1956–1963, RG 84, NARA; ALUSNA, Saigon to the Department of State, Telegram 102114Z, November 10, 1960, CDF 751K.00/11-1060; and, Durbrow to the Department of State, MAGCH 1422, November 10, 1960, CDF 751K.00/11-1060. Junior officers within the airborne brigade had initiated the coup d'état. They were led by Vương Văn Đông, who complained of political infighting within the military and a lack of progress in fighting the Việt Cộng activity, though he and his conspirators had been passed over for promotion during the recent October 26 Independence Day celebrations. See Durbrow to the Department of State, Telegram 1029, November 11, 1960, CDF 751K.00/11-1160. See also Nguyễn Công Luận, *Nationalist in the Viet Nam Wars*, 188–189 and Dommen, *The Indochinese Experience of the French and Americans*, 418–420.

24. Upon being woken after the attack commenced, Mendenhall correctly guessed that it was a coup d'état, though there is no evidence that he had any forewarning. See Joseph A. Mendenhall's letter to his parents reprinted as an editorial note in *FRUS, 1958–1960: Volume I: Vietnam*, 660–661. See also Durbrow to Department of State, Telegram 994, November 11, 1960, Folder 350 "Internal Political Affairs: Vietnam–November Coup d'etat," Box 5, Entry 3340B-Vietnam, Saigon Embassy, General Records, 1956–1963, RG 84, NARA.

25. A detailed analysis of the military units involved in the coup attempt is located in McGarr to Department of the Army CX-166, November 17, 1960, Folder 83 "VN 1960—Attempted Coup d'Etat" Box 1 Entry 5155, General Records of the Department of State, Bureau of East Asian Affairs, Vietnam Desk, Vietnam Subject Files, 1955–1962.

26. The group expected the use of forty tanks from the Thủ Đức Military Academy but were denied them by its Commandant, General Lê Văn Nghiêm. Another battalion surrendered to the 7th ARVN Division near Biên Hòa before it could complete its mission of cutting the northern road. See "Abortive Coup as Told by Rebel Officer," *Vietnam Press* (Evening), November 25, 1960, H4. See also Lâm Quang Thi, *The Twenty-Five Year Century*, 97–99.

27. Saigon to the Secretary of State, Telegram Critic 3, November 10, 1960, CDF 751K.00/11-1060; and, Durbrow to the Department of State, Telegram 996, November 11, 1960, CDF 751K.00/11-1160. See also Miller, *Misalliance*, 202–204.

28. Durbrow to Department of State, Telegram 993, Folder 350 "Internal Political Affairs: Vietnam—November Coup d'etat," Box 5, Entry 3340B-Vietnam, Saigon Embassy, General Records, 1956–1963, RG 84, NARA. See also "Chronology of November 11–12 Events," *Vietnam Press* (Evening), November 21, 1960, H6–H8.

29. This was confirmed by both Colby and Nguyễn Đình Thuận. See Durbrow to Department of State, Telegram 998, November 11, 1960, CDF 751K.00/11-1160; and, Saigon to Secretary of State, Telegram 4, November 10, 1960, CDF 751K.00/11-1060 HBS.

30. Durbrow to Department of State, Telegram 1035, November 12, 1960, CDF 751K.00/11-1260. See also Durbrow to the Department of State, Telegram 1000, November 11, 1960, CDF 751K.00/11-1160.

31. "Saigon Radio Mirrors Course of Coup," FBIS, November 14, 1960, G1–G6. The *Voice of the Republic of Vietnam* broadcast began at approximately 8:45 a.m. and continued until approximately 10:15 a.m.

32. De Jaeger served as the General Representative of the Free Pacific Association, Far East Area. OUSARMA, Saigon to the Secretary of State, CX-154, November 11, 1960, CDF 751K.00/11-1160. See also OUSARMA, Saigon to the Secretary of State, CX-156, November 11, 1960, CDF 751K.00/11-1160; and, Saigon to the Secretary of State, CIA Message Critic 8, November 11, 1960, CDF 751K.00/11-1160.

33. Durbrow to Department of State, Telegram 1015, November 11, 1960, CDF 751K.00/11-1160.

34. Critic CIA Saigon Number 1645, Folder 350 "Internal Political Affairs: Vietnam–November Coup d'etat," Box 5, Entry 3340B-Vietnam, Saigon Embassy, General Records, 1956–1963, RG 84, NARA. Colby offers two accounts of the November 11–12 events in *Lost Victory*, 76–79 and *Honorable Men*, 163–165.

35. "Chronology of November 11–12 Events," *Vietnam Press* (Evening), November 21, 1960, H6–H8. See also Saigon to the Secretary of State, CIA Message 5, November 10, 1960, CDF 751K.00/11-1060.

36. Saigon to the Secretary of State, CIA Message 5, November 10, 1960, CDF 751K.00/11-1060.

37. "Chronology of November 11–12 Events," *Vietnam Press* (Evening), November 21, 1960, H6–H8; and, McGarr to Department of the Army CX-166, November 17, 1960, Folder 83 "VN 1960—Attempted Coup d'Etat" Box 1 Entry 5155, General Records of the Department of State, Bureau of East Asian Affairs, Vietnam Desk, Vietnam Subject Files, 1955–1962. See also Critic CIA Saigon Number 1645, Folder 350 "Internal Political Affairs: Vietnam—November Coup d'etat," Box 5, Entry 3340B-Vietnam, Saigon Embassy, General Records, 1956–1963, RG 84, NARA.

38. Toland to the Chief of Staff, United States Air Force Lieutenant General Isaac White, Telegram C-115, November 11, 1960. *FRUS, 1958–1960: Volume I: Vietnam*, 638–639. The Australian military attaché reported that the attackers had penetrated the Palace walls while the British military attaché maintained that no loyal forces had responded to Ngô Đình Diệm's plea. Saigon to the Secretary of State, CIA Message 6, November 10, 1960, CDF 751K.00/11-1060.

39. Critic CIA Saigon Number 1645, Folder 350 "Internal Political Affairs: Vietnam—November Coup d'etat," Box 5, Entry 3340B-Vietnam, Saigon Embassy, General Records, 1956–1963, RG 84, NARA; Durbrow to the Department of State, Telegram 1009, November 11, 1960, CDF 751K.00/11-1160; and,.

40. Ngô Đình Diệm had been broadcasting an appeal every three minutes on the radio for troops loyal to the government to come to his aid. See Meloy to Department of State, November 12, 1960, Folder 350 "Internal Political Affairs: Vietnam—November Coup d'etat," Box 5, Entry 3340B-Vietnam, Saigon Embassy, General Records, 1956–1963, RG 84, NARA. Details of the events around 10:30 a.m. are located in OUSARMA, Saigon to the Department of State, CX-155, November 10, 1960, CDF 751K.00/11-1060. See also USARMA Saigon to CINCPAC, CX-155 and CX-156, November 11, 1960, Folder 84 "VN 1960—Attempted Coup d'Etat," Box 1, Entry 5155 General Records of the Department of State, Bureau of East Asian Affairs, Vietnam Desk, Vietnam Subject Files, 1955–1962; and, Durbrow to Department of State, Telegram 1006, November 11, 1960, Folder 350 "Internal Political Affairs: Vietnam—November Coup d'etat," Box 5, Entry 3340B-Vietnam, Saigon Embassy, General Records, 1956–1963, RG 84, NARA. The Telegram is also located in CDF 751K.00/11-1160. See also McGarr to the Department of State, MAAG-CH 1426, November 10, 1960, CDF 751K.00/00-1060.

41. "Saigon Radio Mirrors Course of Coup," FBIS, November 14, 1960, G1–G6. Durbrow to the Department of State, Telegram 1007, November 11, 1960, CDF 751K.00/11-1160. Soon afterwards, Durbrow sent a telegram in which it was revealed that Generals Lê Văn Ty and Thái Quang Hoàng were prisoners to Colonel Nguyễn Chánh Thi. Durbrow to the Department of State, Telegram 1012, 1960, CDF 751K.00/11-1160. See Kahin, *Intervention*, 123–125.

42. Durbrow to Department of State, Telegram 1035, November 12, 1960, CDF 751K.00/11-1260. See also Saigon to the Secretary of State, CIA Message 9, November 11, 1960, CDF 751K.00/11-1160; and, Saigon to the Secretary of State, CIA Message 10, November 11, 1960, CDF 751K.00/11-1160. The Revolutionary Council consisted of the coup d'état leader: General Phạm Xuân Chiểu, General Lê Văn Kim, Vương Văn Đông, and Hoàng Cơ Thụy. Colonel Nguyễn Chánh Thi was thought to be a leader though it was revealed that he was forced into action after the process had begun. Other leaders included Lieutenant Colonels Vương Văn Đông, Hoàng Cơ Thụy, Nguyễn Triệu Hồng, Phạm Văn Liệu, Nguyễn Văn Lợi, and Major Nguyễn Văn Lộc. See "Names of Officers of 'Revolutionary Committee' Revealed," *Vietnam Press* (Evening), November 17, 1960, H5; and, "Real Nature of Abortive Coup Revealed at News Conference," *Vietnam Press* (Morning), November 18, 1960, H5–H8.

43. Durbrow to Department of State, Telegram 1015, November 11, 1960, CDF 751K.00/11-1160; and, Durbrow to the Department of

State, Telegram 1012, November 11, 1960, CDF 751K.00/11-1160. See Bùi Diễm, with David Chanoff. *In the Jaws of History*, 95. Bùi Diễm argued that the abortive coup d'état called for reforms just as had the Caravelle Manifesto. Both Durbrow and McGarr agreed that they should not become involved in the politics of the coup while it was ongoing.

44. Joseph A. Mendenhall's letter to his parents reprinted as an editorial note in *FRUS, 1958-1960: Volume I: Vietnam*, 662-663. Durbrow did recall speaking to Generals Dương Văn Minh and Nguyễn Khánh as well as Nguyễn Đình Thuận.

45. Excerpt of Mendenhall Oral History with members of the Office of the Historian, December 27, 1983, *FRUS, 1958-1960: Volume I: Vietnam*, 662. Durbrow maintained throughout the crisis that Ngô Đình Diệm should try to reach a compromise with the rebels so that the Saigon Government could be united in its fight against the Communist insurgency. He also made it clear to Nguyễn Đình Thuận that there would be no United States Marines. In the meanwhile, Durbrow and Parsons settled on Vice President Nguyễn Ngọc Thơ to replace Ngô Đình Diệm should the President leave the position. See Durbrow to Department of State, Telegram 1019, November 11, CDF 751K.00/11-1160; and, Parsons to Durbrow, Telegram 774, November 11, 1960, CDF 751K.00/11-1160. See also Harris, *Vietnam's High Ground*, 50.

46. "Chronology of November 11-12 Events," *Vietnam Press* (Evening), November 21, 1960, H6-H8.; McGarr to CINCPAC, MAGER 1444, November 12, 1960, Folder 83 "VN 1960—Attempted Coup d'Etat" Box 1 Entry 5155, General Records of the Department of State, Bureau of East Asian Affairs, Vietnam Desk, Vietnam Subject Files, 1955-1962; and, McGarr to Department of the Army CX-166, November 17, 1960, Folder 83 "VN 1960—Attempted Coup d'Etat" Box 1 Entry 5155, General Records of the Department of State, Bureau of East Asian Affairs, Vietnam Desk, Vietnam Subject Files, 1955-1962. Students from the NCO academy and units stationed at the Headquarters of the Vietnamese Military Academy in Dalat, at least two battalions from War Zone D, and seven Ranger companies from Tây Ninh headed towards Saigon. Trần Thiện Khiêm also organized another four ARVN battalions, two marine battalions, one tank company, field artillery, and some Ranger units to fight the rebels. When the coup d'état was thwarted, elements from the 2nd, 5th, 8th, and 21st ARVN Divisions had answered Ngô Đình Diệm's call. The loyalty of the ARVN troops and their ability to arrive on the scene was far greater than the rebels had anticipated. See also "Cong Hoa Youth Given Recognition," *Vietnam Press*, November 17, 1960, H14.

47. Durbrow to Department of State, Telegram 1019, November 11, CDF 751K.00/11-1160; and, Durbrow to Department of State, Telegram 1035, November 12, 1960, CDF 751K.00/11-1260.

48. Durbrow to Department of State, Telegram 1019, November 11, CDF 751K.00/11-1160; and, Durbrow to the Department of State, Telegram 1022, November 11, 1960, CDF 751K.00/11-1160.

49. Durbrow to the Department of State, Telegram 1025, November 11, 1960, CDF 751K.00/11-1160.

50. McGarr to Department of the Army CX-166, November 17, 1960, Folder 83 "VN 1960—Attempted Coup d'Etat" Box 1 Entry 5155, General Records of the Department of State, Bureau of East Asian Affairs, Vietnam Desk, Vietnam Subject Files, 1955-1962; "Viet Cong fails in Attack on Government Troops at Phuoc Long," *Vietnam Press* (Morning), November 17, 1960, H3; and, "Chronology of November 11-12 Events," *Vietnam Press* (Evening), November 21, 1960, H6-H8.

51. "Chronology of November 11-12 Events," *Vietnam Press* (Evening), November 21, 1960, H6-H8; McGarr to Felt, MAGTN-PO 1432, November 12, 1960, CDF 751K.00/11-1160; and, Durbrow to Department of State, Telegram 1082, November 15, 1960, CDF 751K.00/11-1560.

52. Telephone Conversation from CIA, November 11, 1960, Folder 84 "VN 1960—Attempted Coup d'Etat," Box 1, Entry 5155 General Records of the Department of State, Bureau of East Asian Affairs, Vietnam Desk, Vietnam Subject Files, 1955-1962.

53. McGarr to CINCPAC, MAGCH-CS 13061, November 11, 1960, Folder 83 "VN 1960—Attempted Coup d'Etat" Box 1 Entry 5155, General Records of the Department of State, Bureau of East Asian Affairs, Vietnam Desk, Vietnam Subject Files, 1955-1962. See also Durbrow to the Department of State, Telegram 1031, November 11, 1960, CDF 751K.00/11-1160.

54. McGarr to CINCPAC, MAGCH-CS 13061, November 11, 1960, Folder 83 "VN 1960—Attempted Coup d'Etat" Box 1 Entry 5155, General Records of the Department of State, Bureau of East Asian Affairs, Vietnam Desk, Vietnam Subject Files, 1955-1962. See also McGarr to the Department of State, MAGTN-PO 1433, November 11, 1960, CDF 751K.00/11-1160; and, Durbrow to the Department of State, Telegram 1034, November 12, 1960, CDF 751K.00/11-1260.

55. Durbrow to Department of State, Tele-

gram 1029, November 11, 1960, Folder 83 "VN 1960—Attempted Coup d'Etat" Box 1 Entry 5155, General Records of the Department of State, Bureau of East Asian Affairs, Vietnam Desk, Vietnam Subject Files, 1955–1962; Mendenhall to Department of State, Telegram 1034, November 12, 1960, Folder 350 "Internal Political Affairs: Vietnam—November Coup d'etat," Box 5, Entry 3340B-Vietnam, Saigon Embassy, General Records, 1956–1963, RG 84, NARA; McGarr to Department of the Army CX-166, November 17, 1960, Folder 83 "VN 1960—Attempted Coup d'Etat" Box 1 Entry 5155, General Records of the Department of State, Bureau of East Asian Affairs, Vietnam Desk, Vietnam Subject Files, 1955–1962.

56. "Chronology of November 11–12 Events," *Vietnam Press* (Evening), November 21, 1960, H6–H8. See also OUSARMA, Saigon to the Secretary of State, Telegram CX-158, November 11, 1960, CDF 751K.00/11-1160.

57. McGarr to Felt, MAGTN-PO 1434, November 12, 1960, November 12, 1960, CDF 751K.00/11-1260; and, Durbrow to Department of State, Telegram 1045, November 11, 1960, Folder 350 "Internal Political Affairs: Vietnam—November Coup d'etat," Box 5, Entry 3340B-Vietnam, Saigon Embassy, General Records, 1956–1963, RG 84, NARA. Durbrow offers a summary of the day's events in Telegram 1065, November 12, 1960, CDF 751K.00/11-1260.

58. Durbrow to the Department of State, Telegram 1042, November 12, 1960, CDF 751K.00/11-1260.

59. OUSARMA to the Secretary of State, CX-161, November 12, 1960, CDF 751K.00/11-1260; and, McGarr to Department of the Army CX-166, November 17, 1960, Folder 83 "VN 1960—Attempted Coup d'Etat" Box 1 Entry 5155, General Records of the Department of State, Bureau of East Asian Affairs, Vietnam Desk, Vietnam Subject Files, 1955–1962. See also McGarr to the Department of State, Telegram MAGTN/PO 1429, November 11, 1960, CDF 751K.00/11-1160; McGarr to the Department of State, Telegram MAGCH-CH 1430, November 11, 1960, CDF 751K.00/11-1160; and, November 14, 1960 Durbrow Off-the-Record Press Conference, Folder 350 "Internal Political Affairs: Vietnam—November Coup d'etat," Box 5, Entry 3340B-Vietnam, Saigon Embassy, General Records, 1956–1963, RG 84, NARA.

60. Durbrow requested instructions from Washington on how to deal with the new government, suggesting that the United States needed to recognize it immediately in order to maintain continuity in the fight against the Viet Cong. See Joseph A. Mendenhall letter to his parents reprinted as an editorial note in *FRUS, 1958–1960: Volume I: Vietnam*, 661; "Saigon Radio Mirrors Course of Coup," FBIS, November 14, 1960, G1-G6.

61. "Saigon Radio Mirrors Course of Coup," FBIS, November 14, 1960, G1-G6; and, Jacobs, *Cold War Mandarin*, 118.

62. The demonstrators were asked to carry signs reading "Down with feudalism and dictatorship! Support the army! Support the Revolutionary Council: The entire nation unites against the communists!" See "Saigon Radio Mirrors Course of Coup," FBIS, November 14, 1960, G1-G6.

63. At least four were killed and eight wounded, though the exact under is not available. See Telegram MAGCH-CS 1435 to the Secretary of State, November 12, 1960, CDF 751K.00/11-1260; and, CX-160 to the Secretary of State, November 12, 1960, CDF 751K.00/11-1260.

64. Durbrow to Department of State, Telegram 1049, November 12, 1960, CDF 751K.00/11-1260; and, McGarr to CINCPAC, MAGCH-CS 1438, November 12, 1960, Folder 83 "VN 1960—Attempted Coup d'Etat" Box 1 Entry 5155, General Records of the Department of State, Bureau of East Asian Affairs, Vietnam Desk, Vietnam Subject Files, 1955–1962.

65. Durbrow to Department of State, Telegram 1049, November 12, 1960, November 12, 1960, CDF 751K.00/11-1260. It is perhaps fortunate that Ngô Đình Diệm was not aware of the Durbrow-Parsons exchange in which Parsons instructed Durbrow to warn Ngô Đình Diệm not to seek retribution. Parsons also instructed Durbrow to reinforce the October 14 démarche as it was clear the attempted coup d'état reaffirmed Ngô Đình Diệm's lack of support in the military and within Saigon. See Parsons to Durbrow, Telegram 782, November 12, 1960, CDF 751K.00/11-1260.

66. There is evidence that many of the rebel paratroopers had been tricked into attacking. Francis Cunningham reported that his neighbor, a Vietnamese Air Force Lieutenant, told him after the coup d'état that they had been informed that Ngô Đình Diệm was under attack by communists and believed they had been sent to rescue him. See Cunningham Memorandum of Conversation, November 13, 1960, Folder 71 "VN 1960—Political Affairs (General), Box 1, Entry 5155 General Records of the Department of State, Bureau of East Asian Affairs, Vietnam Desk, Vietnam Subject Files, 1955–1962; and, Durbrow to Department of State, Telegram 1082, November 15, 1960, CDF 751K.00/11-1560.

67. Durbrow to the Department of State, Telegram 1043, November 12, 1960, CDF 751K.00/11-1260; CX-160 to the Secretary of State,

November 12, 1960, CDF 751K.00/11-1260; and, Mendenhall to Department of State, Telegram 1043, November 12, 1960, Folder 350 "Internal Political Affairs: Vietnam—November Coup d'etat," Box 5, Entry 3340B-Vietnam, Saigon Embassy, General Records, 1956-1963, RG 84, NARA.

68. "Chronology of November 11-12 Events," *Vietnam Press* (Evening), November 21, 1960, H6-H8; and, Radio Broadcasts, November 12, 1960, Folder 350 "Internal Political Affairs: Vietnam—November Coup d'etat," Box 5, Entry 3340B-Vietnam, Saigon Embassy, General Records, 1956-1963, RG 84, NARA. See also Durbrow to the Department of State, Telegram 1050, November 12, 1960, CDF 751K.00/11-1260; Durbrow to the Department of State, Telegram 1051, November 12, 1960, CDF 751K.00/11-1260; MAGCH-CS 1436 to the Secretary of State, November 12, 1960, CDF 751K.00/11-1260; and, "Saigon Radio Mirrors Course of Coup," FBIS, November 14, 1960, G1-G6.

69. "Air Traffic Resumes at Tan Son Nhut," *Vietnam Press* (Morning), November 15, 1960, H16. See also USARMA, Saigon to the Secretary of State, CX-162, November 12, 1960, CDF 751K.00/11-1260. McGarr to CINCPAC, MAGCH-CS 1439, November 12, 1960, Folder 83 "VN 1960—Attempted Coup d'Etat" Box 1 Entry 5155, General Records of the Department of State, Bureau of East Asian Affairs, Vietnam Desk, Vietnam Subject Files, 1955-1962; Durbrow to the Department of State, Telegram 1054, November 12, 1960, CDF 751K.00/11-1260; and, Durbrow to the Department of State, Telegram 1056, November 12, 1960, CDF 751K.00/11-1260.

70. Durbrow to the Department of State, Telegram 1066, November 12, 1960, CDF 751K.00/11-1260; and, Parsons to Durbrow, Telegram 788, November 12, 1960, CDF 751K.00/11-1260. Durbrow then telephoned Nguyễn Đình Thuận with the same message. See Durbrow to the Department of State, Telegram 1067, November 12, 1960, CDF 751K.00/11-1260.

71. Albert Jenkins, Regional Planning Adviser in the Far East to Cleveland, November 14, 1960, CDF 751K.00/11-1460.

72. A list of the plane's occupants is located in William Trimble to the Department of State, Telegram 540, November 16, 1960, CDF 751K.00/11-1460.

73. McGarr to CINCPAC, MAGTN-PO 1445, November 12, 1960, Folder 83 "VN 1960—Attempted Coup d'Etat" Box 1 Entry 5155, General Records of the Department of State, Bureau of East Asian Affairs, Vietnam Desk, Vietnam Subject Files, 1955-1962. Priority cable 175 from Phnom Penh to the Department of State confirmed that the aircraft had requested an emergency landing in Phnom Penh, Folder 350 "Internal Political Affairs: Vietnam—November Coup d'etat," Box 5, Entry 3340B-Vietnam, Saigon Embassy, General Records, 1956-1963, RG 84, NARA. See also "Coup Leaders arrested in Phnom Penh," *Vietnam Press* (Morning), November 14, H7; and, "Negotiations Under Way with Cambodia for Extradition of Treacherous Officers," *Vietnam Press* (Morning), November 18, 1960, H2.

74. "Major Ngo Xuan Soan Killed by Rebels For Opposition to Coup," *Vietnam Press* (Evening), November 17, 1960, H2. See also Trimble to the Department of State, Telegram 530, November 13, 1960, CDF 751K.00/11-1360; and, Trimble to the Department of State, Telegram 531, November 14, 1960, CDF 751K.00/11-1460. General Thái Quang Hoàng was eventually released on November 15, 1960. See Trimble to the Department of State, Telegram 535, November 15, 1960, CDF 751K.00/11-1560; and, Trimble to the Department of State, Telegram 537, November 16, 1960, CDF 751K.00/11-1660.

75. Durbrow to the Department of State, Telegram 1075, November 14, 1960, CDF 751K.00/11-1460. Only these four were arrested, though historians have made claims or implied that all were arrested because of their activities associated with the Caravelle Manifesto. See Herring, *America's Longest War*, 84.

76. MAAG (Richard P. Scott) to CINCPAC, MAGCH-SO 13066, November 12, 1960, Folder 350 "Internal Political Affairs: Vietnam—November Coup d'etat," Box 5, Entry 3340B-Vietnam, Saigon Embassy, General Records, 1956-1963, RG 84, NARA; MAGCH-CS 1441 to the Secretary of State, November 12, 1960, CDF 751K.00/11-1260; Durbrow to the Department of State, Telegram 1063, November 12, 1960, CDF 751K.00/11-1260; and, Durbrow to Department of State, Telegram 1088, November 16, 1960, CDF 751K.00/11-1660 CS.

77. Durbrow to the Department of State, Telegram 1064, November 12, 1960, CDF 751K.00/11-1260. See also "Saigon Radio Mirrors Course of Coup," FBIS, November 14, 1960, G1-G6.

78. Durbrow to Department of State, Telegram 1082, November 15, 1960, CDF 751K.00/11-1560.

79. See also the November 16 *Voice of the Republic of Vietnam* broadcast, "Paratroopers Blameless in Coup Attempt," FBIS, November 17, 1960, G1-G2; and, "Rebels Were Instigated by Colonialists," *Times of Vietnam*, November 15, 1960, FBIS, November 17, 1960, G2. The suggestion that the paratroopers, who had been considered the most loyal force to Ngô Đình Diệm, had nearly driven him from office was an indication of how poorly Ngô Đình Diệm

fared is a common one in Vietnam War historiography. While this is technically true, the missing part of the story is that the paratroopers remained loyal to Ngô Đình Diệm and were guided into their attack because of that loyalty. That is, they were told that they were going to rescue Ngô Đình Diệm from an attempted coup d'état rather than initiating one. Once word of this duplicity reached the troops, there was a general inclination to switch sides to those who were fighting for Ngô Đình Diệm and the Republic of Vietnam, See Jacobs, *Cold War Mandarin*, 119; and, Herring, *America's Longest War*, 83.

80. Ngô Đình Diệm called Vương Văn Đông a troublemaker and Nguyễn Chánh Thi unbalanced. He blamed their condition on poor marriages, as each wife was under French influence. See Durbrow to Department of State, Telegram 1082, November 15, 1960, CDF 751K.00/11-1560.

81. McGarr to CINCPAC, MAGTN-PO 1451, November 13, 1960, and MAGCH-CS 13075, November 13, 1960. Both documents located in Folder 83 "VN 1960—Attempted Coup d'Etat" Box 1 Entry 5155, General Records of the Department of State, Bureau of East Asian Affairs, Vietnam Desk, Vietnam Subject Files, 1955–1962. See also Durbrow to the Department of State, Telegram 1076, November 14, 1960, CDF 751K.00/11-1460. Several major organizations were represented in the march such as National Revolutionary Movement Civil Service League, the Christian Labor Confederation, National Revolutionary Movement, Students' Federation, Workers' Union Confederation, Catholic and Buddhist associations, Socialist Party, Labour Union, Society for the Study of Confucius, and the Anti-Communist Peoples' League. Elements of the 5th, 7th, and 21st ARVN Divisions, Marines, and the Psychological Warfare Battalion were also in the group. See "People Fete Failure of Coup d'Etat," *Vietnam Press* (Single), November 14, H1.

82. Lansdale to Douglas, Vietnam" November 15, 1960. *FRUS, 1958–1960: Volume I: Vietnam*, 667–668. Douglas passed along Lansdale's thoughts to Secretary of Defense Thomas Gates.

83. French to Lansdale, Telegram SGN 239, November 17, 1960. *FRUS, 1958–1960: Volume I: Vietnam*, 669–670. French had a good working relationship with many important Vietnamese.

84. "People's Committee Against Rebels and Communists Set Up," *Vietnam Press* (Evening), November 14, 1960, H4. The People's Counter-Coup d'État Committee was organized by professional organizations and political, military, and religious leaders in Saigon. The group was led by the Dean of Faculty of Pedagogy at the University of Saigon and First Vice President of the National Assembly, Trương Công Cửu. Other members of the central executive committee included vice chairmen Colonel Nguyễn Văn Y and Ngô Trọng Hiếu, secretary general Lieutenant Colonel Nguyễn Văn Châu and several members, including Brigadier Generals Lê Văn Nghiệm, Tôn Thất Đính. During the fighting, the group passed out pamphlets asking for an end to the fighting and a return of those rebels fighting to the side of the government and performed other acts of loyalty during the crisis. See "Counter-Coup D'Etat Committee Chairman Meets the Press," *Vietnam Press* (Morning), November 15, 1960, H5; "Saigon Radio Mirrors Course of Coup," FBIS, November 14, 1960, G1–G6; "Antirebel Committee Issues Communique," *Sài Gòn Mới*, November 15, 1960, November 16, 1960, G1–G2; Durbrow to the Department of State, Airgram G-219, November 21, 1960, CDF 751K.00(W)/11-2160; Durbrow to the Department of State, Telegram 1054, November 12, 1960, Folder 350 "Internal Political Affairs: Vietnam—November Coup d'etat," Box 5, Entry 3340B-Vietnam, Saigon Embassy, General Records, 1956–1963, RG 84, NARA; and, "Flags Out to Fete Crushing of Rebels," *Vietnam Press* (Single), November 13, H10. For additional details of the new committee see "People's Counter Coup D'Etat Committee's Officers Named," *Vietnam Press*, November 15, 1960, H2–H3. See also Durbrow to the Department of State, Telegram 1090, November 16, 1960, CDF 751K.00/11-1660; and, Durbrow to the Department of State, Telegram 1091, November 16, 1960, CDF 751K.00/11-1660. See also Dommen, *The Indochinese Experience of the French and Americans*, 412.

85. The committee was renamed the People's Committee Against Rebels and Communists. See also Memorandum of Conversation between Joseph Mendenhall and Trần Văn Lắm, November 16, 1960, Folder 90 "VN 1960—Government (General), Box 1, Entry 5155, General Records of the Department of State, Bureau of East Asian Affairs, Vietnam Desk, Subject Files, 1955–1962. Mendenhall to the Department of State, Despatch 210, "People's Committee Against Rebels and Communists" November 28, 1960, CDF 751K.001/11-2660 contains a detailed study of the group.

86. Durbrow to Department of State, Telegram 1096, CDF 751K.00/11-1760.

87. During the coup d'état, Vương Văn Đông asked McGarr to join him when he went to the Presidential Palace to negotiate with Ngô Đình Diệm. His motive was to use McGarr to ensure safe passage. See Press Conference transcript, November 14, 1960, 6–8, Folder

350 "Internal Political Affairs: Vietnam—November Coup d'etat," Box 5, Entry 3340B-Vietnam, Saigon Embassy, General Records, 1956–1963, RG 84, NARA. See also Durbrow to Department of State, Telegram 1015, November 11, 1960, CDF 751K.00/11-1160; Durbrow to Department of State, Telegram 1019, November 11, CDF 751K.00/11-1160; and, Durbrow to Department of State, Telegram 1025, November 11, CDF 751K.00/11-1160. Ngô Đình Nhu also later found out that a CIA operative had met with rebels and forced Colby to have him removed from Vietnam. When Colby complied, doing so because the operative's family began receiving threats, Ngô Đình Nhu most likely saw the action as an admission of guilt. See Colby, William and Peter Forbath, *Honorable Men: My Life in the CIA*, 164–165; Ahern, *House of Ngo*, 142–143.

88. "Drastic Measures Against Rebels Demanded," *Vietnam Press*, November 15, 1960, H4.

89. "Two Saigon Dailies Under Seals," *Vietnam Press*, November 15, 1960, H3. See also "Offices of Several Newspapers Sealed," *Tự do*, November 13, 1960, FBIS, November 15, 1960, G2. A November 15 broadcast on *Voice of the Republic of Vietnam* by members of The Committee for Struggle against the Rebels and Communists also signaled out these papers and *Đại chúng* as ones that distorted the truth and "heightened the role of the traitorous acts of the rebels." "Four Saigon Newspapers Are Suspended," *Voice of the Republic of Vietnam*, November 15, FBIS, November 16, 1960, G3.

90. Durbrow to Department of State, Telegram 1088, November 16, 1960, CDF 751K.00/11-1660; and, Durbrow to Department of State, Telegram 1081, November 14, 1960, CDF 751K.00/11-1460. A 34-page transcript of the November 14, 1960 exchange is available at Folder 350 "Internal Political Affairs: Vietnam—November Coup d'etat," Box 5, Entry 3340B-Vietnam, Saigon Embassy, General Records, 1956–1963, RG 84, NARA.

91. Press Conference transcript, November 14, 1960, Folder 350 "Internal Political Affairs: Vietnam—November Coup d'etat," Box 5, Entry 3340B-Vietnam, Saigon Embassy, General Records, 1956–1963, RG 84, NARA. See also Durbrow to the Department of State, Telegram 1081, November 14, 1960, CDF 751K.00/11-1460; and, Durbrow to the Department of State, Telegram 1088, November 16, 1960, CDF 751K.00/11-1660.

92. Press Conference transcript, November 14, 1960, Folder 350 "Internal Political Affairs: Vietnam–November Coup d'etat," Box 5, Entry 3340B-Vietnam, Saigon Embassy, General Records, 1956–1963, RG 84, NARA.

93. Durbrow to the Department of State, Telegram 1089, November 16, 1960, CDF 751K.00/11-1660.

94. Durbrow to the Department of State, Telegram 1091, November 16, 1960, CDF 751K.00/11-1660.

95. Mendenhall to the Department of State, Despatch 208, "Conversation between Chief MAAG and Assistant Secretary of State for National Defense," November 26, 1960, CDF 751K.5/11-2660. A memorandum of conversation between McGarr and Nguyễn Đình Thuận is attached as enclosure 1.

96. Nguyễn Đình Thuận Press Conference at the Điện Hồng Palace, November 17, 1960, 3–12, Folder 98 "VN 1960—Internal Security", Box 1, Entry 5155, General Records of the Department of State, Bureau of East Asian Affairs, Vietnam Desk, Subject Files, 1955–1962. See also "No Foreign Government Involved in Nov. 11 Coup, Presidency Secretary Says," *Vietnam Press* (Morning), November 18, 1960, H1; and, Durbrow to the Department of State, Telegram 1104, November 18, 1960, CDF 751K.00/11-1860.

97. The text of the leaflet is reported in Durbrow to the Department of State, Telegram 1093, November 17, 1960, CDF 751K.00/11-1760; and, Durbrow to the Department of State, Telegram 1096, November 17, 1960, CDF 751K.00/11-1760. See also Nguyễn Đình Thuận Press Conference at the Điện Hồng Palace, 3, November 17, 1960, Folder 98 "VN 1960—Internal Security," Box 1, Entry 5155, General Records of the Department of State, Bureau of East Asian Affairs, Vietnam Desk, Subject Files, 1955–1962.

98. McGarr to Durbrow "Record of Conversation with President Diem," November 17, 1960, *FRUS, 1958–1960: Volume I: Vietnam*, 677–678.

99. Mendenhall offered a handwritten comment on the memorandum of conversation submitted by McGarr of the conversation with Ngô Đình Diệm. He wrote "There is no question that more and more VN'ese are against entourage, arbitrary gov't, lack of coordinated effort against V.C, lack of some press freedom, corruption and arbitrary action by GVN functionaries. Does Diem have any dope to refute this?" Footnote 2 in McGarr to Durbrow "Record of Conversation with President Diem," November 17, 1960, *FRUS, 1958–1960: Volume I: Vietnam*, 677. Mendendall would continue to report conversations of corruption by the Ngo family that he had with Vietnamese, see Folder 92 "VN 1960—Presidency," Box 2, Entry 5155, General Records of the Department of State, Bureau of East Asian Affairs, Vietnam Desk, Subject Files, 1955–1962.

100. Memorandum of Conversation, "Viet-

namese Pamphlet Alleging Americans Involved in Coup Attempt," November 18, 1960, CDF 751K.00/11-1860. Trương Công Cừu, announced on November 29 that the Committee would receive no more contributions from the public starting on December 1. It ceased to be a factor in Saigon politics after that time. See Mendenhall to the Department of State, Despatch 220, "December 1, 1960, WEEKA 49, for State, Army, Navy, and Air Departments from SANA," December 2, 1960, CDF 751K.00(W)/12-260.

101. Memorandum of Conversation, "Vietnamese Pamphlet Alleging Americans Involved in Coup Attempt," November 18, 1960, CDF 751K.00/11-1860.

102. State Department to Durbrow, Telegram 1103, November 18, 1960, CDF 751K.11-1860.

103. Durbrow met with Parkes, Lalouette, Forsyth, Republic of Korean ambassador General Choi Duk Shin, and the chairman of the International Supervisory and Control Commission Gopala Menon of India. All agreed that Ngô Đình Diệm needed to be restrained from a violent response to the attempted coup d'état, that the influence of Ngô Đình Nhu and Madame Nhu must diminish, and that reforms were necessary. See Durbrow to the Department of State, Telegram 1105, November 18, 1960, CDF 751K.00/11-1860.

104. Durbrow to the Department of State, Telegram 1114, November 21, 1960, CDF 751K.00/11-2160; and, Durbrow to the Department of State, Telegram 1115, November 21, 1960, CDF 751K.00/11-2160. Durbrow wanted instructions to speak with Ngô Đình Diệm based on the following points: The United States would consider the 20,000-man increase in the military, but not until Ngô Đình Nhu's role was changed. See Durbrow to the Department of State, Telegram 1105, November 18, 1960. *FRUS, 1958–1960: Volume I: Vietnam*, 685. Durbrow was overruled and instead instructed to meet with Ngô Đình Diệm and encourage him to announce the already agreed to reforms as a first step. The Department of State instructions are located in Telegram 806 to Saigon as noted in Footnote #10, *FRUS, 1958–1960: Volume I: Vietnam*, 685. These actions included the establishment of a National Economic Council, greater freedom of the press, and a reorganization of the Cabinet. The United States also wanted the Civil Guard under the Ministry of Defense so that it could be better trained and equipped. See Durbrow to the Department of State, Telegram 1119, November 23, 1960, CDF 751K.00/11-2260.

105. Memorandum on the substance of discussion at a Department of State-JCS meeting in the Pentagon, Washington, "Ambassador Durbrow's Philosophy Vis-à-vis Attempted Coup in Vietnam (JCS Initiative)," November 18, 1960. *FRUS, 1958–1960: Volume I: Vietnam*, 681–682. See also "Call for Surrender of Traitors," *Voice of the Republic of Vietnam*, November 15, 1960, FBIS, November 16, 1960, G2, which helped Durbrow justify his concerns about a bloodbath occurring.

106. Durbrow to the Department of State, Telegram 1130, November 27, 1960, CDF 751K.5811/11-2760 HBS.

107. Durbrow to the Department of State, Telegram 1130, November 27, 1960, CDF 751K.5811/11-2760 HBS.

108. Durbrow maintained the conditions were justified because he believed Lansdale had already become involved in the process. He argued that Lansdale had sent Jerome French, a member of the Office of the Assistant to the Secretary of Defense for Special Operations, to Saigon to gather information. French, according to Durbrow, had unscheduled meetings with Vietnamese and failed to report these interactions to the Embassy. French was not made aware of this "controversy" until the author had an opportunity to speak with him at the 2008 Texas Tech University Vietnam War conference. He was surprised that his visit had caused such a problem as it was informal in nature and he made visits for personal rather than official reasons. See Lansdale to Parsons, November 29, 1960. *FRUS, 1958–1960: Volume I: Vietnam*, 692–693. For French's version of the episode, see the Memorandum from French to the Secretary of Defense's Assistant for Special Operations, General Graves B. Erskine, 'Report Trip to Asia, 28 October 1960 to 26 November 1960," December 6, 1960. *FRUS, 1958–1960: Volume I: Vietnam*, 713–717. Lansdale also found Durbrow's position strange, as French's trip had been previously planned, though it was interrupted by the coup d'état. French's presence in Saigon after the November 11–12 event was more a coincidence of timing rather than a calculated plan to bypass Durbrow. See French to the Secretary of Defense's Assistant for Special Operations, General Graves B. Erskine, "Report Trip to Asia, 28 October 1960 to 26 November 1960," December 6, 1960. *FRUS, 1958–1960: Volume I: Vietnam*, 713–717.

109. Durbrow to the Department of State, Telegram 1129, November 26, 1960. *FRUS, 1958–1960: Volume I: Vietnam*, 688–691. Durbrow believed Ngô Đình Diệm refused to meet with him on November 22 as a consequence of Durbrow's actions during the attempted coup d'état. Ngô Đình Diệm had actually been sick.

110. "Defence Department to Train Civil Guard," *Vietnam Press* (Morning), November 23, 1960, H3.

111. Memorandum for File, Interview with the President of the Republic of Vietnam G.P. Case and S.M. Strasburger, December 30, 1960, Folder 91 "VN 1960—Chief of Executive Ngo Dinh Diem" Box 1, Entry 5155, General Records of the Department of State, Bureau of East Asian Affairs, Vietnam Desk, Subject Files, 1955–1962. Statements by international leaders include Australian Minister for External Affairs, Sir Robert G. Menzies remarks to the Australian House of Representatives, December 6, 1960, Folder 30 "VN 1960 GVN Australian Relations," Box 1, Entry 5155, General Records of the Department of State, Bureau of East Asian Affairs, Vietnam Desk, Subject Files, 1955–1962; and, "Australian Premier Urges More Western Understanding and Support for Viet Nam," *Vietnam Press* (Evening), December 8, 1960, H1.

112. Outline Plan prepared by the Military Assistance Advisory Group, Vietnam, "U.S. Plan for Counterinsurgency in South Vietnam," October 27, 1960. *FRUS, 1958–1960: Volume I: Vietnam*, 613–620. Durbrow had called for the study while Williams was still in Vietnam. Speculatively, its purpose was to keep Williams busy so that he could not interfere with Durbrow's plans.

113. Durbrow to Parson, November 8, 1960. *FRUS, 1958–1960: Volume I: Vietnam*, 626–631.

114. This would involve MAAG training all 54,000 Civil Guard instead of its current load of 32,000. Durbrow asserted that this would take less time than training an additional 20,000 troops.

115. McGarr to Felt, November 21, 1960, with MAAG Comments on Recommended 20,000 Increase in the Vietnamese Armed Forces Level, Folder 16 "VN 1960—Embassy Saigon, Official-Informal Miscellaneous Letters," Box 1, Entry 5155, General Records of the Department of State, Bureau of East Asian Affairs, Vietnam Desk, Subject Files, 1955–1962.

116. McGarr to Felt, November 21, 1960. Box 1, Entry 5155, General Records of the Department of State, Bureau of East Asian Affairs, Vietnam Desk, Subject Files, 1955–1962. The Joint Chiefs of Staff concurred with the MAAG study. Vice Chief of Staff for the United States Air Force General Curtis E. LeMay suggested that the Department of the Army provide eleven H-34 helicopters with ground support equipment and spare parts. See Durbrow to Parsons, November 30, 1960. *FRUS, 1958–1960: Volume I: Vietnam*, 694–703. See also Eisenhower's approval of the request. See Special Staff Note prepared by the Department of Defense on December 1, 1960 as noted in Footnote #2, *FRUS, 1958–1960: Volume I: Vietnam*, 705.

117. Durbrow to Parsons, November 30, 1960, Folder 16 "VN 1960—Embassy Saigon, Official-Informal Miscellaneous Letters," Box 1, Entry 5155, General Records of the Department of State, Bureau of East Asian Affairs, Vietnam Desk, Subject Files, 1955–1962.

118. When Ngô Đình Diệm issued a Presidential Decree on November 22 that suspended the discharge of reserve officers and Non-Commissioned Officers (NCO) and recalled recently discharged men, Durbrow argued that it was a ploy to get support for the increase. See Durbrow to the Department of State, Telegram 1156, December 7, 1960, CDF 751K.00/12-760. The actual decree is located in Airgram G-245, December 8, 1960, CDF 751K.00/12-860. Durbrow did not consider that the need was a result of the increased Việt Cộng activity at the end of the year.

119. Durbrow to the Department of State 1143, December 1, 1960, CDF 751K.00/12-160.

120. Durbrow to the Department of State, Telegram 1204, December 22, 1960, CDF 751K.00/12-2260. See also Mendenhall to the Department of State, Despatch 249, "Suspension of Conscription," December 16, 1960, CDF 751K.5511/12-1660 HBS.

Chapter 16

1. Durbrow to the Department of State, Telegram 1150, December 4, 1960, CDF 751K.00/12-460. See also Karnow, *Vietnam: A History*, 235; and, Anderson, *Trapped by Success*, 195.

2. Mendenhall to the Department of State, Despatch 244, "Whereabouts of Dr. Phan Quang Dan, and Phan Huy Quat," December 15, 1960, CDF 751K.00/12-1560. A memorandum of conversation between Mendenhall and Andre Lane, President of Brownell, Lane International, Ltd. is attached. Joseph Buttinger, *Vietnam: A Dragon Embattled* (New York: Praeger, 1967).

3. A December 15 English broadcast from Phnom Penh maintained that he had been arrested and offered the rumor that he had been convicted in a secret trial. "Doctor Dan Reported Arrested, Tried," FBIS, December 16, 1960, G2.

4. Huỳnh Sanh Thông to Secretary of State Christian Herter, December 27, 1960, CDF 751K.00/12-2760; and, Durbrow to the Department of State, Telegram 1151, December 4, 1960, CDF 751K.00/12-460. Mendenhall specifically responded to a Bangkok report, which quoted a conversation between the Charge d'Affaires of the Vietnamese Embassy, Đặng Độc Khối and United Nations Economic Commission for Asia and the Far East representa-

tive Ben Dixon, in which Đảng Độc Khối asserted that the Vietnamese situation had improved after November 11. See Dixon to the Department of State, Despatch 343, "Conversation with Dang-Doc-Khoi concerning the Past Coup Government of President Diem of Vietnam," November 8, 1960, CDF 751K.00/12-860. A memorandum of conversation is attached. Wolf Ladejinsky also argued that Đảng Độc Khối suffered from a too positive attitude. See United States ambassador to Thailand, U. Alexis Johnson, to the Department of State, Airgram G-208, December 13, 1960, CDF 751K.00/12-1360.

5. Mendenhall to the Department of State, Despatch 259, "Conversation with Nguyen Dinh Quat," December 22, 1960, CDF 751K.00/12-2260. A memorandum of conversation between Mendenhall and Nguyễn Đình Quát is attached. Mendenhall to the Department of State, Despatch 261, "Political Views of Nguyen Phuong Thiep, Member of the National Assembly," December 23, 1960, CDF 751K.00/12-2360. Three memoranda of conversation between Mendenhall and Nguyễn Phương Thiệp dated December 5, December 12, and December 20 are attached. See also Durbrow to the Department of State, Despatch 269, "Conversation with Chinese Ambassador Concerning Situation in Viet-Nam," December 28, 1960, CDF 751K.00/12-2860. A memorandum of conversation between Durbrow and Yuen Tse Kien is attached.

6. Herter to Durbrow, Telegram 862, December 9, 1960. *FRUS, 1958–1960: Volume I: Vietnam*, 720–721.

7. Daniel V. Anderson to Parson, "Memorandum on Talk with Mr. Merchant on Vietnamese Force Level," December 6, 1960, Folder 108 "VN 1960–National Defense Affairs (General)," Box 2, Entry 5155, General Records of the Department of State, Bureau of East Asian Affairs, Vietnam Desk, Subject Files, 1955–1962.

8. Durbrow to the Department of State, Airgram G-257, December 17, 1960, CDF 751K.5-MSP/12-1760.

9. Wood to Anderson, "Diem's Resentment," December 2, 1960, Folder 91 "VN 1960—Chief of Executive Ngo Dinh Diem," Box 2, Entry 5155, General Records of the Department of State, Bureau of East Asian Affairs, Vietnam Desk, Vietnam Subject Files, 1955–1962.

10. Durbrow to the Department of State, Telegram 1175, December 15, 1960, CDF 751K.00/12-1560. See also Durbrow to the Department of State, Telegram 1176, December 15, 1960, CDF 751K.00/12-1560.

11. Acting Secretary of State Steeves to Durbrow, Telegram 898, December 16, 1960, CDF 751K.00/12-1560. This included actions such as the new National Economic Council, Village Council elections, greater freedom for the press, a reconciliation with the foreign correspondents, and more responsibility for the National Assembly.

12. Acting Secretary of State Steeves to Durbrow, December 20, 1960. *FRUS, 1958–1960: Volume I: Vietnam*, 737–738.

13. Durbrow to the Department of State, Telegram 1216, December 24, 1960, CDF 751K.00/12-2360; and, Durbrow to the Department of State, Despatch 264, "Memorandum Handed to President Diem on Liberalization," December 27, 1960, CDF 751K.00/12-2760. The memorandum is attached.

14. Acting Secretary of State Steeves letter to Durbrow, December 20, 1960. *FRUS, 1958–1960: Volume I: Vietnam*, 737–738.

15. On December 19, the Department of State requested all Far East ambassadors or principle to submit a review of the country for which they represented and offer recommendations on how these actions would follow current United States diplomacy. Durbrow to the Department of State, Telegram 1217, December 24, 1960, CDF 751K.00/12-2460.

16. Parsons to Durbrow, Telegram 961, December 29, 1960, CDF 751K.00/12-2960.

17. Central Intelligence Agency Information Report, "Alternate Political Leadership for Vietnam," December 9, 1960. *FRUS, 1958–1960: Volume I: Vietnam*, 721–728.

18. Possible military leadership included Generals Lê Văn Ty, Dương Văn Minh, Nguyễn Khánh, Trần Văn Đôn, Thái Quang Hoàng, and Tôn Thất Đính were mentioned though all but Dương Văn Minh was dismissed because of loyalty to Ngô Đình Diệm or an inability to rally other military leaders to their side. Among cabinet members, Nguyễn Ngọc Thơ had a Constitutional claim though it was thought his ascendancy would serve as a catalyst for an internal struggle with Ngô Đình Nhu. The best Nguyễn Ngọc Thơ could offer to Vietnam was that of a figurehead. Opposition leaders Phan Quang Đán and Phan Khắc Sửu were also mentioned though neither fared well during and after the attempted coup d'état. See Memorandum of Conversation between Pauline Thọ, Nguyễn Vạn Thọ, and Joseph Mendenhall, "Phan Khac Suu and Activities of National Assembly," December 2, 3, and 6, 1960, Folder 94 "VN 1960—Legislative Branch–National Assembly," Box 2, Entry 5155, General Records of the Department of State, Bureau of East Asian Affairs, Vietnam Desk, Subject Files, 1955–1962. Various political groups, such as the Cần Lao Party, the Hòa Hảo, Cao Đài,

and Bình Xuyên were also dismissed as either too loyal to Ngô Đình Diệm or too disorganized to act.

19. On December 20, groups opposed to Ngô Đình Diệm met in Tây Ninh province and formed the National Liberation Front of South Vietnam (NLF). Inspired by the Third National Congress, which met in Hanoi in September 1960, the NLF offered a ten-point program designed to rally the Vietnamese people against Ngô Đình Diệm and the Americans. The NLF was recognized in a Hanoi Broadcast on January 26, 1961. Gerald DeGroot, *A Noble Cause: America and the Vietnam War*, 69–70; Duiker, *Sacred War*, 128–134; Cooper, *Lost Crusade*, 158; Colby, *Lost Victory*, 81; and, Race, *War Comes to Long An*, 121–122. There was also evidence that the Soviet Union was present in Laos and had been delivering materials using IL-14 transport along the North Vietnamese-Laotian border. See Durbrow to the Department of State, Telegram 1231, December 29, 1960. *FRUS, 1958–1960: Volume I: Vietnam*, 749–750; and, "Republic of Viet Nam Protests Against Violations of Geneva Agreements by Viet Cong," *Vietnam Press* (Evening), December 19, 1960, H3–H4.

20. Durbrow's 60th birthday message sent on January 3 recalled their successes when faced with challenging obstacles. On January 4, he participated in the ceremony honoring Ngô Đình Diệm with a Paul Revere silver bowl from the people of Boston for his fight against the Communist. See Durbrow to the Department of State, January 3, 1961, Folder 361.1 "Executive. Royal Family Vietnam: Ngo Dinh Diem, 1951–1961," Box 6, Entry 3340B, RG 84, NARA; and, Presentation of Paul Revere Bowl to President Ngô Đình Diệm, Folder 361.1 "Executive. Royal Family Vietnam: Ngo Dinh Diem, 1951–1961," Box 6, Entry 3340B, RG 84, NARA; and, "President Receives Gift from Boston," *Vietnam Press* (Evening), January 4, 1961, H1–H2.

21. Anderson to Parsons, "General Lansdale's Call at 3 p.m. Today," December 19, 1960, Folder 20 "GVN 1961–General Lansdale," Box 3, Entry 5155, General Records of the Department of State, Bureau of East Asian Affairs, Vietnam Desk, Subject Files, 1955–1962.

22. Felt to the Office of the Secretary of Defense, Telegram 102203Z, December 10, 1960. *FRUS, 1958–1960: Volume I: Vietnam*, 729.

23. Lansdale to Douglas, "Trip to Asia," December 14, 1960. *FRUS, 1958–1960: Volume I: Vietnam*, 730. See also Footnote #3 in the same document that refers to message Def 987217 to CINCPAC dated December 14, 1960 that contains Douglas' reply to Felt.

24. Lansdale to Gates, January 17, 1961, Folder 20 "GVN 1961–General Lansdale," Box 3 Entry 5155, General Records of the Department of State, Bureau of East Asian Affairs, Vietnam Desk, Vietnam Subject Files, 1955–1962. See Anderson, *Trapped by Success*, 175, 195–196.

25. Lansdale to Gates, January 17, 1961, Folder 20 "GVN 1961–General Lansdale," Box 3 Entry 5155, General Records of the Department of State, Bureau of East Asian Affairs, Vietnam Desk, Vietnam Subject Files, 1955–1962. See also Jones, *Death of a Generation*, 20–22.

26. Lansdale argued that it must be a non-military man so that MAAG could do its job unhindered and that he, "must not be a 'clever' type who is out to gain a reputation as a 'manipulator' or a word-smith who is more concerned about the way his reports will look in Washington than in implementing U.S. policy in Vietnam." See Lansdale to Gates, January 17, 1961, Folder 20 "GVN 1961–General Lansdale," Box 3 Entry 5155, General Records of the Department of State, Bureau of East Asian Affairs, Vietnam Desk, Vietnam Subject Files, 1955–1962.

27. *Basic Counterinsurgency Plan for Viet Nam* prepared by the Country Team Staff Committee, January 4, 1961. *FRUS, 1961–1963: Volume I: Vietnam*, 1961, 1–12. A copy of Appendix IV to Annex C is located in CDF 751K.5-MSP/1-661. Tab A to this Appendix is located in CDF 751K.5/MSP/1-961. Tab C to this Appendix is located in CDF 751K.5/MSP/1-2561. Tab A to Appendix IV of Annex B is located in CDF 751K.5-MSP/2-1361. The agencies involved in its development were MAAG, USOM, United States Information Service (USIS), and the Embassy in Saigon.

28. Summary Record of a Meeting, The White House, January 28, 1961. *FRUS, 1961–1963: Volume I: Vietnam*, 1961, 13–15. See also Kahin, *Intervention*, 129–131; and, Karnow, *Vietnam: A History*, 248–249.

29. See Joseph Morgan, *The Vietnam Lobby: The American Friends of Vietnam, 1955–1975*, 8 and 41; and, James T. Fisher, "The Second Catholic President: Ngo Dinh Diem, John F. Kennedy, and the Vietnam Lobby, 1954–1963" *U.S. Catholic Historian* 15, No. 3, Catholics in a Non-Catholic World, Part Two (Summer 1997), 130–132.

30. At Kennedy's request, Lansdale outlined three requirements that needed to be accomplished in order to turn the tide in Vietnam. Lansdale asserted that American diplomats needed to adhere to a winning strategy that worked with, rather than above, their Vietnamese counterparts. He argued that the Vietnamese needed to act quickly to stem the advance of the Viet Cong, and the Americans must make Ngô Đình Diệm realize that the opposition in Saigon needed to have a public

voice in order to limit their private scheming. See Memorandum from the President's Deputy Special Assistant for National Security Affairs, Walt W. Rostow to the President's Special Assistant for National Security Affairs William P. Bundy, January 30, 1961, Folder "General, 1/61–3/61," Box 193, National Security Country Files, Vietnam Files, John F. Kennedy Presidential Library, Boston Massachusetts [hereafter referred to as NSF: Vietnam, JFK].

31. Notes on a Meeting between Rusk and Parsons, January 28, 1961. *FRUS, 1961–1963: Volume I: Vietnam*, 19–20. See also Jones, *Death of a Generation*, 23–38.

32. Kennedy authorized U.S. $28.4 million for the Vietnamese Armed Forces and U.S. $12.7 million for the Civil Guard. See Memorandum for Rusk and McNamara, January 30, 1961, Folder "General, 1/61–3/61," Box 193, NSF: Vietnam, JFK; and, Cooper, *Lost Crusade*, 169–170. On February 3, Rusk informed Durbrow that the *Basic Counterinsurgency Plan for Viet Nam* had been approved and requested that he present it to Ngô Đình Diệm with the recommendation to approve it. See Department of State to Durbrow, Telegram 276, February 3, 1961, Folder "General, 1/61–3/61," Box 193, NSF: Vietnam, JFK. See also Mann, *A Grand Delusion*, 227–228.

33. Lansdale to Ngô Đình Diệm, January 30, 1961. *FRUS, 1961–1963: Volume I: Vietnam*, 20–24.

34. Lansdale to CINCPAC, Telegram 172157Z as noted in Footnote #2. *FRUS, 1961–1963: Volume I: Vietnam*, 1961, 25.

35. Durbrow to the Department of State, Telegram 1329, January 31, 1961, CDF 751K.00/1-3161.

36. Durbrow to the Department of State, Telegram 1349, February 7, 1961, Folder 350 "Internal Political Affairs: Vietnam, 1959–1961," Box 5, Entry 3340B, RG 84, NARA; Parsons to Rusk, "Viet-Nam–President Ngo Dinh Diem's Reforms (For Use on Hill Today)," February 15, 1961, Box 2, Entry 5155, General Records of the Department of State, Bureau of East Asian Affairs, Vietnam Desk, Vietnam Subject Files, 1955–1962; and, Durbrow to the Department of State, Telegram 1351, February 8, 1961, CDF 751K.00/2-861. See also "Changes in Ministerial Department Envisaged," *Vietnam Press* (Morning), February 7, 1961, H8–H9.

37. Ngô Đình Diệm introduced the Department of Civic Action and the Department of Rural Affairs during the conference.

38. Durbrow to the Department of State, Telegram 1351, February 8, 1961, CDF 751K.00/2-861.

39. Memorandum of Conversation between Bowles and Trần Văn Chương, February 13, 1961, CDF 751K.00/2-1361; and, Memorandum of Conversation, "Viet-Nam–Discussion with the British," February 21, CDF 751K.00/2-2161.

40. Memorandum of Conversation, "Viet-Nam—Discussion with the British," February 21, 1961, CDF 751K.00/2-2161.

41. Durbrow to the Department of State, Telegram 1414, February 28, 1961, CDF 751K.5-MSP/2-2861 HBS. On February 22, Durbrow complained that he had not heard from the Vietnamese and called Nguyễn Đình Thuận to discuss the matter. See Durbrow to the Department of State, Telegram 1391, February 22, 1961, CDF 751K.5-MSP/2-2261 HBS.

42. Ngô Đình Diệm had also promised judicial reform and, in February, the National Assembly merged three draft bills on the subject that had been under discussion since 1958. It passed the first five articles of Bill 36/II on February 26. See "Assembly Divided on Composition of high Judiciary Council," *Vietnam Press* (Morning), February 23, 1961, H2. These articles established the High Council of the Judiciary. See "Assembly's Two Groups Discuss Draft Bill Separately," *Vietnam Press* (Morning), February 23, 1961, H3; "Assembly Passes First Five Articles of Judiciary Bill," *Vietnam Press* (Morning), February 24, 1961, H2–H3; "Barrister Vuong Quang Nhuong First Chairman of Constitutional Court," *Vietnam Press* (Morning), February 25, 1961, H3; and, "Barrister Vuong Quang Nhuong Confirmed Constitutional Court Chairman," *Vietnam Press* (Evening), March 6, 1961, H1. On February 24, the National Assembly passed the remaining fourteen articles of draft bill 36/II, which established the guidelines for electing members and operating the day-to-day functions of the court. See "Assembly Passes Judiciary High Council Law," *Vietnam Press* (Morning), February 25, 1961, H1–H2. Another promised reform, the National Economic Council, was discussed in the National Assembly starting on March 2. Ngô Đình Diệm promulgated Laws 5/61 and 6/61, on March 17 establishing the National Economic Council and the High Court of the Judiciary.

43. "New U.S. Ambassador Named," *Vietnam Press* (Morning), February 20, 1961, H1. News of Durbrow's actual departure was made public on April 7. He would become the Deputy Chief of Missions in Paris. See Durbrow to the Department of State, Telegram 1626, April 21, 1961, CDF 751K.5-MSP/4-2161.

44. Department of State to Durbrow, Telegram 1115, March 1, 1961. *FRUS, 1961–1963: Volume I: Vietnam*, 1961, 40–42.

45. The Containment Strategy originated in the immediate period following the Second World War when the United States shifted its

strategy in dealing with the Soviet Union and Communism by trying to contain it within its existing borders. The Containment Strategy served as the guiding force for American diplomacy as it evaluated to what extent it should become involved in affairs around the world. For details on other Kennedy actions during his first year in office, see Stephen Pelz, "John F. Kennedy's 1961 Vietnam War Decisions." *Journal of Strategic Studies* [Great Britain] 1981 4 (4): 356–385.

46. See Footnote #4, Department of State to Durbrow, Telegram 1115, March 1, 1961. *FRUS, 1961–1963: Volume I: Vietnam*, 1961, 42.

47. McGarr to General Williston Palmer, Director of Military Assistance in the Office of the Assistant Secretary of Defense. March 3, 1961. *FRUS, 1961–1963: Volume I: Vietnam*, 1961, 43–44.

48. Durbrow to the Department of State, Telegram 1414, March 11, 1961, Folder "General, 1/61–3/61," Box 193, NSF: Vietnam, JFK.

49. McGarr to Nguyễn Đình Thuần, March 13, 1961. *FRUS, 1961–1963: Volume I: Vietnam*, 1961, 44–46.

50. McGarr enumerated nine parts of the plan that needed to be accomplished together. These included a more effective logistical system with less duplicate technical services, as well as improved border and coastal surveillance, psychological warfare, and communication. When Nguyễn Đình Thuận and Nguyễn Khánh, now ARVN Chief of Staff, met with Mendenhall and the Country Team on March 24, he informed them that Ngô Đình Diệm had begun to implement some of the military recommendations in the *Basic Counterinsurgency Plan for Viet Nam*. See Mendenhall to the Department of State, Telegram 1523, March 27, 1961, Folder "General, 1/61–3/61," Box 193, NSF: Vietnam, JFK.

51. Durbrow to the Department of State, Telegram 1466, March 16, 1961, CDF 751K.5-MSP/3-1661.

52. Other points raised by Durbrow were improving the intelligence network and Cambodian relations, which had suffered after the C-47 transport aircraft which carried the rebel leadership to Phnom Penh became publicized. See Durbrow to the Department of State, Telegram 1447, March 11, 1961. Folder "General, 1/61–3/61," Box 193, NSF: Vietnam, JFK. There was also a March 4 incident in Tịnh Biên district, An Giang province. Vietnamese security forces clashed with a group that included between twenty to thirty armed individuals who fled with approximately 150 Vietnamese prisoners in Cambodia. The Vietnamese denied that the prisoners had voluntarily left Vietnam for Cambodia. See "Report on Exodus to Cambodia Is Groundless Authorities Say," *Vietnam Press* (Evening), March 8, 1961, H4. This incident was at the forefront through March.

53. Memorandum of Conversation, "Situation in Vietnam," March 27, 1961. *FRUS, 1961–1963: Volume I: Vietnam*, 1961, 52–57; and, Mendenhall to the Department of State, Telegram 1523, March 27, 1961, Folder "General, 1/61–3/61," Box 193, NSF: Vietnam, JFK.

54. Memorandum of Conversation, "Call of the Ambassador of Viet-Nam on Mr. Steeves," April 8, 1961, CDF 751K.00/4-0861.

55. After receiving Thomas Trapnell's report on the American helicopters in Vietnam, he advocated their more active use. See Rostow to Kennedy, "Counter-Guerrilla Programs," April 3, 1961. *FRUS, 1961–1963: Volume I: Vietnam*, 1961, 61–62.

56. "Inter-Departmental Committee Works on Presidential Election Bill," *Vietnam Press* (Evening), October 13, 1960, H1.

57. Saigon Lawyer Trương Đình Dzu told Cunningham that a National Assembly committee, half named by Ngô Đình Diệm, would make all of the campaigning decisions. Trương Đình Dzu argued that his would allow Ngô Đình Diệm to control all aspects of the process. See Mendenhall to the Department of State, Despatch 319, "Presidential Elections Law," January 27, 1961, CDF 751K.00/1-2761. A copy of the 43-article election law is attached to the Despatch. A copy of the March 25, 1961 Special Issue of the *Vietnam Press* is also available as an attachment to Mendenhall to the Department of State, Despatch 439, "Reference Material for the 1961 Presidential Election in South Viet-Nam," April 3, 1961, CDF 751K.00/4-361.

58. "President Inspects Central Provinces," *Vietnam Press* (Morning), January 18, 1961, H1; and, "President Inspects Phuoc Long Province," *Vietnam Press* (Evening), January 19, 1961, H1. See also Nguyễn Công Luận, *Nationalist in the Viet Nam Wars*, 192–193.

59. "University Teachers Request President Ngo to Run for Another Term of Office," *Vietnam Press* (Evening), February 3, 1961, H1–H2; "University Teachers Request President Ngo to Run for Another Term of Office," *Vietnam Press* (Evening), February 3, 1961, H1–H2; "People Throughout Nation Request President to Stand for Re-Election," *Vietnam Press* (Morning), February 4, 1961, H1–H2; and, "More Groups Call on President to Seek Re-Election," *Vietnam Press* (Evening), February 4, 1961, H1–H2. While it would be easy to be skeptical of the overwhelming support, Ngô Đình Diệm did have a well-organized political party and had been the only leader the Republic had known. See "People in Province Ask President to Seek Reelection," *Vietnam Press*

(Morning), February 1, 1961, H2; "People in Provinces Demand President Ngo Dinh Diem to Run for Re-election," *Vietnam Press* (Morning), January 31, 1961, H1; and, "People in Vinh Long and Binh Long Ask President Ngo Dinh Diem to Seek Re-election," *Vietnam Press* (Evening), January 31, 1961, H1–H2; "People in Province Ask President to Seek Reelection," *Vietnam Press* (Morning), February 1, 1961, H1–H2; "More Civic Groups in Provinces Call on President to Seek Re-Election," *Vietnam Press* (Morning), February 2, 1961, H2–H3; and, "More Resolutions Asking President to Seek Re-Election," *Vietnam Press* (Morning), February 3, 1961, H2–H3; "112 More Petitions Asking President to Seek Re-Election," *Vietnam Press* (Morning), February 6, 1961, H1–H3; and, "Workers Unions—Many Other's Pledge Loyalty to Chief Executive—Ask Him to Stand for Re-Election," *Vietnam Press* (Morning), February 7, 1961, H10–H13.

60. Durbrow to the Department of State, Telegram 1352, February 8, 1961, CDF 751K.00/2-861 HBS. "President Ngo Seeks Re-Election," *Vietnam Press* (Evening), February 7, 1961, H1; and, "President Ngo's Letter to the Nation," *Vietnam Press* (Morning), February 8, 1961, H1–H2.

61. Nguyễn Đình Quát was from Hà Tĩnh Province in the north central coast region of then North Vietnam. Nguyễn Thành Phương served as the Vietnamese Minister of State until May 1955 and was a former commander of the Cao Đài forces. He was known as a strong nationalist. Hồ Nhật Tân practiced oriental medicine. Nguyễn Thế Truyền was an engineer. Nguyễn Ngọc Bích and Nguyễn Văn Thỏa were expected to form a fourth Slate but they did not adhere to the election procedures and failed to file their intent by the February 7 deadline. See enclosures 4 and 5, Mendenhall to the Department of State, Despatch 429, "1961 Presidential Election Campaign Gets Under Way," March 29, 1961, CDF 751K.00/3-2961; and, "Six Candidates Slated for Elections," *Vietnam Press* (Morning), February 8, 1961, H3. Nguyễn Đình Quát had earlier sought American approval for his candidacy. See Durbrow to the Department of State, Despatch 315, "Possible Opposition Candidate in GVN Presidential Elections," January 24, 1961, CDF 751K.00/1-2461. A January 11 memorandum of conversation between Mendenhall and Nguyễn Đình Quát is attached to the Despatch. See also Mendenhall to the Department of State, Airgram G-337, February 11, 1961, CDF 751K.00/2-1161 HBS.

62. "Presidential Candidates Choose Emblems," *Vietnam Press* (Evening), February 20, 1961, H4.

63. "Election Campaign Procedures Explained," *Vietnam Press* (Morning), March 9, 1961, H1–H3. See also *Sài Gòn Mới* editorial, March 7, 1961 FBIS, G1.

64. "April 9 Presidential Election 'A Success,' Predicts University Leader," *Vietnam Press* (Morning), March 13, 1961, H4–H8. See also *Dan Viet* editorial, March 10, 1961, FBIS, March 13, 1961, G2.

65. "First Posting Indicates 6,948,466 Voters," *Vietnam Press* (Evening), March 13, 1961, H1.

66. Memorandum of Conversation, April 1, 1961, Folder 14 "C-GVN 1961 Elections," Box 2, Entry 5155, General Records of the Department of State, Bureau of East Asian Affairs, Vietnam Desk, Vietnam Subject Files, 1955–1962.

67. There was some logistical issues, such as at one polling station where there was only one door to enter and exit, which caused a bottleneck. Saigon police and Republic Youth members also assisted in the process. Two voters in Saigon were arrested for trying to vote twice for Slate I but were released later in the day. See "Saigon Begins to Vote in Calm," *Vietnam Press* (Morning), April 9, 1961, H2–H3.

68. "Saigon Begins to Vote in Calm," *Vietnam Press* (Morning), April 9, 1961, H2–H3. There were moments of inspiration as individuals declared their right to vote. Patients from the Saigon hospital went to polling stations, sometimes with help, as did disabled war victims and a group of residents who lived on Nguyễn Văn Kiến Islet who had to leave by boat to cast their ballots at the nearest polling station. See "70.7 Per Cent of Saigon Vote in at 3 P.M," *Vietnam Press* (Evening), April 9, 1961, H4.

69. "65–70 Per Cent of Registered Voters Go to the Polls in Provinces," *Vietnam Press* (Evening), April 9, 1961, H2.

70. Durbrow to Ngô Đình Diệm, April 12, 1961, This letter is included as enclosure 1 in Despatch 465, Folder 350 "Internal Political Affairs: Vietnam, 1959–1961," Box 5, Entry 3340B, RG 84, NARA. See also "National Assembly Confirms Victory of Slate I," *Vietnam Press* (Morning), April 19, 1961, H1–H3.

71. "U.S. Ambassador Honored at Dinner," *Vietnam Press* (Morning), April 20, 1961, H4; and, "U.S. Ambassador Addresses Lions' Club," *Vietnam Press* (Morning), April 26, 1961, H2–H3.

72. "'U.S. Will Do Everything It Can to Support Viet Nam,' Mr. Dean Rusk Says," *Vietnam Press* (Evening), April 22, 1961, H1.

73. "Presidential Inauguration," *Vietnam Press* (Morning), April 29, 1961, H1–H6. See also the 98-page *Vietnam Press* Inauguration Special dated April 29.

Bibliography

Abramson, Rudy. *Spanning the Century: The Life of W. Averell Harriman, 1891–1986.* New York: Morrow, 1992.
Adamson, Michael R. "Ambassadorial Roles and Foreign Policy: Elbridge Durbrow, Frederick Nolting, and the U.S. Commitment to Diem's Vietnam, 1957–61." *Presidential Studies Quarterly* 32, No. 2 (Jun., 2002), 229–255.
Allen, Luther, "Crisis in Saigon: The Sunday Morning Visitor Returns." *The Massachusetts Review* 3, No. 1 (Autumn, 1961), 170–187.
Anderson, David L. *Trapped by Success: The Eisenhower Administration and Vietnam, 1953–1961.* New York: Columbia University Press, 1991.
Appy, Christian G. *Patriots: The Vietnam War Remembered from All Sides.* New York: Viking, 2003.
Bayless, Robert M. *Vietnam: Victory Was Never an Option.* Victoria, B.C., Canada: Trafford, 2005.
Berman, Larry. *Planning a Tragedy: The Americanization of the War in Vietnam.* New York: W. W. Norton, 1982.
Blight, James G., Janet M. Lang, and David A. Welch. *Vietnam if Kennedy Had Lived: Virtual JFK.* Lanham, MD: Rowman & Littlefield, 2009.
Bouscaren, Anthony T. *Last of the Mandarins: Diem of Vietnam.* Pittsburgh, PA.: Duquesne University Press, 1965.
Bradley, Mark Philip. *Vietnam at War.* New York: Oxford University Press, 2009.
Browne, Malcolm. *The New Face of War.* Indianapolis, IN: Bobbs-Merrill, 1965.
Bui Diem, with David Chanoff. *In the Jaws of History.* Boston: Houghton Mifflin, 1987.
Buttinger, Joseph. *Vietnam: A Dragon Embattled.* New York: Praeger, 1967.
_____. *Vietnam: A Political History.* New York: Praeger, 1968.
_____. *Vietnam: The Unforgettable Tragedy.* New York: Horizon Books, 1977.
Cao Noọc Phuong. *Learning True Love: How I Learned and Practiced Social Change in Vietnam.* Berkeley, CA: Parallax Press, 1993.
Cao Van Vien. *Leadership.* McLean, VA: General Research Corporation, 1978.
Catton, Philip E. *Diem's Final Failure: Prelude to America's War in Vietnam.* Lawrence: University Press of Kansas, 2002.
Chomsky, Noam. *Rethinking Camelot: JFK, the Vietnam War, and U.S. Political Culture.* Boston: South End Press, 1993.
Colby, William, with James McCargar. *Lost Victory.* Chicago: Contemporary Books, 1989.
Dallek, Robert. *An Unfinished Life: John F. Kennedy, 1917–1963.* Boston: Little, Brown, 2003.
David Lan Pham. *Two Hamlets in Nam Bo: Memoirs of Life in Vietnam Through Japanese Occupation, the French and American Wars, and Communist Rule, 1940–1986.* Jefferson, NC: McFarland, 2000.
Davidson, Phillip B. *Vietnam at War: The History, 1946–1975.* Novato, CA: Presidio Press, 1988.

DeGroot, Gerald J. *A Noble Cause? America and the Vietnam War*. London: Longman, 1999.
Dockery, Martin J. *Lost in Translation: Vietnam: A Combat Advisor's Story*. New York: Presidio Press, 2003.
Dommen, Arthur J. *The Indochinese Experience of the French and the Americans: Nationalism and Communism in Cambodia, Laos, and Vietnam*. Bloomington: Indiana University Press, 2001.
Donnell, John C. "National Renovation Campaigns in Vietnam." *Pacific Affairs* 32, No. 1 (Mar., 1959), 73–88.
Dooley, Thomas A. *Deliver Us from Evil: The Story of Viet Nam's Flight to Freedom*. New York: Farrar, Straus and Cudahy, 1956.
———. *The Edge of Tomorrow*. New York: Farrar, Straus and Cudahy, 1958.
———. *The Night They Burned the Mountain*. New York: Farrar, Straus and Cudahy, 1958.
Duiker, William J. *Sacred War: Nationalism and Revolution in a Divided Vietnam*. New York: McGraw-Hill, 1995.
Elkind, Jessica. *Aid Under Fire: Nation Building and the Vietnam War*. Lexington: University Press of Kentucky, 2016.
Elliott, Duong Van Mai. *The Sacred Willow: Four Generations in the Life of a Vietnamese Family*. New York: Oxford University Press, 1999.
Ernst, John P. *Forging a Fateful Alliance: Michigan State University and the Vietnam War*. East Lansing: Michigan State University Press, 1998.
Fall, Bernard. *The Two Viet-Nams*. New York: Praeger, 1964.
———. *Viet-Nam Witness, 1953–1966*. New York: Praeger, 1966.
Fay, Paul B., Jr., *The Pleasure of His Company*. New York: Harper & Row, 1966.
Fisher, James T. *Dr. America: The Lives of Thomas A. Dooley, 1927–1961*. Amherst: University of Massachusetts Press, 1997.
———. "The Second Catholic President: Ngo Dinh Diem, John F. Kennedy, and the Vietnam Lobby, 1954–1963." *U.S. Catholic Historian* 15, No. 3, Catholics in a Non-Catholic World, Part Two (Summer, 1997), 119–137.
Fitzgerald, Frances. *Fire in the Lake: The Vietnamese and the Americans in Vietnam*. New York: Random House, 1972.
Fontaine, Ray. *The Dawn of Free Vietnam: A Biographical Sketch of Doctor Phan Quang Dan*. Brownsville, TX: Pan American Business Services, 1992.
Fulbright, J. William. *The Arrogance of Power*. New York: Random House, 1966.
Gardner, Lloyd C., and Ted Gittinger, eds. *Vietnam: The Early Decisions*. Austin: University of Texas Press, 1997.
Gelb, Leslie H., with Richard K. Betts. *The Irony of Vietnam: The System Worked*. Washington, D.C.: The Brookings Institution, 1979.
Givhan, John B. *Rice and Cotton: South Vietnam and South Alabama*. Philadelphia: Xlibris, 2000.
Goodman, Allan E. *Politics in War: The Bases of Political Community in South Vietnam*. Cambridge, MA: Harvard University Press, 1973.
Halberstam, David. *The Making of a Quagmire*. New York: Random House, 1965.
Hall, Mitchell K. *The Vietnam War*. New York: Longman, 2013.
Hammer, Ellen J. *A Death in November: America in Vietnam, 1963*. New York: E.P. Dutton, 1987.
Harris, John. P. *Vietnam's High Ground: Armed Struggle for the Central Highlands, 1954–1965*. Lawrence: University Press of Kansas, 2016.
Haycraft, William Russell. *Unraveling Vietnam: How American Arms and Diplomacy Failed in Southeast Asia*. Jefferson, NC: McFarland, 2006.
Hearden, Patrick J. *The Tragedy of Vietnam*. New York: HarperCollins, 2008.
Herring, George C. *America's Longest War: The United States and Vietnam, 1950–1975*. New York: McGraw-Hill, 2002.
Herrington, Stuart. *Silence Was a Weapon: The Vietnam War in the Villages*. Novato, CA: Presidio Press, 1982.

Hess, Gary R. *Vietnam and the United States: Origins and Legacy of War.* Boston: Twayne, 1990.
———. *Vietnam: Explaining America's Lost War.* Malden and Oxford: Blackwell Publishing, 2009.
Hess, Martha. *Then the Americans Came: Voices from Vietnam.* New York: Four Walls Eight Windows, 1993.
Higgins, Marguerite. *Our Vietnam Nightmare.* New York: Harper & Row, 1965.
Hilsman, Roger. *To Move a Nation.* New York: Doubleday, 1967.
Hoang Ngoc Thanh, and Than Thi Nhan Duc. *President Ngo Dinh Diem and the US: His Overthrow and Assassination.* San Jose, CA: Tuan-Yen and Quan-Viet Mai-Nam Publishers, 2001.
Hoang Van Chi. *From Colonialism to Communism: A Case History of North Vietnam.* New York: Praeger, 1964.
Honey, P. J. "The Problem of Democracy in Vietnam." *The World Today* 16, No. 2 (Feb. 1960), 71–79.
Hunt, Richard A. *Pacification: The American Struggle for Vietnam's Hearts and Minds.* Boulder, CO: Westview, 1995.
Jacobs, Seth. *America's Miracle Man in Vietnam: Ngo Dinh Diem, Religion, Race, and U.S. Intervention in Southeast Asia, 1950–1957.* Durham, NC: Duke University Press, 2004.
———. *Cold War Mandarin: Ngo Dinh Diem and the Origins of America's War in Vietnam, 1950–1963.* Lanham, MD: Rowman & Littlefield, 2006.
Jamieson, Neil L. *Understanding Vietnam.* Berkeley: University of California Press, 1993.
Joes, Anthony J. *Why South Vietnam Fell.* Lanham, MD: Lexington Books, 2016.
Joiner, Charles A., and Roy Jumper. "Organizing Bureaucrats: South Viet Nam's National Revolutionary Civil Servants' League." *Asian Survey* 3, No. 4 (Apr., 1963), 203–215.
Jones, Howard. *Death of a Generation: How the Assassinations of Diem and John F. Kennedy Prevented the Withdrawal of American Troops from Vietnam.* New York: Oxford University Press, 2003.
Kahin, George McTurnan. *Intervention: How America became Involved in Vietnam.* New York: Knopf, 1986.
Karnow, Stanley. *Vietnam: A History.* New York: Viking, 1983.
Kauffman, Christopher J. "Politics, Programs, and Protests: Catholic Relief Services in Vietnam, 1954–1975." *The Catholic Historical Review* 91, No. 2 (Apr., 2005), 223–250.
Kolko, Gabriel. *Anatomy of a War: Vietnam, the United States, and the Modern Historical Experience.* New York: Pantheon, 1985.
Krall, Yung. *A Thousand Tears Falling: The True Story of a Vietnamese Family Torn Apart by War, Communism, and the CIA.* Atlanta, GA: Longstreet, 1995.
Labin, Suzanne. *Vietnam: An Eye-Witness Account.* Springfield, VA: Crestwood, 1965.
Lacouture, Jean. *Vietnam: Between Two Truces.* New York: Vintage Books, 1966.
Langguth, A.J. *Our Vietnam: The War, 1954–1975.* New York: Simon & Schuster, 2000.
Latham, Michael E. "Redirecting the Revolution? The USA and the Failure of Nation-Building in South Vietnam." *Third World Quarterly* 27, No. 1, From Nation-Building to State-Building (2006), 27–41.
Levine, Alan J. *The United States and the Struggle for Southeast Asia, 1945–1975.* Westport, CT: Praeger, 1995.
Lind, Michael. *Vietnam the Necessary War: A Reinterpretation of America's Most Disastrous Military Conflict.* New York: The Free Press, 1999.
Lindholm, Richard W., ed. *Vietnam, The First Five Years: An International Symposium.* East Lansing: Michigan State University Press, 1959.
Logevall, Fredrik. *Choosing War: The Lost Chance for Peace and the Escalation of War in Vietnam.* Berkeley: University of California Press, 1999.
———. *The Origins of the Vietnam War.* New York: Longman, 2001.
Lomperis, Timothy J. *The War Everyone Lost—and Won: America's Intervention in Viet Nam's Twin Struggles.* Baton Rouge: Louisiana State University Press, 1984.

Maclear, Michael. *The Ten Thousand Day War: Vietnam, 1945–1975.* New York: St. Martin's Press, 1981.
Maneli, Mieczyslaw. *War of the Vanquished.* New York: Harper & Row, 1971.
Mann, Robert. *A Grand Delusion: America's Descent into Vietnam.* New York: Basic Books, 2001.
Mecklin, John. *Mission in Torment.* New York: Doubleday, 1965.
Meyer, Harold J. *Hanging Sam: A Military Biography of General Samuel T. Williams from Pancho Villa to Vietnam.* Denton: University of North Texas Press, 1990.
Miller, Edward. *Misalliance; Ngo Dinh Diem, the United States, and the Fate of South Vietnam.* Cambridge, MA: Harvard University Press, 2013.
Morgan, Joseph G. "A Change of Course: American Catholics, Anticommunism, and the Vietnam War." *U.S. Catholic Historian* 22, No. 4, Catholic Anticommunism (Fall, 2004), 117–130.
_____. *The Vietnam Lobby: The American Friends of Vietnam, 1955–1975.* Chapel Hill: University of North Carolina Press, 1997.
Morrison, Wilbur H. *The Elephant and the Tiger: The Full Story of the Vietnam War.* New York: Hippocrene, 1990.
Moyar, Mark. *Triumph Forsaken: The Vietnam War, 1954–1965.* New York: Cambridge University Press, 2006.
Murti, B.S.N. *Vietnam Divided: The Unfinished Struggle.* New York: Asia Publishing House, 1964.
Nashel, Jonathan. *Edward Lansdale's Cold War.* Boston: University of Massachusetts Press, 2005.
Neale, Jonathan. *The American War: Vietnam 1960–1975.* London: Bookmarks, 2001.
Neu, Charles E. *America's Lost War: Vietnam: 1945–1975.* Wheeling, IL: Harlan Davidson, 2005.
Newman, John M. *JFK and Vietnam: Deception, Intrigue, and the Struggle for Power.* New York: Warner, 1992.
Nguyen Dinh Hoa. *From the City Inside the Red River: A Cultural Memoir of Mid-Century Vietnam.* Jefferson, NC: McFarland, 1999.
Nguyen Ngoc Ngan, with E. E. Richey. *The Will of Heaven.* New York: E. P. Dutton, 1982.
Nguyen Qui Duc. *Where the Ashes Are: The Odyssey of a Vietnamese Family.* Reading, MA: Addison-Wesley, 1994.
Nguyen Thai. "South Vietnam." *The Asian Newspapers' Reluctant Revolution,* edited by John A. Lent. Ames: The Iowa State University Press, 1971: 234–257.
Nguyen Thị Thu Lam, with Edith Kreisler and Sandra Christenson. *Fallen Leaves: Memoirs of a Vietnamese Woman from 1940 to 1975.* New Haven, CT: Yale Center for International and Area Studies, 1989.
Nguyen Thi Tuyet Mai, ed. by Monique Senderowicz. *The Rubber Tree: Memoir of a Vietnamese Woman Who Was an Anti-French Guerrilla, an Aide to the First President of the Republic of Vietnam, a Publisher and a Peace Activist.* Jefferson, NC: McFarland, 1994.
Nguyen Tuyet Mai. "Electioneering: Vietnamese Style." *Asian Survey* 2, No. 9 (Nov. 1962), 11–18.
Nilsson, Jan. *Walking the Tightrope.* Queensland, Australia: Terebra, 2012.
Nolting, Frederick, Jr., *From Trust to Tragedy.* New York: Praeger, 1989.
O'Leary, Bradley S., and Edward Lee. *The Deaths of the Cold War Kings: The Assassinations of Diem & JFK.* Baltimore, MD: Cemetery Dance, 2000.
Olson, James S., and Randy Roberts. *Where the Domino Fell: America and Vietnam, 1945–1990.* New York: St. Martin's Press, 1991.
Palmer, Bruce, Jr. *The 25-Year War: America's Military Role in Vietnam.* Lexington: University Press of Kentucky, 1984.
Palmer, Dave Richard. *The Summons of the Trumpet.* San Rafael, CA: Presidio Press, 1984.
Parmet, Herbert S. *JFK: The Presidency of John F. Kennedy.* New York: Dial, 1983.
Pauker, Guy J. "Political Doctrines and Practical Politics in Southeast Asia." *Pacific Affairs* 35, No. 1 (Spring, 1962), 3–10.

Podhoretz, Norman. *Why We Were in Vietnam*. New York: Simon & Schuster, 1982.
Porter, D. Gareth. *The Perils of Dominance: Imbalance of Power and the Road to War in Vietnam*. Berkeley: University of California Press, 2005.
Prados, John. *Vietnam: The History of an Unwinnable War, 1945–1975*. Lawrence: University Press of Kansas, 2009.
Prouty, L. Fletcher. *JFK: The CIA, Vietnam and the Plot to Assassinate John F. Kennedy*. New York: Carol, 1992.
Quinn-Judge, Sophie. "Giving Peace a Chance: National Reconciliation and a Neutral South Vietnam, 1954–1964." *Peace & Change* 38, No. 4 (Oct. 2013), 385–410.
Race, Jeffrey. *War Comes to Long An*. Berkeley: University of California Press, 1972.
Record, Jeffrey. *The Wrong War: Why We Lost in Vietnam*. Annapolis, MD: Naval Institute Press, 1998.
Rosenau, William. *US Internal Security Assistance to South Vietnam: Insurgency, Subversion and Public Order*. London: Routledge, 2005.
Rust, William J. *Kennedy in Vietnam*. New York: Scribner's, 1985.
Schandler, Herbert Y. *America in Vietnam: The War That Couldn't Be Won*. Lanham, MD: Rowman & Littlefield, 2009.
Schulzinger, Robert D. *A Time for War: The United States and Vietnam, 1941–1975*. New York: Oxford University Press, 1997.
Scigliano, Robert G. "The Electoral Process in South Vietnam: Politics in an Underdeveloped State." *Midwest Journal of Political Science* 4, No. 2 (May 1960), 138–161.
_____. "Political Parties in South Vietnam Under the Republic." *Pacific Affairs*, 33, No. 4 (Dec. 1960), 327–346.
_____. *South Vietnam: Nation Under Stress*. Boston: Houghton Mifflin, 1963.
Shaplen, Robert. *The Lost Revolution: The U.S. in Vietnam, 1946–1966*. New York: Harper & Row, 1965.
_____. *Time Out of Hand: Revolution and Reaction in Southeast Asia*. New York: Harper & Row, 1969.
Shaw, Geoffrey. "Laotian 'Neutrality': A Fresh Look at a Key Vietnam War Blunder." *Small Wars & Insurgencies* (Spring 2002) 13, Issue 1, 25–57.
_____. *The Lost Mandate of Heaven: The American Betrayal of Ngo Dinh Diem, President of Vietnam*. San Francisco: Ignatius Press, 2015.
Sheehan, Neil. *A Bright Shining Lie: John Paul Vann and America in Vietnam*. New York: Random House, 1988.
Short, Anthony. *The Origins of the Vietnam War*. New York: Longman, 1989.
Smith, Ralph B. *Revolution versus Containment, 1955–61*. New York: St. Martin's Press, 1985.
Spector, Ronald H. *Advice and Support: The Early Years, 1941–1960*. Honolulu: University Press of the Pacific, 2005.
Statler, Kathryn C. *Replacing France: The Origins of American Intervention in Vietnam*. Lexington: University Press of Kentucky, 2007.
Stewart, Geoffrey C. *Vietnam's Lost Revolution: Ngo Dinh Diem's Failure to Build an Independent Nation, 1955–1963*. New York: Cambridge University Press, 2017.
Strober, Gerald S., and Deborah Hart Strober. *Let Us Begin Anew: An Oral History of the Kennedy Presidency*. New York: HarperCollins, 2003.
Sullivan, William H. *Obbligato: Notes on a Foreign Service Career*. New York: W. W. Norton, 1984.
Tran Van Don. *Our Endless War*. San Rafael, CA: Presidio Press, 1978.
Tregaskis, Richard. *Vietnam Diary*. New York: Holt, Rinehart and Winston, 1963.
Trullinger, James. *Village at War*. New York: Longman, 1980.
Tucker, Spencer. *Vietnam*. Lexington: University Press of Kentucky, 1999.
Turley, William S. *The Second Indochina War: A Short Political and Military History, 1954–1975*. Boulder, CO: Westview, 1986.
Walinsky, Louis J., ed. *Agrarian Reform as Unfinished Business: The Selected Papers of Wolf Ladejinsky*. New York: Oxford University Press, 1977.

Warner, Denis. *The Last Confucian*. Baltimore, MD: Penguin, 1964.
Warner, Geoffrey. "The United States and Vietnam 1945–65: Part II: 1954–65." *Royal Institute of International Affairs* 48, No. 4 (Oct. 1972), 593–615.
Weist, Andrew, and Michael J. Doidge, eds. *Triumph Revisited: Historians Battle for the Vietnam War*. New York: Routledge, 2010.
Westheider, James E. *The Vietnam War*. Westport, CT: Greenwood, 2007.
Wilbanks, James. *Vietnam War Almanac: An In-Depth Guide to the Most Controversial Conflict in American History*. New York: Skyhorse Publishing, 2013.
Winters, Francis X. *The Year of the Hare: America in Vietnam, January 25, 1963–February 15, 1964*. Athens: University of Georgia Press, 1997.
Wintler, Justin. *The Viet Nam Wars*. New York: St. Martin's Press, 1991.
Woodruff, Mark R. *Unheralded Victory: The Defeat of the Viet Cong and the North Vietnamese Army, 1961–1973*. Arlington, VA: Vandamere Press, 1999.
Wright, James. *Enduring Vietnam: An American Generation and its War*. New York: Thomas Dunn Books, 2017
Wurfel, David. "The Saigon Political Elite: Focus on Four Cabinets." *Asian Survey* 7, No. 8, Vietnam: A Symposium (Aug. 1967), 527–539.
Young, Marilyn B. *The Vietnam Wars, 1945–1990*. New York: HarperCollins, 1991.
Zasloff, Joseph J. "Rural Resettlement in South Viet Nam: The Agroville Program." *Pacific Affairs* 35, No. 4 (Winter, 1962–1963), 327–340.

Index

Agence Kampuchea Presse 44
Agrovilles 12, 148–149, 152, 155, 164–165, 229n18
Alphand, Hervé 102
American Friends of Vietnam 12, 16, 78, 121, 134, 188, 224n60
American Trading Company of Vietnam 226n57
An Giang province 26, 42, 248n52
An Xuyên province 135
Anderson, Daniel 6, 8, 10, 16, 120, 159, 185, 201n5
Anderson, George 205n50
Armstrong, Hamilton Fish 103–104, 220n32
Army of the Republic of Vietnam (ARVN) 26, 43, 52, 74–76, 100, 142–144, 147–149, 151, 154, 162, 169, 171–172, 175–178, 182, 186, 191, 200n18, 201n7, 230n22, 234n5, 236n26, 238n46, 241n81, 248n50
Askew, Laurin 158
Australia 28, 31, 51, 100–102, 108, 237n38, 244n111

Ba Cụt *see* Lê Quang Vinh
Bác dạy 24
Bacon, Leonard 28, 89, 91, 204n25
Ban Kapai village 88
Ban Mê Thuột 5–6, 33, 39
Ban Mê Thuột–Ninh Hòa road 33
Ban Pak Nhay village 73–77
Ban Tarouna village 88
Ban Tavigne village 88
Bangkok 118, 192, 244n4
Bảo Đại 83, 128, 155, 229n11
Barbour, Robert 34–35, 53–54, 69, 113, 209n10
Barnes, Thomas 170
Barre, Jean 99, 119
Barrows, Leland 33–34, 36, 38, 50, 56–62, 84, 86–87, 211n44
Basic Counterinsurgency Plan for Viet Nam 188, 190–194, 246n27, 247n32, 248n50
Beakley, Wallace Morris 47

Bến Giang 86
Biên Hòa 118, 122, 235n26
Bình Dương province 143
Bình Lớn Second Constituency 236n21
Bình Xuyên 13, 31–32, 120, 155, 246n18
Blackburn, Paul 114
Blakeney, Frederick 100
Bloc for Library and Progress *see* Caravelle Manifesto
Bổ Túc 40, 50
Bonesteel, Charles H. 158
Bong Souvannavong 204n23
Bowie, Thomas 26–27, 31, 70, 205n37, 206n55, 213n38
Bowles, Chester 190
Brèthes, Jean 234n52
Brucker, Wilber M. 81–82, 84, 141–142, 144, 228n27, 227, 28, 228n29
Bùi An Tuấn 125
Bùi Quang Ngô 137
Bùi Văn Lương 235n17
Buis, Dale R. 119
Bunting, Frederick 202n11
Buổi sang 66, 68, 125, 137, 148, 178, 225n25
Burgess, W. Randolph 85

Cà Mau peninsula 25, 27, 33
Cabell, Charles 231n33
Cách mạng Quốc gia 32, 42, 47, 87, 90–91, 97, 100, 104, 119, 205n41, 217n25, 218n63, 221n62
Cái Nước district 135
Cambodia 11, 18, 20, 24–30, 34–35, 37, 42–47, 51–52, 54–56, 58, 64, 71–80, 83, 88–89, 91, 96–110, 112–119, 121–122, 129–131, 135, 142, 144, 152, 158, 160, 171, 190, 203n10, 207n27, 210n21, 214n66, 217n25, 218n2, 219n15, 221n62, 221n66, 223n51, 248n52
Campbell, Alan 213n38
Cần Lao Nhân Vị Cách Mạng Đảng (Cần Lao Party) 64, 83, 113, 138, 147–148, 153–155, 159–160, 166, 179, 190, 192, 245n18

Cần Thơ 173
Canada 14, 75, 93
Cao Đài 6, 13, 128, 155, 208n54, 209n1, 245n18, 249n61
Caravelle Manifesto 155–159, 164, 171, 227n12, 238n43
Carlson, Gunnar 70–71
Central Intelligence Agency (CIA) 25, 42, 45, 80, 82–83, 89, 92–93, 99, 101, 113, 171, 174, 186–187
Châu Đốc province 24, 26, 72
Chea Sim 203n10
chi bộ của Đảng Lao động Việt Nam (Worker's Party of Vietnam) see Lao động Party
China (Communist) see People's Republic of China
China, Republic of (Taiwan) 17, 20
Choi Duk Shin 243n103
Cholon 124, 173
Chuông Mai 121, 125, 127, 178
Chương Văn Dĩnh 205n37
Church, Marguerite 226n55
Citizens Rally 79
Civil Guard 17, 24, 26–27, 33, 37, 39, 50, 52, 59–65, 74–75, 81, 86, 88, 118, 139, 144, 146, 149–150, 165, 169, 181–182, 185–186, 189, 201n7, 211n44, 213n38, 230n23, 230n30, 232n9, 234n5, 235n5, 243n104, 244n113, 247n32
Colby, William 113, 136, 171–173, 189, 222n12, 236n29, 242n87
Colegrove, Albert 119–122, 124, 132–134, 155, 226n57
Committee for the Defense of the National Interests (CDNI) 80
Communist China see People's Republic of China
Communist Denunciation Campaign (1957) 53
Comstock, Richard 154–156
Công nhân 68, 203n4, 207n26, 210n13
Constitutional Court 12
Country Team (U.S.) 39, 59–60, 63–64, 68, 71, 78, 80–83, 86, 88, 112–114, 135–139, 143, 146, 148, 151, 155, 161–162, 164, 166, 169, 175–177, 180, 183, 186, 189, 192, 206n8, 211n29, 229n12, 233n27, 235n6, 248n50
Coup d'état (November 1960) 171–175
Court of Appeals 65
Cunningham, Francis 239n66
Curtis, Thomas 226n55

Đa Nhim Hydroelectric Project 17
Dai Ha Jih Pao 90
Đại Lộc Affair 53
Đại Việt Party (Đại Việt Quốc dân đảng) 121, 199n5, 224n61
Đắk Lê 86
Dalat 29, 113

Dân chúng 6, 32, 42, 46, 66–67, 178
Đan Nguyên 32, 45–46, 105, 204n41
Đảng Độc Khối 244n4
Đặng Văn Sung 224n14
Đào Hưng Long 231n46
Dap Chhuon 100–106, 219n5, 219n9, 219n15
Dầu Tiếng 80
De Jaeger, Raymond J. 172, 237n32
Democratic Opposition Bloc 46
Democratic Republic of Vietnam (North Vietnam) 10, 12, 27, 45, 52, 56, 65, 80, 88–97, 104, 121, 128, 141, 144, 158, 170, 185, 190
Department of Civic Action (Vietnamese) 247n37
Le Dépêche du Cambodge 26, 101
Desai, Manilal Jagdish 96, 218n59
Development Loan Fund 47, 49, 171
Diệm, Ngô Đình see Ngô Đình Diệm
Dillon, C. Douglas 93, 107, 146
Dillon, James 161
Định Tường province 213n38
Dixon, Ben 245n4
Độ Mặn Quát 123
Đỗ Văn Công 5
Dolan, John 160
Douglas, James 177
du Berrier, Hilaire 46
Đức Lập village 135
Dulles, John Foster 7, 20, 91, 95, 202n12, 202n13, 216n3
Dương Văn Minh 162, 238n44, 245n18
Durbrow, Elbridge: Arthur Gardiner meetings 90–91, 113–114, 127; Basic Counterinsurgency Plan for Viet Nam 191–194; Cambodia 25–27, 37, 42–46, 51, 56, 75, 78–80, 88–89, 97, 100–110, 112–119, 130–131, 144, 160; Caravelle Manifesto 155–156; Civil Guard 17, 26, 33, 39, 59–63, 144, 146, 149–150, 165, 169, 181–182, 185–186, 189; Colegrove Affair 119–121, 132–134; Coup d'état (November 1960) 171–175; Edward Lansdale controversy 2, 146–147, 157–159, 161–163, 166, 168, 181, 234n3, 243n108, 246n26; Henry Hohler meetings 169, 234n52; Lionel McGarr meetings 168–169, 174–176, 178–179, 182, 238n43; Ngô Đình Nhu 55, 89, 166, 169–170, 180; Nguyễn Đình Thuần 36, 110–111, 118, 127, 141, 149, 153, 169, 174, 179, 190–192; Nguyễn Ngọc Thơ 45, 127–128, 140, 148, 153, 164, 169; Roger Lalouette meetings 97, 100, 115–118, 130, 160, 169, 222n25, 234n52, 243n103; Samuel Williams 25, 27, 32–33, 36, 39, 48, 81–82, 90–91, 94, 110, 141, 160–162; Wilber Brucker visits 81–82, 84, 141–142, 144; William Colby 71–173

Economic Police Service (Vietnam) 66
Eisenhower, Dwight D. 7–8, 10, 19–20, 22, 103, 106, 119, 169, 180, 197
Elections, National Assembly (1959) 66, 85,

94, 120, 122–129, 131, 135, 139, 145, 225n20, 225n21
elections, presidential (1961) 138, 187, 189, 192–195, 225n21, 248n57, 249n61
Elting, Howard 62–64, 66–69, 71–72, 91, 119, 123
Exodus, Operation 22, 203n21

Felt, Harry 84, 94, 182, 186
Flesch, Joseph 159
Fong, Hiram 226n55
Forces Armées Royales 73
Forsyth, William Douglas 243n103
Fox, Mary Joan 202n11
France 8, 11–13, 17, 20–21, 24–25, 29, 32–33, 39, 43–44, 48, 52, 54, 56, 75, 78, 80, 83–85, 89, 91, 93–95, 97, 99, 100–102, 104–105, 107–109, 111–113, 116–118, 121, 127–128, 136, 138, 140, 148, 152, 155, 160, 164, 166, 169–170, 178–179
French, Jerome 177, 243n108

Gardiner, Arthur 68, 86, 90, 113–114, 120–121, 127, 183, 188
Garner, Frederic 222n26
Gassouin, Oliver 95
Gates, Thomas 241n82
Gazette de Saigon 85
Geneva Conference and Agreements (1954) 11–14, 29, 88, 92–97, 101, 107, 110, 115, 117, 119, 141,162, 203n21, 204n29, 222n16
Gia Long 136
Gonder, Frank 133, 155–156, 164, 226n57
Gorce, Pierre 104, 115–117, 223n45
Gore, Al 140, 227n9
Great Britain *see* United Kingdom
Gregory, Gene 44
Gulf of Thailand 159

Hà Tĩnh province 249n61
Hammarskjold, Dag 91–93, 95–97, 104–105, 218n48
Hanoi 41, 46, 82, 90–93, 95–97, 105, 120, 125, 128, 153, 155, 181, 246n19
Hartshorn, Edwin 74, 104
Heavner, Theodore 84, 120, 148, 164, 233n37
Helble, John 194
Herter, Christian 95, 102, 130–131, 184, 216n3
Hickenlooper, Bourke 134
Hitchcock, David 84
Hồ Liêm 53
Hồ Nhật Tân 193, 249n61
Hồ Văn Nhựt 155
Hồ Viết Điểu 231n46
Hoà bình Trung lập 108
Hòa Hảo 13, 26, 44, 120, 155, 203n4, 222n21, 245n18
Hỏa Lựu 148–149
Hoàng Cơ Thụy 66, 125, 172, 237n42
Hoàng Huy 194

Hoàng Lập 89
Hoàng Văn Lạc 38
Hohler, Henry 169, 183, 234n52
Hood, Lord Samuel 190
Houghton, Amory 21, 234n52
Huế 34–35, 38, 53–54, 56, 69, 71, 84–85, 113, 120, 164, 168, 170, 196
Huỳnh Công Hậu 83
Huỳnh Thành Vị 137
Huỳnh Văn Điểm 19, 201n5

India 28, 51, 75, 91–93, 96–97, 204n2, 206n8, 218n58, 243n103
International Control Commission (ICC) 14, 90–93, 96–98
International Supervisory and Control Commission 243n103

Jelley, Robert 35, 84, 206n55
Johnston, Myriam 113
Joint Chiefs of Staff (U.S.) 168, 180, 234n5, 244, 116
Journal d'Extreme Orient 71
Judd, Walter 226n55

Karnow, Stanley 179
Katun 50
Kellogg, Edmund 26, 44–45, 96, 102, 105–106, 203n11
Kennedy, John F. 2, 37, 188–192, 195, 197, 246n30, 247n32
Kent, Sherman 234n2
Khamphan Panya 92, 94, 96
Khánh An village 42
Khmer Issarak 105
Kidder, Randolph 83–85, 113
Kiên Giang province 233n41
Kiến Hòa province 143
Knight, Robert 159, 161
Kompadon village 73
Kompong 51
Kontum 33, 49–50, 56
Kontun-Mo Doc Road 49
Korea, Republic of 28, 51, 203n15, 243n103

Ladejinsky, Wolf 22, 38, 49, 134, 147, 153, 160, 164, 169, 231n39, 245n4
Lại Từ 129
Lalouette, Roger 97, 100, 102, 115–118, 130, 160, 169, 222n25, 234n52, 243n103
Lam Lê Trinh 235n17
Lâm Quang Thơ 173
Lâm Văn Tết 231n46
Lambert, Didier 71
Lambert, J.B. 112–113
Land Reform/Redistribution (Vietnam) 11, 139, 190, 229n18, 230n18
Lane, Andre 244n2
Lansdale, Edward 2, 114, 146–147, 150–152, 157–159, 161–163, 166, 168, 177–178, 180–

181, 187–189, 191, 222n16, 229n1, 230n23, 233n27, 234n3, 243n108, 246n26, 246n30
Lao động Party 10
Lao Hak Xat 89
Lao Lam Lao Party 80
Laos 11, 18, 20, 27–29, 37, 41, 45–46, 56, 80, 88–98, 100–102, 107–108, 110, 114, 121, 128–129, 171, 186, 202n13, 217n25, 231n33, 232n12, 246n19
LeMay, Curtis 244n116
Lemnitzer, Lyman Louis 180–181
Lê Quang Luật 205n37
Lê Quang Vinh 24, 115, 203n4, 222n21
Lê Quang Vy 84
Lê Si Ngạc 123, 224n3, 225n3
Lê Sống 45, 66, 124, 127, 205n41, 207n26
Le Tri village 72
Lê Trọng Quát 236n21
Lê Văn Đông 147
Lê Văn Kim 38, 237n42
Lê Văn Nghiệm 175, 236n26, 241n84
Lê Văn Trọng 102
Lê Văn Ty 237n41, 245n18
Lincoln, Anthony 217n39
Lodge, Henry Cabot, Jr. 96, 196, 218n48
Lon Nol 73, 108, 119, 223n42
Long An province 135, 143
Long Điền district 66, 212n15
Luang Prabang 97
Lucas, James 133–134
Lyon, Cecil 102

Madame Nhu 7, 64, 124, 166, 169–170, 188, 231n46, 243n103
Mai Hữu Xuân 68
Malaya 151–152, 158, 204n21
Manac'h, Etienne 234n52
Mansfield, Mike 10, 121, 162
Matsui, Victor 219n5
Marcy, Carly 28
May Jih Luan Zan 32, 42
McDowell, Harris 226n55
McGarr, Lionel C. 2, 162, 168–169, 174–176, 178–182, 186, 189, 191–193, 196, 234n5, 235n7, 238n43, 241n87
McGee, Gale 140
Mekong Delta 25, 40, 150–151, 234n52
Mekong River 72, 108, 116, 118
Mendenhall, Joseph 72, 124, 132, 136, 138, 146, 156, 166, 173, 184, 187–188, 236n24, 242n99, 244n4, 245n5, 248n50
Menon, Gopala 243n103
Menzies, Austin 134
Merchant, Livingston 181, 185
Michel Nguyễn Văn Lanh *see* Nguyễn Long Châu
Michigan State University Group 13, 39, 59, 64, 230n23
Military Assistance Advisory Group (MAAG) 2, 37, 39, 47, 60, 70, 73–74, 78, 80, 86, 99, 104, 114, 118, 122, 143–144, 154, 161–162, 169, 179, 182–183, 191, 203n15, 206n8, 228n30, 231n40, 235n5, 244n114, 244n115, 246n26, 246n27
Military Assistance Program (MAP) 86
Minh Thành 52
Montagnards 89, 110, 123, 210n24
Mounier, Emmanuel 209n2
Movement of the Free Khmer 129–131, 159, 232n12
Mỹ Tho 173
Myers, Samuel L. 230n22

National Assembly (Laos) 91–92, 204n23
National Assembly (Vietnam) 7, 12, 35, 70, 85, 123–129, 137–138, 148, 165–166, 169, 171, 177, 190, 192–193, 195, 225n20, 227n9, 2236n21, 245n11, 247n42, 248n57
National Assembly elections (1959) *see* elections, National Assembly (1959)
National Congress of the People's Socialist Community 117
National Economic Council 12, 155, 243n104, 245n11, 247n42
National Liberation Front of South Vietnam *see* Việt Cộng
National Revolutionary Movement 47, 79, 124–126, 129, 137, 193, 205n41, 225n20, 227n9, 229n11, 241n81
National Security Council (Vietnam) 165, 234n52
Nehru, Jawaharlal 204n20, 218n58
Neo Lao Hak Xat 80, 89–90, 92, 96–97, 218n63
Nghệ An province 89
Nghiêm Xuân Thiện 212n7
Ngô Đình Cẩn 34–35, 53–54, 69, 79, 85, 101–102, 148, 164, 229n11
Ngô Đình Diệm: Agrovilles 148–149, 155; Army of the Republic of Vietnam 43, 100, 142–144, 151, 154, 162, 175, 186; Brucker Affair 141–144; Cambodia 2, 11, 18, 20, 25–28, 33–34, 37, 42–45, 51, 54–56, 58, 73, 75–77, 100–109, 112–119, 122, 130–131, 160; Caravelle Manifesto 155–159, 164, 171; Civil Guard 26–27, 33, 39, 59–64, 81, 86, 139, 144, 149–150, 181–182, 185–186; coup d'état (November 1960) 171–175; Edward Lansdale meetings 114, 146–147, 150–2, 157–159, 161–163, 166, 168, 177–178, 180–181, 187–189, 191; elections (National Assembly, 1959) 94, 122, 126, 131; elections (presidential, 1961) 189, 192–195; Lionel McGarr meetings 174–176, 179, 186, 192; Ngô Đình Nhu's influence 7, 104, 148, 166, 169–170; Norodom Sihanouk meetings 76–77, 79, 99–106, 110, 112, 114–119, 129–131, 160; Samuel Williams meetings 27, 32–33, 36, 38–41, 43–45, 48–51, 54–58, 60–64, 67–68, 70–71, 80–82, 84, 86–88, 90, 94, 99–100,

104, 106, 110, 112, 114, 121, 125, 127–129, 136, 140–144, 149–151, 154–155, 157–166; Wolf Ladejinsky meetings 22, 38, 49, 134, 147, 153, 160, 164, 169
Ngô Đình Luyện 164
Ngô Đình Nhu 5, 7–10, 26, 35, 44, 55, 69, 71, 75–76, 79, 83, 89–91, 101–102, 104–105, 109, 119, 124, 148, 157, 159, 164, 166, 169–170, 177, 180, 183–184, 188, 196, 199n6, 200n13, 233n37, 242n87, 243n103, 243n104, 245n18
Ngô Đình Thục 52
Ngô Hữu Thời 236n21
Ngô Sách Vinh 125
Ngô Trọng Hiếu 26, 43–44, 55, 72–73, 83, 99–100, 102, 106, 129, 203n11, 219n2, 219n5, 241n84
Ngô Xuân Soạn 176
Ngôn luận 31–32, 42, 46, 65, 67
Người Việt Tự Do 71, 76, 120
Nguyễn Chánh Thi 176–177, 237n41, 237n42, 241n80
Nguyên Châu Group 27
Nguyễn Chí 213n44
Nguyễn Đình Gia 201n5
Nguyễn Đình Quát 193, 245n5, 249n61
Nguyễn Đình Thuần 36, 62–64, 100, 110–111, 118, 127, 130, 140–142, 149–150, 152–153, 166, 169, 172, 174, 179–180, 183, 190–192, 228n32, 230n33, 231n33, 232n16, 232n22, 236n29, 238n44, 238n45, 240n70, 247n41, 248n50
Nguyễn Duy Liên 158
Nguyễn Hòa Phạm 53
Nguyễn Hữu Châu 17–19, 36–39, 45, 48, 57, 59–64, 85, 201n5, 202n12, 206n8, 211n29
Nguyễn Khánh 121, 150, 165, 171, 230n26, 238n44, 245n18, 248n50
Nguyễn Long Châu 26
Nguyễn Ngọc Bích 249n61
Nguyễn Ngọc Chạch 70
Nguyễn Ngọc Khôi 154
Nguyễn Ngọc Liên 205n37
Nguyễn Ngọc Thơ 29–30, 36, 45, 58, 108, 115–116, 127–128, 138, 140, 148, 153, 164, 166, 169, 193, 238n45, 245n18
Nguyễn Phương Thiệp 85, 129, 166, 245n5
Nguyễn Thân 135, 139
Nguyễn Thành Phương 193, 249n61
Nguyễn Thế Truyền 193, 249n61
Nguyễn Trân 126–128, 213n38, 224n14
Nguyễn Triệu Hồng 237n42
Nguyễn Văn Báu 35, 70, 206n55
Nguyễn Văn Bưu 233n37
Nguyễn Văn Cẩn 85, 125
Nguyễn Văn Châu 241n84
Nguyễn Văn Đông 233n37
Nguyễn Văn Hoan 29
Nguyễn Văn Kiến islet 249n68
Nguyễn Văn Kim 224n14
Nguyễn Văn Liên 137, 235n17

Nguyễn Văn Lộc 237n42
Nguyễn Văn Lợi 237n42
Nguyễn Văn Lưỡng 235n17
Nguyễn Văn Mạnh 70–71
Nguyễn Văn Nhieu 101
Nguyễn Văn Sỹ 235n17
Nguyễn Văn Tâm 29
Nguyễn Vạn Thọ 245n18
Nguyễn Văn Thỏa 249n61
Nguyễn Văn Thời 166
Nguyễn Văn Thuận 70–71
Nguyễn Văn Xuân 29
Nguyễn Văn Y 138
Nhà Trắng 33, 154
Nhu, Ngô Đình see Ngô Đình Nhu
Nishiyama, Takehiko 84
Nolting, Frederick E. 13, 191, 193, 195–196
Nong Kimny 223n51
Norodom Sihanouk 26, 44–45, 72–73, 75–77, 79–80, 83, 88, 99–110, 112, 114–119, 129–131, 160, 203n10, 210n13, 219n2, 219n3, 219n9, 219n15, 220n33, 222n19, 223n46, 232n12
Norodom Surmarit 129, 203n10
Norodom Vakrivan 129

O'Daniel, John 78, 87
O'Donnell, Edward 114
Office of Strategic Services (OSS) 46
ordinance 53 31
Ourot Souvannavong 92, 95–97
Ovnand, Chester 119
Oyadao village 73

Parkes, Roderick 63, 97, 130, 243n104
Parsons, J. Graham 93, 111–113, 120, 130–131, 134, 152–154, 162, 165, 169–170, 180, 183–189, 228n28, 232n16, 238n45, 239n65
Pathet Lao 20, 29, 41, 45, 47, 90, 93, 97, 121, 204n25
Payart, Jean 75
Penn Nouth 42, 56, 72, 76, 119
People's Committee Against Communists and Rebels 178–179, 184, 241n85
People's Counter-Coup d'état Committee 178
People's Republic of China 17, 55, 77, 90, 97, 102, 106, 116, 216n10
personalism 52, 209n2
Personalist Labor Revolutionary Party see Cần Lao Party
Phạm Công Tắc 6
Phạm Huy Cơ 83
Phạm Ngọc Vinh 148, 229n11
Phạm Trọng Nhân 102
Phạm Văn Đồng 89
Phạm Văn Liễu 237n42
Phạm Xuân Áng 53
Phạm Xuân Chiểu 237n42
Phan Huy Quát 176, 184
Phan Khắc Sửu 126, 137, 165, 176, 184, 227n12, 231n46, 236n21, 245n18

Phan Phụng Tiên 176
Phan Quang Đán 30–32, 46, 66, 79, 83, 124–129, 131, 134–135, 139, 165, 175, 184, 205n41, 212n7, 245n18
Phi Vân 66
Philippines 20, 64, 108, 151, 215n17
Phnom Penh 24, 26, 46, 72–76, 99, 102, 104–106, 108, 112, 114, 116, 118, 130–131, 176, 219n5, 219n15, 232n12, 240n73, 244n3, 248n52
Phong Dinh province 148–149
Phong Saly province 45, 208n44
Phoui Sananikone 80, 91–92, 94, 217n39
Phoumi Vongvichit 45
Phú Quốc Island 25
Phục Quốc Hội 208n54
Phùng 5–6, 199n5
Phước Tuy province 66
Pilcher, John 132–134, 226n55
Pleiku province 33, 40, 50, 206n12
Poland 75, 90, 93
Poulo Panjang islands 51
Pracheaserey 210n13
presidential election (1961) *see* elections, presidential (1961)
Price, C. Hoyt 202n11
Price, Darrell 113

Quảng Nam province 53
Quảng Trị Province 233n37

Rạch Giá 26
Radio Hanoi 121
Radio Saigon 172, 174
Réalités Cambodgiennes 73, 104, 105–107, 115, 119–120
Republican Youth Movement 152, 201n7, 233n37
Revolutionary Committee (November 1960 coup d'état attempt) 174–176, 178
Revolutionary Workers' Party 34
Riley, Herbert D. 134
Robertson, Walter 21, 72
Rockefeller III, John D. 103–104
Rostow, Walt W. 192–193, 247n30
Rusk, Dean 188, 191–192, 247n32
Russia *see* Soviet Union

Sài Gòn Mới 66, 76, 90, 178, 212n13, 219n15
Saigon-Biên Hòa Project 33
Saigon Military Mission 146, 161222n16, 229n1
Sam Neua province 45
Sam Sary 99, 101, 105, 219n3, 219n15, 232n12
Sangkum *see* National Congress of the People's Socialist Community
Sasorith, Katay Don 20, 28, 89
Savannakhet province 88
Scott, Richard 240n76
Sedgwick, Charles 202n12

Self-Defense Corps 201n7, 213n38
Self-Defense Force 27, 39–40, 47–48, 86, 140, 211n4
Shuff, Charles 86
Siem Hieng 105
Sihanouk, Norodom *see* Norodom Sihanouk
Sim Var 25–26, 43, 45, 73, 75
Sisowath Kossamak 129, 203n10
Slat Peou 219n5
Smith, Horace 92, 94–97, 217n39
Sóc Trăng 33
La Societe des Cauotehouc d'Extrême Orient 52
Sơn La province 89
Son Sann 106–108, 116–118, 220n55
Sống chung 42
South Korea *see* Republic of Korea
Southeast Asia Treaty Organization (SEATO) 18, 20, 90–91, 192, 216n18, 217n25
Souvanna Phouma 45, 80, 204n23
Soviet Union 10, 38, 55, 90, 92–93, 97, 103, 105–106, 191, 246n19, 248n45
Sparkman, John 28
Spellman, Francis 52
Sprague, Mansfield 10, 204n20
Steeves, John 94, 161, 185, 192
Strom, Carl 25–26, 43, 55–56, 73–76, 102, 109, 207n32
Stuart, Francis Hamilton 102
Stump, Felix B. 27, 44, 112, 159, 202n17
Stung Treng province 73
Sukarno 116–117
Sun Wun Jih Pao 32
Sûreté 55, 171, 176, 208n54
Svay Rieng province 105

Taiwan *see* Republic of China
Tân Dân 31–32, 66
Tân Hoá province 89
Tân Lược 164
Tân Sơn Nhứt 14, 24, 171–172, 176
Tây Ninh province 6, 50, 57, 142, 209n71, 238n46, 246n19
Temporary Equipment Recovery Team (TERM) 141, 162
Thái Quang Hoàng 176, 237n41, 240n74, 245n18
Thailand 20, 28, 37, 51, 73, 88, 102, 105–106, 116, 118, 190
Thiết Thực 66
Thời luân 31–32, 46, 65–67, 205n42, 208n54
Thủ Đức Military Academy 236n25
Thừa Thiên Citizen's Rally 148, 229n11
Tiếng Chuông 125
Times of Vietnam 31, 44–45, 83, 90, 120, 209n1
Tin Mới 125, 178, 217n25, 219n15
Tịnh Biên district 248n52
Tioulong, Nhiek 108, 115–116, 119
Toland, Butler 172

Tôn Thất Đính 150, 241n84, 245n18
Tôn Thất Thiện 201n5
Tourane see Danang
Trà Vinh province 44
Trần Chánh Thành 120, 127, 127, 204n21, 228n32
Trần Kim Tuyến 166, 169–170
Trần Lê Quang 68, 201n5, 212n33
Trần Lệ Xuân see Madame Nhu
Trần Thế Xương 125
Trần Thiện Khiêm 173, 175–176, 238n46
Trần Trung Dũng 27, 36, 154, 235n17
Trần Văn An 201n5
Trần Văn Chương 7, 47, 152, 160–161, 171, 180, 190, 192, 202n12, 202n17, 232n16
Trần Văn Dĩnh 235n17
Trần Văn Đỗ 176, 231n46
Trần Văn Đôn 201n5, 245n18
Trần Văn Hữu 29
Trần Văn Lắm 12
Trần Văn Văn 155, 165, 176
Trảng Sụp, attack on 142–143, 149
Trì Bình village 6
Tri Ton district 72
Trimble, William 102, 107–109, 115–118, 130–131
Trụ Gian (targeted assassinations) 135
Trương Cảng 76
Trương Công Cừu 129, 241n84, 243n100
Trương Đình Dzu 248n57
Trương Vĩnh Lễ 79, 129, 165
Tự do 30–32, 46–47, 53, 65, 68, 71, 76, 93, 97, 115, 120, 124, 148, 204n29, 205n42, 207n18, 212n7, 217n25

United Kingdom 94–95, 97, 102, 158, 164, 169, 179, 191, 222n19, 237n38
United Nations 10, 25, 42, 55–56, 73, 91–97, 104
United States Information Service (USIS) 41, 66, 82, 84, 113, 215n17, 246n27
United States Operations Mission (USOM) 16–17, 19, 33, 36–39, 47–48, 56–58, 64, 68, 71, 81, 86–87, 110–111, 134, 150, 165, 188, 205n50, 210n24, 230n23, 246n27
Usher, Richard 158

Văn Hoan 68
Van Juo Jih Pao 93
Vị Thanh 148–149
La Vie Française 71

Vientiane 89, 92–97, 107, 115
Việt Cộng 42, 74, 80–81, 94, 100, 110, 113–114, 118, 125–126, 135, 138, 141–142-145, 147–149, 151–152, 160, 169, 171, 174–175, 177, 182, 184–189, 191, 205n50, 230n30, 234n3, 236n23, 239n60, 244n118, 246n30
Việt Minh 10, 53, 210n24
Vietnam General Confederation of Labor 42, 68
Vietnam Press 32, 74, 76, 100, 106, 120
Vietnamese Socialist Party 126, 231n46, 241n81
Vietnamese Socialist Union 79
Vietnamese Women's Association 124
Vietnamese Women's Solidarity Movement 7
Vĩnh Long province 164
Võ Lang 113
Võ Văn Hải 113, 147, 160, 201n5
Voice of Khmer Freedom Movement 118, 129–131, 134
Voice of the National Salvation Movement 41, 199n5
Voice of the Republic of Vietnam 236n31, 242n89
Von Wendland, Baron 160
Vũ Văn Mẫu 72, 74, 90–91, 100, 103–104, 106–108, 115–117, 119, 130, 195, 213n48
Vũ Văn Thái 19, 58, 127, 201n5
Vương Văn Đông 171–172, 176–177, 236n23, 237n42, 241n80

Washington Daily News 119
Wilde, James 134, 172
Willams, Samuel 2, 8–9, 25, 27, 32–33, 36, 38–41, 43–45, 48–51, 54–58, 60–64, 67–68, 70–72, 74, 80–82, 84, 86–88, 90–91, 94, 99–100, 104, 106, 110, 112–114, 119–121, 125, 127–129, 136–138, 140–144, 146–147, 149–152, 154–155, 157–166, 168–169, 171, 177, 180, 182, 191, 210n24, 211n30, 216n18, 228n27, 228n29, 230n22, 230n25, 232n9, 232n22, 233n27, 244n112
Wintrebert, Michel 39, 54
Wood, Chalmers B. 79, 83, 85, 123, 141, 151–152, 159–161, 165–166, 185, 190, 231n33

Young, Kenneth 19, 232n16
Yuan Tung Jinh Pao 32, 212n7
Yuan Tze-Chien 22

Zasloff, Joseph 164, 233n41

www.ingramcontent.com/pod-product-compliance
Ingram Content Group UK Ltd.
Pitfield, Milton Keynes, MK11 3LW, UK
UKHW041932140426
5217IPUK00014B/439